Fourth Edition

Public Communication Campaigns

Fourth Edition

Public Communication Campaigns

Editors

Ronald E. Rice
University of California, Santa Barbara

Charles K. Atkin
Michigan State University

Los Angeles | London | New Delhi
Singapore | Washington DC

SSAGE

Los Angeles | London | New Delhi
Singapore | Washington DC

FOR INFORMATION

SAGE Publications, Inc.
2455 Teller Road
Thousand Oaks, California 91320
E-mail: order@sagepub.com

SAGE Publications Ltd.
1 Oliver's Yard
55 City Road
London, EC1Y 1SP
United Kingdom

SAGE Publications India Pvt. Ltd.
B 1/I 1 Mohan Cooperative Industrial Area
Mathura Road, New Delhi 110 044
India

SAGE Publications Asia-Pacific Pte Ltd
3 Church Street
#10-04 Samsung Hub
Singapore 049483

Acquisitions Editor: Matthew Byrnie
Editorial Assistant: Stephanie Palermini
Production Editor: Astrid Virding
Copy Editor: Pam Schroeder
Typesetter: Hurix Systems Pvt. Ltd.
Proofreader: Dennis W. Webb
Indexer: Molly Hall
Cover Designer: Candice Harman
Marketing Manager: Kelley McAllister
Permissions Editor: Karen Ehrmann

Printed in the United States of America

Library of Congress Cataloging-in-Publication Data

Public communication campaigns / editors, Ronald E. Rice, Charles K. Atkin.–4th ed.
    p. cm.
  Includes bibliographical references and index.
  ISBN 978-1-4129-8770-7 (pbk.)
  1. Publicity. 2. Advertising, Public service. 3. Public relations. 4. Advocacy advertising. I. Rice, Ronald E. II. Atkin, Charles K.
  HM1226.P83 2013
  659–dc23

                                                2011048277

This book is printed on acid-free paper.

SUSTAINABLE FORESTRY INITIATIVE
Certified Chain of Custody
Promoting Sustainable Forestry
www.sfiprogram.org
SFI-01268
SFI label applies to text stock

12 13 14 15 16 10 9 8 7 6 5 4 3 2 1

Contents

List of Tables and Figures

Preface and Acknowledgments

MISSION

This new, fully revised and expanded fourth edition provides readers with a comprehensive, up-to-date look into the field of public communication campaigns. The subject of campaigns has become increasingly high profile in the academic world in the decade since the last edition, and hundreds of new studies on campaign theory and practice have been published since 2001. Moreover, the rise of new media has expanded the array of strategies for designing and implementing campaigns. Largely rewritten to reflect the latest theories and research, this text continues in the tradition of ongoing improvement and expansion into new areas, including AIDS; sun protection; organ donation; human rights; social norms; corporate social responsibility; risky sex; communities; ocean environment; entertainment–education (E–E); Internet, web-based or digital interventions; fear messages; and media advocacy. Classic chapters are updated on topics such as campaign history, theoretical foundations, formative evaluation, systems approaches, input–output persuasion matrix, design and evaluation, meta-analysis, and Sense-Making Methodology (SMM).

Public Communication Campaigns, 3rd edition, was a substantial extension and updating of the prior two editions. Interest in, research on, and implementation of public communication campaigns continues to grow in terms of application areas, theories and methods, international examples, and implications of new media. *Public Communication Campaigns, 4th edition,* has been significantly revised to reflect these changes while continuing classic and central topics and themes. While more books on specific aspects or areas of communication campaigns have appeared over the years, *Public Communication Campaigns* has provided a broad as well as comprehensive resource for students, researchers, and implementers. The fourth edition will continue in this tradition.

MARKET

This volume will be a valuable resource for students, researchers, and practitioners in the fields of communication, journalism, public relations, mass media, advertising, and public health programs. The book is intended primarily for advanced undergraduate and master's-level courses. Researchers and practitioners will continue to find this a useful resource; the previous edition is the most widely cited work on the subject of communication campaigns. *Public Communication Campaigns, 4th edition,* will be especially relevant to departments in mass communication, public relations, social marketing, marketing, and public health.

MAJOR FEATURES AND BENEFITS

Key features include state-of-the-art literature reviews; a broad range of campaign examples from specific at-risk populations to global population, both U.S. and international; contributors with extensive expertise and experience; shorter chapters; and more online resources. The contributions apply and explain a wide range of methodological approaches and research designs, both qualitative and quantitative, from longitudinal studies to meta-analyses. This edition provides insight into new theories, campaign applications, methods, research, and results from prior and new contributors. Updated or revised chapters include 2, 4, 5, 6, 7, 9, 10, 20, 22, and 23; new chapters include 1, 3, 8, 11, 12, 13, 14, 15, 16, 17, 18, 19, and 21.

New topics covered include human rights, fear appeals, social norms, sun protection, condom use, organ donation, ocean sustainability, risk and efficacy, corporate social responsibility, and digital games.

The chapters are organized into sections on overview and history, design and evaluation, theory foundations, and applying theory and evaluation. These sequenced chapters treat all stages of public communication campaign motivation, design, implementation, and evaluation so that readers and teachers can sequence or combine chapters to emphasize different stages or the overall process.

CHANGES FROM THE THIRD EDITION

We conducted extensive research on how to best revise and update *Public Communication Campaigns*. This involved conducting a citation analysis of every entry, summarizing the reviewers' comments as to the top chapters to keep, reviewing recent International Communication Association programs and online databases for authors and topics in the area of public communication campaigns, searching for campaign resources in journals and online, identifying more recent treatments of central campaign topics, and applying our own awareness of both central and new topics and approaches. This broad review identified many more researchers and topics than could possibly be included in one book, of course. So, we then compared and discussed all the possibilities to arrive at a set of authors and topics that provide fairly comprehensive coverage within the nearly 75-page shorter limit of the fourth edition compared to the third edition. We also discussed with the contributors ways to include or focus on some of the topics raised by our review.

Not only is there a chapter devoted specifically to new media (online games, interactive digital media), but where appropriate, other chapters integrate the role of online and digital media in both campaign development and implementation. The fourth edition features fresh perspectives and 21st-century cases with chapters by new authors and substantial updates by returning authors. But, it also maintains key chapters that have been highly cited in the literature or that offer fundamental conceptual contributions to understanding campaigns. This edition has been designed to make the book more student friendly as a text for advanced undergraduate courses without sacrificing the scholarly priorities. This has been accomplished primarily through more careful editing of material, reducing the length of chapters, and emphasizing topics of interest to students. The book's design presents a more coherent communication campaign resource by providing an appropriate sequence of sections: Overview and History, Design and Evaluation, Theoretical Foundations, and Applying Theory and Evaluation.

ACKNOWLEDGMENTS

We are grateful for all the students, teachers, researchers, and professionals who have used *Public Communication Campaigns* over the years.

John A. Banas (University of Oklahoma), Tomasz A. Fediuk (Illinois State University), Muhiuddin Haider (University of Maryland), Michel M. Haigh (The Pennsylvania State University), Marjorie Kruvand (Loyola University Chicago), John K. Mayo (Florida State University), Michael D. Slater (The Ohio State University), and Itzhak Yanovitzky (Rutgers University) provided incisive and helpful reviews of the third edition and recommendations for this fourth edition.

Todd Armstrong, Nathan Davidson, Elizabeth Borders, and Liz Thornton of SAGE Publications, Inc., managed the great support for and administration of the entire process, from development through production and marketing. We thank Pamela Schroeder for superb copyediting and Molly Hall for the very useful index.

It was a pleasure working with all the contributors to this edition. It's a humbling yet very collegial opportunity to be surrounded by so much expertise, experience, and goodwill. Finally, we thank Claire B. Johnson and Sandi W. Smith for their enduring encouragement, tactful feedback on our conceptions of campaigns, forbearance of our late-night editing, and cordial recognition of our unremitting updates about the arduous hurdles to accomplishing the fourth edition.

PART I

Overview and History

CHAPTER 1

Theory and Principles of Public Communication Campaigns

Charles K. Atkin and Ronald E. Rice

Public communication campaigns can be defined as purposive attempts to inform or influence behaviors in large audiences within a specified time period using an organized set of communication activities and featuring an array of mediated messages in multiple channels generally to produce noncommercial benefits to individuals and society (Rice & Atkin, 2009; Rogers & Storey, 1987).

The campaign as process is universal across topics and venues, utilizing systematic frameworks and fundamental strategic principles developed over the past half century. Campaign designers perform a situational analysis and set objectives leading to development of a coherent set of strategies and implement the campaign by creating informational and persuasive messages that are disseminated via traditional mass media, new technologies, and interpersonal networks.

THEORETICAL FOUNDATIONS OF CAMPAIGNS

Although no specific theory has been developed to explain and predict public communication campaigns, a number of theoretical perspectives are regularly invoked to guide campaign strategies. The most comprehensive applicable conceptualizations are the *social marketing* framework and the *Communication-Persuasion Matrix*.

Campaigns across the spectrum of health, prosocial, and environmental domains share some similarities to commercial advertising campaigns. Thus, it is useful to apply social marketing, which emphasizes an audience-centered consumer orientation and calculated attempts to attractively package the social product and utilize the optimum combination of campaign components to attain pragmatic goals (Andreasen, 1995, 2006; Kotler, Roberto, & Lee, 2002; McKenzie-Mohr, 2011). Social marketing offers a macro perspective, combining numerous components, notably the multifaceted conceptions of product, costs, and benefits, as well as audience segmentation, policy change, and competition (see Bracht & Rice in Chapter 20 and Rice & Robinson in Chapter 16).

In McGuire's (Chapter 9) classic *Communication-Persuasion Matrix,* or input–output model, the communication *input variables* include source, message, channel, and audience; these factors, which are central to most communication models, will be discussed at length in subsequent sections. The *output process* posits audience responses to campaign stimuli as proceeding through the basic stages of exposure and processing before effects can be achieved at the learning, yielding, and behavior levels. *Exposure* includes the simple reception of a message and the degree of attention to its content. *Processing* encompasses mental comprehension, pro- and counterarguing, interpretive perceptions, and cognitive connections and emotional reactions produced by the campaign message. *Learning* comprises information gain, generation of related cognitions, image formation, and skills acquisition. *Yielding* includes acquisition and change in attitudes, beliefs, and values. *Behavior* in the campaign context involves the bottom-line enactment of the actions recommended in messages.

Specific central theories that are applicable to various aspects of public communication campaign strategies, processes, and implementation include:

Agenda setting (McCombs, 2004). The phenomenon of topical salience applies to campaign impact on the perceived importance of societal problems and the prominence of policy issues.

Diffusion of innovations (Rogers, 2003). This theory introduces the ideas of relative advantage and trialability of recommended behaviors, and the individual adoption decision process, as well as opinion leadership that shapes diffusion through interpersonal channels and social networks via multistep flows.

Elaboration Likelihood Model (ELM) (Petty & Cacioppo, 1986) and *Heuristic Systematic Model (HSM)* (Eagly & Chaiken, 1993). ELM and HSM highlight the role of audience involvement level as it shapes cognitive responses, thought generation, and central versus peripheral routes to persuasion.

Extended Parallel Process Model (Stephenson & Witte, 2001). Effectiveness of fear appeals is enhanced by understanding cognitive processes that control danger versus emotional processes, which control the fear via denial or coping; perceived efficacy influences type of response.

Health Belief Model (HBM) (Becker, 1974). Several concepts from HBM pertain specifically to the potency of health threat appeals: susceptibility multiplied by seriousness of consequences and the self-efficacy and response efficacy of performing the recommended behavior.

Instrumental learning (Hovland, Janis, & Kelley, 1953). As adapted to mediated communication, this learning mechanism features message-related concepts of source credibility, reinforcement incentives, and repetition of presentation.

Integrative Theory of Behavior Change (Cappella, Fishbein, Hornik, Ahern, & Sayeed, 2001). The multifaceted model integrates HBM, Social Cognitive Theory (SCT), and Theory of Reasoned Action (TRA) to specify how external variables, individual differences, and underlying beliefs contribute to differential influence pathways for outcome behaviors, intentions, attitudes, norms, and self-efficacy.

Message frames (O'Keefe & Jensen, 2007; Quick & Bates, 2010). This framework focuses on how message appeals are packaged in terms of gain-frame promotion of positive behavior versus loss-frame prevention of negative behavior, especially for audiences likely to display reactance.

Self-Efficacy (Bandura, 1997). This key construct highlights the role of the individual's perceived capability of successfully performing behaviors; those who are confident of carrying out recommended actions are more likely to attempt and sustain behavioral enactment efforts.

Social Cognitive Theory (Bandura, 1986). SCT emphasizes the processes by which source role models, explicitly demonstrated behaviors, and depiction of vicarious reinforcement enhance the impact of mediated messages.

Theory of Reasoned Action (Ajzen & Fishbein, 1980; Ajzen, Albarracin, & Hornik, 1997). The TRA and the ensuing *Theory of Planned Behavior (TPB)* formulate a combination of personal attitudes, perceived norms of influential others, and motivation to comply as predictors of intended behavior. A key underlying mechanism is based on the *expectancy–value* equation, which postulates attitudes are predicted by beliefs about the likelihood that given behavior leads to certain consequences, multiplied by one's evaluation of those consequences.

Transtheoretical Model (Prochaska & Velicer, 1997). This stage-of-progression model identifies subaudiences on the basis of their stage in the process of behavior change with respect to a specific health behavior (precontemplation, contemplation, preparation, action, or maintenance), which shapes the readiness to attempt, adopt, or sustain the recommended behavior.

Uses and gratifications (Katz, Blumler, & Gurevitch, 1974; Rubin, 2002). This offers concepts useful in understanding audience motivations for selecting particular media, attending to media messages, and utilizing learned information in enacting behaviors.

AUDIENCE SEGMENTATION AND CAMPAIGN DESIGN

Identifying the Audience

Campaign design begins with a conceptual assessment of the situation to determine opportunities and barriers and to identify which outcome behaviors would be performed by which people (Atkin & Salmon, 2010; see also Dervin & Foreman-Wernet, Chapter 10). Rather than attempting to reach the broad public, campaign designers typically identify specific (often "at risk") segments of the overall population. There are two major strategic advantages of subdividing the public in terms of demographic characteristics, predispositions, personality traits, and social contexts. First, message efficiency can be improved if subsets of the audience are prioritized according to their centrality in attaining the campaign's objectives as well as receptivity to being influenced. Second, effectiveness can be increased if message content, form, style, and channels are tailored to the attributes and abilities of subgroups.

closest & most distant

The design specifies *focal segments* of the population whose practices are at issue and the primary *focal behaviors* that the campaign ultimately seeks to influence. The next step is to trace backward from the focal behaviors to identify the proximate and distal determinants and then create *models* of the pathways of influence via attitudes, beliefs, knowledge, social influences, and environmental forces (ideally grounded in one or more theoretical models). The next phase is to examine the model from a communication perspective, specifying *target audiences* that can be directly (or, as noted below, indirectly) reached and *target behaviors* that can be influenced by campaign messages. A sophisticated campaign will seek to affect the most promising pathways guided by a comprehensive plan for combining manifold components and an appropriate theoretical framework matched to the desired outcome and the relevant audiences and social systems.

which? how choose?

how choose?

Direct Effects on Focal Audience Segments

The nature of the substantive problem dictates the broad parameters of the focal audience to be influenced. Most campaigns aim messages directly at the focal segments, which are subpopulations who might benefit from the campaign because they are at risk for harm or in need of help or improvement. The potential for achieving direct effects depends on the relative prevalence of various types of receptiveness among target audience segments. A fundamental receptivity factor is stage of readiness to perform the practice; campaigns typically achieve the strongest impact via triggering or reinforcing messages intended for people who are already favorably predisposed (as argued by the Transtheoretical Model). Another key audience segment includes those who have not yet tried the undesirable behavior but whose background characteristics suggest they are at risk in the near future; many may be receptive to persuasive messages. Those committed to unsuitable practices are not readily influenced by directly targeted campaigns, so a heavy investment of resources to induce discontinuation tends to yield a marginal payoff. Among focal targets, there are demographic, social, and psychological-based subgroups such as higher versus lower income strata, high versus low sensation seekers, those experiencing psychological or social obstacles in accomplishing certain behaviors, and members of different cultures.

Indirect Effects on Interpersonal Influencers and Policy Makers

Rather than relying predominantly on direct persuasion, campaigners may attain greater impact by investing effort and resources in campaign components affecting indirect or secondary target audiences who can 1) exert interpersonal influence on focal individuals or 2) help reform environmental conditions that shape behavior. Media campaigns have considerable potential for motivating interpersonal influencers in close contact with focal individuals as well as producing effects on institutions and groups at the national and community levels (Atkin & Salmon, 2010).

Thus, a second effects strategy is to initiate a multistep flow by disseminating messages to potential *interpersonal influencers* or opinion leaders who are in a position to personally influence focal individuals. Campaigns aim at opinion leader audiences because they tend to be more receptive to campaign messages, and their indirectly stimulated influences are likely to be more effective than campaign messages directly targeted to the focal segment (Rogers, 2003). Interpersonal influencers can impact behavior through activities such as dispensing positive and negative reinforcement, exercising control via rule making and enforcement, facilitating behavior with reminders at opportune moments, and serving as role models. A major advantage of the interpersonal relationships is that the influencer can customize the messages to the unique needs and values of individuals in a more precise and context-relevant manner than most media messages. The effectiveness of social network-oriented media campaigns, typically targeted to friends and family members of the focal individuals to be influenced, is reviewed in the health domain by Abroms and Maibach (2008).

In a third effects strategy, the campaign may seek to alter the environment indirectly by providing messages to societal and organizational policy makers who are responsible for devising constraints and creating opportunities that shape focal individuals' decisions and behaviors. Individuals' decisions are strongly shaped by the constraints and opportunities in their societal environments, such as monetary expenses, laws, industry practices, entertainment role models, commercial messages, social forces, and community services. Policy makers in government, business, educational, medical, media, religious, and community organizations can initiate interventions that alter the environment.

Some reformers combine community organizing and media publicity to advance healthy public policies via *media advocacy*. The media advocacy approach seeks to frame public health issues to emphasize policy-related environmental solutions rather than the usual focus on individual responsibility for good health. Media advocacy is "the strategic use of mass media in combination with community organizing to advance healthy public policies" (Dorfman & Wallack, Chapter 23). It explicitly attempts to associate social problems with social structures and inequities, change public policy rather than individual behavior, reach opinion leaders and policy makers, work with groups to increase involvement in the communication process, and reduce the power gap instead of simply providing more information. The four primary activities involved in media advocacy include 1) develop an overall strategy, which includes formulating policy options, identifying the stakeholders that have power to create relevant change, applying pressure to foster change, and developing messages for these stakeholders, 2) set the agenda, including gaining access to the news media through stories, news events, and editorials, 3) shape the debate, including framing the public health problems as policy issues salient to significant audiences, emphasizing social accountability, and providing evidence for the broader claims, and 4) advance the policy, including maintaining interest, pressure, and coverage over time.

Activists generate news media coverage to mobilize the public to influence policy makers to enact reforms to address health problems, particularly relating to smoking and drinking. Gaining consistent visibility in the news media is a key to achieving an agenda-setting effect, which is particularly important in media advocacy strategies targeted to opinion leaders and policy makers in society. Through agenda setting on health issues, news coverage can mold the public agenda and the policy agenda pertaining to new initiatives, rules, and laws. An important element involves strengthening the public's beliefs about the efficacy of policies and interventions that are advanced, which leads to supportive public opinion (and direct pressure) that can help convince institutional leaders to formulate and implement societal constraints and opportunities.

A related means of integrating media and interpersonal communication is to organize campaign activities at the community level (Bracht & Rice, Chapter 20). Community-based campaigning can engage stakeholders at all stages of the process, from contributing design inputs to assisting in implementation to active involvement in consequences; some campaigns explicitly seek to empower communities and activate voluntary associations, government agencies, schools, or businesses to achieve short-term success and help attain sustainability and institutionalization of campaign initiatives. Organizing community campaigns encompasses assessing assets and capacities, developing a collaborative organizational structure, generating cooperation of multiple partners and broad citizen participation, and consolidating program maintenance.

CAMPAIGN MESSAGES AND MEDIA

Strategic Approaches: Prevention Versus Promotion

In seeking to influence behavior, campaigners may decide to promote positive behaviors (e.g., eat fruit, buckle safety belts, recycle paper) or to prevent problematic behaviors (e.g., consuming fats, driving while intoxicated, burning forests). Traditionally, prevention campaigns present fear appeals to focus attention on negative consequences of a detrimental practice rather than promoting the desirability of a positive alternative. This approach is most potent in cases where harmful outcomes are genuinely threatening or positive products are insufficiently compelling.

The social marketing perspective is especially applicable to promoting desirable behavior, which involves offering rewarding gains from attractive "products" (such as tasty fruit, the designated driver arrangement, or staircase exercising). In developing behavioral recommendations in promotional campaigns, designers can draw upon an array of options from the "product line." These target responses vary in palatability associated with degree of effort, sacrifice, and monetary expense; a central strategic consideration in determining the degree of difficulty is receptiveness of the focal segment. The prolonged nature of campaigns enables the use of gradually escalating sequential approaches over a period of months or years.

Message Content: Informational Versus Persuasive

In many campaign situations, informational messages that seek to create awareness or provide instruction play an important role. *Awareness messages* present relatively simple content that informs people what to do, specifies who should do it, or provides cues about when and where it should be done. Even superficial messages can stimulate the audience to seek out richer, in-depth content from elaborated informational resources such as webpages, books, and opinion leaders. The more complex *instruction messages* present how-to-do-it information in campaigns that need to produce knowledge gain or skills acquisition, including enhancing personal efficacy in bolstering peer resistance and acquiring media literacy skills.

However, the central type of content in campaigns features *persuasive* messages. Most campaigns present persuasion appeals emphasizing reasons why the audience should adopt the advocated action or avoid the proscribed behavior. For audiences that are favorably inclined, the campaign has the easier persuasive task of reinforcing existing predispositions: strengthening a positive attitude, promoting postbehavior consolidation, and motivating behavioral maintenance over time. Because a lengthy campaign generally disseminates a broad array of persuasive messages, strategists often develop a variety of appeals built around motivational incentives designed to influence attitudes and behaviors.

Message Appeals: Persuasive Incentives

Persuasive messages in public communication campaigns frequently utilize a basic expectancy-value mechanism by designing messages to influence beliefs regarding the subjective likelihood of various outcomes occurring; attitudinal and behavioral effects are contingent upon each individual's valuation of these outcomes. The operational formula for preventing risky behaviors is *susceptibility* multiplied by *severity,* using a loss frame to motivate the audience with a high likelihood of suffering painful consequences. The incentive appeals often build on existing values of the target audience, so the messages tend to reinforce the predispositions or change beliefs about the likelihood of experiencing valued consequences.

For campaigns in the health domain, the primary incentive dimensions are physical health, time and effort, economic, moral, legal, social, and psychological. Rather than over-emphasizing the narrow dimension of physical health threats (e.g., death, illness, injury), campaigners are increasingly diversifying loss-framed incentive strategies to include other negative appeals (e.g., monetary expense, psychological regret, social rejection), as well as emphasizing gain-framed positive incentives (e.g., valued states or consequences, such as physical well-being, saving money, social attractiveness).

Message Design and Implementation: Qualitative Dimensions

Designing messages involves the strategic selection of substantive material and the creative production of stylistic features. In developing the combination of message components, the campaign designer seeks to emphasize one or more of five influential message qualities. First, *credibility* is primarily conveyed by the trustworthiness and competence of the source and the provision of convincing evidence. Second, the style and ideas should be presented in an *engaging* manner via selection of interesting or arousing substantive content combined with attractive and entertaining stylistic execution. The third dimension emphasizes selection of material and stylistic devices that are personally *involving* and *relevant,* so receivers regard the behavioral recommendation as applicable to their situations and needs. The fourth element is *understandability,* with simple, explicit, and detailed presentation of content that is comprehensive and comprehensible to receivers. For persuasive messages, the fifth factor is *motivational incentives,* as described above. Atkin and Freimuth (Chapter 4) provide much greater detail on the formative evaluation stage of message design.

Message Sources

The *messenger* is the presenter who appears in the message to deliver information, demonstrate behavior, or provide a testimonial. Messengers help enhance each qualitative factor by being engaging (attractiveness, likability), credible (trustworthiness, expertise), and relevant to the audience (similarity, familiarity). These attributes can 1) attract attention and facilitate comprehension by personalizing message concepts, 2) elicit positive cognitive responses during processing, 3) heighten emotional arousal via identification or transfer of affect, and 4) increase retention due to memorability. The key categories of public communication campaign messengers are celebrities, public officials, topical expert specialists, professional performers, ordinary people, specially experienced individuals (e.g., victims or beneficiaries), and unique characters (e.g., animated or costumed).

Mediated Communication Channels: Mass and Digital

In disseminating messages, most campaign designers still rely on traditional broadcast and print channels that carry public service messages, entertainment–education (E–E) placements, and news coverage. Websites displaying prepackaged informational pages have also been a central campaign vehicle since the late 1990s, although campaigns have increasingly utilized interactive technology (whether online or via DVDs or mobile devices) in recent years.

   In assessing the dozens of options for channeling campaign messages, campaign designers take into consideration advantages and drawbacks along a number of communicative dimensions. Salmon and Atkin (2003) discuss channel differences in terms of *reach* (proportion of population exposed to the message), *specializability* (narrowcasting to specific subgroups or tailoring to individuals), *interactivity* (receiver participation and stimulus adaptation during processing), *meaning modalities* (array of senses employed in conveying meaning), *personalization* (human relational nature of source–receiver interaction), *decodability* (mental effort required for processing stimulus), *depth* (channel capacity for conveying detailed and complex content), *credibility* (believability of material conveyed), *agenda setting* (potency of channel for raising salience priority of issues), *accessibility* (ease of placing messages in channel), and *economy* (low cost for producing and disseminating stimuli).

   Channel selection is most often determined by the usage patterns of target audiences and the nature of the message and topic within the constraints of available resources. Public communication campaigners find it more practical to stage a pseudo event that generates news coverage than to raise funds to purchase time or space in the ideal media vehicle, more feasible to achieve a minor product placement in an entertainment program than to capture the whole plotline, and more economical to place a public service announcement (PSA) on a low-rated, mature adult radio station than on a hot teen station. Certain topics pertaining to health, safety, and the environment are inherently attractive to professionals working in traditional media such as local newspapers, women's magazines, and radio talk shows. The related practice of E–E (Singhal, Cody, Rogers, & Sabido, 2004), which involves embedding campaign topic-related material in entertainment programming, is widely welcomed by media gatekeepers in developing nations but not the United States.

Health interventions and campaigns are increasingly emphasizing digital media technologies (Edgar, Noar, & Freimuth, 2007; Parker & Thorson, 2009; Rice & Atkin, 2009). New media offer additional dimensions of campaigning through interactivity, tailoring, and narrowcasting. *Interactivity* has two primary dimensions, direction of communication and level of receiver control over the communication process, which yield four kinds of relationships between the user and the source (monologue, feedback, responsive dialogue, and mutual discourse). Each of these relationships can be associated with specific design features, such as surveys, games, purchasing products or services, e-mail, hyperlinks, and chat rooms. Interactive media facilitate *tailoring* of customized messages that reflect the individual's predispositions and abilities (Noar, Harrington, & Aldrich, 2009; Rimer & Kreuter, 2006). Online screening questionnaires assess factors, such as readiness stage, stylistic tastes, knowledge levels, and current beliefs, and then direct them to *narrowcast* messages. Not only does this approach increase the likelihood of learning and persuasion, but it decreases the possibility of boomerang effects.

The Internet has become a major source for information, discussion, therapy, and access to physicians (Rice, 2006; Rice & Katz, 2001). Online health-related support groups can increase social support, quality of life, and self-efficacy in managing one's health condition. The value of anonymity inherent in web information search and online discussion groups is valuable for private or sensitive topics (e.g., STD/HIV prevention and testing). A meta-analysis of 75 randomized controlled health trials involving computer-delivered intervention found improved knowledge, attitudes, intentions, health behaviors, and general health maintenance across a variety of health domains (Portnoy, Scott-Sheldon, Johnson, & Carey, 2008). Another meta-analysis of 85 studies of using the Internet for health behavior change reported an overall small but significant positive effect, with stronger results for interventions applying theory in general and TPB in particular for those applying behavior change techniques and those using other communication approaches, especially text messaging (Webb, Joseph, Yardley, & Michie, 2010). Mobile phone calling and texting are well suited to offer tailored, wide-reaching, interactive and continuing campaign interventions. Cole-Lewis and Kershaw's (2010) review found consistent evidence of the positive effects of text messaging on behavioral changes across demographic and national differences.

Campaigns may utilize online public service promos, typically in the form of brief banner ad messages or solicitations to click through to a website. However, these messages have severe content capacity limitations, the sponsors have little control over placement of their banner ads, and ads are often blocked by computer software. Paid health promotion ads on social media sites have greater potential for impact because of more prominent placement and more precise targeting. Health PSA spots and long-form video messages attract modest viewership on YouTube, although unhealthy portrayals and parodies of the health messages are also featured among the mix of messages accessible on this site.

Blogs serve an important role in linking users with similar information needs and concerns to share their views and experiences, while wikis support collaboration among campaign members. Podcasts can provide relevant audio information (such as social support, variations on the persuasive message, or related health news) to motivated audiences at their convenience. Twitter can be used to provide updates and protocol reminders to campaign-specific followers.

Voice response systems, interactive video, DVD, CD-ROM, mobile phones, and computer games can be effective in reaching young people. Lieberman (Chapter 19) recommends that computer-mediated campaigns feature youthful genres, support information seeking, incorporate challenges and goals, use learning by doing, create functional learning environments, and facilitate social interaction. Video game learning relevant to campaigns includes skill acquisition from interactive games, improved self-efficacy through success in vicarious experiences, and role-playing and modeling. Baranowski, Buday, Thompson, & Baranowski (2008)'s meta-analysis of 25 studies of using video games to affect health behavior (chronic disease management, exercise, and diet) found improvements in nearly all outcomes.

To maximize quantity, campaigners seek to gain media access via monetary support from government and industry (to fund paid placements and leveraged media slots), aggressive lobbying for free public service time or space, skillful use of public relations techniques for generating entertainment and journalistic coverage, and reliance on low-cost channels of communication such as websites and social media. The Ad Council helps develop a select number of nonprofit messages each year, both responding to and influencing campaign agenda items. For example, its current public service campaign topics include 11 community issues (from energy efficiency to pet shelters), eight education issues (from college access to lifelong literacy), and 27 health and safety issues (from autism awareness to nutrition education) (see http://www.adcouncil.org/default.aspx?id=15). Moreover, the reach of a campaign is often boosted by sensitizing audiences to appropriate content already available in the media and by stimulating information seeking from specialty sources.

Quantitative Dissemination Factors

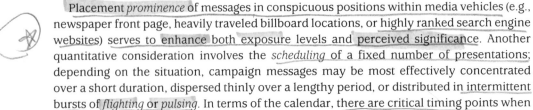

Five major aspects of strategic message dissemination are the total volume of messages, the amount of repetition, the prominence of placement, the scheduling of message presentation, and temporal length of the campaign. A substantial *volume* of stimuli helps attain adequate reach and frequency of exposure as well as comprehension, recognition, and image formation. Message saturation also conveys the significance of the problem addressed in the campaign, which heightens agenda setting and salience. A certain level of *repetition* of specific executions facilitates message comprehension and positive affect toward the product, but high repetition produces wear out and diminishing returns.

Placement *prominence* of messages in conspicuous positions within media vehicles (e.g., newspaper front page, heavily traveled billboard locations, or highly ranked search engine websites) serves to enhance both exposure levels and perceived significance. Another quantitative consideration involves the *scheduling* of a fixed number of presentations; depending on the situation, campaign messages may be most effectively concentrated over a short duration, dispersed thinly over a lengthy period, or distributed in intermittent bursts of *flighting* or *pulsing*. In terms of the calendar, there are critical timing points when the audience is more likely to be attentive or active in information seeking.

Regarding the overall *length* of the campaign, the realities of public service promotion and problem prevention often require exceptional persistence of effort over long periods of time to attain a critical mass of exposures. In many cases, perpetual campaigning is necessary because focal segments of the population are in constant need of influence as newcomers enter the priority audience, backsliders revert to prior misbehavior, evolvers gradually adopt practices at a slow pace, and vacillators need regular reinforcement.

CAMPAIGN EVALUATION METHODS

Formative Evaluation

The applicability of general campaign design principles depends on the specific context (especially types of audiences to be influenced and types of product being promoted), so effective design usually requires extensive formative evaluation inputs (Atkin & Freimuth, Chapter 4). In the early stages of campaign development, designers collect background information about the focal segments and interpersonal influencers using statistical databases and custom surveys to learn about audience predispositions, channel usage patterns, and evaluations of prospective sources and appeals. As message concepts are being refined and rough versions are created, qualitative reactions are obtained in focus group discussion sessions, and supplemental quantitative ratings can be measured in message testing laboratories.

Process Evaluation

While the campaign is underway, *process evaluation* assesses the extent to which designed elements are actually implemented and ways in which the campaign program can be improved for subsequent designers and implementers (Steckler & Linnan, 2006). Process evaluation is useful for determining effectiveness of campaign management and identifying lessons for overcoming social and structural obstacles.

Summative or Outcome Evaluation

After a campaign has been implemented (but planned and integrated from the beginning), summative evaluation research is performed to assess outcomes. Valente and Kwan (Chapter 6) summarize the basic methodologies, including field experimental, cross-sectional, cohort, panel, time-series, or event-history designs, although qualitative components and mixed-methods evaluations provide unique, additional, and triangulated insights. Summative research can be conducted both during and after major campaign phases.

Campaign Effectiveness

Research findings suggest that campaigns are capable of generating moderate to strong influences on cognitive outcomes, less influence on attitudinal outcomes, and still less influence on behavioral outcomes (Atkin, 2001; Snyder & LaCroix, Chapter 8). Further, behavioral outcomes tend to vary in proportion to such factors as the dose of information, qualitative potency of messages, integration of mass and interpersonal communication systems, and integration of social-change strategies (enforcement, education, and engineering; see Paisley & Atkin, Chapter 2).

A campaign may not attain a strong impact for many reasons. Audience resistance barriers arise at each stage of response from exposure to behavioral implementation. A major problem is simply reaching the audience and attaining attention to the messages (Hornik, 2002). Exposed audience members are lost at each subsequent response stage due to defensive responses such as misperception of susceptibility to threatened consequences, denial of applicability of message incentives to self, defensive counterarguing against persuasive appeals, rejection of unappealing behavioral recommendations, and sheer inertial lethargy. Public communication campaign outcomes tend to diminish for receivers who regard messages as offensive, disturbing, boring, stale, preachy, confusing, irritating, misleading, irrelevant, uninformative, useless, unbelievable, or uninspiring.

Salmon and Murray-Johnson (Chapter 7) make distinctions among various types of campaign effectiveness, including *definitional effectiveness* (e.g., getting a social phenomenon defined as a social problem or elevating it on the public agenda), *contextual effectiveness* (e.g., impact within particular contexts such as education vs. enforcement vs. engineering), *cost-effectiveness* comparison (e.g., prevention vs. treatment, addressing certain problems over others), and *programmatic effectiveness* (e.g., testing campaign outcomes relative to stated goals and objectives).

FUTURE CHALLENGES

Despite considerable progress in recent years, a variety of theoretical and practical challenges and tensions remain to be addressed. Future research is needed to better understand the issues pertaining to campaign design, implementation, and resource allocation outlined in this section.

What is the optimum mix of message incentives? Most campaigns use multiple persuasive appeals, but not enough is known about the most effective combination of gain-frame versus loss-frame messages and of fear appeals versus other negative appeals. What should be the relative emphasis on short-term versus long-term objectives and effects, and how can campaigns achieve longer-term outcomes? How can campaigns successfully promote a *prevention* approach in order to avoid the more expensive *treatment* approach typically favored by organizations, government agencies, and the electorate?

What is the most effective balance of *direct* versus *indirect strategies* in various contexts? Campaigns increasingly rely on messages targeted to interpersonal influencers and on media advocacy approaches aimed at the general public and policy makers, but the appropriate blending of these approaches has not been identified. Beyond the predominant focus on individual benefits, campaigns must address important social problems involving community and collective benefits. What are the relative influences of individual differences versus social structure on the problems motivating communication campaigns? How can campaigns communicate effectively with young people who exhibit fundamentally different evaluations of risk and future consequences, who are using radically different interactive and personal media, and who are deeply embedded in peer networks?

interesting

What is the impact of various quantities of campaign messages? Research should examine the minimum volume of stimuli needed to achieve meaningful effects on key outcomes and the quantitative point of diminishing returns from larger volumes. With respect to repetition, it would be helpful to know at what point wear out occurs for a particular message execution.

Finally, what is the relative impact of various channels for disseminating messages? Specifically, researchers need to assess the influence of each new communication technology that is introduced to determine the cost-effectiveness of paid advertisements, to fine-tune the mixture of education and entertainment in *infotainment* that's embedded in commercial media, and to examine the roles of diverse options such as television, posters, websites, mobile devices, and personal outreach. Intriguingly, the ease of users creating their own messages, and the involvement of those users in a variety of online and mobile media, provide the potential for much more engagement by focal audiences and their communities in future campaigns. In particular, the constantly evolving landscape of mediated communication will revolutionize the campaign of the future; research is needed to monitor opportunities and assess the potential of new applications. Moreover, campaigns will need to devise approaches for overcoming the simultaneous pervasive negative influence of counterproductive mass media messages on campaign issues such as drinking, violence, and environmental damage.

Conclusion

Most experts conclude that contemporary public communication campaigns attain a modest rather than strong impact, notably on the health behaviors. This is partially due to meager dissemination budgets, unsophisticated application of theory and models, and poorly conceived strategic approaches. It is also due to the difficulty of the task facing the campaigner, who may be promoting complex or difficult behaviors, targeting resistant audience segments, or coping with limited resources, while at-risk audiences are constantly exposed to peer influences, entertainment portrayals, and advertisements that highlight, encourage, and positively frame detrimental behaviors. In these situations, more emphasis should be given to relatively attainable impacts by aiming at more receptive focal segments, by promoting more palatable positive products perceived to have a favorable benefit-cost ratio, by creatively generating free publicity, and by shifting campaign resources to indirect pathways that facilitate and control behavior of the focal segment via interpersonal, network, organizational, and societal influences. More generally, the degree of campaign success can be improved via greater diversification of pathways, products, incentives, and channels beyond the approaches conventionally used in public communication campaigns.

Despite the array of barriers that diminish campaign effectiveness, the research literature shows many success stories over the past several decades. Health campaigns have made significant contributions to the progress in addressing important problems such as smoking, seat belt use, drunk driving, AIDS, drug use, and heart disease. These effective campaigns tend to be characterized by theoretical guidance and rigorous evaluation, substantial quantity of message dissemination over sustained periods, widespread receptivity to the advocated action and accompanying persuasive incentives, and supplementation of mediated messages by campaign-stimulated factors such as informal interpersonal influences and social engineering policy initiatives.

Greater success can be attained if campaigners play to the strengths of the mass media for influencing cognitively oriented variables (e.g., by imparting new knowledge, enhancing salience of a problem or product, teaching people new techniques, and stimulating information seeking). Moreover, the relatively small collection of packaged messages such as PSAs can be augmented by generating publicity and by sensitizing audiences to respond to congruent content available in the media. Quantity can be increased by pursuing monetary resources to enable paid placements and by using creative and political resources to generate free publicity and engineer healthy entertainment portrayals.

With the increasing adoption of sophisticated strategies and the rising priority of healthy and prosocial practices for individuals and society, there is a sound basis for optimism that campaigns can produce stronger impacts in the future. The ideas outlined in this chapter (and elaborated in the following chapters) offer some promising approaches for designers to consider in developing the next generation of campaigns for addressing societal problems.

ADDITIONAL RESOURCES FOR CAMPAIGN DESIGN AND RESEARCH INFORMATION

Theories, designs, and impacts of media-based public campaigns are summarized in chapters by Abroms and Maibach (2008); Atkin and Salmon (2010); Randolph and Visnawath (2004); Rice and Atkin (2009, 2011); Salmon and Atkin (2003), and Silk, Atkin, and Salmon (2011). Key book-length theoretical perspectives and reviews include Atkin and Wallack (1990); Backer, Rogers, and Sopory (1992); Edgar, Noar, and Freimuth (2007); Green and Tones (2010); Hornik (2002); Kotler, Roberto, and Lee (2002); Lundgren and McMakin (2009); Maibach and Parrott (1995); O'Keefe (2002); Perloff (2003); Rice and Atkin (2001); Rogers (2003); Salmon (1989); Stiff and Mongeau (2003); and Witte, Meyer, and Martell (2001). The encyclopedic overview of the broad topic of communication campaigns by Rice and Atkin (2011) provides a useful resource listing of annotated publications and websites organized into 17 sections: basic source books, pertinent academic journals, summary of major theoretical perspectives, social marketing, campaign design, new media, formative evaluation, campaign implementation, community and media advocacy issues, general health topics, HIV/AIDS, nutrition, drugs, smoking, human rights, environment, and evaluation of campaign impact. Additional links to online resources are available at http://www.comm.ucsb.edu/faculty/rrice/ricelink.htm#CAMPAIGN.

References

Abroms, L. C., & Maibach, E. W. (2008). The effectiveness of mass communication to change public behavior. *Annual Review of Public Health, 29,* 219–234.

Ajzen, I., & Fishbein, M. (1980). *Understanding attitudes and predicting social behavior.* Englewood Cliffs, NJ: Prentice Hall.

Ajzen, I., Albarracin, D., & Hornik, R. C. (2007). *Prediction and change of health behavior: Applying the reasoned action approach.* Mahwah, NJ: Lawrence Erlbaum.

Andreasen, A. (1995). *Marketing social change: Changing behavior to promote health, social development, and the environment.* San Francisco: Jossey-Bass.

Andreasen, A. (2006). *Social marketing in the 21st century.* Thousand Oaks, CA: Sage.

Atkin, C. K. (2001). Theory and principles of media health campaigns. In R. E. Rice & C. K. Atkin (Eds.), *Public communication campaigns* (3rd ed., pp. 49–68). Thousand Oaks, CA: Jossey-Bass.

Atkin, C. K., & Salmon, C. (2010). Communication campaigns. In C. Berger, M. Roloff, & D. Roskos-Ewoldsen (Eds.), *Handbook of communication science* (2nd ed., pp. 419–435). Thousand Oaks, CA: Sage.

Atkin, C. K., & Wallack, L. (1990). *Mass communication and public health: Complexities and conflicts.* Newbury Park, CA: Sage.

Backer, T., Rogers, E. & Sopory, P. (1992). *Designing health communication campaigns: What works?* Newbury Park, CA: Sage.

Bandura, A. (1986). *Social foundations of thought and action: A social cognitive theory.* Englewood Cliffs, NJ: Prentice Hall.

Bandura, A. (1997). *Self-efficacy: The exercise of control.* New York: W.H. Freeman.

Baranowski, T., Buday, R., Thompson, D. I., & Baranowski, J. (2008). Playing for real: Video games and stories for health-related behavior change. *American Journal of Preventive Medicine, 34(1),* 74–82.

Becker, M. H. (1974). *The health belief model and personal health behavior.* San Francisco: Society for Public Health Education.

Cappella, J., Fishbein, M., Hornik, R., Ahern, R. K., & Sayeed, S. (2001). Using theory to select messages in anti-drug media campaigns: Reasoned action and media priming. In R. E. Rice & C. K. Atkin (Eds.), *Public communication campaigns* (3rd ed., pp. 214–230). Thousand Oaks, CA: Sage.

Cole-Lewis, H., & Kershaw, T. (2010). Text messaging as a tool for behavior change in disease prevention and management. *Epidemiologic Reviews, 32*(1), 59–69. Retrieved from http://epirev.oxfordjournals.org/cgi/content/abstract/mxq004v1

Eagly, A., & Chaiken, S. (1993). *Psychology of attitudes.* New York: Harcourt Brace Jovanovich.

Edgar, T., Noar, S., & Freimuth, V. (2007). *Communication perspectives on HIV/AIDS for the 21st century.* Mahwah, NJ: Lawrence Erlbaum.

Green, G., & Tones, K. (2010). *Health promotion: Planning and strategies* (2nd ed.). London: Sage.

Hornik, R. (2002). *Public health communication.* Mahwah, NJ: Lawrence Erlbaum.

Hovland, C., Janis, I., & Kelley, H. (1953). *Communication and persuasion.* New Haven, CT: Yale University Press.

Katz, E., Blumler, J. G., & Gurevitch, M. (1974). Utilization of mass communication by the individual. In J. G. Blumler & E. Katz (Eds.), *The uses of mass communications: Current perspectives on gratifications research* (pp. 19–32). Beverly Hills, CA: Sage.

Kotler, P., Roberto, N., & Lee, N. (2002). *Social marketing: Improving the quality of life.* Thousand Oaks, CA: Sage.

Lundgren, R. E., & McMakin, A. H. (2009). *Risk communication: A handbook for communicating environmental, safety, and health risks.* Hoboken, NJ: Wiley.

Maibach, E., & Parrott, R. (1995). *Designing health messages: Approaches from communication theory and public health practice.* Thousand Oaks, CA: Sage.

McCombs, M. (2004). *Setting the agenda: The mass media and public opinion.* Malden, MA: Blackwell.

McKenzie-Mohr, D. (2011). *Fostering sustainable behavior: An introduction to community-based social marketing.* Gabriola Island, British Columbia, Canada: New Society Publishers.

Noar, S. M., Harrington, N. G., & Aldrich, R. (2009). The role of message tailoring in the development of persuasive health communication messages. In C. S. Beck (Ed.), *Communication yearbook 33* (pp. 73–133). New York: Lawrence Erlbaum.

O'Keefe, D. J. (2002). *Persuasion: Theory and research.* Thousand Oaks CA: Sage.

O'Keefe, D. J., & Jensen, J. D. (2007). The relative persuasiveness of gain-framed and loss-framed messages for encouraging disease prevention behaviors: A meta-analytic review. *Journal of Health Communication, 12,* 623–644.

Parker, J. C., & Thorson, E. (2009). *Health communication in the new media landscape.* New York: Springer.

Perloff, R. M. (2003). *The dynamics of persuasion: Communication and attitudes in the 21st century* (2nd ed.). Mahwah, NJ: Lawrence Erlbaum.

Petty, R., & Cacioppo, J. (1986). *Communication and persuasion: Central and peripheral routes to attitude change.* New York: Springer-Verlag.

Portnoy, D. B., Scott-Sheldon, L. A. J., Johnson, B. T., & Carey, M. P. (2008). Computer-delivered interventions for health promotion and behavioral risk reduction: A meta-analysis of 75 randomized controlled trials, 1988–2007. *Preventive Medicine, 47*(1), 3–16.

Prochaska, J., & Velicer, W. (1997). The Transtheoretical Model of health behavior change. *American Journal of Health Promotion, 12,* 38–48.

Quick, B., & Bates, B. (2010). The use of gain- or loss-frame messages and efficacy appeals to dissuade excessive alcohol consumption among college students: A test of psychological reactance theory. *Journal of Health Communication, 15,* 603–628.

Randolph, W., & Visnawath, K. (2004). Lessons learned from public health mass media campaigns: Marketing health in a crowded media world. *Annual Review of Public Health, 25,* 419–437.

Rice, R. E. (2006). Influences, usage, and outcomes of Internet health information searching: Multivariate results from the Pew surveys. *International Journal of Medical Informatics, 75*(1), 8–28.

Rice, R. E., & Atkin, C. K. (Eds.). (2001). *Public communication campaigns* (3rd ed.). Thousand Oaks, CA: Sage.

Rice, R. E., & Atkin, C. K. (2009). Public communication campaigns: Theoretical principles and practical applications. In J. Bryant & M. Oliver (Eds.), *Media effects: Advances in theory and research* (3rd ed., pp. 436–468). Hillsdale, NJ: Lawrence Erlbaum.

Rice, R. E., & Atkin, C. K. (2011). Communication campaigns. *Oxford Bibliographies Online (Communication).* DOI: 10.1093/OBO/9780199756841–0055. 28pp.

Rice, R. E., & Katz, J. E. (Eds.). (2001). *The Internet and health communication: Expectations and experiences.* Thousand Oaks, CA: Sage.

Rimer, B., & Kreuter, M. W. (2006). Advancing tailored health communication: A persuasion and message effects perspective. *Journal of Communication, 56,* S184–S201.

Rogers, E. M. (2003). *Diffusion of innovations* (5th ed.). New York: Free Press.

Rogers, E. M., & Storey, J. D. (1987). Communication campaigns. In C. Berger & S. Chaffee (Eds.), *Handbook of communication science* (pp. 817–846). Newbury Park, CA: Sage.

Rubin, A. M. (2002). The uses-and-gratifications perspective of media effects. In J. Bryant & D. Zillmann (Eds.), *Media effects: Advances in theory and research* (2nd ed., pp. 525–548). Mahwah, NJ: Erlbaum.

Salmon, C. (1989). *Information campaigns: Balancing social values and social change.* Newbury Park, CA: Sage.

Salmon, C., & Atkin, C. K. (2003). Media campaigns for health promotion. In T. L. Thompson, A. M. Dorsey, K. I. Miller, & R. Parrott, R. (Eds.), *Handbook of health communication* (pp. 472–494). Mahwah, NJ: Lawrence Erlbaum.

Silk, K., Atkin, C. K., & Salmon., C. (2011). Developing effective media campaigns for health promotion. In T. L. Thompson, R. Parrott, & J. Nussbaum (Eds.), *Handbook of health communication* (2nd ed., pp. 203–219). Hillsdale, NJ: Lawrence Erlbaum.

Singhal, A., Cody, M., Rogers, E., & Sabido, M. (2004). *Entertainment-education and social change: History, research, and practice.* Mahwah, NJ: Lawrence Erlbaum.

Steckler, A., & Linnan, L. (Eds.). (2006). *Process evaluation for public health interventions and research.* New York: John Wiley and Sons.

Stephenson, M., & Witte, K. (2001). Creating fear in a risky world: Generating effective health risk messages. In R. E. Rice & C. K. Atkin (Eds.), *Public communication campaigns* (3rd ed., pp. 88–102). Thousand Oaks, CA: Sage.

Stiff, J. B., & Mongeau, P. (2003). *Persuasive communication* (2nd ed.). New York: Guilford Press.

Webb, T. L., Joseph, J., Yardley, L., & Michie, S. (2010). Using the Internet to promote health behavior change: A systematic review and meta-analysis of the impact of theoretical basis, use of behavior change techniques, and mode of delivery on efficacy. *Journal of Medical Internet Research, 12*(1), e4. Retrieved from http://www.jmir.org/2010/1/e4

Witte, K., Meyer, G., & Martell, D. (2001). *Effective health risk messages.* Thousand Oaks, CA: Sage.

Public Communication Campaigns—The American Experience

William Paisley and Charles K. Atkin

Public communication campaigns are a familiar and essential part of American civic culture. Campaign topics range from personal issues, such as health, to social issues, such as equal opportunity, energy conservation, and environmental protection. Campaigns are regarded as public service programs if their goals are widely supported by the public and policy makers. However, if their goals are controversial, then campaigns are regarded as advocacy strategies. As societal values change, some campaign topics (e.g., race and gender equality) move from the second category to the first. Some topics (e.g., the traditional American diet now regarded as unhealthy) move from the first category to the second.

CAMPAIGN STAKEHOLDERS

This volume, written by social scientists, tells how public communication campaigns have matured in recent decades thanks in part to the contributions of social science to campaign planning and implementation. However, social scientists are only the latest group of stakeholders to be involved in public communication campaigns. Prior to World War II, the principal stakeholders were voluntary associations, the mass media, and the federal government. These stakeholders are as active as ever. Three other stakeholders, foundations, trade unions, and corporations, became increasingly involved in public communication campaigns following World War II.

Voluntary associations—professional, service-oriented, religious, and social, such as the American Cancer Society, the Catholic Church, Mothers Against Drunk Driving (MADD)—are often the lead organizations in public communication campaigns. In the public's view, associations possess *entitlement* to address particular issues.

The mass media publish and broadcast an *agenda* of issues that are thought to be important to the public. Via editorials and investigative reporting, publishers and broadcasters advocate action with respect to certain issues. One editorial does not a campaign make, but with tenacity and courage (in the face of possible revenue losses), the media have conducted effective campaigns for more than a century.

Government agencies also conduct and sponsor public communication campaigns. Direct government involvement in campaigns was once rare. However, beginning with the expansion of federal social programs in President Franklin Roosevelt's New Deal, it became common for agencies to use communication campaigns to foster public awareness and favorable attitudes toward federal social programs.

Foundations, such as the Bill & Melinda Gates Foundation and Robert Wood Johnson Foundation, are similar to government agencies in their methods of sponsoring public communication campaigns. Foundations tend to be less politicized than government agencies and more able to undertake controversial campaigns, support innovative methods, and address issues continuously across political cycles. On the other hand, the officers of large foundations tend to be more conservative than their counterparts in government. As a result of these contrasting tendencies, a groundbreaking campaign may make its surprising debut in either sector.

Trade unions owe much of their success and, in some cases, their very existence to communication campaigns that persuade the public to support their goals. One key public action is the consumer boycott, which was effectively employed during the 1970s by labor organizer César Chávez. He inspired a national boycott of grapes to gain recognition of the United Farm Workers of America union in California's agricultural valleys.

Corporations and industry councils promote awareness of activities that have public benefits, such as Anheuser-Busch's "Know When to Say When" campaign. Social scientists' main contribution is their theory-grounded approach to planning and conducting campaigns, beginning in the last half of the 20th century. Social scientists are the catalysts of a new era of cooperation among the stakeholders of campaigns, and their research confirms the roles played by other stakeholders.

This chapter is largely devoted to campaigners who came before the social scientists. Over three centuries of American public communication campaigns, there are more similarities than differences in the objectives and methods of campaigners. The chapter begins with some defining characteristics of public communication campaigns then summarizes some major reform movements and campaigns in the colonial, national, and modern eras. The final section explores three challenges to public communication campaigns that arose between the postwar years and the beginning of the 21st century.

DEFINING CHARACTERISTICS OF PUBLIC COMMUNICATION CAMPAIGNS

Two different but complementary definitions of public communication campaigns are in use. Definition in terms of *objectives* focuses on one group's intention to change another group's beliefs or behaviors. This definition comes to the fore when intentions are controversial, such as campaigns about family planning or global warming. Its most important implication is that the change objectives may be accomplished through a communication campaign or through noncommunication strategies, such as behavioral engineering.

Public communication campaigns are also defined in terms of the *methods* they employ. Their most important implication is that a public communication campaign may involve a conventional mix of brochures, posters, advertisements, and commercials or a different array of communication methods. In industrialized nations, the crowded communication environment favors unusual methods that draw attention to themselves, such as guerilla theater, provocative billboards, murals, and issue mascots.

Reform, defined as action that makes society or the lives of individuals better, is a unifying principle of public communication campaigns. *Better* is defined by emerging values in a society during each period in its history. Public consciousness of a social issue generally increases over time. Today's definition of better may have been too extreme yesterday and may be too moderate tomorrow. In addition, when an issue involves contending interests, the negotiated settlement of those interests is adjusted through experience—that is, over time.

Thus the definition of public communication campaigns can focus either on objectives—strategies of social control insofar as one group intends to influence the beliefs or behaviors of another group—or on methods—a genre of communication that could be called *noncommercial advertising.*

Implications of the Social Control Definition

If campaigns are defined as strategies of social control, then their relationships to other social control strategies is thought provoking. Strategists have developed a paradigm of the *three Es* to categorize approaches to influence behavior: *education, engineering,* and *enforcement.* Public communication campaigns tend to focus on the education part of this triad; for example, safety belt messages warn that unbuckled passengers will be injured in a crash. Safety belt campaigns can also be used to implement enforcement by influencing public opinion to support buckling laws and motivating policy makers to aggressively enforce the laws; enforcement enables additional education message appeals, such as the threat of monetary fines for not being buckled. Engineering solutions, such as noxious buzzers to trigger buckling or airbags that deploy on impact, are typically developed without the direct influence of campaigns.

Each society in each era of its development has an ideology that guides its use of education, engineering, and enforcement to promote change. In the United States, if engineering promises a quick solution, as was often the case in the 19th and 20th centuries, then education and enforcement may not be tried until engineering has had its chance. The first hope is that a miracle drug or equivalent technology will be developed. Education is often the second strategy to be tried. Enforcement is the third, and usually unpopular, strategy.

It is important to note that the social control definition is only a heuristic for planning campaigns and not a judgment of campaign planners' motives. In fact, it is assumed that campaign planners do intend to influence the beliefs and behaviors of others. Most public communication campaigns are regarded as prosocial and are overseen by responsible advisers. Even so, many campaign issues are characterized by two or more contending perspectives (e.g., abortion, nuclear power, health care policy), with each side claiming prosocial benefits.

During the last half of the 20th century, the intertwined strategies of education, engineering, and enforcement could be seen in operation. In the 1950s, civil rights activists innovated new forms of protest that exploited the mass media coverage of their movement. Television provided a national showcase for the principles of nonviolence and the dignity of the oppressed that were borrowed from Gandhi's Indian independence movement and the nonviolent disruptions and hunger strikes of British and American suffragists. Enforcement emerged in the form of a Supreme Court decision striking down the doctrine of "separate-but-equal" services for African-Americans and deployment of federal militia to enforce access to lunch counters, voting booths, and schools. The 1950s saw a burst of engineering creativity in medicine with development of antibiotics, polio vaccines, and oral contraceptives.

The 1960s were marked by an eager faith in engineering solutions, such as Lyndon Johnson's social engineers, who created programs to combat poverty, illiteracy, inequality, and so on. The favored solution in the 1970s was enforcement. Harmful or wasteful conditions were targeted for regulation. Richard Nixon signed a bill banning cigarette advertising on television and radio. With the blessing of the Supreme Court, the Federal Trade Commission expanded its antitrust powers to ban deceptive advertising. Agencies such as the Occupational Safety and Health Administration and the Equal Employment Opportunity Commission took their turns as enforcers during that decade.

Dissatisfaction with both the engineering and enforcement strategies became evident in the 1980s. Engineering often fails because of a faulty analysis of the problem or lack of available knowledge to produce a solution. Enforcement fails when policies are difficult to enforce and when the policies overreach the problem (e.g., some policies that are lampooned for "political correctness").

The 1990s restored a promising balance in the three social change strategies. Engineering improvements range from new medicines (e.g., for HIV remission) to energy-saving products (e.g., compact fluorescent lightbulbs). New laws have significantly reduced smoking in workplaces and public spaces, and new policies of inclusiveness have increased the participation of many groups in the social mainstream.

However, the most dramatic developments of the 1990s involved communication technology with the rise of personal computers, the proliferation of cable and satellite television channels, and the emergence of the Internet. Hundreds of Internet websites are now devoted to certain high-profile campaign issues such as abortion, firearms, or nuclear power. It is clear that the Internet is now one of the venues of public debate and that other competing points of view are only a click away.

Implications of the Process Definition

When engineering and enforcement are less feasible and education is the only strategy that is worth pursuing, attention shifts to the process of communicating. Modern campaigns draw upon the techniques of journalists, media producers, educators, small group specialists, and others. Campaign planners synthesize these techniques into a variety of approaches designed for different target audiences because each audience lives in its own communication environment that filters the messages that reach it. Each audience responds in its own way to appeals based on altruism, self-interest, desire, fear, and so on.

The process-based discipline of planning campaigns leads to conceptual frameworks for understanding what a campaign should accomplish in terms of objectives, messages, contexts, and audiences. These frameworks enable the planner to: clarify the objectives and roles of the campaign's stakeholders; choose and adapt approaches according to audience differences; sequence and coordinate campaign activities; monitor the campaign's possible failure points; improve the campaign on the basis of field trials; and transfer the successes of one campaign in one setting to other campaigns in other settings.

THE ESSENTIAL CONCEPTS OF AGENDA AND ENTITLEMENT

The success of a campaign depends on public perception that the campaign issue is an important one, according to its position on the ever-changing public agenda of issues, and that the campaigners have an entitlement to be involved with the issue.

The concepts of agenda and entitlement originate in a *social contract*. Limits on authority in early America, combined with the diverse goals and customs of American settlers, created a primary role for persuasion and consensus in the American social contract.

The public agenda, when measured by pollsters, always contains some gut issues, such as disease, and some pocketbook issues, such as taxes. However, few issues are truly universal. At any time, issues rise on the public agenda because the problem has gotten worse (e.g., global warming), because changes in the society have made the problem relevant to more people (e.g., heart disease), because public consciousness has caught up with the problem (e.g., rights of disabled persons), or because a solution for the problem has become more feasible (e.g., pollution-reducing technologies).

We come to the question of entitlement to become an advocate of an issue. Is entitlement mainly a question of law, public policy, or public acceptance? Constitutional entitlement is a given in the United States. Within the modern era, however, Margaret Sanger was indicted for sending birth control tracts through the mail. Authorities and citizens still harass unpopular campaigns, but the courts affirm the First Amendment right of the campaigns to proceed.

Public policy affects entitlement when there is a jurisdictional or "ownership" debate over issues. For example, a recently formed agency or association may have a more activist charter and more funds for its cause than an established agency or association.

Public acceptance is the final test of entitlement. The public is ready with the American comeback, "This is none of your business," unless the communicator is clearly a stakeholder in the issue. Aggrieved groups have *first-party* entitlement to communicate in their own interests. *Second-party* entitlement is suspect; we wonder why a group wants to be involved in someone else's grievance.

However, some issues have no first-party group to claim entitlement. Whales, seal pups, and future generations of Americans are the first parties of campaigns, but they are not their own advocates. In such cases, second-party groups step forward to serve as advocates, sometimes putting themselves at risk as surrogate first parties. For example, some save-the-whales groups increased their entitlement when the public saw them risking harm on the ocean. Even when first parties are their own advocates, other groups, such as white civil rights workers in the South during the 1960s, Vietnam draft protesters who were beyond draft age, and straight supporters of gay and lesbian causes, all gained entitlement according to the personal risk or cost of their actions.

Entitlement based on expertise is subject to public acceptance as well. Expert entitlement is a limited license that can be used up if experts publicize too many issues or issues outside their fields. In the 1980s, the Surgeon General (C. Everett Koop) skillfully spent his entitlement by focusing on only the major issues of smoking and AIDS, resisting the temptation to use his "bully pulpit" on behalf of all health issues.

THREE CENTURIES OF AMERICAN PUBLIC COMMUNICATION CAMPAIGNS

The history of the United States is interwoven with communication campaigns from the colonial era to the present day. The communication campaign is only one means of influencing public knowledge, attitudes, and behaviors. However, the limited authority of early American governments, both colonial and national, created a reliance on the communication campaign as an instrument of social change.

The French writer Alexis de Tocqueville (1835/1961) was one of the first to describe how communication informed and mobilized public action in America. He noted "the skill with which the inhabitants of the United States succeed in proposing a common object to the exertions of a great many men, and in getting them voluntarily to pursue it" (p. 129).

Reform was accomplished differently in America than in England or France, according to de Tocqueville: "Wherever, at the head of some new undertaking, you see the Government of France or a man of rank in England, in the United States you will be sure to find an association. . . . If it be proposed to advance some truth or foster some feeling by the encouragement of a great example, [Americans] form a society" (pp. 128–129).

In his American travels, de Tocqueville witnessed the blossoming of the abolition, temperance, and women's rights movements as well as the ferment of Jacksonian democracy and westward expansion. The public agenda of the 19th century was crowded with other issues as well: treatment of the insane, reform of prisons, education of children, opportunities for the deaf and blind, better housing for workers, control of gambling and prostitution in the cities, construction of libraries, and the latest news on experimental utopian communities.

Individual Reformers in the 18th Century

Prior to 1800, American public communication campaigns were often conducted by strong-willed individuals who reached the public through the pulpit or the printing press. An important example from the colonial era was Reverend Cotton Mather's campaign to promote inoculation during Boston's smallpox epidemic of 1721 to 1722. Mather was able to show that death from smallpox was nine times more prevalent among the uninoculated than among the inoculated. Mather's pamphlets and personal appeals foreshadowed the role of the CDC by almost three centuries.

Philadelphia was the headquarters of many types of campaigns in the late 1700s. The first slavery abolition society in America was founded there by Benjamin Franklin and

Benjamin Rush. Thomas Paine published the first American defense of women's rights in his *Pennsylvania Magazine*. In addition, Paine's *Common Sense* booklets, the rallying call of American independence, were widely read through the 13 colonies.

The first significant temperance tract, *Inquiry Into the Effects of Spiritous Liquors on the Human Body and Mind*, was written by Benjamin Rush. Rush also wrote *Thoughts on Female Education*, which argued that the education of women was necessary to ensure that children would be instructed properly in citizenship. Three intertwined issues of American social reform in the 19th century—abolition, women's rights, and temperance—were thus brushed by the 18th century quill of the Philadelphia physician Benjamin Rush.

Rush also published *Medical Inquiries and Observations Upon the Diseases of the Mind.* However, actual reform in the treatment of the mentally ill did not begin until Dorothea Dix's crusade in the 1840s. While teaching Sunday School at a Massachusetts jail, she witnessed treatment of mentally ill persons that stunned her; she visited many other jails and prisons throughout the state to gather facts for a deposition to the Massachusetts legislature. Her goal was humane treatment of the mentally ill in new institutions created for them. She worked effectively behind the scenes, seldom speaking in public. Subsequently, her cause broadened to prison reform, particularly the need to establish separate facilities for women. Dix is a transitional figure in American reform. She was a lone crusader in a century that saw increasing reliance on associations and mass media to move voters and legislators toward the unavoidable decisions on abolition and suffrage.

Associations and Reform in the 19th Century

Issues that are entrenched in law or custom may require decades of lobbying, campaigning, and confronting the opposition. The numeric strength and continuity of associations have proved to be invaluable in achieving reform over the long term.

Abolition associations were the first to adopt the modern form of local chapters coordinated by a headquarters office. The American Anti-Slavery Society was founded in 1833. Its membership grew with each act of violence against the movement, such as the mob beating of abolitionist publisher William Lloyd Garrison and the murder of another abolitionist publisher, Elijah Lovejoy. By 1838, the American Anti-Slavery Society had more than 1,000 chapters and a quarter-million members.

When Lucretia Mott and Elizabeth Cady Stanton were rebuffed because of their gender as delegates to the 1840 World Anti-Slavery Conference in London, they realized that their loyalties were divided between Negro rights and women's rights. Several years of increasingly public protest led to the Seneca Falls (New York) Convention on Women's Rights in 1848, where 68 women and 32 men signed a Declaration of Principles for women's suffrage.

The intertwined character of 19th-century reform movements is evident also in the lifelong temperance campaigning of feminists. Mott, Stanton, Lucy Stone, Susan B. Anthony, and Frances Willard spoke on suffrage one day and on temperance the next. The "evil" of alcohol was not primarily a moral issue for the feminists but an economic one. Not until legislatures began to pass property reform laws could married women retain title even to real estate they had owned prior to marriage. Nor were women guaranteed a share of their own earnings. A drunkard husband could bring economic disaster to the household. The Women's Christian Temperance Union (WCTU) was founded in 1874, and activities initially focused on Home Protection Drives to petition state legislatures for local options on the manufacture and sale of alcoholic beverages.

The coalition against women's suffrage drew its oratory from southern politicians and its funds from the liquor lobby. The politicians were determined to deny the vote to black women, while the liquor manufacturers were determined to keep protemperance women away from the polls. The suffragists' communication strategy was multifaceted. Susan B. Anthony's New York campaign of 1854 was the first to use county captains to gather petition signatures. In the same New York campaign, Stanton testified before the state legislature.

Mass communication was another strategy of the suffragists. Several suffrage newspapers were published after the Civil War, notably Anthony's *The Revolution,* the masthead of which proclaimed, "Men, their rights and nothing more; women, their rights and nothing less."

A book is not regarded as a public communication campaign in itself. However, a few books became the texts of campaigns in America. The importance of Harriet Beecher Stowe's tract, *Uncle Tom's Cabin* (1852), was such that Abraham Lincoln greeted her 10 years later as "the little woman who wrote the book that started this great war." Through this best-selling book, Stowe brought the issue of slavery back to a moral foundation when it had become a pawn of sectional rivalry.

In addition to grassroots organizing, legislative testimony, and mass communication, a fourth strategy of the reformers was confrontation, which brought publicity in newspapers that ignored their peaceful efforts. In the general election of 1872, Anthony led a party of 16 women to the polls in Rochester, New York, where they registered and voted illegally. President Ulysses S. Grant's administration chose to make an example of Anthony; she was tried and convicted in 1873.

Confrontation was a strategy of other 19th-century movements as well. The abolitionists did not need to seek confrontation, which awaited them in many northern cities. Neither did they avoid confrontation by meeting only in safe settings such as churches. The temperance movement did not have an official confrontation policy, but Carry Nation made headlines in Kansas and New York. Her saloon-bashing hatchet was a newspaper cartoonist's delight. Saloon owners and patrons dreaded the sight of her 6-foot frame at the door. She was repeatedly beaten during her forays, and she was arrested at least 30 times.

The growing power of the mass media to shape public opinion after the Civil War is illustrated by cartoonist Thomas Nast's campaign to unseat Boss Tweed and the Tammany Hall political machine in New York. Nast's famous cartoons "Tammany Tiger Loose" and "Group of Vultures Waiting for the Storm to Blow Over," both published in 1871, led to probes that toppled Tweed and sent him to prison.

Across the continent, a one-person campaign to preserve wilderness areas was evolving into a major national organization. Scottish-born John Muir came to California in 1868, imbued with a transcendental respect for wilderness. In the 1870s, Muir began to gather public and government support for national parks in the Sierra Nevada mountains. This was a hard sell because almost no one in the Eastern establishment had seen the wonders of the Yosemite Valley or the sequoia groves of the Sierra Nevada. Muir's strategy was to describe in articles and books what others had not seen. Some of Muir's books, such as *The Mountains of California* (1894) and *The Yosemite* (1912), rank among the finest of American nature writing.

Yosemite and Sequoia National Parks were established by Congress in 1890, followed within a few years by other national parks and national forests adjacent to them. During the 1890s, business interests were partly successful in delaying Congressional implementation of these land protection measures. Conservationists, led by Muir, countered by establishing the Sierra Club in 1892. With Muir as its president until his death in 1914, the Sierra Club became an effective voice for conservation.

Mass Media and Reform in the 20th Century

The role that mass media would play in America's increasingly pluralistic society was anticipated by de Tocqueville's (1835/1961) observation:

> When men are no longer united amongst themselves by firm and lasting ties, it is impossible to obtain the concurrence of any great number of them, unless you can persuade every man whose concurrence you require that his private interest obliges him voluntarily to unite his exertions to the exertions of all the rest. This can only be habitually and conveniently effected by means of a newspaper; nothing but a newspaper can drop the same thought into a thousand minds at the same moment. (p. 134)

At the end of the 19th century, the initiative for reforming many social problems shifted from associations to the mass media. Many of the problems, by their very nature, were not the rallying causes of organized activity. The muckrakers writing for *McClure's, Cosmopolitan, Collier's, Hampton's, Pearson's, Everybody's,* and other magazines first had to convince the public that impure food, price collusion, child labor, tenement squalor, and unavailable health care for the poor were social evils.

New printing technologies, the rise of literacy, and momentous national events combined to put more publications in the public's hands than ever before in history. Newspaper circulation rose from one for every five households in 1850 to more than one for one in 1910. To sustain the rapid growth in circulation, newspapers and magazines began to create news on causes of their own choosing.

Muckrakers such as Lincoln Steffens, Ida Tarbell, Upton Sinclair, David Graham Phillips, Ray Stannard Baker, and Samuel Hopkins Adams made new enemies with each story. The publications risked economic sanctions; their strategy for survival was to build readerships too large for advertisers to boycott them.

The muckrakers' issues comprised a new century's agenda for social reform. The main issues of 19th-century reform—slavery, women's lack of franchise, and the threat of alcohol to the family—were recognized as evils in light of America's original social contract. Issues of 20th-century reform entailed a new interpretation of social responsibility: food producers should not adulterate their products; corporations should not collude to fix prices; children should be in schools, not in factories; and so on.

Another difference between 19th- and 20th-century reform is apparent now as we acknowledge that many reforms begun in the 20th century were left incomplete at its end. The 19th-century reformers believed that an issue was resolved when legislative or judicial action was taken. The abolitionists' accomplishments consisted of the Thirteenth, Fourteenth, and Fifteenth Amendments (abolition of slavery, equal protection under the law, and suffrage for former slaves). The suffragists first achieved reform in state property laws, then secured suffrage in a few western states, and capped their struggle with the Nineteenth Amendment (suffrage for women). Temperance advocates won local prohibition referenda, then swept the country with the Eighteenth Amendment (prohibition of intoxicating liquors). Many abolitionists, suffragists, and temperance advocates "retired" when their amendments were ratified. The freed slave, the enfranchised woman, and the family of the former drunkard could now work out their own fortunes.

It was soon apparent that legislative and judicial actions were necessary but not sufficient conditions for the changes that 20th-century reformers wanted to achieve. In the new century, reformers came to know the ambiguity of a "solution." A solution might be nullified (as in the repeal of the Eighteenth Amendment by the Twenty-First) or might not be implemented substantively for years after it was decided upon. Moreover, the opposition's legal staff might find loopholes, and compliance would be token and evasive. Finally, the solution to one problem might generate another problem.

The muckrakers savored few victories; there was a limit to how far they could carry their reforms. They were journalists, not administrators. They could conceive a reform and even attend its birth, but they could not rear it. Ironically, they investigated government corruption and ineptitude, yet their writings played a major role in building today's bureaucracy. Inadequate health care required a board of health; impure food required a pure food agency; labor abuses required a department of labor; and so on. Most of the reforms conceived by the muckrakers had to be reared by government officials. In this way 20th-century reform passed into the hands of the civil service.

Enter the Federal Government

Responding to pressure from reformers, muckrakers, and public opinion at the dawn of the 20th century, the federal government was drawn into causes that were far removed from its original charter. After passage of the Interstate Commerce Act in 1887, the federal government's right to regulate interstate commerce became the slim thread for tying the 1906 Pure Food and Drug Act, the 1910 White Slave Traffic Act, the 1916 Child Labor Act, and many other social reform laws to the Constitution. The Supreme Court struck down some of these laws but sustained others.

The two other watersheds of reform legislation in the 20th century occurred during the early years of Franklin Roosevelt's New Deal and Lyndon Johnson's Great Society administrations. These completed the pattern of federal involvement in almost every issue that formerly occupied the associations and mass media, as well as a new 20th-century emphasis on issues such as pollution, environmental protection, and health care (significantly extended by the Health Care Reform Act in 2010).

A NEW CENTURY OF PUBLIC COMMUNICATION CAMPAIGNS

Amazingly, public communication campaigns have now entered their fourth century in America. They are adapting, as always, to new social forces. Three challenges for today's campaigns are *public distrust, episodic issues,* and the *rise of issue literacies.*

Public Distrust

The last third of the 20th century in the United States saw a crisis in public trust that threatened to undermine public communication campaigns. Within a period of a few years, criticism of public officials, public agencies, corporations, and other powerful entities such as labor unions and agricultural interests found its voice.

One timeline of distrust begins with the publication of Vance Packard's *The Hidden Persuaders* in 1957, followed by *The Status Seekers* in 1959 and *The Waste Makers* in 1960. Packard reached large audiences because he used plain language to criticize those who abused the capitalist system rather than intellectually attacking capitalism itself. Rachel Carson's *Silent Spring,* published in 1962, warned the public that the pesticide DDT was being used in agriculture without regard for its effect on other living things. In 1963, Jessica Mitford described practices of the funeral industry that preyed upon bereaved families in *The American Way of Death.* Betty Friedan's *The Feminine Mystique,* published in 1963, continued the theme of manipulation. Ralph Nader's indictment of the automobile industry, *Unsafe at Any Speed,* was published in 1965. Mark Lane's critique of the Warren Commission report on the Kennedy assassination, *Rush to Judgment,* appeared in 1966.

The ultimate cynicism is a lack of surprise, and the instant history of Richard Nixon's victory over Hubert Humphrey, *The Selling of the President—1968,* written by Joe McGinnis and published in 1969, evoked no public outcry over the methods by which Nixon was packaged and sold to the voters. Nor was there much surprise when David Halberstam's *The Best and the Brightest,* published in 1973, indicated that U.S. leaders during the Vietnam conflict were neither. By the time that Carl Bernstein and Bob Woodward reported the Watergate scandal as a detective mystery in *All the President's Men* (1974), there was little that the public could not imagine happening in corporate or political America.

The national conscience had to reflect on past wrongs when Dee Brown wrote *Bury My Heart at Wounded Knee,* which was the number one best seller for 25 weeks in 1971. This book, together with the activism of Native American leaders like Russell Means, focused the public's attention on the continuing injustices that Native Americans have endured.

Notwithstanding the wrongs revealed in this second era of American muckraking, many negative events after World War II had positive consequences. The political terror of McCarthyism brought courageous journalists like Edward R. Murrow to the fore. The character flaws of John F. Kennedy and Bill Clinton have not deterred American youth from social activism that flourishes to this day. The criminality of the Nixon administration ultimately proved that the rule of law extends to the highest office. Civil rights strife from Selma to Stonewall showed that the main legacy of discrimination was not hatred or separatism but a desire to move forward in the mainstream.

Under the media microscope, the flaws of individuals and institutions were enormous but not monstrous. At century's end, it was not the idealist but the cynic who was being told to "get over it."

Episodic Issues

Issues rise and fall on the agenda according to external factors such as crises, incidents, and the appearance of effective advocates on the national scene. Some issues are solved by actions or events; they drop off the national agenda until they become unsolved again. Many persisting issues are subject to issue fatigue; they leave the agenda for a time then return with new advocates or proposals.

Analyses of the amount of coverage received by representative public issues in U.S. magazines from 1960 to 2000 show that only a few issues were at their highest levels at the beginning or end of this time period. Some issues rose and then fell within one decade more or less, such as Vietnam in the 1960s, desegregation in the 1960s, nuclear energy in the 1970s, apartheid in the 1980s, drug abuse in the 1980s, sexual harassment in the 1990s, and gay and lesbian issues in the 1990s. The decline in coverage is dramatic among issues that are regarded as "over" such as Vietnam or apartheid. Communism and disarmament did not remain high on the agenda after the political rebirth of Russia.

An issue by any other name is a different issue. For example, the desegregation issue of the 1960s became the busing issue of the early 1970s and the affirmative action issue of the late 1970s. Similarly, the smoking issue of past decades evolved into the issue of the tobacco industry, complete with corporate wrongdoing and cover-ups; this is the rare topic that hit peaks in both the early 1960s (health harm) and the late 1990s (restrictions on the tobacco industry). Several issues that emerged in the late 1980s have maintained their positions on the agenda, including global warming, breast cancer, and Alzheimer's disease. These types of persistent problems, along with earlier-emerging topics, such as heart disease and pollution, may defy the label of *episodic* and outlast normal issue fatigue. Current leading topics, such as child obesity, may persist or decline.

Ideological-based issues tend to fluctuate according to which political party is in ascendance. For example, health care reform and the role of gays and lesbians in the military peaked during both the Bill Clinton and Barack Obama presidencies.

The Rise of Issue Literacies

The problem of *too many issues, too little time* has led to creative strategies to reclaim our attention. Many advocates now contend that their concern is not an issue but a *literacy*. In recent decades, the public has been urged to attain scientific literacy, technological literacy, legal literacy, sexual literacy, multicultural literacy, computer literacy, ecological literacy, and health literacy.

At one level, the redefinition of issues as literacies is only a strategy to regain attention in the crowded marketplace of issues. At another level, this trend acknowledges the complexity of issues like cancer prevention and treatment. Although a few issues like forest fire prevention and safety belt promotion can still be addressed by posters and slogans, public communication campaigns have matured into many differentiated forms. At the other extreme, the potentially relevant knowledge about a complex topic such as breast cancer is very extensive and conditional with respect to individual factors. It is reasonable to refer to familiarity with this knowledge as a literacy.

Furthermore, relationships between knowledge gain and behavior change as the goals of a campaign are altered when the most appropriate behavior for any member of the target audience must be determined by weighing individual factors. At this historic juncture, a public communication campaign no longer exhorts. Instead, it informs and advises.

Conclusion

Public communication campaigners may wish that the organizing skill of a Susan B. Anthony, the charisma of a William Lloyd Garrison, or the appalling disclosures of an Upton Sinclair could be as effective now as in the past. The world of cancer, AIDS, drug abuse, the toxic environment, bioengineered food, tobacco control, domestic violence, corporate finance malfeasance, and a host of other issues has moved beyond these appealing simplicities.

However, the world of modern campaigns contains solutions as well as problems. Campaigns learn from the successes and failures of other campaigns. Thanks to the relatively detached perspective of social science, campaigns can be documented, compared, and evaluated for the new concepts and techniques they offer.

As we begin a new century, the science of public communication campaigns comes to the fore and generates its own excitement. As the agenda of social issues changes, so too will campaigns continue to change in adaptive ways to meet the new challenges.

Reference

De Tocqueville, A. (1961). *Democracy in America*. New York: Schocken. (Original work published 1835).

CHAPTER 3

Why Can't We Sell Human Rights Like We Sell Soap?

Robert C. Hornik

In 1951, Wiebe asked whether we can sell brotherhood like we sell soap; he thought we could if we just worked like commercial marketers do. More than a half century after Wiebe's question, what seemed like a straightforward proposition has turned out not to be. In some cases, public communication has been a successful strategy in influencing "good" behavior; in many more, it has turned out be ineffective (Hornik, 2002; Wakefield, Loken, & Hornik, 2010). What have we learned from that experience that might be applied to issues of human rights?

My purpose in this chapter is to describe some current thinking and some evidence in the field of communication for social and behavioral change and consider how those findings may relate to interventions to affect human rights. I begin with a brief review of three intellectual traditions that have dominated research examining the role of communication in social change and then move to discussions of three major topics: how do communication and social change scholars think about behavior; when do we think that communication programs are likely to work; and what are the human rights implications of key conceptualizations of communication for social change.

Before discussing human rights campaigns, it will be helpful to address briefly what is meant by the term *human rights*. The essential idea that people have rights that are inherent in their humanness and not contingent on states appears in the preamble of the 1948 Universal Declaration of Human Rights, which declares "recognition of the inherent dignity and of the equal and inalienable rights of all members of the human family is the foundation of freedom, justice and peace in the world." The Declaration itself goes on in 30 articles to detail a wide range of both positive (e.g., education, medical care) and negative (not subject to torture, no slavery) human rights. Human rights is a philosophical construct but clearly also a political construct; while internal and external critics may insist on the essentialness of a particular human right, the decision of a state to codify and enforce a particular human right reflects its own political dynamic as well as that of states around it, which can establish human rights expectations and take actions to demand their fulfillment (cf. Ishay, 2004; Lauren, 2003).

In order to be able to consider this issue in the context of communication campaigns, I have deliberately stepped away from the philosophical complexities of the broad term and argue that the relevance of communication interventions to human rights requires that we focus on a given human right (e.g., the right of prisoners to vote after their release) and then on a particular behavior likely to influence that right (e.g., encouraging the introduction of legislation to support that right). This then becomes a familiar problem, the sort of behavior change focus that communication campaign scholars are accustomed to addressing.

THREE TRADITIONS OF COMMUNICATION AND SOCIAL CHANGE SCHOLARSHIP

Investments in Information Technology and in Communication Institutions

The oldest tradition of scholarship (and of applied investments in communication) focused on the role of communication infrastructure rather than on the content of communication; it was not interested in deliberate, persuasive campaigns but only in building up the capacity to do communication. Scholars in this tradition argued that, if access to information technology was high and governments assured the free flow of information and a free press, this would create "modern societies" featuring "democratic institutions" (e.g., Pye, 1963).

In the post-WWII period, this strong argument led, for example, to Western foreign aid agencies assisting in the diffusion of newspaper presses, then radio towers and television studios, and even later to investments in telephone systems and in satellite transmission capacity (Hornik, 1988), and more recently to increasing Internet (Wilson, 2004) or social media access and to the distribution of cute, cheap computers to developing countries (One laptop per child, 2011).

A similar argument focused less on the technology and more on the institutional rules for the use of technology. The assumption here was that, if the free press could maintain surveillance over the government and attack its failings, then the government would have no choice but to be responsive (cf. Sen, 1999). A parallel argument can be made with regard to Internet access—it provides ordinary citizens with the opportunity for surveillance, shared communication with others, and a channel for criticism of actions by authorities and, thus, to influence policy.

In each of these cases, the optimistic argument for investment in technology is that broader access to communication capacity is supportive of the development of human rights. However, there are two major countercurrents: that enhancement of communication technological capacity does not define how it will be used and that, even when technology advances provide access to communication by a wider range of constituencies, there is no assurance that they will use it to enhance human rights.

If communication capacity is to fulfill its "best" human rights role, then it would seem as though it ought to involve something beyond the ability to receive broadcast messages; it ought to assure broadened access to a diversity of messages and to the production of messages as well. In the case of messages distributed by mass-mediated channels, are there a range of interests represented in the messages typically consumed by the population (see, for example, Rice, 2008)? There is nothing in the technology itself that assures representation of a breadth of constituencies. Additionally, in an obvious way, the Internet clearly expands the ability of individuals or institutions to produce messages at lower cost, but this implies only the capacity to produce messages; it does nothing to assure wide circulation of such messages. The assessment of communication production capacity has to weigh literal production capacity against actual consumption—does the creation of an Internet webpage (one of billions of such pages) assure reception by more than a tiny fraction of the population?

Perhaps it is more useful to consider the role of the Internet in shaping policy debate as broader than its simple enhancement of mass access to specific site pages. The content of a blog or site page may reach a small percentage of the population directly, but may have substantial influence if other sources—political elites, mass circulation media—are attending to those sources and are shaped by them (for example, presenting information that might have been suppressed except that it will surely be uncovered by bloggers.) Direct exposure to Internet-produced messages can be minimal, but indirect exposure may be substantial (Mitchelstein & Boczkowski, 2009).

Undermining optimistic interpretations of increasing diffusion of communication technology are questions about who actually has the ability to receive and produce messages (e.g., the broad digital divide issue; Katz & Rice, 2002). No less of a concern is the question about how the technology would be used even if both reception and production capacities were widely diffused. Optimists may focus on the Internet as an important political organizing tool or on the free press and blogs as methods for assuring a responsive political elite. However, these are not the only possibilities. Political movements that make use of newly available communication capacities to organize their paths to power may turn out to support human rights but may also limit them if they come to power. For example, the Islamic revolution in Iran made use of taped messages from the Ayatollah Khomeini to organize its opposition to the Shah (Sreberny-Mohammadi, 1990), yet its human rights record is widely criticized, and the groups opposed to Khomeini's successors have turned to the web and its video sharing technology to organize their opposition.

Majorities may find that enhanced communication capacity increases their ability to organize the suppression of minorities (for an extreme example, consider the Hutu use of radio broadcasts to spread their messages encouraging murder of Tutsis in Rwanda). The 24-hour news cycle, and the "gotcha" approach of partisan bloggers and talk show hosts, may constrain the willingness of political leaders to support politically unpopular human rights policies. For a recent example, there is the wariness of U.S. politicians to support immigrant rights in recent years. It is clear that enhanced communication capacity can be used to support human rights or it can be used to undermine them.

"Natural" Media Effects

The second tradition of research extends the focus on technology diffusion and institutional rules around technology to consider the effects of the content spread by the technology. It is not concerned, especially, with deliberate efforts to "sell brotherhood like soap" but rather with the effects of content typically diffused by media sources. After all, most exposure to communication content is not to content shaped to inform, educate, or persuade. Yet, that nonpurposive content may well have effects on noncommercial outcomes, including perceptions of and actions relating to specific human rights issues. The media effects literature is very substantial, and there can be no reasonable attempt here to present it or even outline its dimensions. However, the following paragraphs briefly consider agenda setting, framing, social network and context, and cultivation effects.

One of the most important influences of media may not be to persuade audiences as to which position on an issue to adopt but rather to convince them that they ought to be paying attention to an issue altogether (called *agenda setting;* McCombs & Shaw, 1972) or to convince them that, when they think about an issue, they ought to be understanding it in a particular way (called *framing;* Dearing & Rogers, 1996; Tewksbury & Scheufele, 2009). Both of these are quite relevant to thinking about communication influences on human rights.

Should U.S. voters elect their next president because of his or her position on a human rights issue (e.g., immigrants' rights), or should they weigh his or her position on another issue (e.g., war in the Middle East) more heavily? Even outside of the election context, politicians may be unwilling to focus their attention on an issue unless it matters to the public, and the public interest may be a reflection of media interest.

Even if a topic gains public interest, the way that people consider it may also reflect media coverage of the issue—the way that media *frame* the issue. Is immigration to be understood in terms of legal status of immigrants, as a demand for labor issue, or in terms of the human costs of children long established in the U.S. being forced to return to "home" countries they do not know? Clearly, media coverage of the issue will affect what frames are available for debate.

A particularly intriguing version of the framing hypothesis has been called the *spiral of silence* (Noelle-Neumann, 1974; Scheufele & Moy, 2000). The hypothesis suggests that many people have a tendency to be unwilling to express their opinions if they believe them to be minority opinions because they are likely to be badly received if voiced publicly. However, if minority opinions are not voiced or covered in the media, then others who may hold similar opinions are even less likely to express such opinions, reducing even further their presence and legitimacy in the public debate and strengthening the opposite position. Eventually, according to this hypothesis, such views are likely to be silenced.

Another frequent concern of media effects research that bears on the issue of human rights is the idea that much of the influence of media is interpreted in the context of social network affiliations. This research tradition has argued that audience members are not isolates responding as individuals to hypodermic media messages but rather that we are embedded in social relationships that affect how we interpret and are affected by media (cf. Katz & Lazarsfeld, 1955/2006). There are two major elements of this argument. The first says that how we interpret what we see or hear reflects the frameworks of understanding that come from our social networks. For example, perhaps prior discussions in one individual's social network have focused on the human costs of returning undocumented families to their home countries; new messages from media sources focusing on the illegality of immigrants' statuses do not resonate with that individual's framework for thinking about this issue. The second element argues that our social networks are responsible for passing on, suppressing, or reinterpreting messages that we may not have been exposed to directly. A friend quotes a media source on immigration approvingly or disapprovingly or does not pass the message on at all.

A distinct thread of mass media research is worth attention in the context of human rights concerns. Gerbner and Gross (1976), in their *cultivation effects* theory, argued that the stories that are the core of media content may reinforce social status inequalities and the existing distribution of power in a society. If such inequalities and power statuses limit public interest in addressing human rights issues, then this research tradition deserves further attention in this context. For example, Gerbner showed, as others have, how prevalent violence is on television. Yet, while others argued that such violence would lead viewers to aggressive behavior, he argued that the effects might be quite different: The exposure to violence on television would create in its audience an increase in fear of the world around them, and this fear would increase their willingness to support law and order policies (the *mean world hypothesis*). It is not hard to see how this argument might be extended to expect a reluctance to support human rights concerns if such concerns need to compete with media-reinforced fears about how dangerous a place the world is.

[handwritten in margin: Texans—rich or redneck]

Purposive, Content-Specific Uses of Communication Technology

The third major research tradition, and the one that bears most directly on building interventions to ameliorate human rights concerns, is about purposive uses of communication technology to educate, persuade, and produce social change—what are called *public communication campaigns* (e.g., the focus of this volume). This is a tradition of research that goes beyond the diffusion of technology and beyond the effects of the typical media content toward deliberate attempts to influence behavior. There are substantial literatures that deal with using media to teach in schools (or do school-equivalent education); for agricultural innovation diffusion; for public health communication; and, more recently, as communication in support of governance and environmental issues.

The rest of this chapter provides an overview of some of the major concerns of this field and relates those concerns to thinking about construction of efforts to influence human rights. The section is organized around a series of major questions: How do purposive communication and social change scholars and practitioners think about behavior? What does the evidence say about when communication programs will work (and what are the risks of doing communication interventions)? What issues will efforts to affect human rights through communication need to address?

HOW DO SCHOLARS OF PURPOSIVE COMMUNICATION AND SOCIAL CHANGE THINK ABOUT BEHAVIOR?

Specific Behavior, Not Categories of Behavior

It would be advantageous if it were possible to develop communication campaigns that might influence a broad mind-set among individuals and that such a mind-set would then turn into a variety of specific behaviors. For example, it would be efficient if it were possible to gain a commitment to a healthy lifestyle and then expect that people will turn that commitment into good lifestyle decisions across the board—no smoking, regular exercise, maintenance of a healthy weight, consumption of a diet heavy in fruit and vegetables, and so on. However, behavior change theory and health behavior theory have been more focused on thinking about determinants of specific behaviors (smoking cessation, condom use with the next casual partner, recycling of paper goods, choice of low trans-fat foods) than it has been in thinking about categories of behavior (healthy lifestyles, safe sex, pro-environmental behavior, obesity control). We know a fair amount about how to change specific behaviors—there is good evidence, for example, for communication campaigns to reduce smoking initiation (National Cancer Institute, 2008) and encourage condom use (cf. Palmgreen, Noar, & Zimmerman, Chapter 14; Valente & Kwan, Chapter 6). However, we don't have evidence supporting the effects of campaigns to increase healthy lifestyles or engage in safer sex when those abstract categories are not defined by specific behaviors. We know much less about how to change categories of behaviors. There are two likely explanations for this mismatch between what we would like to do (see many behaviors adopted in response to categorical advocacy) and what we have been more successful in doing (stimulating targeted behavior change).

The behaviors that interventionists and policy advocates may see as fitting into a category and as appropriately adopted as a coherent set of behaviors are not always seen as similar behaviors by ordinary people. Human rights advocates may see immigration issues, prisoners' rights, political participation, free speech, and access to smoke-free homes as all human rights issues. However, ordinary people may see those issues as quite distinct—their support for one of those issues may not generalize to support for others, and one may see oneself as a supporter of human rights but not accept that support for a particular immigrant right fits into that category.

Also, it may be that the behaviors that fall into a single category for outsiders are distinct in the factors that influence them for the individuals who might consider performing them. Fishbein and Ajzen's (2009) Integrative Model (IM) brings together constructs from their own prior theories (Theory of Reasoned Action, Theory of Planned Behavior) and those of other health behavior scholars (Social Cognitive Theory, Health Belief Model) in defining a common set of likely categories of influence on behavior. The IM argues that there are three central determinants of behavior: beliefs about the good and bad outcomes of a behavior, beliefs about what important others do and expect the individual to do with regard to the behavior, and beliefs about whether or not one has the skills and the opportunity to engage in a behavior successfully. Each of these is assumed to influence behavior, either directly or through the intention to engage in the behavior. This model can be applied to thinking about human rights advocacy.

Human rights supporters seek not merely abstract support for an ideal but want to see specific behaviors to enact that support. For example, one can consider the issue of support for the restoration of voting rights for felons after serving their prison terms. Perhaps a human rights group would like to develop a public communication campaign to advocate for this goal, encouraging people to write supporting letters to the editor in local newspapers or to send letters to legislators when the issue is up for debate. The influences on individuals' willingness to write letters to the editor may reflect their belief that voting rights for felons is a good thing (which may reflect a broader commitment to human rights), but it also may reflect their belief that a letter to the editor is likely to influence the attainment of those rights, their belief that they have the time and the ability to compose a persuasive letter that will be published, and their belief that important social network members will respond positively to them if they see a letter under their signature supporting felons' voting rights. The influences on the writing to a legislator may be quite distinct; for example, given that letters to legislators do not involve public advocacy, the role of the expectations from a social network may be quite different. More broadly, the set of influences that come into play when a quite different human rights-related behavior is the target may be substantially different.

The implications for human rights advocacy of this set of arguments encouraging a focus on specific behaviors are twofold. There may be little expectation that a broad campaign for human rights will have any important behavioral effects, absent a focus on specific issues. This may not be much of a challenge to current human rights work; it would seem that most human rights campaigns are about specific issues already and not about some generic human rights goal. However, the second implication may have more traction. It is rarely the case that human rights advocates' goals are merely attitudinal. Goals are typically behavioral—that individuals should take specific actions or sets of actions—that are expected to lead to a change in institutional policy or practice. Successful advocacy campaigns need first to define the specific behaviors they want to encourage and then understand what is likely to influence each behavior. Crucially, they need to understand that different behaviors (even if they are meant to address the same issue) will have different influences, and that the influences on each behavior may be weighted differently across the people who are addressed. In particular, general support for human rights may be relevant to some issues and irrelevant to others, and even where it may be relevant, it may be an essential determinant or a minor determinant of the likelihood that people will engage in desired behaviors.

What Does the Evidence Say About When Communication Programs Will Work?

This section considers evidence about two types of communication efforts: deliberate or controlled communication campaigns and public relations or media advocacy programs. *Controlled communication campaigns* are campaigns where producers develop specific messages and transmit them through well-defined channels with an expectation that they will produce measureable behavior change. *Public relations campaigns* make use of press releases and other materials to encourage attention to an issue by media and other institutions. They also may hope for behavior change, but they do not expect to control how many messages are received by audiences or through what channels. They may have a goal of changing broad social norms concerning an issue and, in some cases, may focus on mobilizing public support to achieve policy change.

The literature on deliberate public communication campaigns is quite substantial (as this volume shows). This chapter provides only a very high-level summary of some major conclusions based in that literature (Snyder & LaCroix, Chapter 8; Wakefield et al., 2010). There are three types of campaigns for which there is decent positive evidence of influence on behavior: when the focus behavior is high reward and low cost to implement; when the communication campaign can complement substantial changes in the material environment, affecting adoption of the behavior; and when the communication campaign can be long-lived and operate through multiple channels with an expectation of incremental change.

Campaigns Focused on Low-Cost, High-Reward Behaviors

There are (rare) cases where behavior change is simple and highly rewarding and otherwise unknown to an audience. Adoption of these behaviors can be sharply affected by conventional communication campaigns. One useful example is the effort to encourage parents to put their infants on their backs to sleep. As evidence accumulated that Sudden Infant Death Syndrome (SIDS) might be reduced if children slept on their backs rather than their stomachs, a number of agencies mounted campaigns to encourage this shift in behavior. However, because the promised reward associated with the behavior was highly valued (reducing the otherwise unknown risk of SIDS), the behavior was simple and easy to adopt (putting the baby on his or her back rather than prone, otherwise not a common practice), and the costs were probably low (some possible increased fussiness), it was quickly adopted by many parents, and deaths from SIDS declined rapidly by 50% or more in a number of countries (Willinger, Hoffman, & Hartford, 1994).

Campaigns Linked to Substantial Changes in the Material Environment

Communication campaigns have been effective when they were mounted to facilitate behavior change and when that communication effort complemented a change in the behavior environment (or, as Paisley & Atkin, Chapter 2, explains, when education is joined with enforcement and/or engineering, and as in several other chapters, social marketing principles propose; see also Rice & Foote, Chapter 5). Communication is used to publicize some "real" change in the environment that has clear implications for behavior change.

For example, in urban areas of the Philippines, on-time immunization rates were lower than desired. The Ministry of Health improved its policies around delivering health services (creating a focus vaccination day, allowing clinic staff to open vials of serum even for a single child, and others). However, it complemented such changes in the material environment around provision of vaccination with intense advertising programs letting parents know about where and when vaccines were available. If clinics had not been ready to serve increased demand, then it is unlikely that the communication efforts would have been worthwhile; at the same time, the policy changes alone were not able to increase the rates. Complementing material changes with communication meant a jump in one year in timely complete vaccination from 32% to 56% (Zimicki et al., 1994).

Long-Lived, Long-Term Programs

The third type of communication program with some consistent evidence for success is a group of long-lived, high-exposure, multiple-channel programs that work to affect individual preferences as well as social support and institutional policies that support such preferences. These programs are rarely limited to communication efforts alone but typically complement communication efforts with other changes and also expect to achieve effects over the long term.

A distinct version of this long-term, large-scale intervention program is the antismoking movement in the United States. There are specific, shorter-lived communication interventions with some evidence of immediate success (Farrelly, Davis, Haviland, Messeri, & Healton, 2005), but the most striking results come from taking a 50-year perspective (National Cancer Institute, 2008). The proportion of U.S. adults who smoked in 2011 was less than half the proportion that smoked in 1958. It can be argued that this reflects not a single effort by a single authority but the often uncoordinated efforts of a movement that produced slow but, over-the-long-term, large change. Sometimes, this movement involved identifiable mass media campaigns; sometimes it involved deliberate public relations efforts by antismoking groups to affect policy decisions at all levels of institutions; sometimes it involved legal actions; and sometimes it involved community groups pressing their cases on policy makers (Warner, 1989). All of these reflected a massive shift in social norms around smoking even as tobacco companies fought those changes. These activities were not part of one integrated, specific communication campaign but, at the core, were the diffusion of the idea that smoking was dangerous and merited public action.

This antismoking effort exemplifies also a last type of communication program that seems relevant to human rights campaigns: *public relations* and *media advocacy programs* (see Taylor, Chapter 18; and Dorfman & Wallack, Chapter 23). Agencies may seek to use what is called *earned media* to influence the public. They meet with journalists and editorial boards, put out press releases, organize press conferences, encourage demonstrations, or create other attention-getting events all in the hope that news media will both cover the issues of concern to the agency and within a framework that favors the agency's position. In contrast to the controlled intervention programs described above, they do not buy advertising time or seek free media time for PSAs. They can control the message that gets to the public at large only if their public relations campaign is successful in shaping what the media outlets say. There are two versions of these programs. Some intend to shape public sentiment in the belief that policy makers will be responsive to shifts in public opinion. Media advocacy is a particular type of public relations that seeks to use to use media coverage to galvanize grassroots organizations and to use media coverage of grassroots demonstrations to put pressure on policy makers. Others try to short-circuit that policy influence process by using the fact of press coverage of an issue to convince policy makers that public sentiment is on their side whether or not there has actually been a shift in sentiment (cf. Walker, 2010). As noted above, the antismoking movement has been particularly adept at gaining favorable press coverage and, in turn, affecting policy decisions. There has been a massive and continuing shift in institutional policies meant to discourage smoking: smoke-free buildings, bars, and airplanes; tax increases on tobacco products; and enhanced enforcement of underage smoking laws.

Digression: At Least Communication Can Do No Harm—Well, Not Quite

Historically, when groups have proposed to undertake communication programs, they have assumed that they will either be unsuccessful or successful, where being unsuccessful meant not producing any behavior change (see Salmon & Murray-Johnson, Chapter 7, on varieties of campaign effectiveness). However, a recent experience raises an additional caution flag. The U.S. government invested something over $1 billion in its National Youth Antidrug Media Campaign. The evaluation of that campaign reported that either there were no effects on youth beliefs and behavior around drugs (particularly marijuana) or possibly *boomerang effects* (Hornik, Jacobsohn, Orwin, Piesse, & Kalton, 2008): Nonmarijuana-using youth who were most exposed to antidrug ads at baseline were more likely one year later to have beliefs and social norms consistent with drug use and, in some cases, to have initiated marijuana use.

The likely mechanism for the observed boomerang effects is of particular interest to those considering human rights campaigns. It appeared that the effects were probably associated with repeated exposure to messages. Even though each message encouraged rejecting the behavior, the repeated exposure may have led to the acceptance of a contrary *meta-message* (or framing), a perception that marijuana use was highly prevalent because why else would so many messages be used to attack it? These findings are consistent with a theoretical argument put forward by Cialdini (2003), who has shown that such prevalent information about noncompliance can undermine compliance.

Implications for Human Rights Campaigns

What are the implications of this brief summary of evidence relating to other communication campaigns for the development of human rights-related campaigns? First, if there is low-hanging fruit of the sort exemplified by the Back to Sleep (SIDS) campaigns in a particular human rights context, then it is an obvious target. Second, exposing violations of public norms makes it impossible to continue what is accepted in private. In a sense, the quick media response to the Iraqi Abu Ghraib prison and torture photographs reflected the photos' portrayal of behavior, which was a deep violation of public norms around prisoner treatment (Andén-Papadopoulos, 2008). However, such clearly unacceptable violations may not be uncovered regularly. Third, programs that can use communication to promote awareness of material changes in the environment may be an approach that is more applicable. A communication campaign that lets abused women know about newly available resources available to them will surely be more successful than a communication campaign that merely encourages women to leave their abusing spouses but has no resources to provide.

However, it is likely that many human right issues will not bend to quick communication interventions (although human rights organizations may be able to stimulate donations to their causes through such campaigns). Then, the most important implication of this history may be the example of the smoking campaigns: Many human rights issues will require long-term, large-scale, continuing interventions. It may be that, for example, cementing policy makers' votes to support legalization of undocumented immigrants already in the United States will require a relatively long horizon, a thoroughgoing understanding of the influences on various relevant constituencies, and a multicomponent effort to affect public norms about the issue.

WHAT ISSUES WILL HUMAN RIGHTS COMMUNICATION NEED TO ADDRESS?

This discussion focuses on presenting a small number of typical problems that many communication programs face, and it may well be that human rights-focused communication advocacy and behavior change programs should expect to face them as well: poor messages, too little exposure, a focus on individual persuasion rather than social networks and institutions contexts, that communication isn't the real problem, and confusing communication with action.

Poor Messages

Many communication programs confuse the goal of their program with the messages they need to distribute. Perhaps a program wants to encourage letter writing to legislators. However, a message that merely asks for letters on the basis of what its advocates think are good reasons for writing may be not be successful. The crucial question is this: What are the forces that influence potential letter writers? Is it their belief about whether a letter will affect a desired outcome, their belief that there won't be a bad consequence for their own careers, their beliefs about whether other people they care about think they should write, or their confidence that they can write a persuasive letter? A message emphasizing that letter writers can feel good about their commitment to human rights may not matter if reluctant writers need to be convinced that writing can actually convince policy makers. Message producers need to choose messages that are persuasive to their target audiences, and the arguments that are likely to influence them are not always what program producers might guess. Nonetheless, programs often put a lot of resources into producing pretty messages (nice formats, good fonts, balanced designs, and attention-getting images) but spend too little on understanding how target audience members think about the behavior of concern (see chapters discussing formative evaluation by Atkin & Freimuth, Chapter 4; Rice & Foote, Chapter 5; and Valente & Kwan, Chapter 6).

Too Little Exposure

Good programs may eventually sort out the need for careful message design. However, the next problem looms large. Many serious communication efforts fail because their good messages are not seen or heard at all or are not seen or heard with sufficient frequency to be persuasive. Even when substantial effort goes into message creation, there may not be sufficient funding to purchase exposure or no adequate strategy to earn free exposure. If, for example, a program is aimed at audiences in the United States, it faces the daunting task of competing with massive media noise for audience attention: public service advertising, if aired at all, is often relegated to times of the day when few are in the audience. Purchasing advertising time at a level that can be recalled by the target viewer is likely to be beyond the budget of many human rights advocacy programs. This often means that public relations strategies—efforts to earn free media time by making news—are the only viable approach. At the same time, public relations is an approach where control over the actual content of messages is reduced, and there is rapid wear out of the willingness of news media to pay attention to an issue. Getting sufficient continuing message exposure is a crucial problem to be solved for any human rights agency that intends to make use of public communication.

Individual Persuasion When the Behavior Belongs to Social Networks or Institutions

Much of the history of communication for social change has been focused on persuading individuals to change their behaviors. Even for issues when individual behavior is the focus of a campaign, this may not always be the most efficient strategy. If a behavior is open to influence from an individual's social network, then it may prove productive to focus a campaign on changing social norms and only through social norm change try to influence individual behavior. For example, it has often been argued that adolescent binge drinking reflects social norms, and the best strategy for reducing such drinking is through changing the norm (and the perception of the norm) within social networks (see DeJong & Smith, Chapter 12). In a parallel way, if a behavior is substantially influenced by institutional policies and structures, convincing institutions to change policies may be a more efficient way of changing individual behavior than efforts at individual persuasion (see Dorfman & Wallack, Chapter 23). The efforts to complement individual antismoking messages with advocacy to change institutional policies around smoking are a clear example of this strategy. It is more difficult for individuals to maintain a smoking habit when they have to step outside their workplaces every time they want to light up.

This logic applies to human rights issues in two ways. There are some individual behaviors that can support a human rights agenda that will happen quickest if they are influenced by shared norm change in a social network or supportive institutional policy changes. Communication interventions designed to affect those social network norm changes and to encourage institutional policy change will look different than interventions designed only to persuade individuals directly. Thus, a communication campaign to afford women the "right" to breast-feed might focus on building social support for workplace breast-feeding as a human right. If colleagues endorsed this right, and if institutions built private lactation rooms, exercise of the right becomes possible. Perhaps of greater relevance, many human rights issues are about institutional change, per se. In contrast to a health communication campaign that may be using institutional or social routes to get to individual behavior change (smoke-free workplaces to get individuals to stop smoking), human rights campaign are often directly about institutional policy changes (changing the legal status of undocumented immigrants).

It Is Not Really a Communication Problem

Thus far, this chapter has made the assumption that there is a communication solution to a particular problem, and the challenge is creating an effective communication strategy. Communication interventions often assume that, if only the right people or policy makers knew or believed the right things, then the needed changes would come about. However, agencies considering communication interventions need to ask a hard question first: If the problem is one of lack of material resources to permit changes, or if current circumstances are consistent with interests reflecting the distribution of power in a society, is communication really a solution? Sometimes, it is the interests of policy actors not to change policy; they fully understand the issues and the human rights arguments behind change, but they think that change is not in their own interests or the interest of the constituencies who support them (an issue especially relevant to environmental campaigns; see Rice & Robinson, Chapter 16). This idea is closely linked to the next one.

Confusing Communicating With Doing Something About a Problem

Communication efforts can make actors feel like they are doing something, which is not the same as doing something. When agencies (and in this case, particularly political actors) turn to public communication to address an issue, there are (at least) two outcomes they may be seeking. Ideally, they are trying to make things better. However, they also may be trying to look like they are doing something to make things better. A government ministry can invest in a public communication campaign to encourage families to send their daughters to school, and that may be an important intervention. But, if the problems with sending girls to school reflect institutional constraints—unwillingness of religious authorities in local areas to countenance mixed schooling or the need for school-age girls to care for younger siblings because of the lack of affordable child care alternatives—the public communication campaign may bring credit for its sponsors but have little impact on the participation of girls in schooling. Because communication is a public intervention, it carries with it a particular risk of allowing the appearance of action to replace effective action or to create other outcomes (see Salmon & Murray-Johnson, Chapter 7).

Conclusions

We know how to address and try to influence a specific behavior, but we do not know how to address behavioral categories. We do not know how to address human rights attitudes broadly, and it is not obvious that a broad commitment to human rights will translate into specific behaviors in support of a specific human right. Rather, human rights campaigns, if they follow the history of other intervention areas, will focus on specific outcomes, will consider what behaviors need to be influenced for the outcomes to be achieved, and specify what the likely influences on those specific behaviors are. Communication efforts will then focus on addressing the relevant influences.

Rarely, there will be a behavioral target that is easy to influence. More often, purposive communication is likely to be effective because it influences behavior over the long run through lots of exposure, through the use of multiple channels, and because it produces incremental rather than dramatic change. Large-scale change may come because of action by multiple agencies rather than the short-term, focused campaign by a single actor.

Communication is one tool for human rights advocates, but if it is to be effective, it will require skilled and focused use, reasonable expectations, and patience. Use of communication interventions requires hard thinking about relevance and then specifically about models of behavior change that are assumed, messages that promise to be persuasive for audiences, and strategies to gain sufficient exposure to those messages.

References

Andén-Papadopoulos, K. (2008). The Abu Ghraib torture photographs: News frames, visual culture, and the power of images. *Journalism, 9,* 5–30.

Cialdini, R. B. (2003). Crafting normative messages to protect the environment. *Current Directions in Psychological Science, 12*(4), 105–109.

Dearing, J., & Rogers, E. M. (1996). *Agenda-setting.* Thousand Oaks, CA: Sage.

Farrelly, M. C., Davis, K. C., Haviland, M. L., Messeri, P., & Healton, C. G. (2005). Evidence of a dose: Response relationship between "truth" antismoking ads and youth smoking prevalence. *American Journal of Public Health, 95*(3), 425–431.

Fishbein, M., & Ajzen, I. (2009). *Predicting and changing behavior: The reasoned action approach.* New York: Taylor & Francis.

Gerbner, G., & Gross, L. (1976). Living with television: The violence profile. *Journal of Communication, 26*(2), 172–194.

Hornik, R. (1988). *Development communication: Information, agriculture and nutrition in the Third World.* New York: Longman.

Hornik, R. (Ed.). (2002). *Public health communication: Evidence for behavior change.* Mahwah, NJ: Lawrence Erlbaum.

Hornik, R., Jacobsohn, L., Orwin, R., Piesse, A., & Kalton, G. (2008). Effects of the National Youth Antidrug Media Campaign on youth. *American Journal of Public Health, 98*(12), 2229–2236.

Ishay, M. R. (2004). *The history of human rights: From ancient times to the globalization era.* Berkeley: University of California Press.

Katz, E., & Lazarsfeld, P. (2006). *Personal influence: The part played by people in the flow of mass communication* (2nd ed.). London: New Brunswick and London Transaction Publishers.

Katz, J. E., & Rice, R. E. (2002). *Social consequences of Internet use: Access, involvement and interaction.* Cambridge, MA: The MIT Press.

Lauren, P. G. (2003). *The evolution of international human rights: Visions seen.* Philadelphia: University of Pennsylvania Press.

McCombs, M., & Shaw, D. (1972). The agenda-setting function of mass media. *Public Opinion Quarterly, 36*(2), 176–187.

Mitchelstein, E., & Boczkowski, P. (2009). Between tradition and change: A review of recent research on online news production. *Journalism, 10*(5), 562–586.

National Cancer Institute. (2008). The role of the media in promoting and reducing tobacco use. *Tobacco control monograph,* 19 (NIH Pub. No. 07–6242). Bethesda, MD: Author.

Noelle-Neumann, E. (1974). The spiral of silence: A theory of public opinion. *Journal of Communication, 24*(2), 43–51.

One laptop per child. (2011). Retrieved May 1, 2011, from http://one.laptop.org/stories

Pye, L. (Ed.). (1963). *Communications and political development.* Princeton, NJ: Princeton University Press.

Rice, R. E. (Ed.). (2008). *Media ownership: Research and regulation.* Cresskill, NJ: Hampton Press.

Scheufele, D. A., & Moy, P. (2000). Twenty-five years of the spiral of silence: A conceptual review and empirical outlook. *International Journal of Public Opinion Research, 12*(1), 3–28.

Sen, A. (1999). Democracy as a universal value. *Journal of Democracy, 10*(3), 3–17.

Sreberny-Mohammadi, A. (1990). Small media for a big revolution: Iran. *International Journal of Politics, Culture and Society, 3*(3), 341–372.

Tewksbury, D., & Scheufele, D. A. (2009). News framing theory and research. In J. Bryant & M. B. Oliver (Eds.), *Media effects: Advances in theory and research* (3rd ed., pp. 17–33). New York: Routledge/Taylor & Francis.

Wakefield, M. A., Loken, B., & Hornik, R. C. (2010). Use of mass media campaigns to change health behavior. *Lancet, 376*(9748), 1261–1271.

Walker, E. (2010). Industry-driven activism. *Contexts, 9*(2), 44–49.

Warner, K. E. (1989). Effects of the antismoking campaign: An update. *American Journal of Public Health, 79*(2), 144–151.

Wiebe, G. D. (1951). Merchandising commodities and citizenship on television. *Public Opinion Quarterly, 15*(4), 670–691.

Willinger, M., Hoffman, H. J., & Hartford, R. B. (1994). Infant sleep position and risk for sudden infant death syndrome. (Report of a National Institutes of Health meeting, January 13 and 14, 1994, Bethesda, MD). *Pediatrics, 93,* 814–819.

Wilson, E. J. III. (2004). *The Information Revolution and developing countries.* Cambridge, MA: The MIT Press.

Zimicki, S., Hornik, R. C., Verzosa, C. C., Hernandez, J. R., De Guzman, E., Dayrit, M., Fausto, A., & Lee, M. B. (1994). Improving vaccination coverage in urban areas through a health communication campaign: The 1990 Philippines Experience. *Bulletin of the World Health Organization, 72*(3), 409–422.

PART II

Design and Evaluation

CHAPTER 4

Guidelines for Formative Evaluation Research in Campaign Design

Charles K. Atkin and Vicki Freimuth

Public communication campaigns have achieved a varied record of success in influencing health and prosocial behavior as reflected by the diverse array of cases cited in this book. Designing and implementing effective campaigns requires a disciplined approach where the campaign team performs a thorough situational analysis, develops a theory-based but pragmatic strategic plan, and implements the creation and placement of messages in accordance with principles of effective media campaign practices. Moreover, diligent efforts are needed to enhance the working relationship between campaign designers and evaluators versus creative professionals who translate concepts in messages. A key role of the strategist in the collaborative process is to develop a framework for setting specifications and providing feedback as messages are prepared. Using a research-based approach in the public service domain is challenging when the mind-set of personnel in sponsoring organizations entails rigid advocacy of unpalatable, ideal behavior, devotion to politically correct message content, and self-indulgent artistic expression. Furthermore, specialists in domains such as health, environment, or altruism aren't always conscious of the fact that they differ substantially from their audiences in topical knowledge, values, priorities, and level of involvement, so they lack the perspective of the "average" person. Research data from samples of the intended audiences can help overcome the gulf between sender and receiver (see Dervin & Foreman-Wernet, Chapter 10).

Over the life of a campaign, evaluation research encompasses collection of information about audiences at the *formative* stage, followed by *process* evaluation to assess implementation as the campaign unfolds, and finally *summative* evaluation to track campaign impact (see Valente & Kwan, Chapter 6; Salmon & Murray-Johnson, Chapter 7). Formative evaluation research inputs can enhance campaign effectiveness by guiding the development of sophisticated strategies and effective messages. This preliminary phase of research is useful for determining which approaches are most promising and for revealing whether certain components are ineffective or even counterproductive. According to Palmer (1981), formative research provides data and perspectives to improve messages during the course of creation. He divides this type of evaluation into two phases. The first involves *preproduction research,* "in which data are accumulated on audience characteristics that relate importantly to the medium, the message, and the situation within which the desired behavior will occur" (p. 227). The second type of formative research is *production testing,* also known as pretesting, in which draft prototype messages are evaluated to obtain audience reactions prior to final production.

Public communication campaigners increasingly utilize elaborate formative evaluation techniques, particularly for major campaigns sponsored by government agencies, foundations, and organizations promoting health and social progress. Reviews of the media health campaign literature conclude that formative evaluation contributes to more successful campaigns (Noar, 2006; Rogers, 1996). Recent exemplars of sophisticated formative research include Bauman, Smith, Maibach, and Reger-Nash (2006); Berkowitz, Huhman, Heitzler, Potter, Nolin, and Banspach (2008); Cho and Witte (2005); Parrott, Steiner, and Goldenhar (2008); Smith, Atkin, Martell, Allen, and Hembroff (2006); and Uhrig, Bann, Wasserman, Guenther-Grey, and Eroglu (2010).

Information about the audience is most often utilized to identify specialized subgroups to be reached, to devise message appeals and presentation styles, and to select sources and channels. Furthermore, the formulation of campaign goals and objectives is increasingly based on research identifying priority areas of concentration, prospects for attaining certain types of impact, and critical stages of the communication process that must be addressed.

The campaign designer must adeptly overcome audience resistance manifested as receivers progress through exposure to processing to learning to yielding to behaving. Perhaps the most elemental problem is reaching the audience and engaging attention to the messages. Other key barriers include underestimating susceptibility to threats, counterarguing persuasive appeals, displaying reactance to compliance attempts, and exhibiting inertia (Knowles & Linn, 2004; McGuire, Chapter 9). Campaign designers are vigilant of unintended side effects that undermine campaign objectives (see Salmon & Murray-Johnson, Chapter 7). Concerns about boomerang effects especially shape the selection and presentation of behavioral recommendations, negative persuasive incentives, and source messengers (see Hornik, Chapter 3). Avoiding counterproductive responses from the audience requires careful formative evaluation inputs, both preproduction research and production testing.

CONCEPTUAL FRAMEWORK FOR CAMPAIGN PERSUASION

Communication–Persuasion Matrix

A fundamental organizing framework for developing campaign strategies is McGuire's matrix, which arrays source, message, channel, receiver, and destination variables as inputs and a series of information-processing and response variables as outputs (2001, Chapter 9). The first three input components are subject to manipulation by the campaign designer. The *source* concept includes both the organization that sponsors the campaign and the messenger who delivers the message, which can be characterized in terms of demographics (age, sex, socioeconomic status), credibility (expertise, trustworthiness), and attractiveness. Each *message* may feature a variety of content dimensions (themes, appeals, claims, evidence, and recommendations) using various formats of arranging material and styles of packaging, while the overall series of messages in a campaign can vary in volume, repetition, prominence of placement, and scheduling. The *channel* variables comprise the basic medium of transmission (e.g., television, social media sites), the content modes (e.g., news item, PSA), and the particular media vehicles (e.g., specific radio station, magazine title, website).

Although *receiver* factors are not subject to manipulation, sensitivity to the background attributes, abilities, and predispositions of individuals enhances the effectiveness of campaign stimuli. Finally, the *destination* encompasses the array of impacts that the campaign aims to produce, such as immediate versus long-term change, prevention versus cessation, direct versus two-step flow of influence, and intermediate responses versus ultimate behavioral outcomes.

The output variables have been conceptualized in a number of ways, typically beginning with exposure and processing, followed by the hierarchy of cognitive, affective, and behavioral consequences of the campaign inputs, such as skill acquisition, attitude change, and decision to act. Formative research can help identify what types of content and style will attract audience attention, facilitate comprehension, elicit emotional reactions and elaborations, impart knowledge gain and skills acquisition, influence the formation or change of affective orientations such as beliefs and attitudes, and affect pertinent behavioral performance.

Key Theoretical Approaches

Formative evaluation draws upon concepts and influence processes from theories, models, and frameworks in communication, social psychology, marketing, and health education. A number of key perspectives described in Chapter 1 provide pertinent guidance regarding the types of information researchers should collect to facilitate media campaign strategies.

Public service campaigns differ from other leading forms of media content, such as news and entertainment, because the messages are purposively focused on knowledge, attitudes, and behavior. In many respects, though, campaigns in the health and prosocial domains are similar to commercial advertising campaigns. Thus, it is useful to adapt concepts from the *social marketing* framework, which emphasizes an audience-centered consumer orientation and calculated attempts to attractively package the social product and utilize the optimum combination of campaign components that will attain pragmatic goals (see Bracht & Rice, Chapter 20; Rice & Robinson, Chapter 16). Social marketing offers a macro perspective, combining numerous components to be assessed at the formative stage, notably the multifaceted conceptions of "product," costs, and benefits (particularly nonsubstantive incentives), as well as audience segmentation, policy change, and competition.

The *uses and gratifications* perspective helps isolate audience motivations for attending media messages and for utilizing learned information in enacting behaviors. Processing concepts are drawn from the *cognitive response* model that emphasizes how audience involvement shapes thought generation and central versus peripheral routes to persuasion. The *instrumental learning* perspective focuses attention on factors such as source credibility, incentives featured in message appeals, and repetition.

Framing theory suggests careful appraisal of packaging message appeals in terms of gain-frame promotion of positive behavior versus loss-frame prevention of negative behavior. The concept of salience is central to the *agenda setting* perspective, particularly related to the prominence of societal problems and importance of issues, and to *media priming,* where certain cognitions associated with a health or social behavior result in short-term activation effects.

Social Cognitive Theory emphasizes the importance of source role models, explicitly demonstrated behaviors, depiction of vicarious reinforcements, and self-efficacy. Expectancy–value formulations, particularly the *Theory of Reasoned Action* and the *Theory of Planned Behavior,* focus on beliefs about the likelihood that performing a behavior leads to certain consequences and highlight the role of subjective norms. Several concepts from the *Health Belief Model* and *Protection Motivation Theory* pertain specifically to health threat appeals: susceptibility multiplied by seriousness of consequences and the self-efficacy and response efficacy of performing behavior. The *Transtheoretical Model* identifies key stages of change for segmenting audiences and for determining readiness to attempt, adopt, or sustain the recommended behavior. The *diffusion of innovations* theory suggests examining the relative advantage and trialability of focal behaviors and allocating media messages to stimulate social influence via multistep flows.

PREPRODUCTION RESEARCH

During the preproduction stage, the strategist seeks to learn as much as possible about the intended audience before articulating goals and developing strategies. Specifically, the research helps identify intended audiences and focal behaviors, specify significant intermediate response variables, ascertain channel exposure patterns, and determine receptivity to potential message components.

To collect pertinent preproduction information, researchers utilize focus groups, surveys, and secondary analysis. *Focus group* sessions are conducted by a moderator who stimulates extensive, open-ended discussions of selected issues in a small group setting (this technique is described in the pretesting section). The *Sense-Making Methodology* (Dervin & Foreman-Wernet, Chapter 10) applies more in-depth interviews and observations. Quantitative data are most often generated via formal surveys of midsize samples representing intended audience segments; standardized items are used to systematically measure a broad array of variables via interviews or questionnaires. In the case of campaigns featuring individually customized message tailoring, researchers utilize a unique type of formative research where the actual audience first completes an online survey instrument measuring numerous variables (Rimer & Kreuter, 2006). The computer program then matches this individual assessment input with appropriate portions of content drawn from a database to create a tailored message that is then delivered on-screen or on printed pages. Finally, secondary data can be accessed from technical report tables and online databases; these resources are described at the end of the preproduction section.

This section outlines basic approaches to selecting audience segments, specifying priority behaviors, elaborating cognitive and affective variables, ascertaining channel usage patterns, and evaluating key message elements. For a detailed illustration of how these methods and concepts are applied to the typical health campaign topic of drunk driving prevention, see Atkin and Freimuth (2001).

Identifying Audience Segments

Rather than attempting to reach a broad cross-section of the population, effective campaigns focus on multiple, specialized audience segments. Formative research is useful in identifying high-priority subgroups by gathering data about which categories of individuals are most relevant to the campaign goals, which are most receptive to media persuasion on the topic (through which media), and which are in a position to influence interpersonally the intended audience. Survey measures with representative samples are typically used to segment the audience along multiple dimensions defined in terms of demographic and psychographic characteristics, social role position, topic-related predispositions and behavioral intentions, readiness for change, and media exposure patterns. Segmenting the population into relatively homogeneous subgroups enables strategists to prepare distinctive messages adapted to the specific characteristics and predispositions of each subgroup and to select appropriate media channels to reach the intended audiences.

Most strategies focus on *primary* audiences composed of people to be directly influenced by the campaign. This approach may be supplemented by messages aimed at *secondary* (or gateway) audiences, such as friends, family members, and authority figures who are in positions to exercise influence over the primary audience (and who may have greater receptivity to campaign messages).

Specifying Focal Behaviors

Formative evaluation seeks to provide strategists with a better understanding of the nature of the existing problematic behaviors to be addressed by the campaign and the "product line" of optimal behaviors to be promoted. Basic behavioral practices are typically composed of specific component actions. Preproduction research helps determine audience receptivity to various discrete actions that could be recommended in a campaign. For example, an impaired driving campaign might promote the designated driver arrangement, companion intervention to take away keys from a drunk driver, one drink per hour for the driver, or abstention by the driver. These data enable designers to identify the promising options that are most amenable to change, to isolate certain unpopular but essential behaviors that will require special persuasive emphasis, and to eliminate from the campaign certain peripheral behaviors that will be widely resisted by the audience. Research may also assess reactions to various forms of symbolic branding of products and of the sponsoring organization. For example, altruistic images may be associated with the designated driver, and tough punishment is the hallmark of the Mothers Against Drunk Driving group.

Elaborating Cognitive and Affective Variables

As a means to attaining the bottom-line behavioral objectives, campaign messages must first have an impact on preliminary or intermediate variables along the response chain, ranging from exposure and processing to learning and yielding to actual utilization. In particular, campaign designers face certain obstacles that must be overcome; these audience resistance points often involve misconceptions, dysfunctional attitudes, and behavioral inhibitions. Isolating the most crucial response stages is facilitated by an understanding of the characteristics and predispositions of the intended audience.

Knowledge and Literacy

Research illuminates the intended audience's entry-level awareness and information holding about the subject matter of the campaign, identifying what is already known, what gaps exist, what confusions must be clarified, and what misinformation must be corrected. It's also helpful to ascertain knowledge about topic-related vocabulary and terminology; research may show that people hold diverse meanings for same concepts and labels or that they lack comprehension of certain claims or evidence. Measuring degree of familiarity with specific behavioral recommendations or awareness of drawbacks of certain behaviors is useful in determining whether to employ one- versus two-sided message strategies or explicit versus implicit conclusions.

Beliefs and Perceptions

Because many campaign message strategies seek to alter subjective conceptions relating to behaviors and expected consequences, it is important to measure precisely the pre-existing cognitive orientations held by individuals. Measures are taken of the audience's beliefs and perceptions pertaining to 1) barriers and opportunities affecting performance of a behavior, 2) the likelihood expectations of experiencing beneficial and harmful outcomes, notably illusions of invulnerability, 3) social support or opposition from the interpersonal network and subgroup norms, and 4) monetary costs and affordability of societal resources.

Attitudes and Values

Affective predispositions are also a significant consideration in message design, particularly evaluations of outcomes associated with practices. Depending on the direction, intensity, and structure of relevant values and attitudes, the campaign may concentrate on creation, conversion, reinforcement, or activation. Attitudinal predispositions may pertain to potential behavioral products and to approval of policy options advanced in advocacy campaigns. Understanding the desirability of promised or threatened outcomes can help formulate strategy, such as emphasizing gain- versus loss-frames and intensifying the degree of negativity or positivity related to the value component of the expectancy–value equation.

Salience Priorities

Research also provides guidance concerning which cognitive and affective orientations should be made more or less important to the audience. Salience measures assess level of involvement in the campaign topic, agenda ranking of a policy issue, and relative weighting of various outcomes that combine to shape behavioral intentions. More basically, research assesses the degree of concern or interest in the topical domain as well as the top-of-the-mind salience of performing the recommended behavior.

Efficacy and Skills

For certain practices, many well-intentioned and highly motivated individuals do not carry out appropriate acts because they lack confidence in their ability to perform the behaviors competently (see Rimal and Limaye, Chapter 17). If research shows that this is a barrier, messages can be designed to enhance personal efficacy or provide training for specific implementation skills.

Ascertaining Channel Usage Patterns

In deciding which channels are most efficient and effective for disseminating campaign messages, strategists need to determine intended audience preferences for traditional and new media and their patterns of interpersonal communication. While basic exposure figures are available from commercial audience measurement services (see "Preproduction Database Resources" in this chapter), customized surveys provide a much more elaborate and relevant array of data.

At a general level, it is useful to know the following information about the intended receivers: 1) amount of time spent watching television, listening to radio, reading magazines and newspapers, surfing the Internet, and visiting social media websites, along with exposure to secondary channels such as direct mail, billboards, or kiosks, 2) usage of specific media vehicles such as TV networks, magazine titles, and blogs and attention to various types of media content such as news stories and PSAs, and 3) patterns of community connections and interpersonal communication with pertinent categories of people.

Topic-specific data are especially pertinent to campaign planning: 1) consumption of news stories, product ads, and entertainment portrayals that directly complement or compete with campaign messages, and 2) interpersonal contacts, such as discussions with specialized opinion leaders, exposure to personal influence and peer pressures, and attempts to influence others on the topic.

Beyond exposure, formative researchers can assess credibility and utility of various media channels, vehicles, and content categories and may also measure audience recall and evaluative reactions to pertinent messages disseminated in previous campaigns. Similarly, audience members can be asked to identify interpersonal influence sources and memorable messages relating to the subject matter of the campaign.

Preliminary Evaluation of Message Elements

Before campaign messages are crafted and pretested, strategic and creative development is facilitated by both informal feedback and formal ratings of prospective components of these messages. Respondents typically rate a checklist of promising options displayed in the final section of an online survey instrument or respond to a set of open-ended queries. A comprehensive preproduction questionnaire might feature listings of three to five examples of various components that are under consideration for use in a campaign: spokespersons, headlines, slogans, persuasive incentives, storyline scenarios, stylistic devices, literacy levels, and supporting evidence. Responses such as credibility, comprehensibility, and subjective effectiveness are measured for each option.

Preproduction Database Resources

In addition to gathering customized information via surveys and focus groups, researchers also access a wide variety of previously collected data from governmental and private sectors. The federal health agencies have numerous databases that contain findings from sample surveys and statistical compilations. The CDC houses the National Center for Health Statistics (www.cdc.gov/hchs/index.htm) and CDC Wonder (www.wonder.cdc.gov), hosting databases on dozens of topics that generally feature demographic subgroups (adolescents, women), health behaviors (exercise, smoking), and diseases and conditions (diabetes, obesity). The Partners in Information Access for the Public Health Workforce (www.phpartners.org/health_stats.html) provides links to a massive array of databases from government agencies and public health organizations.

Companies specializing in public opinion surveys, audience measurement, and evaluation provide free or inexpensive data opportunities that are pertinent to campaign design. Harris Interactive offers low-cost omnibus survey options for general public polls and for specialized samples, such as youth, affluent people, and beltway influentials; it also offers access to findings from hundreds of surveys conducted over the past decade. For Gallup and other major U.S. pollsters, the Roper Center Public Opinion Archives (www.ropercenter.uconn.edu) serves as a repository for the most comprehensive collection of survey datasets emphasizing political opinions, along with data dealing with health, environment, social behavior, crime prevention, cultural attitudes, and media usage.

The Nielsen company (www.nielsen.com) regularly disseminates data on the public's exposure to major categories of media—television, radio, online, and mobile—and posts several white paper reports each month describing trends in use of traditional and new media technologies by the overall public and key audience segments, such as youth and minorities. Certain findings are frequently reported in media industry periodicals and websites, notably *Broadcasting & Cable* (www.broadcastingcable.com). The Arbitron company (www.arbitron.com) conducts the most extensive research on radio audiences, using traditional diaries and portable *people meter* devices. Much of Arbitron's listenership data are available to nonsubscribers; findings include market-wide ratings and useful subgroup comparisons by age, sex, income, education, and race.

One of the leading evaluation research firms is Weststat (www.weststat.com), which frequently conducts social science surveys on topics such as health, education, environmental protection, science, and technology. Their formative projects utilize both quantitative and qualitative methods to guide the development of large-scale communication campaigns, including the CDC's VERB physical exercise campaign and NIDA's antidrug media campaign; methodological techniques and evaluation findings are reported in white papers and journal articles.

Thus, there are a variety of ways to compile background information in the preproduction phase of campaign design. Informed by these data, researchers and strategists are in a position to collaborate with creative specialists in formulating and drafting an array of message themes and styles (and specific elements such as headlines, copy points, layouts, artwork, and music) and selecting source talent to appear in draft messages. As this stimulus construction process progresses, further research inputs are provided in the form of message pretesting.

PRETESTING RESEARCH

The second basic phase of formative evaluation is pretesting, the process of systematically gathering intended audience reactions to preliminary versions of messages before final production (U.S. Department of Health and Human Services, 2008). Pretesting can help determine which of numerous ideas or rough messages are most effective, and it can identify strengths and weaknesses in specific test messages. Because formative pretesting relies on measures of perceived message effects, Dillard, Weber, and Renata (2007) performed a meta-analysis to empirically validate how well pretest appraisals predict actual effects when campaigns are disseminated. They found a correlation of +.41 between perceived and actual message effectiveness, indicating that pretest measures tend to be moderately accurate. Pretesting research is involved in concept development and message creation through gauging sensitive elements.

Developing the Concept

Concepts are partially formulated message ideas consisting of visual sketches and key phrases that convey the main elements to be represented in the finished product. Pretesting at this stage provides direction for eliminating weaker approaches and identifying the most promising concepts, saving considerable time and money during production. Sometimes, entirely new concepts emerge from audience responses; original ideas are revised and refined, as in the case of concept testing feedback that heightened the realism of diverse student groups working together to create a drug prevention video (Freimuth, Plotnick, Ryan, & Schiller, 1997). Another advantage to pretesting rough concepts is the generation of words, phrases, and vernacular used by the intended audience so that appropriate language can be revised. For example, the National Cancer Institute (NCI) conducted concept testing to learn how to present cancer risk information. They learned that the word *risk* raises alarm while *chance* minimizes it. Vague or unfamiliar terms such as *fourfold* and *lifetime risk,* gave people reason to discount the information (U.S. Department of Health and Human Services, 2008).

Creating the Test Message

Complete messages can then be created in rough form for the next stage of pretesting: message creation. For print materials, it is best to test a complete prototype of the final material, including the text, layout, typeface, and visuals. Rough executions of video spots used to rely on animatics (a series of detailed drawings filmed in rapid succession and using camera zooms and pans to give the illusion of movement) or photomatics (similar but using a series of photos), but because of digital photography, web access to stock photographs, and nonlinear editing programs, they have been replaced by much more rapid, computer-based techniques, which are referred to as digimatics. Radio messages and print materials can also be prepared for testing in rough form. If music or sound effects will be used in the final audio product, they should also be included in the rough message. Interactive media, such as websites, CD-ROMs, DVDs, or mobile device applications, should be complete enough to allow basic functionality and design to be assessed. At this stage, pretesting can be used to predict how effectively a message will move the intended audience through key types of reaction to campaign stimuli by 1) assessing the attention value of a message, 2) measuring its comprehensibility, 3) determining its relevance to the intended audience, 4) identifying strengths and weaknesses, and 5) gauging any sensitive or controversial elements.

Assessing Attention

An essential ingredient of messages is their ability to attract the intended audience's attention in the context of competing media and messages. Typically, this criterion is assessed by exposing intended audiences to a clutter format of several similar messages placed within an appropriate medium or context and then asking them to list the messages they remember seeing. For posters, for example, the intended audience might be asked to sit in a waiting room for a few minutes where several posters are hung on the walls. After leaving the room, they would be asked to recall the messages contained in the posters. For video messages, five to seven spot messages might be placed within an entertainment program and, afterwards, the audience asked to list all the ads or public service messages they remember seeing. More direct observational methods also have been used to assess attention, especially with very young children. Children's Television Workshop has used the distracter method, which measures attention by observing whether children are focused on the program or on a competing stimulus. Observational data also are gathered about the children's verbal comments, their singing and dancing in response to the show, and off-task activities, such as talking or playing with their friends (Palmer, 1981).

Measuring Comprehension

Messages must be understood before they can be processed and accepted. Procedures for measuring comprehension range from highly structured, closed-ended questions to open-ended requests for recall of main ideas. When developing the United States Department of Agriculture (USDA) food pyramid, extensive pretesting revealed that the pyramid shape conveyed key concepts more clearly than a bowl or other shapes. In addition, planners learned that representing fats, oils, and sugars as a bottle of salad dressing, a can of soda, and a bowl of sugar created widespread misunderstanding (U.S. Department of Health and Human Services, 2008).

Identifying Strong and Weak Points

Pretesting prior to final production and distribution can help ensure that each element of a message is likely to meet the information needs of the audience. In a test of a booklet on lung cancer, patients could recall on average 2 out of 12 ideas presented; half the patients were not able to recall any, however. Too many technical terms, high density of concepts, concepts unimportant to the audience, and too little differentiation between diagnostic and treatment procedures inhibited intended audience recall (U.S. Department of Health and Human Services, 2008).

Determining Personal Relevance

Intended audiences must perceive that a message personally applies to them for the message to be effective. When the National Bone Health Campaign research team explored the credibility of a spokesperson among girls 9 to 12 years old, the sample said they wanted to hear the message from a girl who was strong, bold, confident, active, healthy, and popular. This advice guided the development of Carla, a cartoon spokes-character who speaks to girls as a peer working to build powerful bones. In the pretesting of a website featuring Carla, girls described her as powerful and fun—someone they'd like to know and be friends with (U.S. Department of Health and Human Services, 2008).

Gauging Sensitive or Controversial Elements

Pretesting can help in determining whether messages may alienate or offend intended audiences, often rejecting sponsors' or interest groups' assumptions about the general public's responses. Pretest results showed that using vernacular language to discuss diarrhea in a booklet on chemotherapy was regarded as offensive by the low literacy-intended audience, who preferred a more technical discussion (U.S. Department of Health and Human Services, 2008).

TYPES OF PRETESTING

The following sections summarize a variety of pretesting techniques in developing public service messages: 1) focus group interviews, 2) individual in-depth interviews, 3) central-location intercept interviews, 4) self-administered questionnaires, 5) theater testing, and 6) other techniques, such as readability testing, usability testing, gatekeeper review, participatory rapid appraisals, and multimethod combinations.

Focus Group Interviews

Focus group interviews are a form of qualitative research adapted by marketing research-ers from group therapy (Krueger & Casey, 2009). They are conducted with a group of approximately 5 to 10 respondents simultaneously. Using a discussion outline, a modera-tor builds rapport and trust and keeps the session on track while allowing respondents to talk freely and spontaneously. As new topics related to the outline emerge, the moderator probes further to gain useful insights. An experienced, capable moderator should lead the groups. The moderator must be well informed about the subject and the purpose of the group sessions.

Focus groups are a very flexible formative research method. Many focus group sessions are conducted in sophisticated facilities with one-way mirrors and video cameras, but they are also carried out in workplaces, in outdoor settings, via telephone, and over the Internet. Online focus groups can be held in modified chat rooms. Participants are recruited by phone or e-mail, and they log onto a designated website at a prearranged time. Once in the "room," the participant's screen is usually divided into two sides: One side has the text of the discussion, and the other shows messages and materials. Although the online setting reduces the in-depth emotional information obtained by personally observing the partici-pants, this method lowers the costs (by eliminating expenses for travel, food, and renting facilities), and discussion threads create an instant transcript (Heckman, 2000). Turney and Pocknee (2005) argue that these virtual focus groups are particularly useful when par-ticipants are difficult to recruit or access in central locations and that this method enables safe, secure, and anonymous environments in which to share ideas and experiences.

Focus group interviews provide insights into intended audience beliefs on an issue, allow program planners to obtain perceptions of message concepts, and help trigger the creative thinking of communication professionals. The group discussion stimulates respondents to talk freely, providing valuable clues for developing materials in the con-sumers' language.

As with any qualitative research approach, care must be taken not to interpret or generalize focus group interview results quantitatively; the testing is indicative and not definitive. Focus group respondents should be typical of the intended audience. Subgroups within the intended audience representing relevant positions on the issues should be included, usually in separate focus groups. For example, in testing message concepts on smoking aimed at a general audience of smokers, it would be helpful to conduct focus groups with some key subgroups, such as males and females, heavy and light smokers, and older and younger ages to determine if the messages were effective across all these groups.

Individual In-Depth Interviews

Individual, in-depth interviews are used for pretesting issues that are very sensitive or must be probed very deeply and for respondents who are difficult to recruit for focus group interviews, such as physicians, dentists, and chief executive officers. Such interviews can be quite long, lasting from 30 minutes to 1 hour, and are used to assess comprehension as well as feelings, emotions, attitudes, and prejudices. Although in-depth interviews are very costly and time-consuming, they may be the most appropriate form of pretesting for sensitive subjects (e.g., breast reconstruction).

Central-Location Intercept Interviews

Central-location intercept interviews involve stationing interviewers at a location frequented by individuals from desired intended audiences and, after asking a few screening questions, inviting qualified respondents to participate in the pretest. If they are willing to participate, each respondent is taken to the interviewing station, shown the pretest messages, and asked a series of questions to assess their reactions to the message concepts or executions. One advantage to this type of pretesting is that a high-traffic area can yield many interviews in a reasonably short time. The second advantage is that using a central location for hard-to-reach intended audiences can be a cost-effective means of gathering data. As with focus groups, sampling is not random, and the results cannot be generalized to a larger population. A significant disadvantage of this method is the obtrusiveness of the study; because respondents know they are participating in a test, their responses may be less valid.

The National Youth Antidrug Media Campaign used the central intercept method in a unique way. This campaign developed a rigorous, quantitative copy testing system to assess near-final ads. The research used an experimental design with respondents recruited in a mall intercept and randomly assigned to two conditions. The test group saw the message, and the control group did not, and both groups filled out brief questionnaires to assess effects. The results had to show significantly greater antimarijuana attitudes and intentions relative to the control group in order for the ad to be aired (Foley & Pechmann, 2004).

Self-Administered Questionnaires

Self-administered questionnaires can also be used to pretest concepts and rough messages. These questionnaires can be mailed to respondents along with pretest materials or distributed at a central location. Each respondent is asked to review the materials, complete the questionnaire, and return it by a certain date. The Internet has enhanced the use of this method. It is now possible to inexpensively conduct these tests on a website, which speeds up the data collection process and encourages broader participation. Disadvantages include a low overall response rate, tendency toward self-selection of individuals who have either strongly positive or negative responses to the pretest materials, and sample biases relating to respondents being Internet users.

An efficient approach for assessing audience responses to messages is a fairly brief set of questionnaire items that can be administered following exposure to a specimen message. The instrument measures the perceived effectiveness of the message for producing an impact on an intended audience (e.g., "How effective is this message in influencing college students to avoid driving drunk?" with response categories such as *Very Effective, Fairly Effective, Slightly Effective,* and *Not Effective*). Then, respondents evaluate the message along, perhaps, a dozen quality dimensions using a numerical scale ("What is your personal reaction to the message? Give ratings using a scale from 0 to 10 on each of these factors."). Typical factors (and accompanying definitions) include *informative* (tells you something new, increases your knowledge), *sensible* (presents wise advice that seems reasonable), *memorable* (vivid image, fascinating fact, and catchy slogan), *enjoyable* (interesting, entertaining, and stimulating message), *useful* (valuable information, helpful advice worth remembering), *imaginative* (style is refreshing, novel, unique, and clever), *believable* (accurate information, sincere and trustworthy characters), *professional* (high production quality), *motivating* (presents influential reasons to prompt changes in behavior), and *relevant* (personally meaningful content, identifiable with characters and situations). Next, respondents provide assessments of whether or not the message has any of these negative features using a simple Yes or No response to a series of questions on factors such as the following: *preachy* (tone of message too moralistic or righteous), *disturbing* (turned off because it is too emotional or threatening), *confusing* (vague or difficult to understand), *irritating* (offensive or annoying), *dull* (boring, stale, or trite style), or misleading (biased arguments or exaggerated claims). These standardized evaluations may be supplemented with open-ended questions soliciting positive or critical comments as well as suggestions for improving the message.

Theater Testing

Theater testing uses forced exposure to test rough television message executions in controlled settings. Testing takes place with several hundred randomly recruited respondents representative of the message's intended audience; they are seated in groups of approximately 25 around large TV monitors. The test spots are embedded among other commercials in TV program material to camouflage the intent of the testing situation and simulate the home viewing context, and all questions are prerecorded and administered over TV monitors.

Respondents are asked to recall, on an unaided basis, all the messages they remember by brand name, product type, or public service (the attention measure). They are then asked to write down the central point each message was trying to convey (the main idea communication measure). Subsequently, respondents are exposed to the embedded test messages for a second time, followed by diagnostic questions that probe respondent reactions, including personal relevance and a believability measure. Theater testing also provides an opportunity to use electronic devices to record and display moment-to-moment evaluations of messages, which can later be overlaid on the actual messages to identify particularly positive or negative components.

Other Techniques: Readability, Usability, and Gatekeeper Review

Readability testing is critical when producing print materials because it estimates the educational level required for intended populations to adequately comprehend written text. Readability tests are available on many standard word processing packages, or a score can easily be computed by hand (U.S. Department of Health and Human Services, 2008).

To ensure that users will find a website or mobile phone app well designed and easy to use, *usability testing* is performed during the development of the site or app. People representing the intended audience actually sit down and use the site to complete tasks, while a research aide observes how they interact with the site and asks them questions following completion of the tasks.

Public communication campaigns often rely on *gatekeepers* to disseminate materials, such as PSA directors or station managers who select and schedule broadcast messages and health professionals who hand out or display print messages. In order to enhance cooperation, gatekeepers may be asked to review and evaluate rough materials concurrently with audience pretesting.

The traditional formative research methods described in the previous sections have been criticized because the audiences are seldom involved in problem identification that sensitively meets their information needs. Some campaigns employ participatory rapid appraisal as a semistructured process of learning from, with, and by underserved or remote population segments such as residents of rural or foreign locales (Clift & Freimuth, 1997) or the sense-making methodology (Dervin & Foreman-Wernet, Chapter 10).

Finally, multiple formative evaluation methods are frequently combined as the campaign is developed. The VERB campaign, the CDC effort to increase physical activity among *tweens* (9- to 13-year-olds), made extensive use of formative evaluation methods to develop the brand, test messages, and materials and decide on which media outlets to place campaign advertising (Berkowitz et al., 2008). The brand development process used interviews with triads of tweens, focus groups with parents of tweens, and adults who work with this age group and in-depth interviews with industry professionals. In addition, this campaign conducted both semiotic analyses of ads and brands targeting tweens and hedonic analyses of these brands to reveal the elements that inspire tween affinity from a pleasure-seeking perspective. Another innovative formative technique used in developing the VERB brand was diaries kept by tweens and their parents depicting tweens' after-school experiences, expressing ideas, feelings, hopes, and fears through words and pictures.

Conclusion

By collecting preproduction information and feedback reactions to pretest theoretically derived versions of the message concepts and executions, campaign designers are in a much better position to devise more effective campaign plans and messages before final production and full-scale dissemination. Formative evaluation facilitates the development of more sophisticated campaign strategies, helps avoid pitfalls, and improves the quality and effectiveness of the created messages.

References

Atkin, C., & Freimuth, V. (2001). Formative evaluation research in campaign design. In R. E. Rice & C. Atkin (Eds.), *Public communication campaigns* (pp. 125–145). Thousand Oaks, CA: Sage.

Bauman, A., Smith, B. J., Maibach, E. W., & Reger-Nash, B. (2006). Evaluation of mass media campaigns for physical activity. *Evaluation and Program Planning, 29,* 312–322.

Berkowitz, J., Huhman, M., Heitzler, C., Potter, L., Nolin, M., & Banspach, S. (2008). Overview of formative, process, and outcome evaluation methods used in the VERB™ campaign. *American Journal of Preventive Medicine, 34*(6), S222–S229.

Cho, H., & Witte, K. (2005). Managing fear in public health campaigns: A theory-based formative evaluation process. *Health Promotion Practice, 6*(4), 482–490.

Clift, E., & Freimuth, V. S. (1997). Changing women's lives: A communication perspective on participatory qualitative research techniques for gender equality. *Journal of Gender Studies, 6*(3), 289–296.

Dillard, J. P., Weber, K. M., & Renata, G. V. (2007). The relationship between the perceived and actual effectiveness of persuasive messages: A meta-analysis with implications for formative campaign research. *Journal of Communication, 57*, 613–631.

Foley, D., & Pechmann, C. (2004). National youth antidrug campaign copy testing system. *Social Marketing Quarterly, 10*(2), 34–42.

Freimuth, V. S., Plotnick, C. A., Ryan, C. E., & Schiller, S. (1997). Right turns only: An evaluation of a video-based, multicultural drug education series for seventh graders. *Health Education & Behavior, 24*(5), 555–567.

Heckman, J. (2000). Turning the focus online. *Marketing News, 34*(5), 15.

Knowles, E. S., & Linn, J. A. (2004). *Resistance and persuasion.* Mahwah, NJ: Lawrence Erlbaum.

Krueger, R. A., & Casey, M. A. (2009). *Focus groups: A practical guide for applied research* (4th ed.). Thousand Oaks, CA: Sage.

McGuire, W. (2001). Input and output variables currently promising for constructing persuasive communications. In R. E. Rice & C. Atkin (Eds.), *Public communication campaigns* (pp. 22–48). Thousand Oaks, CA: Sage.

Noar, S. M. (2006). A 10-year retrospective of research in health mass media campaigns: Where do we go from here? *Journal of Health Communication, 11*(1), 21–42.

Palmer, E. (1981). Shaping persuasive messages with formative research. In R. E. Rice & W. Paisley (Eds.), *Public communication campaigns* (pp. 227–242). Beverly Hills, CA: Sage.

Parrott, R., Steiner, C., & Goldenhar, L. (2008). Georgia's harvesting healthy habits: A formative evaluation. *The Journal of Rural Health, 12*, 291–300.

Rimer, B., & Kreuter, M. (2006). Advancing tailored health communication: A persuasion and message effects perspective. *Journal of Communication, 56*, S184–S201.

Rogers, E. M. (1996). Up-to-date report. *Journal of Health Communication, 1*, 15–24.

Smith, S. W., Atkin, C., Martell, D., Allen, R., & Hembroff, L. (2006). A social judgment theory approach to conducting formative research in a social norms campaign. *Communication Theory, 16*, 141–152.

Turney, L., & Pocknee, C. (2005). Virtual focus groups: New frontiers in research. *International Journal of Qualitative Methods, 4*(2), 1–10.

Uhrig, J. D., Bann, C. M., Wasserman, J. W., Guenther-Grey, C., & Eroglu, D. (2010). Audience reactions and receptivity to HIV prevention message concepts for people living with HIV. *AIDS Education and Prevention, 22*, 110–112.

U.S. Department of Health and Human Services. (2008). *Making health communication programs work: A planner's guide.* Bethesda, MD: National Cancer Institute. Retrieved September 29, 2010, from the national Cancer Institute: http://www.cancer.gov/pinkbook

A Systems-Based Evaluation Planning Model for Health Communication Campaigns in Developing Countries

Ronald E. Rice and Dennis Foote

The Academy for Educational Development was the project implementer under Project Director Bill Smith, while Stanford University and Applied Communication Technology were the project evaluators, under Foote. Research was funded through the offices of Education and Health of the Bureau of Science and Technology, U.S. Agency for International Development, under project AIDIDSPE-C-0028. Assistance was also generously provided by the USAID missions in Honduras and The Gambia, the Ministry of Public Health in Honduras, and the Ministry of Health, Labour, and Social Welfare in The Gambia.

Systematic evaluation of health and nutrition communication campaigns in less developed countries is of paramount importance because poor health conditions continue to stifle human and national potential, high levels of governmental and individual resources are involved, and the cumulative knowledge about how to design communication interventions effectively in such settings is inconsistent. Salmon and Kroger (1992) argue that most campaigns either explicitly or implicitly focus on 1) the individual level rather than system level, and 2) effects rather than processes and structures of campaigns (see also Dorfman & Wallack, Chapter 23; Salmon & Murray-Johnson, Chapter 7). Thus, this chapter presents a systems-theoretic framework for planning evaluations of health communication campaigns in less-developed countries, to identify relevant variables and processes, and to facilitate more effective and focused efforts.

Systems theory argues that there are common structures and processes operating in phenomena regardless of the research discipline applied (Berrien, 1968; Bertalanffy, 1968; Buckley, 1968). These structures include a system (a set of interacting and interdependent elements, components, or subsystems functioning within a common boundary), some common goal(s), and a surrounding environment (a set of inputs and constraints). A system such as a rural community exists in an *initial state* in an environment (such as the state of high infant morbidity and mortality in a developing country), obtains or receives *inputs* such as a health campaign, processes them according to *goals and constraints* (such as improved health, insufficient water, or cultural norms concerning illness and maternal care), develops *outputs* (such as lower infant mortality or a reorganized health care delivery system), and receives *feedback* from the environmental actors and elements (such as increased support, political opposition, changed social norms, competition from other systems, need for maintenance, etc.). One of the six theoretical approaches to corporate and social issues campaigns explicated by Bridges (2004) is *systems theory*, a common foundation for public relations and issues management processes. This approach emphasizes the interdependency of an organization in larger economic, political, and social systems, the tendency toward homeostasis, and adaptation based on feedback from the environment relative to a goal state.

Health communication campaigns, for example, are appropriately conceived of as systems of influence, both with respect to the multiple media, message, audience, community, and environmental systems and with respect to the campaign organizations and actors as production and political systems (McLeroy, Bibeau, Steckler, & Glanz, 1988; Ray & Donohew, 1990; Salmon & Kroger, 1992; Winett, 1986). Campbell, Steenbarger, Smith, and Stucky (1982) applied this systems perspective in evaluating a community counseling project, concluding that taking a systems perspective leads to a widening of the scope of the original evaluation questions, increasing the range of evaluation tools necessary to understand the system. Rudd, Goldberg, and Dietz (1999) also proposed and analyzed a comprehensive systems-based approach for sustaining community campaigns. Salmon and Kroger (1992) analyzed the National AIDS Information and Education Program as both an organizational system and a (campaign) system of influence. The Centers for Disease Control and Prevention (2009) provides very detailed guidelines and resources (what they call Procedural Guidance) for a range of community-based campaigns and interventions related to HIV/AIDS. Both social marketing and community campaigns implicitly presume an interdependent system of actors, subsystems, environments, resources, and values (see also Bracht & Rice, Chapter 20).

The proposed evaluation planning model derived from Suchman (1967) involves the following (often interrelated, iterative, and interactive) stages: 1) specifying the goals, assumptions, and related projects, 2) specifying the system and the process model, 3) specifying prior states and system phases, 4) specifying system constraints and intervention inputs, 5) specifying immediate and long-term goals, 6) specifying the process model at the individual level, 7) choosing among research approaches appropriate to the system, and 8) assessing implications for design.

SPECIFYING THE GOALS, ASSUMPTIONS, AND RELATED PROJECTS

One of the major causes of infant mortality in developing countries is diarrheal disease. It occurs at significant levels in practically every country, made worse by poor nutrition and bad sanitary conditions. Averaged over studies published between 1992 and 2000, 4.9 children under five years old per 1,000 per year died for a median of 21% of all deaths in this age range (while nearly 20 out of 1,000 die of diarrhea-related dehydration before their second birthdays), and an estimated total of 2.5 million per year (Kosek, Bern, & Guerrant, 2003). Death is typically caused by dehydration—loss of fluids and electrolytes—before the child's natural defenses can defeat the cause of diarrhea. Less acute consequences—malnutrition and waste of human and material resources—are even more common.

Since the 1960s, a diverse set of approaches to reducing diarrhea-related infant mortality has been studied, including immunization, improved water availability, disposal of excreta, weaning education, reduction of infection through animals and insects, and oral rehydration therapy (ORT) (Feachem, 1986; Hornik, 1985, 1993). ORT is a comprehensive approach that includes breast-feeding, improved nutrition, and sanitary practices. In addition, an inexpensive oral rehydration solution (ORS) that treats the dehydration by replacing fluids and electrolytes has been developed. ORT-oriented campaigns have significantly decreased diarrhea-related infant deaths around the world. For example, an ORS program in Egypt reduced deaths attributed to diarrhea 82% for infants and 62% among children, although the program took nearly five years to raise sufficient awareness after lessons learned from the testing of a nurse–mother community pilot program in 29 rural villages (Levine, 2007). There are, however, considerable problems associated with ORS, such as dangers from improperly mixed solutions, worsening of diarrhea symptoms, and difficulties in distributing ingredients (Hornik, 1985). Huttly, Morris, and Pisani (1997) provide a comprehensive review of causes of and interventions for morbidity and mortality effects of infant diarrhea in developing countries.

One of the classic campaigns to improve prevention and treatment of diarrheal infant mortality was a joint effort of USAID and the Ministries of Public Health of Honduras and The Gambia to carry out the large-scale Mass Media and Health Practices (MMHP) project. A subsequent USAID-supported project, HEALTHCOM (Hornik, 1993), expanded the approach to more than 20 countries and helped to carry on the effort in Honduras where ORS (comprising sodium, glucose, potassium, and bicarbonate, called Litrosol) was distributed in packets to be mixed with one liter of water. In The Gambia, ORS was mixed at home, with eight bottle caps of sugar, one cap of salt, and three bottles (one liter) of water, partially due to the expense of ORS packets (over a dime, not including internal distribution costs) and partially to avoid production dependencies.

SPECIFYING THE SYSTEM AND THE PROCESS MODEL

Figure 5.1 presents an overview of the systems-based evaluation planning model. Taking a systems perspective, this model shows that, before any intervention, there exists a prior state (of the people, their family, their community, the environment, the economy, mortality and morbidity rates, sanitary conditions, nutritional levels, etc.) that is the baseline to which ongoing and final evaluation measurements are compared and constraints existing in the system that affect how the population interacts with the intervention.

The prior state, system constraints, and the intersection of system constraints and intervention inputs interrelate and feed into the process component. For example, perhaps

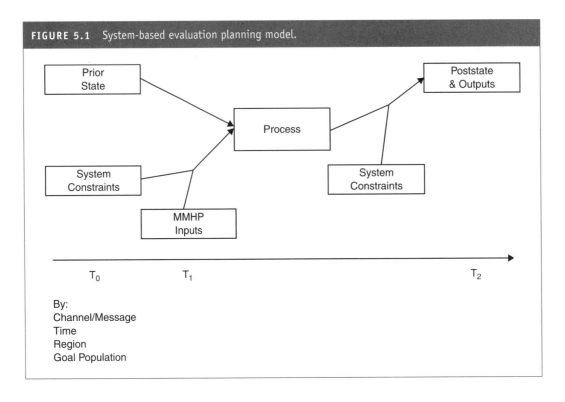

FIGURE 5.1   System-based evaluation planning model.

a family learns new approaches to sanitation and wants to perform them but cannot because personal, cultural, or economic conditions prevent them from buying soap, using sufficiently clean water, or believing in bacteria. Thus, system constraints can block or transform the progression from process to output.

The subsequent condition of the goal population constitutes a new or poststate. This poststate, which includes outputs from the process components, consists of the information, attitudes, behaviors, and health status of individuals, as well as many of the conditions measured in the prior state component. Many of the values of the variables measured may not have changed; some would not be expected to change. And, some new aspects of the system may have been introduced, such as new health communication infrastructures or, in the long run, a rise in population growth, leading to a new set of constraints and conditions. Of course, because such interventions occur over a lengthy period of time, this whole model may repeat itself in various phases.

Perhaps the most important analytical aspect of an evaluation of a complex campaign is the need to consider, measure, and assess the effect of the major variables that help explain why certain outputs occurred as well as why certain others did not. Such explanations are typically couched in terms of *program* or *theory* failure (see Valente & Kwan, Chapter 6). Broadly, program failure results when the program is not or cannot be implemented as planned due to factors such as the use of inappropriate messages or language or dependency on an insufficient distribution system. Theory failure, assuming successful program implementation, occurs when one or more of the hypothesized causal links are not supported by the evaluation data (e.g., when people who know what the appropriate behavior is understand why it might be to their advantage to adopt it and have access to the necessary resources yet nevertheless fail to adopt) or have unexpected effects (e.g., when greater participation in a campaign-related event is associated with decreased learning).

The likelihood of program and theory failure increases as we move along the process components from more immediate outcomes, such as knowledge levels, to longer-term outcomes, such as health status or mortality rates, for three basic reasons. First, we generally hypothesize that the components are causally related and thus those subjects who do not choose to, fail to, or are unable to complete one component become unavailable for the remaining components. Second, the cumulative effect of constraints and intervening variables, over which the implementer has no control, is almost certain to decrease the probability of occurrence of the postulated causal processes. Third, even if each component is accomplished, the relative strength of change is stochastic so that the final outcome from many successful components may still be hard to detect (see McGuire, Chapter 9).

SPECIFYING PRIOR STATES AND SYSTEM PHASES

Specifying the Prior State

The prior state of the environment can be conceptualized as clusters of variables identified by theoretical processes and prior empirical results, including community or population; household; communication; sanitation; information, attitudes, and behaviors; nutrition; general health; and child-care practices.

Specifying System Phases

Fundamental to understanding the evaluation process is the fact that the system, and thus the implementation of the treatments, exists and changes over time. Description and analysis of the prior state and system constraints will lead to specification of variables by system phase, identifying when certain interventions should be applied and for which goal populations.

The MMHP campaigns organized their messages in phases according to temporal fluctuations (the rainy and dry seasons affect the type and amount of diarrhea) and a model of cumulative impact. Activities were phased to train health workers at the beginning and to follow a sequence of information, enabling behaviors, and reinforcement in messages for the general population. During the rainy season of Phase II, diarrhea rates were high, so the central messages, conveyed by intensive media intervention, focused on the purpose, availability, proper mixing, and regimen for ORT. In Phase III, after the rainy season had passed, the intervention messages promoted selected prevention behaviors as well as maintaining the treatment behaviors. Phase IV was during the next rainy season, so the intervention returned to its treatment focus with selected prevention messages. In Phase V, after the rainy season had passed, the role of breast-feeding in ORT and its more general benefits were emphasized.

SPECIFYING SYSTEM CONSTRAINTS AND INTERVENTION INPUTS

Specifying System Constraints

It is necessary to detect and measure system constraints that may block or transform the progression from inputs to outputs, such as resources, cultural beliefs (e.g., diarrhea is often seen as a normal way to purge harmful illnesses such as measles; Green, 1986), medical community, environment, and delivery of interventions. The pervasiveness of system constraints, even as manifested in how interventions are designed, may well prevent any substantive improvement in the population's health status (e.g., a program failure). For example, Cornish and Campbell (2009) noted that results of peer education are inconsistent and highly dependent on the context. They compared two programs in India and South Africa, intended to empower sex workers to require condom use, identifying success factors such as including stable and supportive networks and political and infrastructural resources, engagement of local stakeholders, and community development orientation instead of only a biomedical one.

Once the linkages between intervention inputs and potential outputs are specified theoretically, it becomes crucial to identify distinctions among planned inputs (e.g., media, medical practices, ORS packets), delivery constraints, real inputs, resource and access constraints, engaged inputs, and final engagement by individuals—that is, what is perceived by the intended audience as being input. These engaged inputs must be considered the basis for potential measures of exposure, attention, and recall in analyzing change and poststate measurements and, as such, still do not represent the final basis upon which to assess theory failure or success. Thus tests of program success should use data on planned and real inputs; tests of theory success should use data on real and engaged inputs.

Media Inputs

In The Gambia at the time of the study, 60% of household compounds had at least one working radio receiver; in those compounds, 75% of the women listened to Radio Gambia, which delivers the MMHP spots, so only 45% of the women in the general population could potentially directly engage in processing the campaign's radio messages. Compare this engaged radio input to the 3% literacy rate by individual women, which would prevent any substantial engagement with print messages. Thus one strategy in The Gambia project was to provide color-coded flyers or wall posters with mixing instructions, which were explained and reinforced through radio messages. In Honduras, 67% had a working radio. Averaged over several waves, from 9:00 a.m. to 10:00 a.m., 19% listened to their radios, and 60% of those reported hearing the campaign spot, representing 12% of the population. From noon to 1:00 p.m., the figures were 35%, 81%, and 28%, respectively.

Each planned media input, such as radio spots, can be coded for goal audience and frequency, region, and station. Specific messages can be coded by implementation phase within each specific input. That is, only a few messages in certain media are project inputs in each phase for each subaudience. Therefore, the relative efficacy or recall of those messages, by medium, can be compared to the relative efficacy or recall of different messages, by medium, in later phases.

For example, in The Gambia project, the color-coded instruction flyers were the most significant print media input. The presence of mixing flyers that mothers put up in their homes significantly influenced earlier learning about and use of ORT and later-occurring forgetting or disadoption of ORT, whereas the recalling of radio messages led to earlier forgetting and disadoption (Snyder, 1991). One explanation is that putting the flyer up was associated with taking action concerning ORT, while remembering hearing the message was not necessarily associated with immediate action. When hearing was contemporaneous with learning about ORT or adopting it, then respondents learned earlier and maintained use longer (Snyder, 1991).

Resource Inputs

The distribution of ORS packets with associated print material is considered a planned resource input, which also must be monitored to determine engaged inputs to goal populations. Differential distribution by channel (commercial or public health outlets) or by geographical region (closer or farther from roads) may help explain why intervention efforts are differentially successful in various regions.

Audience Inputs

Relevant populations other than the goal caretaker or child populations—direct contact personnel, such as health workers and physicians, and indirect contacts, such as volunteer care workers—can be viewed as additional inputs or constraints. Goal audiences can be asked about these interpersonal diffusion channels that may help to spread or resist mass media inputs (Coleman, Katz, & Menzel, 1966; Rogers & Kincaid, 1981). For example, local health workers have been shown to be a significant influence in campaigns to teach correct ORS mixing or to support proper weaning as approaches to reducing diarrhea-related infant deaths (Feachem, 1986; Kumar, Monga, & Jain, 1981). For example, in The Gambia, village health volunteers trained by the health workers were identified by red flags outside their compounds. Local mothers could come to these red flag volunteers to learn how to mix the ORS correctly. However, the volunteers were not supported throughout the campaign by health workers, so this indirect interpersonal channel disappeared.

SPECIFYING IMMEDIATE AND LONG-TERM GOALS

In the Honduran and Gambian projects, categories of *cognitive* outcomes included attention to—and recognition, recall, and knowledge of—nutritional and preventive behaviors and

ORT messages. Categories of *behavior* outcomes included response to diarrheal episodes (e.g., administration of ORT, taking child to clinics), infant feeding practices, water quality, prevention, and personal hygiene. Categories of *health* outcomes included nutritional status, morbidity (frequency, severity, and duration of diarrhea), and mortality. Categories of *system* outcomes included the institutionalization of ORT in the health system, improvements in communication about infant health and ORT, distribution of ORT in clinics and through community outlets, and incorporation of ORT in national and local training (for detailed results, see this chapter in the second edition of *Public Communication Campaigns* and McDivitt, Hornik, & Dara, 1994).

SPECIFYING THE PROCESS MODEL AT THE INDIVIDUAL LEVEL

The individual-level process model used in the MMHP projects was derived from three theoretical foundations of health communication campaigns. The HBM considers whether individuals believe they are susceptible, whether the messages are relevant, and whether the individuals have options. Concepts such as self-efficacy, internal information processing, and attitudes are important components of this model (Hornik, 2002). The *social marketing* framework emphasizes the identification of markets and audiences and how to place and price a product (Bracht & Rice, Chapter 20). The *communication/persuasion matrix* (McGuire, Chapter 9) shows communication variables as inputs (source, message, channel, receiver, and destination factors) and the "successive response steps that must be elicited in the public if the communication campaign is to be effective" as outputs. Evaluation efforts should gather information on some factors affecting these prior stages, such as cultural constraints against yielding to a particular argument about, say, the amount of liquids a baby can ingest, or against comprehension of the distinction between bottle- and breast-feeding.

The MMHP evaluation attempted to monitor or measure some of these individual processes (see Figure 5.2). Each of these steps is accompanied by measurement or monitoring of intervening variables and system constraints that prevent full linkage to the next step and of unforeseen outputs of a prior step. The application of this evaluation approach allows insights into the diagnosis of problems within a given project (program failures) and to design principles for this type of project (here subsumed as theory failures). For example, when emphasis and reinforcement of specific messages are not sustained, initial gains can quickly be lost. It was clear that mothers were not following a simple pattern of adoption followed by sustained use. Snyder (1991), analyzing seven aggregated waves of The Gambia data, showed that use of ORT was maintained by 70 % of the initial adopters after five months, 50 % after 13 months, and only 30 % after 21 months. Although only 8 % started using ORT and then stopped permanently, 57 % started, stopped, and started again.

CHOOSING AMONG RESEARCH APPROACHES

The MMHP evaluation used six major study groupings that differed markedly from one another in magnitude, study population, and measurement requirements: 1) a *longitudinal*

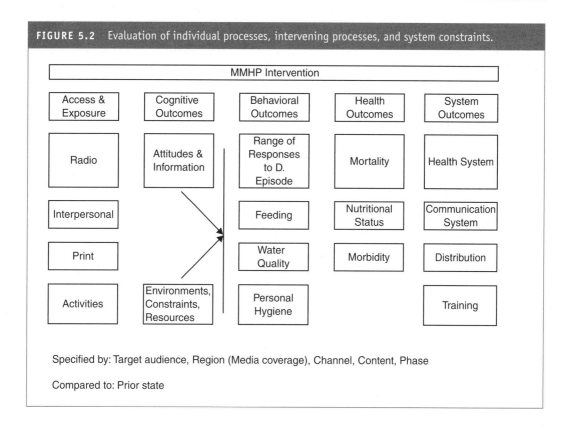

FIGURE 5.2   Evaluation of individual processes, intervening processes, and system constraints.

study including monthly measures and observations and analyses to detect sequencing and linkage among process components, 2) a *mortality* study, in Honduras, an interrupted time-series analysis to detect change in mortality due to infant diarrhea in treatment area, 3) an *opinion leader and health professional* interview study to elicit assessment of project impact and organizational success, 4) an *ethnographic* study to provide more anthropological insights into impacts, customs, and beliefs, 5) an *archival* study to assess clinical and hospital measures of infant mortality, morbidity, treatment, and so on, and 6) a *cost-effectiveness* study to aid in understanding relative payoffs for future programs. For example, the cost-effectiveness of the Egyptian ORS study was estimated between $100 and $200 per death averted (Levine, 2007). An earlier analysis estimated that, for diarrheal diseases in children under five years old, costs were between $30 and $100 for each disability-adjusted life year saved or $3000 per death prevented (Murray, Kreuser, & Whang, 1994). Particular project contexts may lead to emphasis or rejection of one or more of these study approaches as well as the need for triangulation by means of multiple methodologies and data sources to compensate for barriers to one or more planned studies (Kreps, 2008).

IMPLICATIONS FOR DESIGN

Sampling

Issues of sampling and control groups are crucial to any campaign evaluation (see Valente & Kwan, Chapter 6). Insights from analysis of the prior state and system constraints, given a set of project goals, will help establish proper sampling frames and units of analysis.

For example, because health delivery infrastructure and broadcast media are typically in place before project intervention, these often establish treatment, and thus sampling, boundaries. Because the objectives of the MMHP evaluation included developing a transnational model of health communication evaluation, the primary objective of sampling was to enable generalizations to the full range of conditions (e.g., prior states, inputs, and constraints) represented in developing countries rather than to make possible precise statements about aggregate national levels in a given country.

Particular system contexts and constraints will influence the analytical level. For example, noninstitutional infant care is delivered in the home; therefore, all individual variables must be linked to a home unit. But, what is a *home?* In Honduras, a household was defined as a living unit that contains both a place for cooking and a place for sleeping. Thus, in Honduras, 750 mothers were randomly selected from 20 stratified villages. In The Gambia, however, the home is a compound of 10 to 100 people, consisting of physical structures enclosing polygamous multifamily living units. Thus infant care can never be attributed solely to the attitudes and cognitive and behavioral levels of one individual. Thus, in The Gambia, 1,029 mothers were sampled from compounds selected randomly from 20 stratified villages.

Control Groups

Because resources for fieldwork are limited, it is crucial to think through carefully the value of mounting data collection efforts in nontreatment areas (Suchman, 1967). The Gambia project, which was nationwide from the beginning, was able to have 20 treatment villages receiving multiple measurements and eight villages measured only once (to test for measurement effects), but there were no nontreatment controls. In the Honduras project, because the government rapidly expanded from the pilot site to a national campaign to promote the use of ORT, it became impossible to identify a group outside of the treatment area that had not received some kind of treatment, however minor. Furthermore, because the project effort was not uniform within the pilot region, it was not possible to assign households randomly to treatment conditions. Thus, neither project involved nontreatment groups, but both projects incorporated nonrepeated measures groups to test for measurement influences.

Comparisons Within the Treatment Area

Five sources of data within the treatment area from the study groupings could be used for within-treatment control purposes, as in the Honduras project.

1. *Household as its own control.* Local interviewers can return for repeated measurements to households that could then serve as their own controls for many variables.

2. *Making use of staged implementation.* If, because of phases in system constraints, components of the campaign are introduced in different phases in different regions of the treatment area, the study can compare as yet untreated segments of the population within the measurement sample to treated segments.

3. *Natural variations in exposure.* Because of the vagaries that can be expected in mounting a complex intervention, there will be program failure in some components of the campaign. These variations, if inputs are adequately monitored, can be used for comparison purposes.

4. *Self-determination of exposure.* Some people will select not to expose themselves to a health campaign because they do not have access to a radio, because they do not choose to talk to health workers, and so on. Although not necessarily comparable, they can be a source of some kinds of information with which to compare exposed respondents.

5. *Measurement effects.* A smaller sample in both Honduras and The Gambia was interviewed only once or twice across the longitudinal survey to compare to the larger sample, which may have been sensitized by the multiple interviews.

Comparisons With Nontreated Populations

Data about people outside the treatment area can be obtained from several sources, such as archival data, ethnographic studies, other health projects functioning in the region, and standardized data on infant growth and weight. Special one-shot studies may assess the level of a belief or practice in a nontreatment area when results in the treatment area are ambiguous.

The Question of Controls in a Longitudinal Study

Sources of control data for variables falling in each of the outcome categories may vary in accessibility and utility. For example, beliefs, practices, and levels of knowledge can change quickly on exposure to campaign intervention, so repeated measures can capture changes in these outcomes between implementation stages but probably not levels of health status variables, such as changes in mortality due to dehydration.

In the Honduran and Gambian projects, the focus was on infant feeding and child-care practices in traditional communities, areas where rapid changes are not expected to occur in the absence of external stimuli. Thus, it seemed that monitoring other information inputs (via the ethnographic and interview studies) into the treatment villages would be a more efficient way to evaluate rival explanations for change than collecting measures on control populations whose comparability is open to some doubt. If mothers began preparing ORS in the household, this change in behavior could be attributed only to the health education campaign because it represents the adoption of a new behavior.

Conclusion

This chapter has argued that evaluation of purposive communication projects in less-developed countries has much to gain from the use of a generic planning model based upon a systems approach. Using the example of ORT projects in two developing countries, the model highlights the need to identify and measure eight evaluation components from a systems perspective. The use of such a planning model could not only help guide the development and application of evaluation efforts, and provide a common framework for use in related projects, but more importantly, lead to more effective campaign interventions.

References

Berrien, F. (1968). *General and social systems.* New Brunswick, NJ: Rutgers University Press.

Bertalanffy, L. von. (1968). *General systems theory.* New York: Braziller.

Bridges, J. A. (2004). Corporate issues campaigns: Six theoretical approaches. *Communication Theory, 14*(1), 51–77.

Buckley, W. (Ed.). (1968). *Modern systems research for the behavioral scientist.* Chicago: Aldine.

Campbell, D., Steenbarger, B., Smith, T., & Stucky, R. (1982). An ecological systems approach to evaluation: Cruising in Topeka. *Evaluation Review, 6*(5), 625–648.

Centers for Disease Control and Prevention. (2009). *Procedural guidance for community-based organizations.* Washington, DC: Department of Health and Human Services, Centers for Disease Control and Prevention. Retrieved September 22, 2011, from http://www.cdc.gov/hiv/topics/prev_prog/ahp/resources/guidelines/pro_guidance/pdf/ProceduralGuidance.pdf

Coleman, J., Katz, E., & Menzel, J. (1966). *Medical innovation: A diffusion study.* New York: Bobbs-Merrill.

Cornish, F., & Campbell, C. (2009). The social conditions for successful peer education: A comparison of two HIV prevention programs run by sex workers in India and South Africa. *American Journal of Community Psychology, 44,* 123–135.

Feachem, R. (1986). Preventing diarrhoea: What are the policy options? *Health Policy and Planning, 1*(2), 109–117.

Green, E. (1986). *Diarrhea and the social marketing of oral rehydration salts in Bangladesh.* Social Science Medicine, *23*(4), 357–366.

Hornik, R. (1985). *Nutrition education: A state of the art review.* Washington, DC: World Bank.

Hornik, R. (1993). *Development communication: Information, agriculture, and nutrition in the Third World.* Lanham, MD: University Press of America.

Hornik, R. (Ed.). (2002). *Public health communication: Evidence for behavior change.* Mahwah, NJ: Lawrence Erlbaum.

Huttly, S. R. A., Morris, S. S., & Pisani, V. (1997). Prevention of diarrhoea in young children in developing countries. *Bulletin of the World Health Organization, 75*(2), 163–174.

Kosek, M., Bern, C., & Guerrant, R. L. (2003). The global burden of diarrhoeal disease, as estimated from studies published between 1992 and 2000. *Bulletin of the World Health Organization, 81,* 197–204.

Kreps, G. L. (2008). Qualitative inquiry and the future of health communication research. *Qualitative Research Reports in Communication, 9*(1), 2–12.

Kumar, V., Monga, O., & Jain, N. (1981). The introduction of oral rehydration in a rural community in India. *World Health Forum, 2*(3), 364–366.

Levine, E. (Ed.). (2007). Preventing diarrheal deaths in Egypt. *Case studies in global health: Millions saved* (Case 8). Sudbury, MA: Jones & Bartlett Learning. Retrieved September 22, 2011, from http://www.jblearning.com/samples/0763746207/46207_FMxx_Levine.pdf

McDivitt, J., Hornik, R., & Dara, C. (1994). Quality of home use of oral rehydration solutions: Results from seven HEALTHCOM sites. *Social Science & Medicine, 38*(9), 1221–1234.

McLeroy, K., Bibeau, D., Steckler, A., & Glanz, K. (1988). An ecological perspective on health promotion programs. *Health Education Quarterly, 15,* 351–377.

Murray, C. J. L., Kreuser, J., & Whang, W. (1994). Cost-effectiveness analysis and policy choices: Investing in health systems. *Bulletin of the World Health Organization, 72*(4), 663–674.

Ray, E., & Donohew, L. (Eds.). (1990). *Communication and health: Systems and applications.* Hillsdale, NJ: Lawrence Erlbaum.

Rogers, E.M., & Kincaid, D.L. (1981). *Communication networks: Toward a new paradigm for research.* New York: Free Press.

Rudd, R., Goldberg, J., & Dietz, W. (1999). A five-stage model for sustaining a community campaign. *Journal of Health Communication, 4*(1), 37–48.

Salmon, C. T., & Kroger, F. (1992). A systems approach to AIDS communication: The example of the national AIDS information and education program. In T. Edgar, M. Fitzpatrick, & V. Freimuth (Eds.), *AIDS: A communication perspective* (pp. 131–146). Hillsdale, NJ: Lawrence Erlbaum.

Snyder, L. (1991). Modeling dynamic communication processes with event history analysis. *Communication Research, 18*(4), 464–486.

Suchman, E. (1967). *Evaluative research.* New York: Russell Sage Foundation.

Winett, R. (1986). *Information and behavior: Systems of influence.* Hillsdale, NJ: Lawrence Erlbaum.

CHAPTER 6

Evaluating Communication Campaigns

Thomas W. Valente and Patchareeya P. Kwan

This chapter provides an introduction to communication campaign evaluation. The first section briefly defines the nature of campaign evaluation, including debates, functions, and barriers. The chapter then presents an evaluation framework that delineates the steps in the evaluation process and presents study designs used to conduct evaluation research. Sections following the evaluation framework first consider aspects of the formative evaluation phase: theories, study designs, statistical power and sample size, levels of assignment, and analysis. These sections distinguish evaluation procedures based on sample types (cross-sectional vs. panel) and levels of assignment (group, individual, self-selected). The process evaluation phase sections discuss campaign exposure and interpersonal communication. The evaluation phase sections review impact measurement and dissemination. The importance of specifying a theoretical basis for an evaluation is stressed throughout. Examples from both past and recent studies are given throughout the chapter, and it closes with a discussion of impact assessment and dissemination procedures.

THE NATURE OF EVALUATION

Evaluation is the systematic application of research procedures to understand the conceptualization, design, implementation, and utility of interventions (here, communication campaigns). Evaluation research determines whether a program was effective, how it did or did not achieve its goals, and the efficiency with which it achieved them (Boruch, 1996; Mohr, 1992; Rossi, Freeman, & Lispsey, 1998; Shadish, Cook, & Leviton, 1991; see also chapters in this volume by Atkin & Freimuth; Rice & Foote; Salmon & Murray-Johnson; and Snyder & LaCroix). Evaluation contributes to the knowledge base of how programs reach and influence their intended audiences so that researchers can learn lessons from these experiences and implement more effective programs in the future. Rather than assessing staff performances, evaluation is meant to identify sources or potential sources of implementation problems (i.e., *process evaluation*) in addition to finding out whether and how the program worked (i.e., *summative evaluation*) so that corrections can be made for current and future programming purposes. Empirical work on evaluation as a specialty field has blossomed in the past few decades, and today, evaluation is seen as a distinct research enterprise (Shadish, Cook, & Leviton, 1991).

Three major debates often frame an evaluation enterprise. One debate concerns the use of quantitative versus qualitative methodologies. The balance of emphasis between the two methods should be driven by their ability to answer the research questions being posed and the availability of data. In order to evaluate an intervention effectively, evaluators may want to employ both quantitative and qualitative methods as the findings from one will help to supplement the results of another (Guba & Lincoln, 1981). A second debate concerns whether nonexperimental designs can adequately control for selectivity and other biases inherent in the public communication evaluation process (Black, 1996; Victora, Habicht, & Bryce, 2004). With proper theoretical and methodological specification, researchers can use quasi-experimental designs to evaluate campaigns. A third debate concerns the advantages and disadvantages of internal versus external evaluators. External evaluators often have more credibility but are usually less informed than internal evaluators about aspects of the campaign's implementation that may influence its effectiveness. See Valente (2002) for more details on these issues.

Evaluation research serves three functions in any communication campaign. It improves the probability of achieving program success by forcing campaign programmers to specify explicitly in advance the goals and objectives of the campaign and the theoretical or causal relations leading to those expectations. Once the campaign objectives are specified, it becomes possible to create programs to meet these objectives and develop instruments to measure them. The first function of an evaluation, then, is to determine the expected impacts and outcomes of the program. For example, if a campaign was designed to raise the awareness of the dangers of substance abuse, the evaluation proposal should state the percentage increase expected in this awareness. The second function of a campaign evaluation is to help planners and scholars understand how or why a particular campaign worked or did not work. Knowing how or why a program succeeded or failed—that is, the theoretical and causal as well as implementation reasons—increases the likelihood that successes can be repeated and failures avoided in future behavioral promotion programs. Finally, a third function of evaluation is to provide information relevant for planning future activities. Evaluation results can indicate what behaviors or which audiences should be addressed in the next round of activities. In sum, we conduct evaluation (particularly process and summative evaluation) to know whether the program worked, how and why it worked, and how to make future programs better.

There are many barriers to rigorous evaluation. One major barrier is the perceived cost of evaluation. Many programmers argue that money spent on evaluation research should not be diverted from program activities. This argument neglects the fact that evaluation should be an integral part of any program. Research costs should normally be limited to approximately 10% to 15% of the total project budget (Piotrow, Kincaid, Rimon, & Rinehart, 1997). These costs, however, provide a high rate of return to the program by improving its implementation and the basis for explaining and understanding the results. A second barrier to rigorous evaluation is the perception that research takes too much time. To minimize this concern, evaluation results should be available before, during, immediately after, and some later time after the program is completed. Finally, many people object to evaluation on the grounds that it detracts from program implementation. Evaluations should not interfere with programs but rather should be considered an integral part of, and complement to, the program. Indeed, planning and implementing a rigorous evaluation clarifies the timing and objectives of various program components such as when to conduct the program launch, when to start broadcasts, and how to space supplementary activities to maximize reach and effectiveness (Rice & Foote, Chapter 5).

EVALUATION FRAMEWORKS

Figure 6.1 provides a conceptual framework of the campaign evaluation process. Evaluation research is often conducted in three distinct phases: *formative, process,* and *summative* (or *outcome*). The first step in the evaluation process is to identify and assess the needs that drive the desire for a communication campaign. These may be identified by the relevant communities themselves (see Bracht and Rice, Chapter 20). Once needs are identified, formative research is conducted to more clearly understand the subject of the program.

Formative research consists of those activities that define the scope of the problem, gather data on possible intervention strategies, learn about the intended audience, and investigate possible factors that might limit program implementation. Formative research is also used to test message strategy, test the effectiveness of possible communication channels, and learn about audience beliefs, motivations, perceptions, and so on (Atkin & Freimuth, Chapter 4). Programmers need to understand the current problem and intended audience prior to developing interventions to address them. They need to know things such as what the intended audience thinks, how they feel, what they do, why they choose not to perform a certain behavior, and so on (see also Dervin & Foreman-Wernet, Chapter 10). Typically, formative research is conducted using qualitative research methods such as focus group discussions (FGDs), in-depth interviews, and ethnographic observations, though initial surveys are useful as well.

A recent study used FGDs to assess the barriers and facilitators to adopting obesity prevention recommendations among parents of overweight children (Sonneville, La Pelle, Taveras, Gillman, & Prosser, 2009). The study showed that there were many barriers to adopting healthier habits for their children, including perceived cost, lack of information, available transportation, safe facilities, and difficulty with changing habits. However, in the FGDs, parents indicated that availability of physical activity programs and healthier food choices were all facilitators to adopting new behaviors. The results of the FGDs allowed program developers to tap into information that they would otherwise not have known and made it possible to develop an intervention strategy that specifically addressed the concerns of their audience.

Process research (also known as monitoring) consists of those activities conducted to measure the degree of program implementation to determine whether the program was delivered as it was intended. Process research is usually conducted by collecting

FIGURE 6.1   Evaluation framework.

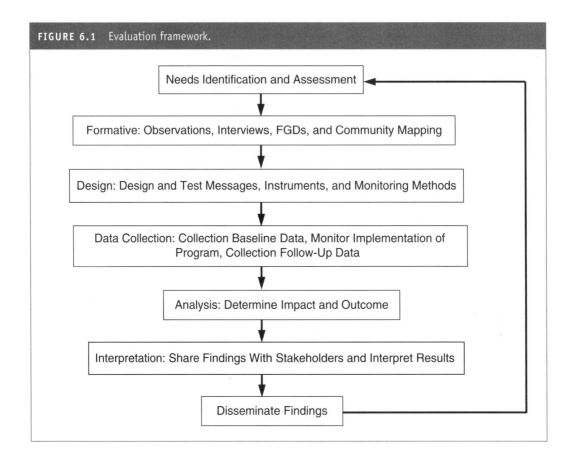

data on when, where, and for how long the campaign is implemented. The evaluator might want to hire individuals to watch TV or listen to the radio at prespecified times to record the program, conduct content analyses of local newspapers, or collect usage data from a campaign website. In the Bolivia National Reproductive Health Program (NRHP) project (Valente & Saba, 1997), we requested logbooks from the advertising agency contracted to produce and broadcast information about reproductive health in Bolivia. We discovered that the campaign was not implemented as intended in the smaller cities, and this warranted a rebroadcast of the campaign (Valente & Saba, 1998).

Summative (or outcome) research consists of those activities conducted to measure the program's impact and the lessons learned from the study and to disseminate research findings (see also Salmon & Murray-Johnson, Chapter 7). Summative research is usually conducted by analyzing quantitative data collected before, during, and after the campaign, depending on the research design (see below). Summative research is an interactive and iterative process in which preliminary findings are shared with program planners and other stakeholders prior to widespread dissemination. The stakeholders provide insight into the interpretation of data and can help set the agenda for specific data analyses. Once the summative research is completed, the findings can be disseminated. The evaluation framework in Figure 6.1 delineates the steps in the evaluation process, but it is theory concerning human behavior that informs it.

SUMMATIVE EVALUATION RESEARCH

Theoretical Considerations

Program goals and objectives should not emerge spontaneously but rather stem from theoretical explanations for behavior (although, indeed, the campaign may also be testing proposed theoretical explanations and causal relations). The choice of a theoretical orientation to develop a model for and explain the behavior under study can drive both the design of the program and the design of the evaluation, particularly the design of the study measures and surveys. If, for example, self-efficacy is theorized to be an important influence on whether individuals use condoms during sex, then the program may try to increase self-efficacy among the intended audience. The evaluation therefore needs to measure self-efficacy before, during, and after the campaign to determine whether the program did indeed deliver self-efficacy messages or training (process evaluation), and change self-efficacy levels in the appropriate communities (summative evaluation). As an example, the Sister-to-Sister: The Black Women's Health Project was a skill-building HIV/STD risk reduction intervention that aimed to increase self-efficacy for impulse control, carrying condoms, and consistent condom use with a partner (O'Leary, Jemmott, & Jemmott, 2008). In order to test program impact, self-efficacy was measured at baseline, posttest, and 3-, 6- and 12-month follow-up.

Weiss (1972) made a useful distinction between successful *theoretical specification* (determined by summative evaluation) and successful *program implementation* (determined by process evaluation) via three different scenarios in which the program or the theory might succeed or fail. In the first scenario, a successful program sets in motion a causal process specified by a theory that results in the predicted and desired outcome. In the second scenario, there is a failure of theory in which there is a successfully implemented program (as measured by process evaluation) that sets in motion a causal process that did not result in the desired outcome. In the third scenario, because of a program failure, the intervention did not start or complete an expected causal sequence, so the theory could not be tested.

Thus, the congruence between theory and program implementation can be very important, and a tight linkage between the two increases the likelihood the program will be judged a success by avoiding cases in which there is a theory failure (Chen & Rossi, 1983). If the program fails, you may not be able to test theory, but if the theory fails, you are left with incorrectly concluding either that the program failed or succeeded. Having set goals and objectives and determining the theoretical underpinnings for the program and the evaluation, the researcher must then specify a study design.

Study Designs

Study design is the specification and assignment of intervention and control conditions; the sampling methodology and sample selection procedures; and the statistical tests to be used to make decisions about the effectiveness of a campaign. An appropriate research design is one that minimizes threats to internal and external validity given the constraints of program implementation and resources. *Threats to validity* are factors that conspire to provide alternative explanations for intervention effects. Examples of threats to validity include history (occurrence of controllable events during the study), maturation (e.g., aging of subjects), testing (effect of surveys on responses), selectivity (bias due to selection process), and sensitization (interaction between pretest and intervention). The following sections address levels of assignment and sampling procedures and then present six study designs.

Levels of Assignment and Sampling

Specification of intervention and control conditions can occur at the individual, group or community, or self-selection level. *Individual assignment* occurs when the researcher can specify which individuals will be exposed to the intervention and which ones will not. Ideally, researchers can identify a population, select a random sample, and then randomly assign individuals to groups that receive the intervention (or different interventions) and groups that do not (control groups). *Group assignment* occurs when the researcher specifies that certain groups such as schools, organizations, or communities will be the focus of the intervention and that the intervention can be restricted to these groups. In such cases, the intervention is applied to one or some groups, while other groups that do not receive the intervention act as comparison groups. *Self-selection assignment* occurs when the study subjects themselves determine who is exposed to the intervention. Self-selection assignment occurs most commonly in mass media campaign studies as a majority of the population has the ability to selectively hear or see the program and many people may selectively recall it. Once the level of assignment is specified, researchers then determine whether it is feasible to collect panel samples (i.e., interviews with the same respondents at multiple points in time) or cross-sectional samples (i.e., interviews with different respondents at one or multiple points in time).

Study Designs

A standard way to depict study designs is to use an X to refer to an intervention condition and an O to refer to a data collection observation (e.g., administration of a survey). Subscripts distinguish different Xs and Os. For example, X_1 and X_2 may refer to two different interventions such as a media-only campaign (X_1) and a media campaign plus supplementary interpersonal counseling (X_2). For observations, subscripts are often used to refer to observations in different conditions (e.g., intervention and control groups) and at different time periods (e.g., before and after a campaign) (Campbell & Stanley, 1963; Cook & Campbell, 1979).

TABLE 6.1 Study Designs				
Design	Baseline	Intervention	Follow-Up	Validity Threats Reduced
1: Postcampaign Only	-	X	0	None
2: Pre/postcomparison	0	X	0	Selectivity
3: Pre/postcomparison & Post-Only Control Group	0 -	X -	0 0	Testing
4: Pre/postcomparison & Predetermined Control Group	0 0	X -	0 0	History & Maturation
5: Pre/postcomparison & Predetermined Control Group & Post-Only Intervention Group	0 0 -	X - X	0 0 0	Sensitization
6: Solomon Four Group	0 0 - -	X - X -	0 0 0 0	All of the above

Note: - = no observation or intervention; X = intervention/campaign; 0 = observation such as a survey.

Table 6.1 arrays the six study designs in descending order in terms of the number of observation groups for each. Design 1, postcampaign only, collects data on the degree of exposure to the campaign, any self-reports of whether respondents feel that the campaign influenced them, and possibly behavioral data. Design 1 is the weakest evaluation design because it only provides data on posttreatment conditions and does not control for any threats to validity.

Design 2, pre- and postcomparison, reduces some threats to validity as it provides a baseline against which to compare the postcampaign scores. Design 2 is often used when identifying or creating a control group is not feasible. A cross-sectional pre- and post-comparison consists of selecting two comparable independent samples before and after the campaign and making population-level comparisons. For example, Kerrigan, Telles, Torres, Overs, and Castle (2008) collected cross-sectional data from about 500 female sex workers in Brazil before and after an HIV/STI prevention intervention that used a community development component. They found that social cohesion and mutual aid were associated with consistent condom use but that only a small number of women participated in community-related activities over the course of the intervention, and thus, there were limited changes in the community and no significant increase in preventive behaviors among the women. The shortcoming of this methodology is that there may be fluctuations in sample characteristics that account for differences in outcomes between the two surveys. Perhaps the first group of women in the Kerrigan and others' study was somehow different than the second group, and these differences were not controllable (e.g., everyone who was eager to participate in community-level activities signed up for the study immediately and completed the pretest, while those who were not so interested did not initially sign up, and thus, the posttest sample consisted of less eager women). Moreover, secular trends, historical events, or other factors may have created the behavior change.

A panel pre- and postdesign can help eliminate some of these rival explanations as the same persons are interviewed and changes can be measured on individuals (i.e., not solely at the population level). For example, in an evaluation of a street theater's effectiveness at reducing family planning misinformation, Valente, Poppe, Alva, de Briceno, and Cases (1994) interviewed passersby about their family planning knowledge before and after the drama. The study found that the drama reduced misinformation by 9.4%. The shortcoming of the panel pre/post design, however, is that, because there is no control group, it is hard to say what would have happened in the absence of the campaign and hard to determine the influence that taking the survey had on respondent's misinformation scores (validity threats of history, testing, and sensitization among others).

Designs 3 and 4 include a post-only control group and a pre- and postcontrol group, respectively. Both of these designs are strong and provide relatively good measures of program impact as the intervention group's scores can be compared to the control group's. For example, Valente and Bharath (1999) interviewed 100 randomly selected people who attended a three-hour drama designed to improve knowledge about HIV/AIDS transmission. The same 100 persons were interviewed immediately after the drama, and an additional 100 persons were interviewed after the drama only. Results indicated that the drama increased knowledge by 26% amongst the first group (i.e., we compared predrama with postdrama knowledge). Comparison of the postdrama scores between those interviewed before and those not interviewed before provided an estimate of the effect of the intervention attributable to taking the pretest (3% in this case). The main limitations of Designs 1 through 3 are that they cannot measure the degree of change due to history or maturation, which are threats to validity that happen over time.

Design 4 enables the comparison of difference scores for both the treatment and control groups and a computation of the difference of differences. Because Design 4 has a group measured before and after the intervention that did not receive the intervention, the scores for the control group can be used to estimate the amount of change attributable to history and maturation. Design 4 enables researchers to subtract pretest scores from the posttest ones for both experimental and control groups and then subtract these differences from one another (the difference of differences). This value provides a measure of program effectiveness, but it does not, however, control for testing and sensitization effects.

Design 5 adds a second intervention group, which does not get pretested, in order to control for the possible effects of the pretest sensitization. Design 5 is quite rigorous as it controls for most threats to validity. The only limitation to Design 5 is that it is restrictive in its ability to determine how much of the effects due to validity threats can be attributed to specific validity threats. For example, the post-only intervention groups may have scores comparable to the control group due to historical factors that the researcher wants to separate from those effects due to the pretest sensitization. As a hypothetical example, suppose a campaign was launched to improve knowledge on the harmful effects of substance abuse. Further suppose that a historical event such as the death of a famous person due to a drug overdose occurs during the study period. Comparisons of group scores will not be able to differentiate whether posttest scores changed due to the interaction between the program and the historical event or interactions between the pretest and the historical event.

Design 6, the Solomon (1949) Four Group Design, adds a final control group that receives no intervention and no pretest survey. The Solomon Four Group Design is the most rigorous as it controls for (or allows measurement of) all threats to validity. These six study designs are usually implemented with panel samples because Designs 4, 5, and 6 cannot be implemented with cross-sectional samples unless groups are used at the level of assignment, requiring a large numbers of groups.

Statistical Power and Sample Size

Once the study design is specified, researchers must determine the needed sample size to conduct the study. Available resources often determine the sample size used for a study because many studies have fixed budgets and researchers often decide that they will spend a portion of that for data collection. However, regardless of the available resources, it is prudent to conduct power analysis to determine 1) the appropriate sample size needed before the study is conducted, and 2) the degree of reliability in the study results. *Power* is the ability of a statistical test to detect a significant association when such an association actually exists, that is, avoiding Type II errors (Borenstein, Rothstein, & Cohen, 1997; Cohen, 1977). For example, suppose a study finds that participants improved their knowledge by 10% but reports that this increase was not statistically significant. Power analysis may show that the power is only 40%, meaning that, out of 100 tests conducted among this population and with this effect size, 40 of the tests would be considered significant. This indicates that a larger sample drawn from the population (or greater control of other variables) would be needed to produce an effect size that is statistically significant.

Power analysis consists of the interrelationship between four components of study design: 1) effect size (magnitude of difference, correlation coefficient, etc., also known as Δ), 2) significance level (Type I error or alpha level—usually .05 or .01), 3) sample size, and 4) power (calculated as 1-beta or Type II error—usually .80 or .90). These four components are related to one another by power formulas (equations) so that, if any three components are known, the fourth can be computed (Hill & Lewicki, 2007). Thus, a researcher can determine the minimum sample size needed for a study by specifying the expected or presumed effect size, the desired significance level, and desired power.

Levels of Assignment and Analysis

Many interventions are developed for specific communities or are tested in multiple communities before being scaled up to regional or national audiences. In many studies, certain communities (schools, organizations, towns, etc.) act as intervention sites, while other communities act as controls (Berkowitz, Huhman, & Nolin, 2008; Fox, Stein, Gonzalea,

Farrenkopf, & Dellinger, 2010; Rogers et al., 1999). Study designs in which the group is the unit of randomization are referred to as *group-randomized trials* (Murray, 1998). In group randomized trials, data are collected on individual and sometimes appropriate group-level behavior, but because individuals are clustered into groups, researchers need to conduct their analysis in a manner that accounts for differences in variation between groups versus variation within groups. Generally, individuals in the same group will be more alike one another (have less variation) than individuals from different groups (have more variation). Given the group difference in variances, statistical clustering correction techniques such as the intraclass correlation should be used (Murray, 1998).

When impact studies are conducted using groups as the unit of assignment, such that some groups or communities are exposed to the campaign and others serve as comparisons, the researcher can compute group-level values for the variables and conduct statistical analysis using the group as the unit of analysis (Kirkwood, Cousens, Victora, & de Zoysa, 1997). This analytic technique provides a test of program impact at the community level.

The more common analytic approach for community-based data is to create dummy variables indicating whether the respondent was in the intervention (or which intervention) or control group. For example, when the campaign is broadcast in multiple communities, a variable is created that indicates which respondents were in intervention groups and which were in comparison groups. A statistical test such as ANOVA is conducted to determine whether outcomes were significantly different between conditions. If there are multiple conditions—for example, mass media supplemented with interpersonal persuasion—then a new variables is created with a value for each condition so that differences across each condition can be tested. Murray (1998) has presented techniques that control for the within-group variations inherent in this type of analysis.

Many mass media campaigns cannot be restricted to intervention and control conditions because they are broadcast to an entire region or even to an entire country. In such cases, comparison between conditions is not possible, and the researcher has to rely on before–after surveys with independent or panel surveys. Although such designs, referred to as quasi-experimental, are usually considered less rigorous, evidence suggests (Berkowitz et al., 2008; Castellanos-Ortega et al., 2010; Snyder, Hamilton, Mitchell, Kiwanuka-Tondo, Fleming-Milici, & Proctor, 2004; Snyder & LaCroix, Chapter 8) that they still provide valid evaluations of campaign effects. The chief threat to validity for quasi-experimental campaign evaluations is that researchers have difficulty determining whether associations between program exposure and outcomes are genuine or spurious. In other words, respondents may report an increase in campaign exposure and state that they started a new behavior, but the researcher cannot attribute this change solely to exposure.

To address the problem of spuriousness and other validity threats with cross-sectional data, researchers can 1) include a time variable to control for any secular trends and sample variations, 2) control for sociodemographic and other characteristics with multivariate statistical techniques, 3) create valid and reliable measures of campaign exposure (verified by process evaluation) that can be linked in a dose–response relationship (Jato,

Simbakalia, Tarasevich, Awasum, Kohings, & Ngirwamungu, 1999), and 4) attempt to eliminate rival or alternative explanations. In panel studies, researchers can also do 1 to 4 above but have the further advantage of controlling for and measuring the influence of past behavior.

No single methodological technique completely solves the spuriousness problem. The best approach is to start with a plausible theoretical model and use multiple sources of data at multiple points in time to construct a coherent explanation for a campaign's impact (or lack thereof).

Campaign Exposure

A critical variable used to evaluate public communication campaigns is campaign exposure. *Campaign exposure* is the degree to which audience members have access to, recall, or recognize the intervention. High levels of campaign exposure can indicate that the intended message reached the audience (or perhaps some segments). High levels of campaign exposure can also lead to campaign success (Berkowitz et al., 2008). Campaign exposure often provides the first step in a behavior change sequence and provides a necessary indicator to distinguish between program and theory failure. Note that *process evaluation* can help identify how much of the planned exposure or treatment is actually engaged by particular audiences (see Rice & Foote, Chapter 5).

A further recommendation when looking at campaign exposure in both panel and cross-sectional studies is to collect data from respondents on their recollections of exactly when or for how long the respondents had been engaging in the behavior. Such data provide a link between self-reports and the timing of programmatic interventions (i.e., exposure). For example, in the Bolivia NRHP campaign, we knew when the specific advertisements promoting contraceptive methods were broadcast, and we asked respondents how long they had been using their current contraceptive method. We linked the two pieces of information and found that the modal month that new adopters of contraceptives started using their method was the same month that the TV and radio spots were first broadcast.

Interpersonal Communication

Public communication campaigns can be very effective at stimulating interpersonal communication (e.g., Valente, Poppe et al., 1994). Campaigns often purposively stimulate interpersonal communication, but the impact of this media-generated communication will not be apparent until the information percolates through interpersonal networks and individuals have time to share their attitudes, experiences, and opinions with one another (Boulay, Storey, & Sood, 2002; Valente, 1995). Valente extended the two-step flow hypothesis (whereby media influence opinion leaders who in turn influence others—Katz, 1957) by developing a threshold model in which the media first influence those with low thresholds who in turn influence others in their personal networks with higher thresholds (Valente, 1995, 1996; Valente & Saba, 1998).

Measuring Impact

A primary goal of summative evaluation research is to measure the effects of an intervention (see Rice & Foote, Chapter 5; Salmon & Murray-Johnson, Chapter 7). The researcher first determines whether outcomes have changed between baseline and follow-up (for example, with a t-test). Change scores can then be computed and analysis of variance tests conducted to determine whether change was different for different demographic and socioeconomic groups, such as between males and females or between different ethnic groups. Typically, the researcher will then compute a regression equation with the follow-up score as the dependent variable and the baseline and intermediate time period scores as independent variables (this is known as *lagged analysis*) and include sociodemographic and system constraint variables as controls. Importantly, campaign researchers should also include variables that measure access to (or literacy of) the media channels over which the campaign is disseminated (perhaps obtained through the process evaluation) and include variables for campaign exposure (see Valente, 2002).

In the Bolivia NRHP campaign evaluation example, we analyzed data from a cross-section and panel sample of respondents who were interviewed before and after the nine-month campaign. Two of the outcomes were an index of awareness of contraceptive methods and self-reported use of a modern method of contraceptives (Valente & Saba, 2001). We hierarchically regressed method awareness using ordinary least squares (OLS) on 1) sociodemographic variables of education, income, gender, marital status, age, and number of children, 2) city method prevalence rate, 3) time (baseline or follow-up), 4) network exposure (number of the respondent's network whom he or she thinks uses a contraceptive method), and 5) campaign exposure.

We regressed contraceptive use using logistic regression because it is a dichotomous variable (i.e., use of a modern method of contraceptives or no use) on the same variables. Results indicate that education, income, being female, network, and campaign exposure were all significantly positively associated with method awareness in the cross-sectional data. Time had a slight negative association, which indicates that the follow-up sample had lower method awareness. For contraceptive use, all variables except number of children, time, and campaign exposure were associated with use of contraceptives. The panel data analysis showed similar results for method awareness with the exception that age and number of children were also significantly associated with method awareness. Method awareness at baseline was significantly associated with method awareness at follow-up. The adjusted odds ratio indicated that persons who used contraceptives at baseline were 4.9 times more likely to use contraceptives at follow-up than those who did not use contraceptives at baseline. Campaign exposure was significantly associated with awareness but not with use, indicating that the campaign influenced knowledge but did not directly influence use. This analysis lends support to an interpretation of the campaign's effect as indirectly influencing behavior through method awareness (but see Valente & Saba, 1998).

DISSEMINATION OF FINDINGS

Once the study has been completed, the researcher should disseminate the results. Dissemination (sometimes referred to as *feedback* or *feed-forwarding*) is often neglected in evaluation plans because researchers are preoccupied with planning and conducting the study and often feel that the results will speak for themselves. Moreover, it is difficult to anticipate the appropriate audiences and channels for dissemination before the findings are known.

Evaluation findings can be disseminated in at least five ways: 1) via scheduled meetings with the programmers, 2) at scientific conferences relevant to the topic, 3) through key findings or technical reports, 4) through academic papers published in refereed journals, and 5) on online websites—which is fast becoming a trend because it is quickly disseminated and has a far reach. Most campaigns not documented in evaluation reports are often forgotten within a year or two.

Conclusion

Public communication campaign evaluation represents an exciting intellectual opportunity to bridge behavioral theory with important practice. The value of these behavior change programs, however, is fundamentally dependent on determining who was reached, how the program influenced them, and how programs can be improved in the future. Without evaluation, the utility of implementing public communication campaigns is subject to debate, criticism, and even ridicule. Disseminating information to foster a more informed and hence more empowered populace represents a significant means to improve the quality of life for all. The challenge for communication campaign evaluators is to implement rigorous evaluations that advance the science of communication and simultaneously provide relevant information to the practice of communication.

References

Berkowitz, J. M., Huhman, M., & Nolin, M. J. (2008). Did augmenting the VERB Campaign advertising in select communities have an effect on awareness, attitudes and physical activity? *American Journal of Preventive Medicine, 34*(6), S257–S266.

Black, N. (1996). Why we need observational studies to evaluate the effectiveness of health care. *British Medical Journal, 312*(7040), 1215–1218.

Borenstein, M., Rothstein, H., & Cohen, J. (1997). *Power and precision: A computer program for statistical power analysis and confidence intervals.* Teaneck, NJ: Biostat.

Boruch, R. (1996). *Randomized experiments for planning and change.* Thousand Oaks, CA: Sage.

Boulay, M., Storey, J. D., & Sood, S. (2002). Indirect exposure to a family planning mass media campaign in Nepal. *Journal of Health Communication, 7*(5), 379–399.

Campbell, D. T., & Stanley, J. C. (1963). *Experimental and quasi-experimental designs for research.* Boston: Houghton Mifflin.

Castellanos-Ortega, A., Suberviola, B., Garcia-Astudillo, L. A., Holanda, M. S., Ortiz, F., Llorca, J., & Delgado-Rodriguez, M. (2010). Impact of the Surviving Sepsis Campaign protocols on hospital length of stay and mortality in septic shock patients: Results of a three-year follow-up quasi-experimental study. *Critical Care Medicine, 38*(4), 1036–1043.

Chen, H. T., & Rossi, P. H. (1983). Evaluating with sense: The theory-driven approach. *Evaluation Review, 7*(3), 283–302.

Cohen, J. (1977). *Statistical power analysis for the behavioral sciences* (Rev. ed.). New York: Academic Press.

Cook, T. D., & Campbell, D. T. (1979). *Quasi-experimentation: Design and analysis issues for field settings.* Boston: Houghton Mifflin.

Fox, S. A., Stein, J. A., Gonzalea, R. E., Farrenkopf, M., & Dellinger, A. (2010). A trial to increase mammography utilization among Los Angeles Hispanic women. *Journal of Health Care for the Poor and Underserved, 9*(3), 309–321.

Guba, E. G., & Lincoln, Y. S. (1981). *Effective evaluation: Improving the usefulness of evaluation results through responsive and naturalistic approaches.* San Francisco, CA: Jossey-Bass.

Hill, T., & Lewicki, P. (2007). *STATISTICS methods and applications.* Tulsa, OK: StatSoft.

Jato, M., Simbakalia, C., Tarasevich, J., Awasum, D., Kohings, C., & Ngirwamungu, E. (1999). The impact of multimedia family planning promotion on the contraceptive behavior of women in Tanzania. *International Family Planning Perspectives, 25*(2), 60–67.

Katz, E. (1957). The two-step flow of communication: An up-to-date report on a hypothesis. *Public Opinion Quarterly, 21,* 61–78.

Kerrigan, D., Telles, P., Torres, H., Overs, C., & Castle, C. (2008). Community development and HIV/STI-related vulnerability among female sex workers in Rio de Janeiro, Brazil. *Health Education Research, 23*(1), 137–145.

Kirkwood, B. R., Cousens, S. N., Victora, C. G., & de Zoysa, I. (1997). Issues in the design and interpretation of studies to evaluate the impact of community-based interventions. *Tropical Medicine and International Health,* I, 1022–1029.

Mohr, L. B. (1992). *Impact analysis for program evaluation.* Newbury Park, CA: Sage.

Murray, D. M. (1998). *Design and analysis of group-randomized trials.* New York: Oxford University Press.

O'Leary, A., Jemmott, L., & Jemmott, J. (2008). Mediation analysis of an effective sexual risk-reduction intervention for women: The importance of self-efficacy. *Health Psychology, 27*(2s), 180–184.

Piotrow, P. T., Kincaid, D. L., Rimon, J., & Rinehart, W. (1997). *Health communication: Lessons for public health.* New York: Praeger.

Rogers, E. M., Vaughan, P. W., Swalehe, R. A., Rao, N., Svenkerud, P., Sood, S., & Alfred, K. (1999). Effects of an entertainment-education radio soap opera on family planning behavior in Tanzania. *Studies in Family Planning, 30,* 193–211.

Rossi, P. H., Freeman, H. E., & Lipsey, M. (1999). *Evaluation: A systematic approach.* Thousand Oaks, CA: Sage.

Shadish, W. R., Cook T. D., & Leviton, L. C. (1991). *Foundations of program evaluation: Theories of practice.* Newbury Park, CA: Sage.

Snyder, L. B., Hamilton, M. A., Mitchell, E. W., Kiwanuka-Tondo, J., Fleming-Milici, F., & Proctor, D. (2004). A meta-analysis of the effect of mediated health communication campaigns on behavior change in the United States. *Journal of Health Communication, 9*(1), 71–96.

Solomon, R. L. (1949). An extension of control group design. *Psychological Bulletin, 46,* 137–150.

Sonneville, K., La Pelle, N., Taveras, E., Gillman, M., & Prosser, L. (2009). Economic and other barriers to adopting recommendations to prevent childhood obesity: Results of a focus group study with parents. *BMC Pediatrics, 9*(81), 1–7.

Valente, T. W. (1995). *Network models of the diffusion of innovations.* Cresskill, NJ: Hampton Press.

Valente, T. W. (1996). Social network thresholds in the diffusion of innovations. *Social Networks, 18,* 69–79.

Valente, T. W. (2002). *Evaluating health promotion programs.* New York: Oxford University Press.

Valente, T. W., & Bharath, U. (1999). An evaluation of the use of drama to communicate HIV/AIDS information. *AIDS Education and Prevention, 11,* 203–211.

Valente, T. W., Poppe, P. R., Alva, M. E., de Briceno, V, & Cases, D. (1994). Street theater as a tool to reduce family planning misinformation. *International Quarterly of Community Health and Education, 15*(3), 279–289.

Valente, T. W., & Saba, W. (1997). Reproductive health is in your hands: The national media campaign in Bolivia. *SIECUS Rep, 25*(2), 10–13.

Valente, T. W., & Saba, W. P. (1998). Mass media and interpersonal influence in the Bolivia National Reproductive Health Campaign. *Communication Research, 25,* 96–124.

Valente, T. W., & Saba, W. (2001). Campaign recognition and interpersonal communication as factors in contraceptive use in Bolivia. *Journal of Health Communication, 6*(4), 1–20.

Victora, C. G., Habicht, J., & Bryce, J. (2004). Evidence-based public health: Moving beyond randomized trials. *American Journal of Public Health, 94*(3), 400–405.

Weiss, C. (1972). *Evaluation research: Methods for assessing program effectiveness.* Englewood Cliffs, NJ: Prentice Hall.

CHAPTER 7

Communication Campaign Effectiveness and Effects

Some Critical Distinctions

Charles T. Salmon and Lisa Murray-Johnson

There is a substantial history of research regarding the success or failure of health communication campaigns. Traditionally, evidence-based data from objective metrics are used to support hypotheses and conclusions, with rational argument as the bridge between goal-oriented objectives and findings. Yet, the arguments used to support the conclusion that a given campaign was or was not effective merit close scrutiny. Campaign effectiveness is a multifaceted construct; there is no universally accepted standard definition or consensus within the scientific community regarding what constitutes an effective campaign. Further, the terms *campaign effects* and *campaign effectiveness* often have been used interchangeably in evaluation reports, thereby obscuring the fact that some campaigns induce harmful or unintended effects. The consequence of idiosyncratic jargon and interpretation has resulted in an ambiguous body of research and commentary that has diminished the opportunity for scientific generalization across the field of campaign research. The purpose of this chapter is to provide evaluators with guidance for assessing commonly overlooked outcomes of campaigns, whether manifest or latent and intended or unintended.

WHAT CONSTITUTES AN EFFECTIVE CAMPAIGN?

In recent years, the term *campaign effectiveness* has been scrutinized by numerous scholars. In an attempt to call forth better understanding of the term, some studies employ economic or epidemiological models, efficacy studies, and theoretical interrogation (i.e., to ensure that conceptual, taken-for-granted assumptions are explored before operational explication is developed) (Dillard, Weber, & Vail, 2007; Dutta-Bergman, 2005; Hutchinson & Wheeler, 2006; Snyder, Hamilton, Mitchell, Kiwanuka-Tondo, Fleming-Milici, & Proctor, 2004). However, in terms of practice, we still see greater emphasis on the method itself rather than conceptualization of what constitutes success. Recent articles have fixed on the inclusiveness of meta-analysis, randomized control trials or quasi-experimental studies with high internal validity, and longitudinal studies when possible. The ascribed process has been on ensuring that the formula by which effectiveness is measured can be consistently applied (Evans, Uhrig, Davis, & McCormack 2009; Noar, Palmgreen, Chabot, Dobransky, & Zimmerman, 2009; Stephenson, Southwell, & Yzer, 2010). Measurement in evaluation work can be challenging: Some prior evaluation studies have been less rigorously developed, and replication may not be plausible, and there are challenges associated with controlling study conditions, or studies are unable to demonstrate lasting influence (Myhre & Flora, 2000; Randolph & Viswanath, 2004; Snyder et al., 2004). High quality and consistency in measurement should be a goal of any endeavor.

Yet, the larger issue should focus on the conceptual nature of what constitutes success. Measurement should follow conceptualization, not precede or be parallel to it. Article titles with the term *effectiveness* are sometimes treated as an ad-hoc supposition, and authors may not clearly explain to readers the criteria by which success is ascribed. We hope that, by revisiting current conundrums of campaign effectiveness, it will motivate scholars and practitioners to solve these dilemmas.

In the original presentation of this chapter, *campaign effectiveness* was conceptualized as the ratio of achievements divided by expectations (Salmon & Murray-Johnson, 2001). In other words, an achievement or accomplishment is deemed successful or unsuccessful relative to what is desired or expected. When the denominator—the expectation—is high, the numerator—the outcome—will have to be of proportionally greater magnitude for it to be judged a success. Conversely, when the expectation is low, even a much lesser outcome or achievement will be interpreted as successful. This paradigm was chosen because, when most models, formulas, and progressive demarcations associated with effectiveness are distilled, campaign evaluators must still return to a ratio of expectations to outcomes. Because there are literally dozens of ways of analyzing data and presenting and interpreting the same statistical results, different evaluators can interpret the same data as evidence of either campaign effectiveness or ineffectiveness. Thus, we find in the campaign literature situations such as the following:

- Specific HIV/AIDS mass media campaigns that claim campaign effectiveness but possess weak designs that lack control for confounding factors, as demonstrated by Noar and colleagues (2009) in a 10-year meta-analysis.

- Domestic violence campaigns that claim effectiveness in building awareness about the severity of and services for those experiencing abuse. For women, perceptions moved in the expected direction, but for men in the study, it was believed gender stereotypes were activated. There was either no change or change in the opposite direction hypothesized (Keller, Wilkinson, & Otjen, 2010).

As Carol Weiss, Murphy-Graham, & Birkeland (2005) have concluded, there are multifold presentations of evaluation used to symbolically, instrumentally, or conceptually give legitimization to an issue or platform. The rhetoric of evaluation is at the mercy of those decision makers who consider the conceptualized and operationalized meaning of "effectiveness" from an existing point of view, and the challenge to scholars is to access knowledge along pathways of influence.

EXPLICATING CAMPAIGN EFFECTIVENESS

Compounding the difficulty in deriving valid generalizations about campaign effectiveness is the exceedingly broad range of possible campaign outcomes (ranging from individual-level outcomes, such as influencing knowledge, skills, attitudes, and behavior, to social-level outcomes, such as stimulating political action, winning the approval of a community coalition, or reducing cost expenditures for short- versus long-term disease treatment). Further, different conceptualizations of effectiveness are used to judge different outcomes. Six conceptualizations are presented in this chapter: definitional, ideological, political, contextual, cost, and programmatic.

Definitional Effectiveness

The first level of effectiveness pertains to the success that groups have in defining a social phenomenon as a social problem. When a certain condition has been accepted as socially problematic, it reflects the ability of some claims-making organization to get an issue onto various agendas (e.g., media, public, etc.) and achieve consensus that one issue is more worthy of political and financial capital than a competitor (Finnegan & Viswanath, 1997). For example, from 1990 to 2005, 1,507 messages were broadcast on ABC, NBC, and CBS news broadcasts to provide the public a greater understanding of organ donation (Quick, Kim, & Meyer, 2009). The authors noted modest but favorable coverage about becoming an organ donor. Nevertheless, the ability for organ donation coalitions to have their messages become a part of the news agenda is significant. As Dearing and Rogers (1996) stated, agenda setting is the media's role of shaping, changing, and reinforcing the target audience's perceptions on a topic. To the extent that campaign planners desired to get organ donation on the media's agenda as a pressing social problem, they were effective in terms of this very basic type of outcome.

The "selling" of a disease or health problem is thus an integral component of the initial phase of the campaign process. Media agendas are limited, for example, in terms of the number of issues for which time, energy, monetary support, and attention that can be devoted to it. Health advocates are placed in a position of competing with each other, each championing a different health cause and vying for limited attention and opportunity attention (Dearing & Rogers, 1996).

To offer another example, health promoters working in the area of cardiovascular medicine emphasize such claims as "Heart and cardiovascular disease is the number one killer of Americans" as a way of gaining attention. Diseases that kill far fewer Americans, such influenza or kidney disease, must still be positioned in such a way that they are perceived as serious, important, and hence, worthy of federal dollars and media attention. The challenge to health communicators is to be effective in this positioning strategy by emphasizing the uniqueness and potential threat of their disease vis-à-vis other diseases that are clamoring for the same limited resources. To the extent that an advocacy group achieves this outcome, it is thus effective in a definitional sense, a type of effectiveness that is often overlooked by evaluators but which is critical to the ultimate success of discrete communication campaigns.

Ideological Effectiveness

Once a social problem has been constructed, it is concomitantly defined at either the *individual* or *social* level of analysis. In most cases, campaigns are designed to modify personal knowledge, attitudes, intentions, and behaviors rather than to modify the political and economic environments in which those attitudes, intentions, and behaviors occur. For example, some social critics contend that the incidence of pregnancy among unwed teenage women constitutes a social problem. To the extent that a group achieves consensus that this is indeed the case, the next query focuses on the cause or source of this problem. If the problem becomes defined at the individual level, as due to sexual promiscuity or lower rates of contraceptive practices, then campaign definitions would focus on educating teens on how to avoid unwanted pregnancies. One could expect a sharp decline in teen pregnancies, as was shown in the late 1990s with a 38% reduction, due to increased condom use among sexually active teens from 40% to 51% from 1991 to 2001 (Santelli, Abma, Ventura, Lindberg, Morrow, Anderson et al., 2004; Santelli, Lindberg, Finer, & Singh, 2007).

In contrast, the problem of teen pregnancy might be defined by other claims makers at the social level. After a decade of falling teen pregnancy rates, by 2007, levels began to increase again. Using a social-level construction, it was argued that rate fluctuation was due to the lack of social services, underfunded youth development programs, and policies governing state Medicaid family planning (Yang & Gaydos, 2010). If this definition were to prevail, social-level solutions would be deployed, such as changes in policy and funding for welfare and other social service programs.

Yet, it is overwhelmingly the case that, more often than not, health problems are defined, at the individual level, as problems of lack of knowledge, "poor" attitudes, or lack of "appropriate" behaviors on the part of individuals who seem destined to suffer the consequences of their actions (Dorfman & Wallack, Chapter 23; Tesh, 1988; Wallack, 1989). An example is the Harvard Alcohol Project, which glorified the collaboration among MADD, Hollywood producers, and university researchers in advocating the designated driver campaign (Montgomery, 1993; see DeJong & Smith, Chapter 12). Television producers were encouraged to have scriptwriters focus on personal responsibility for drunk driving, as demonstrated by the popular phrase "Friends don't let friends drive drunk." Within 15 months, 62 popular sitcoms and dramas wholeheartedly discussed the concept. Yet, to some critics, this "effective" effort to implement the designated driver concept failed to address the "real" problem. Alcohol manufacturers and distributors were left untouched by the campaign (and continued to reap public and governmental goodwill in the process) while blaming individual drinkers for irresponsible behavior.

The attempt to "fix" human actions at the individual level is often preferred because campaigns tend to be perceived as ideologically neutral in contrast to systemic solutions, which are often labeled as *partisan* or *political.* Communication campaigns are actually no less political than other approaches to social change, but rarely are the hidden assumptions and politics of campaigns ever considered or debated to the same degree as are proposals for systemic change.

Political Effectiveness

As has been noted elsewhere, health communication represents a highly visible mechanism for demonstrating that a government cares about a particular social problem or issue (Salmon, 1989, 1992). For example, the classic studies of Stanford Three and Five City Projects, Minnesota Heart Health Program, Project STAR, and other similar campaigns were large-scale, expensive, government grant-sponsored initiatives designed to identify and solve the public health concerns of diet, obesity, physical activity, and drug use (Farquhar et al, 1990; Goldman & Glanz, 1998; Maccoby, Farquhar, Wood, & Alexander, 1977). Their massive media messages and community-driven programs created a very visible and public gesture of caring for the health and welfare of constituents.

As well, in recent years, the government has attempted to show that it is concerned about foreign dependency on oil and the high cost of gasoline by launching information programs to promote the production and use of ethanol. These programs accrue an added political benefit of helping American farmers earn higher prices for their corn crops, which now become sources of fuel rather than merely sources of food. The political benefits of promoting ethanol are therefore substantial. And yet, a political agenda that emphasizes ethanol instead of investment in wind or solar power actually perpetuates a longer-term dependency on oil and contributes to rising food prices and starvation in countries that historically have been reliant on American corn. The success of government efforts to promote ethanol use, in spite of its obvious long-term drawbacks, therefore constitutes a significant political success for proponents of ethanol and the oil industry (Salmon & Fernandez, in press).

In this sense, campaigns constitute a type of symbolic politics (Edelman, 1964). Campaigns are often politically palatable strategies for social change because they resonate with such cherished democratic themes as the value of education, an enlightened populace, a preference for individual-level change through the exercise of free will rather than coercion, and the merits of evolutionary rather than revolutionary change. The passing of the indoor ban for tobacco is a case in point. While it is scientifically accepted that secondhand smoke is a cause of death and disease for those who do not use tobacco (Pirkle, Bernert, Caudill, Sosnoff, & Pechacek, 2006), if there is no local or state indoor ban for smoking, then patrons can continue to expose others in bars and restaurants (O'Dougherty, Forster, & Widome, 2010). In Minneapolis–St. Paul, interviews with local elected officials were conducted to assess what arguments swayed local officials to move toward a smoking ban. Officials needed to appear impartial to both market capitalism (i.e., businesses concerned that patronage would decrease if the ban was consistently enforced) and consumer culture (i.e., advocates and public health officials supporting clean air bills). Considerable resources were marshaled by both sides in communicating these messages. As Paletz, Pearson, and Willia (1977) argue, virtually all government public service campaigns in some way portray the federal government as working in a caring and capable manner to solve social problems and to inspire confidence in political institutions while suppressing political participation. Local officials initially wove messages to appease both sides when the ban was introduced in 2006, but over time, conversations with constituents resonated positively. An ideological shift of business owners with local officials was apparent within 2 1/2 years of the smoking ban as city leaders could claim increased employment in restaurants by 5% in Minneapolis and only a 1% decrease in St. Paul (Klein, Forster, Erickson, Lytle, & Schillo, 2010). While economic arguments may drive political effectiveness, it is crucial to assess intended and unintended outcomes. Some evaluators may fail to assess political effectiveness unless the sponsor's specific political agenda is known and incorporated into the evaluation study and potential long-term consequences of campaigns, such as political apathy, are studied.

Contextual Effectiveness

When evaluators assess the impact of communication campaigns, there is also the opportunity to assess context. For example, we might start with the classic distinctions among three different mechanisms of social change offered by Paisley and Atkin (Chapter 2). An *engineering* solution to a social problem typically occurs with the development of a technology or innovation that can alone remedy the problem (such as the introduction of oral or needle inoculation with attenuated polio virus, which has eradicated polio). *Enforcement,* in contrast, typically involves the passage of laws, the use of coercion, or other forms of mandating change (such as seat belt laws, immigration vaccination laws, and mandated child safety protection). The third mechanism, *education,* typically involves modifying knowledge, attitudes, beliefs, or behavior; it is the predominant communication arm of social change.

When evaluating communication campaigns, one needs to take into account the capabilities of these alternatives: engineering and enforcement. If we find, for example, that antidrug PSAs do not eradicate illegal drug use, we need not instinctively "blame" campaigns or indict them for their ineffectiveness, especially as prior enforcement approaches often have failed (Kang, Cappella, & Fishbein, 2009). Rather, the focus of the evaluation can instead turn to analyses of why the decision to use communication or how to use communication (i.e., Kang et al. look at the use of cue-eliciting urges for smoking)—instead of engineering or enforcement—was made in the first place and whether that decision was an appropriate one. The focus of the evaluation should further consider the role engineering and enforcement play in influencing the effectiveness of communication or vice versa (as an obvious example, a mandatory seat belt law can have a chance of being effective only if the citizenry is made aware that it is in place). Increasingly, various combinations of the three strategies of change are used in unison rather than exclusively, but rarely is this synergy taken into account in most evaluation research.

Context should also be addressed across employed mass media channels. With the advent of multiple technology resources employed in communication campaigns (e.g., web, television, social networks), emergent contextual differences may be marked by channel strength, quality, scope, and reach (Jeong & King, 2010; Leshner, Bolls, & Thomas, 2010).

Cost-Effectiveness

This conceptualization emphasizes whether communication campaigns are more or less cost-effective than other forms of intervention. Prevention is a central component of the contemporary health paradigm as HMOs and other health service organizations are attempting to reduce costs of medical care by reducing the incidence of individuals' health needs. In particular, several cost-effectiveness models can be considered: cost avoidance or minimization, cost benefit, or cost consequence (Hutchinson & Wheeler, 2006).

Cost avoidance and minimization models consider that, when all potential interventions are equal, to utilize the solution that costs the least on the basis of lowest overall costs makes sense. Health systems may consider an avoidance model, for example, to treat heart failure patients. Communication programs and postdischarge meetings to track their care cost considerably less than hospital readmissions. Cost benefit models, in comparison, consider the overall benefits in relation to overall costs. Costs of treating heart failure patients in weekly group meetings for 6 weeks postdischarge may include costs of transport, counselor time, nursing assessment, and materials, but the benefits of personalizing their health care, positive community, social support and well-being, and the ability to manage treatment compliance well outweigh the costs. Cost consequence models, however, compare different types of interventions based on the different types of expected outcomes. In a cost consequence model, the benefits and costs may not be given equal value, which then allows campaign designers and evaluators to give a rating or evaluation based on perceived value. Most communication campaigns, unless specifically stated, tend to gloss over how cost-effectiveness is constructed (Hutchinson & Wheeler, 2006).

In evaluating cost-effectiveness, attention must be given to several potentially competing elements, such as reach and access, campaign message exposure, risk, available resources, and policy and procedures. *Effective* campaigns are those that reach the "right" individuals without similarly motivating the "wrong" individuals (i.e., appropriate audience segmentation and targeting) with a message that reaches them in a palatable manner (i.e., exposure and tailoring). It must occur while reducing potential risk from competing interests or counterarguments (i.e., risk) and all within the available personnel and material resources. When government or sponsor organizations are involved, rules about expenditures must be further justified and legitimized; in short, cost-effectiveness only continues to grow in importance in communication campaigns.

Programmatic Effectiveness

Finally, every information campaign is, or at least ought to be, driven by goals and objectives that specify the nature and degree of impact sought. When campaign performance is measured against these goals and objectives, an assessment of programmatic effectiveness can be made through a direct comparison between objectives and outcomes. This type of effectiveness is described in detail in most standard evaluation research textbooks.

However, one caveat should be mentioned. Critical to the comparison between objectives and outcomes is, of course, awareness of those objectives. For example, PSAs developed by the National AIDS Information and Education Program were designed to encourage individuals to call the National AIDS Hotline, the largest public health hotline in the world. This was done because it was realized that a single 30- or 60-second TV spot could not possibly address all the concerns and questions that an audience member might have about the disease and that the media message needed to be supplemented by a more interactive interpersonal message. If evaluated in terms of programmatic criteria, the ads were effective because they accomplished what they were designed to accomplish. Yet, if evaluated in terms of other criteria applied by outside evaluators not privy to the organization's goals and objectives—such as whether the ads influenced a person's behavioral intention to wear a condom—then the ads could (unfairly) be deemed ineffective.

DISTINGUISHING BETWEEN CAMPAIGN EFFECTS AND EFFECTIVENESS

The terms campaign *effects* and *effectiveness* have long been treated as interchangeable and synonymous, at least as used in numerous studies and review essays about campaigns, yet they are conceptually quite distinct. Both represent interpretations of communication outcomes, but they differ in terms of the key dimension of intentionality. For example, a disproportionate amount of research on media effects has focused on antisocial effects, such as children imitating violence in real life after viewing it on television. However, the imitation of violence would be characterized as evidence of a media effect rather than media effectiveness, for it presumably is not the intention of the creators of the media content to induce violent behavior on the part of children watching their show. On the other hand, if a television show were to adopt entertainment–education (E–E or edutainment; see Singhal, Wang, & Rogers, Chapter 22; Schiavo, 2007) strategies with the specific intention of inducing their viewers to behave in a particular way (e.g., cooperate rather than fight), then such a finding would be evidence of both a media effect and media effectiveness. Thus, *effectiveness* constitutes a subset of the larger category of effects, that is, the subset of effects defined in terms of preexisting goals and intentions. Crossing these two Yes–No dimensions generates the following four cells or categories: The two conventional cases are when Cell 1 is Yes effects and Yes effectiveness and Cell 4 is No effects and No effectiveness; two noteworthy combinations are Cell 3 (Yes effects and No effectiveness) and Cell 2 (No effects and Yes effectiveness).

Cell 1: Effects and Effectiveness

Cell 1 asks the question, "Can we have a situation in which we have an outcome defined as an effect that we also interpret as evidence of effectiveness?" Consider the case where the goal of a cardiovascular health campaign is to increase knowledge of heart disease by 10% in a community and decrease mortality in the process. If, through pre- and posttests with appropriate comparison communities, we determine a 10% increase in knowledge, then we conclude that the educational component of the campaign did have an effect. If the mortality trend and age-adjusted mortality are lower than expected, one can also conclude the campaign was effective. The National High Blood Pressure program, starting in 1972 and trended through 1992, demonstrated increased awareness and knowledge, while reducing the mortality in these 20 years by 59% (i.e., 77,500 Americans were expected to die from a stroke in 1990 alone, yet not only was mortality lowered but also blood pressure control from 116,000 people who reported no cardiovascular events) (Roccella, 2002). Although this type of outcome is fairly straightforward and easily understood, the literature on campaigns contains at least as many reports of campaign failure as campaign success.

Cell 4: No Effects, No Effectiveness

In Cell 4, we have an outcome that we do not recognize as an effect, and the interpretation is a lack of effectiveness. *Ineffectiveness* has been rationalized as the result of poorly constructed or implemented messages or campaigns, the inability to reach the target audience, lack of inoculation with the campaign message, or the inability to produce lasting change in attitudes, knowledge, or behaviors (Backer, Rogers, & Sopory, 1992; Rossi & Freeman, 1993; see Atkin & Freimuth, Chapter 4). Ineffectiveness is a plausible outcome both in theory and in practice (consider, for example, the titles of studies by Hyman & Sheatsley, 1947, and by Robertson, 1976).

Cell 3: Effects but Not Effectiveness

While the first two cells are intuitive and commonly alluded to in the campaign literature, the latter two are not. Starting with Cell 3, it is plausible to have an outcome judged to be evidence of a campaign's effect but not considered to be evidence of campaign effectiveness. This is an unintended effect, for it is not expected in terms of the goals, objectives, and expectations of the campaign planner and, yet, is some outcome attributable to the campaign's intervention (Byrne & Niederdeppe, 2011; Cho & Salmon, 2007; Guttman & Salmon, 2004). Unintended effects may be interpreted as positive or negative, short term or long term, or occurring at an individual or societal level. Often, campaign planners and evaluators attempt to control for unintended effects through extensive formative research and the inclusion of multiple controls. However, it is not always possible to foresee and mitigate all of the different types of unintended effects, such as hysteria or panic, knowledge gaps, discrimination and scapegoating, confusion and misunderstanding, and potential boomerang effects. As an example, Harakeh, Engels, Den Exter Blokland, Scholte, and Vermulst (2009) conducted a study on parental communication with Dutch adolescents as an attempt to reduce smoking. Smoking-specific communication did not alter youth smoking. Study authors evaluated numerous variables, such as parents smoking, quality of communication, quality of the parent–adolescent relationship, and frequency of communication, yet, their findings were contrary to prior research, which demonstrated that parental communication can influence smoking-related decisions (Miller-Day, 2002). While the campaign may not be considered effective, there were notable effects produced from the intervention. When communicating with younger siblings, but not older ones, it appeared that the likelihood of smoking actually increased over time (Harakeh et al., 2009). In general, it is important to note that combinations of campaign effects without effectiveness are very important from the standpoint of future campaign design and that they merit particular attention from campaign evaluators because of their surprising prevalence.

Cell 2: No Known Effects, But Effectiveness

Cell 2 occurs when there is no evidence of a campaign having any tangible effect, but it is nonetheless judged to be effective. There are two contexts in which this outcome might occur. First, placement has long been used as a criterion of effectiveness for publicity and public service efforts. Whereas commercial advertisers pay for space and, hence, are guaranteed control of the placement and timing of their messages in the media, publicity agents and public service campaigners are said to "pray" for space. They must send their materials to media gatekeepers (editors and broadcast news directors) without payment for placement or timing (Wallack, 1989). This publicity model, which serves as the basis of most PSA campaigns, has long relied on the collection of news clippings as evidence that an organization's prayers have been answered—that its messages appeared in the media. This type of evaluation obviously begs the question of whether anyone saw, read, understood, acted on, or remembered the information (are *engaged,* as in Rice & Foote, Chapter 5), but nevertheless it has endured as an accepted form of campaign evaluation.

The second context is characterized by intense competition. In antismoking campaigns, for example, where public service campaigners have active adversaries who are attempting to increase their market shares, reinforcement of existing nonsmoking rates rather than actual reduction—or other types of seemingly null effects—could be considered a type of victory (and hence, effectiveness).

Conclusion

As this chapter has illustrated, there is considerable work for scholars going forward to advance the field of campaign effectiveness. We offer a short list of recommendations as a guide to future work. First, authors should clearly articulate the manner by which success is being conceptualized for their study or research project variable by variable. As has been done with other communication constructs (i.e., compliance gaining or persuasion typologies), we encourage the development of a schematic regarding the nature of campaign effectiveness or success. To study what works means that readers must have an opportunity to debate the conceptual and informational value of how the campaign is designed, measured, and analyzed. While some authors (i.e., see Snyder & LaCroix, Chapter 8) have done an admirable job of bringing meta-analysis into the campaign literature, there is still a need for definitional clarity to provide thoughtful investigation about how campaigns are being measured. Less meticulous studies that list campaign hypotheses and data merely as consistent or inconsistent do not answer the larger questions about the conceptual base of communication campaign effectiveness. The former is a focus on the intended nature of campaign effects, and we hope to show in this chapter that effects are both intended and unintended.

As it goes without saying, most campaigns are complex; they have been constructed based on principles of message design, audience segmentation, channel selection, and often a myriad of goal-oriented outcomes. Analyses and discussions sections that distill this immense informational treasure trove during formative, process, and outcome evaluations do readers a disservice. Although numerous campaign effects can be identified and rationalized, controversies about the parameters of effectiveness and gaps in measurement will continue to surface. But, it is in the sharing of this information that contributions and insight will help all of us to develop more thoughtful narratives and isolation of variables that provide to advance campaign work.

Second, we recommend that authors describe in their work awareness of secular trends and the perceived influence of those trends in assessing the extent to which a campaign should be labeled successful or not. It is not enough to claim that improvement or changes in technology or social networks are behind or hindering claims of effectiveness. Technology formats will continue to necessarily evolve and adapt, and social media networks will continue to grow and expand. The objective for the scholar is to explore in what specific ways, rather than general ones, that these newer options for campaign design and implementation change the definitions and operationalizations of doing this work. Secular trends have always created challenges for campaign designers: Funders become interested in some topics over others, popular culture becomes interested in some findings over others, and news and political agendas demonstrate wealth or dearth of coverage. With the recognition that program sponsors, agency partners, and primary and secondary publics will always ascribe positive or negative dichotomous assessments about campaign results, the scholar must use a critical and independent assessment from which to give accurate coverage of the complex, multilayered work and contradictory findings that may emerge.

It is only by broadening the scope of evaluation research and the conceptualization of campaign effectiveness to incorporate the social construction of health, ideological biases, and conflicting stakeholder agendas that we can fully appreciate the role that campaigns play in society and their realistic potential to shape social change.

References

Backer, T. E., Rogers, E. M., & Sopory, P. (1992). *Designing health communication campaigns: What works?* Newbury Park, CA: Sage.

Byrne, S., & Niederdeppe, J. (2011). Unintended consequences of public health messaging to reduce population rates of obesity. In J. Cawley (Ed.), *Social science of obesity*. Oxford, UK: Oxford University Press.

Cho, H., & Salmon, C. T. (2007). Unintended effects of health communication campaigns. *Journal of Communication, 57,* 293–317.

Dearing, J. W., & Rogers, E. M. (1996). *Agenda-setting*. Thousand Oaks, CA: Sage.

Dillard, J. P., Weber, K. M., & Vail, R. G. (2007). The relationship between real and actual effectiveness of persuasive messages: A meta-analysis with implications for formative campaign research. *Journal of Communication, 57,* 613–631.

Dutta-Bergman, M. H. (2005). Theory and practice in health communication campaigns: A critical interrogation. *Health Communication, 18*(2), 103–122.

Edelman, M. (1964). *The symbolic uses of politics*. Urbana: University of Illinois Press.

Evans, W. D., Uhrig, J., Davis, K., & McCormack, L. (2009). Efficacy methods to evaluate health communication and marketing campaigns. *Journal of Health Communication, 14,* 315–330.

Farquhar, J. W., Fortmann, S. P., Flora, J. A., Taylor, C. B., Haskell, W. L., Williams, P. T., Maccoby, N., & Wood, P. D. (1990). Effects of community-wide education on cardiovascular disease risk factors: The Stanford Five City Project. *JAMA, 264,* 359–365.

Finnegan, J. R., & Viswanath, K. (1997). Communication theory and health behavior change. In K. Glanz, F. M. Lewis, & B. K. Rimer (Eds.), *Health behavior and health education: Theory, research, and practice* (2nd ed., pp. 313–341). San Francisco: Jossey-Bass.

Goldman, L. K., & Glantz, S. A. (1998). Evaluation of antismoking advertising campaigns. *JAMA, 279,* 772–777.

Guttman, N., & Salmon, C. T. (2004). Guilt, fear, stigma and knowledge gaps: Ethical issues in public health communication interventions. *Bioethics, 18,* 531–552.

Harakeh, Z., Engels, R., Den Exter Blokland, E., Scholte, R., & Vermulst, A. (2009). Parental communication appears not to be an effective strategy to reduce smoking in a sample of Dutch adolescents. *Psychology and Health, 23*(7), 823–841.

Hutchinson, P., & Wheeler, J. (2006). The cost effectiveness of health communication programs: What do we know? *Journal of Health Communication, 11*(7), 7–45.

Hyman, H. H., & Sheatsley, P. B. (1947). Some reasons why information campaigns fail. *Public Opinion Quarterly, 10,* 412–423.

Jeong, Y., & King, C. M. (2010). Impacts of website context relevance on banner advertisement effectiveness. *Journal of Promotion Management, 16*(3), 247–264.

Kang, Y., Cappella, J., & Fishbein, M. (2009). The effect of marijuana scenes in antimarijuana public service announcements on adolescents evaluation of ad effectiveness. *Health Communication, 24*(6), 483–493.

Klein, E. G., Forster, J. L., Erickson, D. J., Lytle, L. L., & Schillo, B. (2010). Economic effects of clean indoor air policies on bar and restaurant employment in Minneapolis and St. Paul, Minnesota. *Journal of Public Health Management & Practice, 16*(4), 285–293.

Keller, S. N., Wilkinson, T., & Otjen, A. J. (2010). Unintended effects of a domestic violence campaign. *Journal of Advertising, 39*(4), 53–67.

Leshner, G., Bolls, P., & Thomas, E. (2010). Scare 'em or disgust 'em: The effects of graphic health promotion messages. *Health Communication, 24,* 447–458.

Maccoby, N., Farquhar, J., Wood, P., & Alexander, J. (1977). Reducing the risk of cardiovascular disease: Effects of a community-based campaign on knowledge and behavior. *Journal of Community Health, 3,* 100–114.

Miller-Day, M. (2002). Parent-adolescent communication about alcohol, tobacco, and other drug use. *Journal of Adolescent Research, 17,* 604–616.

Montgomery, K. C. (1993). The Harvard alcohol project: Promoting the designated driver on television. In T. E. Backer & E. M. Rogers (Eds.), *Organizational aspects of health communication campaigns: What works?* (pp. 178–202). Newbury Park, CA: Sage.

Myhre, S. L., & Flora, J. A. (2000). HIV/AIDS communication campaigns: Progress and perspectives. *Journal of Health Communication, 5*(Suppl.), 29–45.

Noar, S. M., Palmgreen, P., Chabot, M., Dobransky, N., & Zimmerman, R. S. (2009). A 10-year systemic review of HIV/AIDS mass media campaigns: Have we made progress? *Journal of Health Communication, 14,* 15–42.

O'Dougherty, M., Forster, J., & Widome, R. (2010). Communicating with local elected officials: Lessons learned from clean indoor air ordinance campaigns. *Health Promotion and Practice, 11*(2), 275–281.

Paletz, D. L., Pearson, R. E., & Willia, D. L. (1977). *Politics in public service advertising on television.* New York: Praeger.

Pirkle, J. L., Bernert, J. T., Caudill, S. P., Sosnoff, C. S., & Pechacek, T. F. (2006). Trends in the exposure of nonsmokers in the U.S. population to secondhand smoke: 1988–2002. *Environmental Health Perspectives, 114*(6), 853–858. Retrieved March 11, 2011, from http://ehp03.niehs.nih.gov/article/fetchArticle.action?articleURI = info:doi/10.1289/ehp.8850

Quick, B. L., Kim, D. K., & Meyer, K. (2009). A 15-year review of ABC, CBS and NBC news coverage of organ donation: Implications for organ donation campaigns. *Health Communication, 24,* 137–145.

Randolph, W., & Viswanath, K. (2004). Lessons learned from public health mass media campaigns. Marketing health in a crowded world. *Annual Review of Public Health, 25,* 419–437.

Robertson, L. S. (1976). The great seat belt campaign flop. *Journal of Communication, 26,* 41–45.

Roccella, E. J. (2002). The contributions of public health education toward the reduction of cardiovascular disease mortality: Experiences from the National High Blood Pressure Education Program. In R. C. Hornik (Ed.), *Public health communication: Evidence for behavioral change* (pp. 97–114). Mahwah, NJ: Lawrence Erlbaum.

Rossi, P. H., & Freeman, H. E. (1993). *Evaluation: A systematic approach* (5th ed.). Newbury Park, CA: Sage.

Salmon, C. T. (1989). Campaigns for social "improvement": An overview of values, rationales, and impacts. In C. T. Salmon (Ed.), *Information campaigns: Balancing social values and social change* (pp. 19–53). Newbury Park, CA: Sage.

Salmon, C. T. (1992). Building theory "of" and theory "for" communication campaigns: An essay on ideology and public policy. *Communication yearbook, 15,* 346–358.

Salmon, C. T., & Fernandez, L. (in press). Biofuels and the law of unintended consequences. In L. Ahern & D. Bortree (Eds.), *Talking green: A guide to contemporary issues in environmental communications.*

Salmon, C. T., & Murray-Johnson, L. (2001). Communication campaign effectiveness: Some critical distinctions. In R. Rice & C. Atkin (Eds.), *Public communication campaigns* (3rd ed., pp. 168–180). Thousand Oaks, CA: Sage.

Santelli, J. S., Abma, J., Ventura, S., Lindberg, L., Morrow, B., Anderson J. E., et al. (2004). Can changes in sexual behavior among high school students explain the decline in teen pregnancy rates in the 1990s? *Journal of Adolescent Health, 35,* 80–90.

Santelli, J. S., Lindberg, L. D., Finer, L. B., & Singh, S. (2007). Explaining recent declines in adolescent pregnancy in the United States: The contribution of abstinence and improved contraceptive use. *American Journal of Public Health, 97*(1), 150–156.

Scherer, C. W., & Juanillo, N. K. (1992). Bridging theory and praxis: Reexamining public health communication. *Communication yearbook, 15,* 312–345.

Schiavo, R. (2007). *Health communication: From theory to practice.* San Francisco: John Wiley & Sons.

Snyder, L. B., Hamilton, M. A, Mitchell, E. W., Kiwanuka-Tondo, J, Fleming-Milici, R, & Proctor, D. (2004). A meta-analysis of the effect of mediated health campaigns on behavior change in the United States. *Journal of Health Communication, 9*(Suppl. 1), 71–96.

Stephenson, M. T., Southwell, B. G., & Yzer, M. (2011). Advancing health communication research: Issues and controversies in research design and data analysis. In T. Thompson, R. Parrott, & J. Nussbaum (Eds.), *Routledge handbook of health communication* (pp. 560–577). New York: Routledge.

Tesh, S. N. (1988). *Hidden arguments: Political ideology and disease prevention policy.* New Brunswick, NJ: Rutgers University Press.

Wallack, L. (1989). Mass communication and health promotion: A critical perspective. In R. E. Rice & C. K. Atkin (Eds.), *Public communication campaigns* (2nd ed., pp. 353–367). Newbury Park, CA: Sage.

Weiss, C. H., Murphy-Graham, E., & Birkeland, S. (2005). An alternate route to policy influence: How evaluations affect D.A.R.E. *American Journal of Evaluation, 26* (1), 12–30. Retrieved March 11, 2011, from http://ehp03.niehs.nih.gov/article/fetchArticle.action?articleURI = info:doi/10.1289/ ehp.8850

Yang, Z., & Gaydos, L. M. (2010). Reasons for and challenges of recent increases in teen birth rates: A study of family planning service policies and demographic changes at the state level. *Journal of Adolescent Health, 46*(6), 517–524.

How Effective Are Mediated Health Campaigns?

A Synthesis of Meta-Analyses

Leslie B. Snyder and Jessica M. LaCroix

The purpose of this chapter is to review what is known about the effectiveness of health communication interventions that use media and the conditions under which they have a greater likelihood of changing health behaviors. We also compare the effectiveness of mediated interventions to other types of interventions that involve communication. Media include little media (e.g., posters and brochures), mass media (e.g., television, radio, billboards, magazines, newspapers), and interactive media (e.g., Internet, telephone, mobile media).

As used here, *media campaigns* are organized communication activity, typically using mass media, directed at a particular target group for a specified period of time to achieve a stated goal. They include social marketing campaigns that use media. *Mediated intervention* refers to any intervention in which media are employed, including mass media, little media, and interactive media. Media campaigns are one type of mediated intervention. *Interpersonal intervention* refers to any intervention using face-to-face or small group communication, including counseling, outreach, and workshops. Interventions that are predominantly interpersonal sometimes use interactive media or little media as well.

We systematically review and meta-analyze the meta-analyses of the relevant literature—a meta-meta-analysis. Meta-analyses quantitatively assess the average effect sizes within a set of studies. The conclusions are more reliable than single studies or narrative reviews because the results are quantitatively pooled across researchers, research settings, populations, methodological variations, and implementation realities. Meta-analysts tightly define the criteria studies must satisfy to be included in their reviews and systematically search the literature (see Johnson, Scott-Sheldon, Snyder, Noar, & Huedo-Medina, 2008; Lipsey & Wilson, 2001).

Estimates of media campaign effect sizes have been useful by providing 1) benchmarks against which to judge the effectiveness of particular campaigns, 2) suggestions for realistic impact levels when writing goals of new campaigns, and 3) bases for power calculations to estimate needed sample sizes when designing campaign evaluations (Snyder, 2001;

Snyder & Hamilton, 2002). The average effect sizes can also help public health organizations decide whether a campaign would help meet their objectives.

Another valuable contribution of meta-analyses is in specifying important moderators of effects. If the studies included in a meta-analysis are statistically similar—homogeneous—then it is appropriate to examine their effect size as a group. If the studies are dissimilar—heterogeneous—there are underlying differences between the studies, supporting the need to find moderating conditions. Knowing the conditions under which media campaign effect sizes are larger or smaller adds greater specificity to recommendations, helping policy makers and intervention designers zero in on which aspects of a campaign led to the most behavior change. Here, we review the effectiveness of interventions using media by different types of moderators, including campaign topic, methodological issues, target population, and channels or media approach. Because one of the most important moderators of media campaign effects has been health topics (Snyder, Hamilton, Mitchell, Kiwanuka-Tondo, Fleming-Milici, & Proctor, 2004), the meta-meta-analysis separates media campaign effects by health topic or, where possible, behavior. The subsequent section reviews additional moderators of campaign effects from the literature, followed by comparative meta-analyses of different intervention approaches.

METHOD

Meta-analyses were included in the present review if they 1) evaluated the effectiveness of interventions or campaigns that used at least one mediated channel to promote primary behavior change or prevention behaviors (as opposed to secondary prevention among those who have been diagnosed as ill), 2) included studies utilizing randomized control trials or quasi-experimental designs (i.e., pre- and posttest design, or post only with comparison group designs), 3) had fewer than 50 % of the included studies used in subsequent meta-analyses in our review, and 4) reported behavioral outcomes using an effect size metric convertible to r, and reported total sample size N. Table 8.1 lists the meta-analyses of mediated interventions that met the inclusion criteria, of which eight focused on media campaign effects. There were no meta-analyses of health advocacy campaigns promoting corporate or regulatory change (for a review, see Freudenberg, Bradley, & Serrano 2009).

The effect sizes were analyzed using Comprehensive Meta Analysis software (Borenstein, Hedges, Higgins, & Rothstein, 2005). For media campaign effects in the next section, we present overall effects using both random and fixed effect models. Given the amount of variation (i.e., populations, intervention intensities, and reliability of measures) across meta-analyses of mediated interventions, random effects models make more conceptual sense than fixed effects models (see Borenstein, Hedges, & Rothstein, 2007). In the subsequent section on comparative effects, most of the effect size estimates in the included meta-analyses used fixed effects models, so that is what is reported.

The results were compared with a meta-meta-analysis of health interventions that focused on interpersonal approaches such as face-to-face counseling, outreach, and small groups and did not include mass media campaigns (Johnson, Scott-Sheldon, & Carey, 2010). We also examined systematic reviews of mediated interventions for their insights on possible moderators of effects.

TABLE 8.1 Papers Included in the Meta-Meta-Analysis		
Reference	**Topic**	**Approach**
Apodaca, T. R., & Miller, W. R. (2003). A meta-analysis of the effectiveness of bibliotherapy for alcohol problems. *Journal of Clinical Psychology, 59,* 289–304.	A	Print
Bien, T. H., Miller, W. R., & Tonigan, J. S. (1993). Brief interventions for alcohol problems: A review. *Addiction, 88,* 315–336.	A	IP
Bonfill Cosp, X., et al. (2004). Strategies for increasing the participation of women in community breast cancer screening. *Cochrane Database of Systematic Reviews, 1,* Article CD002943. Retrieved August 15, 2011, from http://www2.cochrane.org/reviews/en/ab002943.html	M	Phone
Brunner, E., et al. (1997). Can dietary interventions change diet and cardiovascular risk factors? A meta-analysis of randomized controlled trials. *American Journal of Public Health, 87,* 1415–1422.	N	IP
Bruvold, W. H. (1993). A meta-analysis of adolescent smoking prevention programs. *American Journal of Public Health, 83,* 872–880.	S	IP
Carey, K. B., et al. (2009). Computer-delivered interventions to reduce college student drinking: A meta-analysis. *Addiction, 104,* 1807–1818.	A	Computer
Dotson, J. H. (1989). *Physician-delivered smoking cessation interventions: An information synthesis of the literature.* Doctoral dissertation, University of Maryland—College Park.	S	IP
Eyles, H. C., & Mhurchu, C. N. (2009). Does tailoring make a difference? A systematic review of the long-term effectiveness of tailored nutrition education for adults. *Nutrition Reviews, 67,* 464–480.	N	Computer
Feeley, T. H., & Moon, S. (2005). A meta-analytic review of communication campaigns to promote organ donation. *Communication Reports, 22,* 63–73.	O	Campaign
Han, H., et al. (2009). A meta-analysis of interventions to promote mammography among ethnic minority women. *Nursing Research, 58,* 246–254.	M	Campaign
Johnson, B. T., Scott-Sheldon, L. A. J., & Carey, M. P. (2010). A meta-synthesis of health behavior change meta-analyses. *American Journal of Public Health, 100,* 2193–2198.	A, H, M, N, S	IP
Khadjesari, Z., et al. (2010) Can stand-alone computer-based interventions reduce alcohol consumption? A systematic review. *Addiction, 106,* 267–282.	A	Computer
Krebs, P., Prochaska, J. O., & Rossi, J. S. (2010). A meta-analysis of computer-tailored interventions for health behavior change. *Preventive Medicine, 51,* 214–221.	S, M, N	Tailored

(Continued)

TABLE 8.1 (Continued)		
Reference	**Topic**	**Approach**
Lichtenstein, E., Glasgow, R. E., Lando, H. A., Ossip-Klein, D. J., & Boles. (1996). Telephone and counseling for smoking cessation: Rationales and meta-analytic review of evidence. *Health Education Research, 11,* 243–257.	S	Phone
McArthur, D. B. (1998). Heart healthy eating behaviors of children following a school-based intervention: A meta-analysis. *Issues in Comprehensive Pediatric Nursing, 21,* 35–48.	N	IP
Moore, S. D. (1990). *A meta-analytic review of mass media campaigns designed to change automobile occupant restraint behavior.* Doctoral dissertation, University of Illinois, Urbana—Champaign.	O	Campaign
Mullen, P. D., Simmons-Morton, D. G., Ramirez, G., Frankowski, R. F., Green, L. W., & Mains, D. A. (1997). A meta-analysis of trials evaluation patient education and counseling for three groups of preventive health behaviors. *Patient Education and Counseling, 32,* 157–173.	M, S	IP
Myung, S., et al. (2009). Effects of web- and computer-based smoking cessation programs. *Archives of Internal Medicine, 169,* 929–937.	S	Computer
Noar, S. M., Benac, C., N., & Harris, M. S. (2007). Does tailoring matter? Meta-analytic review of tailored print health behavior change interventions. *Psychological Bulletin, 133,* 673–693.	M, N	Tailored
Noar, S. M., Black, H. G., & Pierce, L. B. (2009). Efficacy of computer technology-based HIV prevention interventions: A meta-analysis. *AIDS, 23,* 107–115.	H	Computer
Page, A., Morrell, S., Chiu, C., Taylor, R., & Tewson, R. (2006). Recruitment to mammography screening: A randomized trial and meta-analysis of invitation letters and telephone calls. *Australian and New Zealand Journal of Public Health, 30,* 111–118.	M	Letter
Parcell, L. M., et al. (2007). An analysis of media health campaigns for children and adolescents: Do they work? In R. W. Preiss, B. M. Gayle, N. Burrell, M. Allen, & J. Bryant (Eds.), *Mass media effects research: Advances through meta-analysis* (pp. 345–361). Mahwah, NJ: Lawrence Erlbaum.	S	Campaign
Portnoy, D. B., et al. (2008). Computer-delivered interventions for health promotion and behavioral risk reduction: A meta-analysis of 75 randomized controlled trials, 1988–2007. *Preventive Medicine, 47,* 3–16.	H, S	Computer
Riper, H., et al. (2009). Curbing problem drinking with personalized-feedback interventions. A meta-analysis. *American Journal of Preventive Medicine, 36,* 247–255.	A	Tailored

Reference	Topic	Approach
Rooke, S., et al. (2010). Computer-delivered interventions for alcohol and tobacco use: A meta-analysis. *Addiction, 105,* 1391–1390.	A, S	Computer
Snyder, L. B., et al. (2003). *Meta-analysis of family planning campaigns advised by the Center for Communication Programs at Johns Hopkins University compared to campaigns conducted and advised by other organizations.* Unpublished manuscript.	O	Campaign
Snyder, L. B., Hamilton, M. A., Mitchell, E. W., Kiwanuka-Tondo, J., Fleming-Milici, F., & Proctor, D. (2004). A meta-analysis of the effect of mediated health communication campaigns on behavior change in the United States. *Journal of Health Communication, 9*(Suppl. 1), 71–96.	A, M, O, S	Campaign
Snyder, L. B., Johnson, B. T., Huedo-Medina, T., LaCroix, J. M., Smoak, N. D., & Cistulli, M. (2009, May). *Effectiveness of media interventions to prevent HIV, 1986–2006: A meta-analysis.* Poster presented at the annual meeting of the Society for Behavioral Research, Montreal, Canada.	H	Campaign, IP
Snyder, L. B., Lapierre, M. A., & Maloney, E. K. (2006, November). *Using mass media to improve nutrition: A meta-analytic examination of campaigns and interventions.* Paper presented at the annual meeting of the American Public Health Association, Boston, MA.	N	Mediated
Stead, L. F., Perera, R., & Lancaster, T. (2006). Telephone counseling for smoking cessation. *Cochrane Database of Systematic Reviews, 3,* Article CD002850. Retrieved August 15, 2011, from http://www2.cochrane.org/reviews/en/ab002850.html	S	Phone
Whittaker, R., Borland, Bullen, Lin, McRobbie, Rodgers. (2009). Mobile phone-based interventions for smoking cessation. *Cochrane Database of Systematic Reviews, 4,* Article CD006611. Retrieved August 15, 2011, from http://www2.cochrane.org/reviews/en/ab006611.html	S	Mobile phone
Yabroff, K. R., & Mandelblatt, J. S. (1999). Interventions targeted toward patients to increase mammography use. *Cancer Epidemiology, Biomarkers and Prevention, 8,* 749–757.	M	IP

Note. A = alcohol, H = HIV/STD, M = mammogram, N = nutrition, S = smoking, O = other, IP = Interpersonal.

MEDIA CAMPAIGN EFFECTS BY HEALTH TOPIC

Figure 8.1 shows the average campaign effects by topic from meta-analyses of media campaigns. The error bars on the graph represent the 95% confidence interval around the point estimate and give an indication of the reliability of the estimates. Smaller total sample size and wide spread in point estimates across studies contribute to wider error bars. Nonoverlapping error bars between any two estimates indicate that those two parameters are statistically different. An error bar including zero indicates that the estimate may be zero.

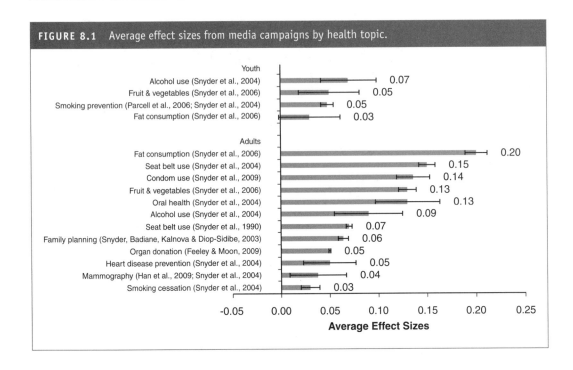

FIGURE 8.1   Average effect sizes from media campaigns by health topic.

There was substantial heterogeneity among the average campaign effect sizes by health behavior and age: for adults $Q(13) = 1789.2$ ($p < .001$); for youth, $Q(4) = 3.58$ ($p < .001$). For adults, the greatest average effect sizes were for reduction of fat consumption, followed by seat belt promotion, condom use, fruit and vegetables, and oral health. The least successful have been smoking cessation campaigns. There are two entries for seat belt campaigns because the later meta-analysis includes enforcement campaigns, while the earlier one does not. The average random effect size for adults was $r = .09$, 95% CI (.07, .11). (The fixed effect size was $r = .05$, 95% CI [.05, .05].) Meta-analyses on youth media campaigns have covered fewer topics. The random effect size for youth was $r = .05$, 95% CI (.04, .06), lower than for adults. (The average fixed effect size for youth was $r = .05$, 95% CI [.04, .05].) Within topics, youth campaigns had lower effect sizes on average than adult campaigns for alcohol use, fruit and vegetables, and fat consumption campaigns. Smoking prevention campaigns for youth were more successful than cessation campaigns for adults, perhaps because prevention is easier to achieve than cessation of an addiction.

ADDITIONAL MODERATORS OF MEDIA CAMPAIGN EFFECTS

The meta-analyses themselves often test moderators of effects. We review key moderators of health-related media campaign effects below.

Enforcement Campaigns

One key moderator of effect sizes was whether or not the campaigns were accompanied by enforcement of laws or regulations, such as police roadside checks for seat belt usage or checks for sale of alcohol to minors, and used messages to that effect. Campaigns that included enforcement had a stronger effect ($r = .17$, 95% CI [.13, .21]), representing a 17% net change in behavior; Snyder & Hamilton, 2002), than campaigns that did not ($r = .06$, 95% CI [.052, .064]); Snyder, Hamilton, & Huedo-Medina, 2009).

A recent meta-analysis covered road safety campaigns promoting seat belts, driving while intoxicated, and speeding (Phillips, Ulleberg, & Vaa, 2011). Although the meta-analysis was not included in Figure 8.1 because of the nature of the outcome variable and an absence of reported sample size, the findings are worth mentioning: a reduction in accidents of 12% (95% CI, .09, .16). The effects were greater for campaigns conducted earlier, of shorter duration, supplemented with personal communication, and including enforcement. Interestingly, the differences between the enforcement campaigns and others were slight. It is possible that the first generation of enforcement campaigns in the 1990s had a much greater impact because of the novelty of the approach and that, by later campaigns, the enforcement message was stale and less effective.

Message Factors

A number of message factors have been found to moderate effect sizes of campaigns and mediated interventions. Media campaigns that present new information are more successful than campaigns repackaging old information (Snyder & Hamilton, 2002). A meta-analysis of online social marketing interventions on topics, such as weight loss, mammogram screening, or smoking cessation, found larger effects for the health interventions employing the following message strategies: tailoring or feedback on performance, source similarity to the targets, information on the consequences of behavior, goal setting, action planning, normative information about others' behavior, arranging for social support, behavioral contracts, self-monitoring of behavioral outcomes, time management, self-talk prompts, rewards for successful behavior, and those focusing on knowledge, norms, and consequences (Cugelman, Thelwall, & Dawes, 2010).

Meta-analyses of interpersonal interventions with some use of media and laboratory studies offer some suggestions as to which message factors might be most beneficial. A meta-analysis of HIV interventions found that messages about attitudes, expectancies, and behavioral skills were more successful than messages about the threat, norms, disease transmission, or disease prevention information; information about the mechanisms of HIV transmission was negatively related to condom use (Albarracin, McNatt, Klein, Ho, Mitchell, & Kumkale, 2003). Among Hispanics, messages emphasizing how to address barriers to condom use, changing peer norms, practicing condom use skills, problem-solving skills such as personal goal setting, and using the culturally appropriate concept of machismo were associated with greater behavioral impact (Herbst, Kay, Passin, Lyles, Drepaz, & Marin, 2006).

Fear appeals may work, but care should be taken in how resulting anxiety will be dealt with. Laboratory studies suggest that fear appeals have more of an impact on behavior if they are accompanied by specific messages about how to control the danger (Witte & Allen, 2000; see Yzer, Southwell, & Stephenson, Chapter 11) and even counseling and testing to relieve anxiety (Earl & Albarracin, 2007).

Additional message factors that need to be addressed by meta-analyses of media campaigns include branding (Evans, Blitstein, Hersey, Renaud, & Yaroch, 2008) and social support (Ammerman, Lindquist, Lohr, & Hersey, 2002). A meta-analysis of formal computer-mediated support groups for people with health problems (secondary prevention) found that the group format led to increased social support, decreased depression, increased quality of life, and increased self-efficacy to manage the condition (Rains & Young, 2009).

Target Group Factors

Tightly defining target groups and designing a media campaign specifically for each group seems to enhance the likelihood of success for HIV and safety campaigns (Snyder, Johnson, Huedo-Medina, LaCroix, Smoak, & Cistulli, 2009; Phillips et al., 2011). Among other types of interventions (e.g., counseling, small groups), targeting appears to be beneficial, too (Albarracin et al., 2003; Pomerleau, Lock, Knai, & McKee, 2005). Other analyses suggest that targeting ethnic minorities or people with lower socioeconomic statuses results in effect sizes at least as large as those for the general population (Feeley & Moon, 2005; Snyder, 2000). Conducting formative research (see Atkin & Freimuth, Chapter 4) was related to greater effect sizes for HIV interpersonal interventions that often included some media (Albarracin et al., 2003; Herbst et al., 2006). Unfortunately, formative research per se has not been tested in meta-analyses of media campaigns because it is typically not reported in evaluations even when it is done.

Environmental Factors

Several environmental factors have been shown to contribute to campaign success, including enforcement (reviewed above) and product distribution. When the behavior is dependent on people using a physical product (like condoms or bike helmets), then *distribution of the product* (presuming it is available or accessible) can contribute to campaign success, particularly among populations with fewer resources (Charania, Crepaz, Guenther-Gray, Henny, Liau, Willis et al., 2010; Snyder, Johnson et al., 2009). Other potentially important factors that have not been tested include the presence of antihealth messages and message clutter in the media environment.

Methodological Issues

In addition to intervention-specific factors mentioned above, the way an intervention is evaluated also affects the magnitude of effect sizes. One fundamental decision evaluators need to make is whether to assess the effects of self-reported exposure or whether to compare communities that have had a campaign to those that have not.

Partition-by-design studies assess the former by examining the effects of measured exposure on behavior (Shadish, Cook, & Campbell, 2002; see also Rice & Foote, Chapter 5, on engaged inputs). A meta-analysis of the methodological factors affecting media campaign effect sizes found that those using a one group partition-by-exposure design had the highest effect sizes $r = .12$, 95% CI (.09, .14) (Snyder, Hamilton et al., 2009). In contrast, studies utilizing pretest–posttest or comparison group (also known as nonequivalent control groups) designs used the group as the measure of exposure—those in the intervention group were considered exposed whether or not individuals were actually exposed. Other analyses showed that the campaign effects were greater when more of the sample was exposed to the campaign (Snyder & Hamilton, 2002). Thus, it should be expected that effects will be greater when, by measurement or design, a greater proportion of the intervention group is exposed to the campaign.

A number of methodological choices that evaluators made did not appear to impact the magnitude of campaign effects (Snyder, Hamilton, et al., 2009), such as research design. Results from one group of pretest–posttest studies, nonequivalent control group studies, and posttest only with nonequivalent control group studies were all similar, with effect sizes ranging from $r = .048$ to $.059$. Panel studies, in which the same people are studied over time, had similar effect sizes to cross-sectional studies in which different people are compared over time. Studies using a physiological measure, such as blood pressure, had a similar effect size as those using self-reported behaviors. The extent to which the intervention community differed at baseline from the control community did not have an impact on the average campaign effect size.

Other methodological issues did affect campaign impacts. The conditions of exposure to the campaign—whether or not research participants or communities were randomly assigned to condition and whether intervention communities were matched with comparison communities or participants self-selected to be exposed—matter. Self-selected samples have greater effect sizes than randomly selected samples (Snyder, Hamilton et al., 2009), which can bias results unless the goal is to reach those who are more motivated to participate rather than a general population. Media campaigns rarely have random assignment to condition at the individual level, but interventions using phone, computers, and other specific technologies sometimes use random assignment to condition in their evaluation studies.

The nature of the control or comparison group is also a very important consideration for evaluation design, meta-analyses, and comparative effect studies. Campaign effect sizes were lower if the comparison group improved over time, whether due to a different intervention, media spillover effects, or nationally improving (secular) trends (Snyder & Hamilton, 2002). In experimental designs, effect sizes can be much smaller if the control group receives some messages rather than none, so the message content should be reported to contextualize the effect sizes (de Bruin, Viechtbauer, Hospers, Schaalma, & Kok, 2009; Noar, Benac, & Harris, 2007).

The differences in methodologies may be extreme when comparing media campaigns to other types of interventions. In the terminology of public health, media campaign evaluations are often Phase 4 trials, measuring effectiveness under real-world conditions, while other types of interventions are often evaluated as Phase 3 trials, measuring the efficacy of an intervention under more controlled conditions (Greenwald

& Cullen, 1985). The former end up with variable rates of exposure, while the latter carefully control "dosage" of exposure and are far more likely to attain exposure levels close to 100% of the intervention group. We know that media campaign effects are greater when exposure to the campaign is greater, but many campaigns fall short of reaching even half the target population (Hornik, 2002; Snyder & Hamilton, 2002). With this in mind, media campaign evaluations should always report levels of exposure to campaign messages in the intervention and comparison communities. Evaluations should also relate difficulties in implementation to avoid a Type III error, concluding campaigns are ineffective when really they were not successfully implemented (Basch, Sliepcevich, & Gold, 1985). Program evaluation can be useful for understanding the real-world conditions affecting implementation (see Salmon & Murray-Johnson, Chapter 7, and Valente & Kwan, Chapter 6).

Evaluators also need to be concerned about participant attrition and incentives. The greater the attrition, the greater the effect size (Albarracin et al., 2003; Snyder, Hamilton, et al., 2009). Paying participants can also inflate effect sizes (Albarracin et al., 2003).

Another methodological concern is the timing of the evaluation relative to the campaign. Media intervention effects decay over time (Grilli, Ramsay, & Minozzi, 2009; Krebs, Prochaska, & Rossi, 2010; Lichtenstein, Glasgow, Lando, Ossip-Klein, & Boles, 1996; Snyder et al., 2008; Vidanapathirana, Abramson, Forbes, & Fairley, 2005; Whittaker, Borland, Bullen, Lin, McRobbie, Rodgers, 2009). The longer the gap in measurement from the end of the campaign to the evaluation, the smaller the average campaign effect size.

COMPARING MEDIA CAMPAIGNS TO OTHER APPROACHES

Meta-analyses were available for media campaigns and other mediated interventions for five of the health behavior domains included in a recent meta-meta-analysis of interpersonal interventions that do not use media (Johnson, Scott-Sheldon, & Carey, 2010): alcohol use, smoking, HIV/STD prevention, mammography screening, and nutrition (much more in-depth analyses for each behavior are available from the authors). Based on the literature in each health domain, we were able to break out a number of different intervention approaches to compare to media campaigns. When feasible, we partitioned interventions based on the channel—such as print, computer, letters, phone, and interpersonal (nonmediated). Tailored interventions, which use individual assessments to select appropriate messages, appeared in the literature in several health domains and are reported separately. We also noted when meta-analyses of interpersonal interventions reported on a specific approach, such as counseling, school-based, or workplace-based communication, or were combined with either small media or mass media. Meta-analyses in Johnson and colleagues (2010) were omitted if they did not meet the inclusion criteria.

Alcohol Use

Alcohol interventions often target youth and adults to decrease the quantity and frequency of drinking. Media campaigns aimed at adults were slightly more successful

$r = 0.11$, 95% CI (0.08, 0.15) than those targeting youth $r = 0.07$, 95% CI (0.04, 0.10). Media campaigns for adults have similar effect sizes to print-based interventions $r = 0.12$, 95% CI (0.08, 0.15) and computer-based interventions $r = 0.10$, 95% CI (0.08, 0.12), both of which typically use tailored messages. Many universities, for example, require incoming students to complete a tailored alcohol program online, such as Alcohol 101. Interpersonal interventions aimed at lessening adult drinking $r = 0.19$, 95% CI (0.17, 0.22) were more effective than campaigns, print-delivered interventions, or computer-based interventions. In fact, the average effect sizes for interpersonal interventions were higher for alcohol than for other health topics. Brief interpersonal interventions on alcohol (Moyer, Finney, Swearingen, & Vergun, 2002) are similar in effectiveness to adult media campaigns, print, and computer interventions.

Smoking Prevention and Cessation

The addictive nature of smoking is a tremendous challenge for smoking cessation interventions. Adult smoking cessation media campaigns have a weak track record, $r = 0.03$, 95% CI (0.02, 0.04), and perhaps media campaigns may be better suited to motivating quit attempts and driving people to interpersonal or tailored smoking cessation programs rather than supporting the lengthy quit process. Mobile phone interventions have great promise, although there were a limited number of studies represented in the meta-analysis literature to date $r = 0.24$, 95% CI (0.19, 0.30). Phone (not mobile), $r = 0.08$, 95% CI (0.07, 0.09), computer-based interventions, $r = 0.07$, 95% CI (0.06, 0.9), and interpersonal interventions, $r = 0.12$, 95% CI (0.09, 0.14) were more successful in promoting adult smoking cessation than media campaigns.

More evidence is needed on the impact of smoking cessation efforts geared toward youth. Web-based interventions appear to be about as successful for youth, $r = 0.09$, 95% CI (0.02, 0.17), as phone and computer interventions have been for adults. The literature suggests that complex interventions using multiple strategies, including motivational approaches may work with youth (Grimshaw & Stanton 2010).

For youth smoking prevention, media campaigns were less successful, $r = 0.05$, 95% CI (0.04, 0.05), than interpersonal interventions, $r = 0.09$, 95% CI (0.08, 0.10). However, it is not known whether ongoing smoking prevention campaigns enhance the effectiveness of interpersonal interventions.

HIV/STD Prevention

Media campaigns for HIV/STD prevention promoting condom use have a higher average effect size than campaigns for other topics, $r = 0.11$, 95% CI (0.10, 0.12). Interpersonal interventions have a much smaller effect size than other approaches, $r = 0.04$, 95% CI (0.04, 0.05). Adding small media such as videos, posters, and brochures to interpersonal interventions greatly increased the average effect size, $r = 0.15$, 95% CI (0.13, 0.16). In fact, the effect size was similar to that of combining interpersonal interventions with large media campaigns $r = 0.14$, 95% CI (0.13, 0.15). Tailored interventions in this domain were the most effective approach, $r = 0.17$, 95% CI (0.14, 0.21), although the confidence intervals show that the effect sizes were close to media campaigns plus interpersonal interventions and interpersonal interventions plus small media. HIV campaigns in less-developed nations were more effective than HIV campaigns in more developed nations (see Snyder, Johnson et al., 2009).

Mammography Screenings

The average effect size for media campaigns promoting mammography screenings was $r = 0.03$, 95% CI (0.00, 0.06), which was lower than that for other types of interventions. Tailored interventions, $r = 0.06$, 95% CI (0.04, 0.07), were slightly more effective than media campaigns, and interpersonal interventions, $r = 0.10$, 95% CI (0.08, 0.01), were slightly more effective than tailored interventions. Much greater effect was shown for interventions that used the phone, $r = 0.21$, 95% CI (0.19, 0.23), and those that used invitation and reminder letters, $r = 0.19$, 95% CI (0.17, 0.22) (see Page, Morrell, Chiu, Taylor, & Tewson, 2006). The results suggest that it would be valuable to test different combinations of approaches, such as using media campaigns to drive people to tailored websites and using phone or letter reminders once contact information is obtained through the web or through other records.

Nutrition

Nutrition behaviors are often a focus of obesity, heart disease, diabetes, osteoporosis, and cancer prevention efforts. In this literature, there was no analysis of media campaign effects, but there was one that analyzed mediated interventions (both media campaigns and other interventions that used media; Snyder, LaPierre, & Maloney, 2008). The average effect size for mediated interventions promoting decreased fat consumption among adults was high, $r = 0.20$, 95% CI (0.19, 0.21), and higher than either tailored interventions, $r = 0.07$, 95% CI (0.06, 0.08), or interpersonal interventions, $r = 0.02$, 95% CI (0.01, 0.03). Mediated interventions for adults promoting fruit and vegetable consumption, $r = 0.13$, 95% CI (0.12, 0.14), were also stronger than tailored interventions, $r = 0.09$, 95% CI (0.07, 0.12). Tailored interventions were more effective if participants were assessed more than once and messages were appropriately updated (Krebs et al., 2010).

For youth, the average effect sizes for mediated interventions for both fat consumption, $r = 0.03$, 95% CI (0.0, 0.06), and fruit and vegetable consumption, $r = 0.05$, 95% CI (0.02, 0.08), were lower than they were for adults. A meta-analysis of school-based, interpersonal interventions that did not specify the nutrition behaviors had a higher average effect size, $r = 0.12$, 95% CI (0.08, 0.16), than mediated interventions for youth. Recent meta-analyses suggest that all body mass index (BMI) reduction interventions aimed at children—mediated, school-based, and other interpersonal approaches—have a difficult time finding effects (Gonzalez-Suarez, Worley, Grimmer-Somers, & Dones, 2009; Stice, Shaw, & Marti, 2006; Snyder et al., 2006).

Conclusions

One way to move a scientific area forward is to be clear about the record—where the research gaps are and what needs to be done methodologically in the future. It is heartening to note that media campaign effects have improved over time—at least in one area that has seen a concentrated effort in the past 20 years—HIV prevention (Snyder, Johnson et al., 2009). More recent HIV media campaigns were more likely to follow recommended design practices, including segmentation of the target population, use of behavioral theories, and greater campaign exposure (Noar, Palmgreen, Chabot, Dobransky, & Zimmerman, 2009). Interpersonal intervention meta-analyses also show that more recent studies and health domains with a longer literature have stronger effects (Johnson et al., 2010).

An important strategic issue for the field is predicting when it is effective to use media strategies and when not. The meta-meta-analysis presented in this chapter found that media campaigns or other mediated interventions were better than interpersonal interventions without media for HIV/STD prevention, mammography, and perhaps smoking. Combined media and interpersonal strategies worked better than media alone for youth substance abuse prevention (Derzon & Lipsey, 2002), HIV campaigns in developing countries (Snyder, Johnson et al., 2009), and organ donor campaigns (Feeley & Moon, 2005). In many domains—including smoking, alcohol, nutrition, and weight loss—media enhances the effectiveness of interpersonal interventions (Mullen, Simmons-Morton, Ramirez, Frankowski, Green, & Mains, 1997).

Given the relatively small differences in the magnitude of the effects between mediated and interpersonal approaches in some domains, decisions on which approach is more efficient may depend on *costs, time to bring to scale,* and *message fidelity.* One advantage of mass media, most Internet-based interventions, and many mobile applications is the scalability of the communication—the marginal costs to reach larger numbers of people are low. Most face-to-face and small group strategies, on the other hand, have very high personnel costs, rendering the marginal costs high. We look forward to more published accounts of the costs and public health benefits of different approaches in the future, rendered easier by the creation of easy-to-use tools to estimate the monetary value to society of health interventions (see http://www.nsmcentre.org.uk/resources/vfm for an example). Mediated interventions also may be brought to scale faster than interpersonal interventions, which are challenging to diffuse from controlled pilot studies to wide-scale adoption in clinical and community settings (Glasgow, Klesges, Dzewaltowski, Estabrooks, & Vogt, 2006). Message fidelity is often greater with mediated interventions—in which the message is largely controlled by campaign planners—than in interpersonal interventions, which may experience message drift over time.

When selecting media to use in an intervention, it is important to consider the match between the goals and needed content or messages, affordability of each medium, and the population's communication habits and preferences. The meta-meta-analysis results show the power of reminder and invitation messages via phone calls and letters to get people into services, such as health screenings. Mediated or face-to-face counseling seems to help many people learn about and stick to more effective strategies to quit smoking. In addition, entertainment formats (e.g., movies, dramas, video games) may be well suited for motivational messages and moving social norms. Other types of messages that are often suited to delivery via media are feedback on people's behaviors, reminders to individuals about their personal goals, and social support. Phones have been an overlooked medium—except in a few domains—until the recent interest in e-health in general (Murero & Rice, 2006) and mobile technologies (or *mhealth*) in particular. There are suggestive findings about the power of mobile media for adult smoking cessation, and we should learn more about its effectiveness as more evaluations of mobile media interventions are published. Given that communication effects decay and risk populations gain and lose members over time, sustainability of behavior change probably depends on periodic communication; which channels are better suited to sustained messaging with a given population may be contextually determined and should be examined in future studies.

The present meta-meta-analysis found that youth remain hard to affect in a number of domains, including nutrition, alcohol, and smoking. It may be that newer approaches using video games, social media, and mobile phones may have a greater impact than the interventions reported here. We may also need improved theoretical models of behavior development and change during childhood and adolescence in order to create more effective interventions.

Into the future, it would be good to model the conditions under which 1) particular media and formats 2) using messages based on which elements of theories are helpful 3) with what specific goals and 4) which people 5) over what time periods.

References

Albarracin, D., McNatt, P. S., Klein, C. T. F., Ho, R. M., Mitchell, A. L., & Kumkale, G. T. (2003). Persuasive communications to change actions: An analysis of behavioral and cognitive impact in HIV prevention. *Health Psychology, 22,* 166–177.

Ammerman, A. S., Lindquist, C. H., Lohr, K. N., & Hersey, J. (2002). The efficacy of behavioral interventions to modify dietary fat and fruit and vegetable intake: A review of the evidence. *Preventive Medicine, 35,* 25–41.

Basch, E. E., Sliepcevich, E. M., & Gold, R. S. (1985). Avoiding Type III errors in health education program evaluations. *Health Education Quarterly, 12,* 315–331.

Borenstein, M., Hedges, L., Higgins, J., & Rothstein, H. (2005). Comprehensive Meta-Analysis (Version 2). [Computer software]. Englewood, NJ: Biostat.

Borenstein, M., Hedges, L., & Rothstein, H. (2007). *Meta-analysis: Fixed effects vs. random effects.* Meta-analysis.com. Retrieved August 15, 2011, from http://www.sciencedownload.net/demodownload/Fixed%20effect%20vs.%20random%20effects.pdf

Charania, M. R., Crepaz, N., Guenther-Gray, C., Henny, K., Liau, A., Willis, L. A., & Lyles, C. M. (2010). Efficacy of structural-level condom distribution interventions: A meta-analysis of U.S. and international studies, 1998–2007. *AIDS and Behavior, 15,* 1283–1297.

Cugelman, B., Thelwall, M., & Dawes, P. (2010). Online interventions for social marketing health behaviour change campaigns: A meta-analysis of psychological architectures and adherence factors. *Journal of Medical Internet Research.* Retrieved August 15, 2011, from http://dx.doi.org/10.2196/jmir.1367

de Bruin, M., Viechtbauer, W., Hospers, H. J., Schaalma, H. P., & Kok, G. (2009). Standard care quality determines treatment outcomes in control groups of HAART-adherence intervention studies: Implications for the interpretation and comparison of intervention effects. *Health Psychology, 28,* 668–674.

Derzon, J. H., & Lipsey, M. W. (2002). A meta-analysis of the effectiveness of mass-communication for changing substance-use knowledge, attitudes, and behavior. In W. D. Crano & M. Burgoon (Eds.), *Mass media and drug prevention: Classic and contemporary theories and research* (pp. 231–258). Mahwah, NJ: Lawrence Erlbaum.

Earl, A., & Albarracin, D. (2007). Nature, decay, and spiraling of the effects of fear-inducing arguments and HIV counseling and testing: A meta-analysis of the short- and long-term outcomes of HIV prevention interventions. *Health Psychology, 26,* 496–506.

Evans, W. D., Blitstein, J., Hersey, J. C., Renaud, J., & Yaroch, A. L. (2008). Systematic review of public health branding. *Journal of Communication, 13,* 721–741.

Feeley, T. H., & Moon, S. (2005). A meta-analytic review of communication campaigns to promote organ donation. *Communication Reports, 22,* 63–73.

Freudenberg, N., Bradley, S. P., Serrano, M. (2009). Public health campaigns to change industry practices that damage health: An analysis of 12 case studies. *Health Education & Behavior, 36,* 230–249.

Glasgow, R. E., Klesges, L. M., Dzewaltowski, D. A., Estabrooks, P. A., & Vogt, T. M. (2006). Evaluating the overall impact of health promotion programs: Using the RE-AIM Framework to form summary measures for decision making involving complex issues. *Health Education Research, 21,* 688–694.

Greenwald, P., & Cullen, J. W. (1985). The new emphasis in cancer control. *Journal of National Cancer Institute, 74,* 543–551.

Grimshaw, G., & Stanton A. (2010). Tobacco cessation interventions for young people. *Cochrane Database of Systematic Reviews, 4,* Article CD003289. Retrieved August 15, 2011, from http://www.thecochranelibrary.com/userfiles/ccoch/file/World%20No%20Tobacco%20Day/CD003289.pdf

Gonzalez-Suarez, C., Worley, A., Grimmer-Somers, K., & Dones, V. (2009). School-based interventions on childhood obesity: A meta-analysis. *American Journal of Preventive Medicine, 37,* 418–427.

Grilli, R., Ramsay, C., & Minozzi, S. (2009). Mass media interventions: Effects on health services utilisation. *Cochrane Database of Systematic Reviews, 1,* Article CD000389. Retrieved August 15, 2011, from http://www2.cochrane.org/reviews/en/ab000389.html

Herbst, J. H., Kay, L. S., Passin, W. F., Lyles, C. M., Crepaz, N., & Marin, B. V. (2006). A systematic review and meta-analysis of behavioral interventions to reduce HIV risk behaviors of Hispanics in the United States and Puerto Rico. *AIDS Behavior, 11,* 25–47.

Hornik, R. (Ed.). (2002). *Public health communication: Evidence for behavior change.* Hillside, NJ: Lawrence Erlbaum.

Johnson, B. T., Scott-Sheldon, L. A. J., & Carey, M. P. (2010). A meta-synthesis of health behavior change meta-analyses. *American Journal of Public Health, 100,* 2193–2198.

Johnson, B. T., Scott-Sheldon, L. A. J., Snyder, L. B., Noar, S. M., & Huedo-Medina, T. (2008). Contemporary approaches to meta-analysis of communication research. In Hayes, A., Slater, M. D., & Snyder, L. B. (Eds.), *The SAGE sourcebook of advanced data analysis methods for communication research* (pp. 311–348). Thousand Oaks, CA: Sage.

Krebs, P., Prochaska, J. O., & Rossi, J. S. (2010). A meta-analysis of computer-tailored interventions for health behavior change. *Preventive Medicine, 51,* 214–221.

Lichtenstein, E., Glasgow, R. E., Lando, H. A., Ossip-Klein, D. J., & Boles, S. M. (1996). Telephone and counseling for smoking cessation: Rationales and meta-analytic review of evidence. *Health Education Research, 11,* 243–257.

Lipsey, M. W., & Wilson, D. B. (2001). *Practical meta-analysis.* Thousand Oaks, CA: Sage.

Moyer, A., Finney, J. W., Swearingen, C. E., & Vergun, P. (2002). Brief interventions for alcohol problems: A meta-analytic review of controlled investigations in treatment-seeking and non-treatment-seeking populations. *Addiction, 97,* 279–292.

Mullen, P. D., Simmons-Morton, D. G., Ramirez, G., Frankowski, R. F., Green, L. W., & Mains, D. A. (1997). A meta-analysis of trials evaluation patient education and counseling for three groups of preventive health behaviors. *Patient Education and Counseling, 32,* 157–173.

Murero, M., & Rice, R. E. (2006). E-health research. In M. Murero & R. E. Rice (Eds.), *The Internet and health care: Theory, research and practice* (pp. 3–26). Mahwah, NJ: Lawrence Erlbaum.

Noar, S. M., Benac, C., N., & Harris, M. S. (2007). Does tailoring matter? Meta-analytic review of tailored print health behavior change interventions. *Psychological Bulletin, 133,* 673–693.

Noar, S. M., Palmgreen, P., Chabot, M., Dobransky, N., & Zimmerman, R., S. (2009). A 10-year systematic review of HIV/AIDS mass communication campaigns: Have we made progress? *Journal of Health Communication, 14,* 15–42.

Page, A., Morrell, S., Chiu, C., Taylor, R., & Tewson, R. (2006). Recruitment to mammography screening: A randomized trial and meta-analysis of invitation letters and telephone calls. *Australian and New Zealand Journal of Public Health, 30,* 111–118.

Phillips, R. O., Ulleberg, P., & Vaa, T. (2011). Meta-analysis of the effect of road safety campaigns on accidents. *Accident Analysis and Prevention, 43,* 1204–1218.

Pomerleau, J., Lock, K., Knai, C., & McKee, M. (2005). Interventions designed to increase adult fruit and vegetable intake can be effective: A systematic review of the literature. *Journal of Nutrition, 135,* 2486–2495.

Rains, S. A., & Young, V. (2009). A meta-analysis of research on formal computer-mediated support groups: Examining group characteristics and health outcomes. *Human Communication Research, 35,* 309–336.

Shadish, W. R., Cook, T. D., & Campbell, D. T. (2002). *Experimental and quasi-experimental designs for generalized causal inference.* New York: Houghton Mifflin.

Snyder, L. B. (2000). *Evidence of the effectiveness of communication interventions across diverse populations.* (Report submitted to the Committee on Communications for Behavior Change in the 21st Century: Improving the Health of Diverse Populations, Institute of Medicine). Washington, DC: National Academy of Sciences.

Snyder, L. B. (2001). How effective are mediated health campaigns? In R. Rice & C. Atkin (Ed.). *Public communication campaigns* (3rd ed., pp. 181–190). Thousand Oaks, CA: Sage.

Snyder, L. B., & Hamilton, M. A. (2002). Meta-analysis of U.S. health campaign effects on behavior: Emphasize enforcement, exposure, and new information, and beware the secular trend. In R. Hornik (Ed.). *Public health communication: Evidence for behavior change* (pp. 357–383). Hillsdale, NJ: Lawrence Erlbaum.

Snyder, L. B., Hamilton, M. A., & Huedo-Medina, T. (2009). Does evaluation design impact communication campaign effect size? A meta-analysis. *Communication Methods and Measures, 3,* 84–104.

Snyder, L. B., Hamilton, M. A., Mitchell, E. W., Kiwanuka-Tondo, J., Fleming-Milici, F., & Proctor, D. (2004). A meta-analysis of the effect of mediated health communication campaigns on behavior change in the United States. *Journal of Health Communication, 9*(Suppl. 1), 71–96.

Snyder, L. B., Johnson, B., Huedo-Medina, T., LaCroix, J. M., Smoak, N. D., & Cistulli, M. (2009, May). *Effectiveness of media interventions to prevent HIV, 1986–2006: A meta-analysis.* Poster presented at the annual meeting of the Society for Behavioral Research, Montreal, Canada.

Snyder, L. B., Lapierre, M. A., & Maloney, E. K. (2006, November). *Using mass media to improve nutrition: A meta-analytic examination of campaigns and interventions.* Paper presented at the annual meeting of the American Public Health Association, Boston, MA.

Snyder, L. B., Li, S., Huedo-Medina, T., Noar, S. M., Kotz, J., D'Alessandro, N., Polonsky, M., & Fuhrel-Forbis, A. (2008). Tailored interventions are more effective than traditional interventions over time: A meta-analysis. Paper presented at the National Conference on Health Communication, Marketing, and Media, Atlanta, GA.

Stice, E., Shaw, H., & Marti, C. N. (2006). A meta-analytic review of obesity prevention programs for children and adolescents: The skinny on interventions that work. *Psychological Bulletin, 132,* 667–691.

Vidanapathirana, J., Abramson, M. J., Forbes, A., & Fairley, C. (2005). Mass media interventions for promoting HIV testing. *Cochrane Database of Systematic Reviews, 3.* Article CD004775. Retrieved August 15, 2011, from http://www2.cochrane.org/reviews/en/ab004775.html

Whittaker, R., Borland, R., Bullen, C., Lin, R. B., McRobbie, H., & Rodgers, A. (2009). Mobile phone-based interventions for smoking cessation. *Cochrane Database of Systematic Reviews, 4,* Article CD006611. Retrieved August 15, 2011, from http://www2.cochrane.org/reviews/en/ab006611.html

Witte, K., & Allen, M. (2000). A meta-analysis of fear appeals: Implications for effective public health campaigns. *Health Education and Behavior, 27,* 591–615.

PART III

Theory Foundations

McGuire's Classic Input–Output Framework for Constructing Persuasive Messages

William J. McGuire

Editors' Note: The late William J. McGuire was a leading social psychologist who developed an interest in media effects, including public campaigns. His chapter in earlier editions of this book is more frequently cited than any other. Thus, we have adapted and updated the present version primarily based on McGuire (1989d), which provides much more elaboration, additional topics, and extensive references.

This chapter identifies promising input and output variables for use in persuasion campaigns based upon the input communication and output persuasion matrix (see Table 9.1). The first column reviews the input variables from which persuasive communications can be constructed, while the second discusses the mediational output behaviors that must be elicited to foster changed behavior (e.g., into adopting a more healthful lifestyle).

PROMISING INPUT TOPICS ON HOW COMMUNICATIONS CAN BE MADE MORE PERSUASIVE

The persuasive communication's promising input variables can conveniently be divided into five classes: source, message, channel, audience, and destination—that is, who says what, via which media, to whom, regarding what (Eagly & Chaiken, 1993; McGuire, 1985).

Source Variables That Increase Persuasive Impact

When choosing a source to deliver the influence message, designers of persuasion campaigns conventionally look for three obvious source characteristics: credibility, attractiveness, and power. These are conventionally assumed to enhance persuasive impact via three processes: *internalization, identification,* and *compliance,* respectively.

TABLE 9.1 The Communication and Persuasion Matrix: Input Communication Variables and Output Mediational Steps That Make Up the Process of Being Persuaded

Input Communication Factors	Output Persuasion Steps
1. Source (number, unanimity, demographics, attractiveness, credibility . . .)	1. Tuning in (exposure to the communication)
	2. Attending to the communication
2. Message (appeal, inclusion or omission, organization, style, repetitiveness . . .)	3. Liking it, maintaining interest in it
3. Channel (modality, directness, context . . .)	4. Comprehending its contents (learning what)
	5. Generating related cognitions
4. Receiver (demographics, ability, personality, lifestyle . . .)	6. Acquiring relevant skills (learning how)
5. Destination (immediacy or delay, prevention or cessation, direct or immunization . . .)	7. Agreeing with the communication's position (attitude change)
	8. Storing this new position in memory
	9. Retrieval of the new position from memory when relevant
	10. Decision to act on the basis of the retrieved position
	11. Acting on it
	12. Postaction cognitive integration of this behavior
	13. Proselytizing others to behave likewise

• Credibility derives from the source's perceived expertise and trustworthiness, that is, the source's appearing to know the facts on the issue and to be reporting them honestly. Credibility and trustworthiness take on somewhat different forms and implications when new media are involved (Metzger, Flanagin, Eyal, Lemus, & McCann, 2003). Perceived attractiveness (likeableness) derives from qualities like the source's pleasantness, beauty, familiarity, and similarity (see Hatfield & Sprecher, 1986, on perceived beauty). Perceived power is a positive function of the source's control over the listener's rewards and punishments, desire for the audience's compliance, and ability to monitor the extent of this compliance.

This conventional approach tends to yield valid but rather obvious hypotheses, such as that sources are more persuasive if the audience perceives them as honest or more similar to themselves. McGuire (McGuire, 1983, 1989b) develops more subtle combinations and interactions involving these source variables. For example, which informational source is most effective in changing health judgments depends on whether the communication is designed to induce a change on the likelihood or the desirability dimension. If we are trying to convince parents that they should have their children immunized, if we are arguing for the likelihood of the child's contracting the illness, it is more effective to communicate information from an outside source. However, if we are arguing for the undesirability of the threatening disease, it is more effective to elicit information from within the parent's own cognitive system (McGuire, W. J., & McGuire, C. V., 1991).

Source–audience similarity (such as age or ethnicity) tends to increase persuasive impact (McGuire, 1989d). Sidanius's (1993) Social Dominance Theory, Tajfel's (1982) Social Identity Theory, and Turner's Social Categorization Theory (Turner & Oakes, 1989) have implications regarding how the in-group versus out-group status of the source will affect persuasive impact (Abrams & Hogg, 1990; Sidanius, 1993).

Message Variables That Increase Persuasive Impact

Message variables constitute the most interesting and heavily investigated category of input factors, with subcategories including structure and type of arguments, type of appeals, message style, humor, repetition, and so on.

The Structure of Argument

Attitude structure assumes that attitudes are organized into interconnected systems so that a persuasive communication that deals explicitly with one issue is likely to have remote ramifications also on unmentioned but related issues. Related attitudes are affected to the extent that they are concurrently *salient*, suggesting that attitudes can be changed not only by presenting new information from an outside source but also by increasing the salience of information already within the audience's own belief system by means of a directed thinking task or by Socratic questioning (McGuire, 1960; McGuire & McGuire, 1991).

Types of Arguments

The ancients (Aristotle, Cicero, Quintilian) were highly interested in the comparative persuasive power of various types of arguments, but contemporary researchers have tended to neglect the topic. The empirical work so far has been confined largely to Aristotle's three types of proof—pathos, ethos, and logos (Edwards, 1990; Millar, & Millar, 1990). Progress has been made on a related issue, the relative merits of various compliance-gaining tactics (Cialdini, 2001).

Types of Appeals

McGuire (McGuire, 1989d) identified 16 types of human needs to which health persuasion campaigns can appeal. The 16 divide into four classes: *cognitive stability* (such as the need for consistency and hermeneutic or attributional needs), *cognitive growth* (such as the need for stimulation and for felt competence), *affective stability* (such as tension reduction and ego defense), and *affective growth* (such as affiliative and identity needs). Public health campaigns may be too narrow in using only appeals to the obvious needs (feeling of well-being, risk avoidance, etc.), when appeals to other motives (beauty, independence) may be more effective, at least in some high-risk groups.

Message-Style Variables

Another set of message variables rich in persuasive potential involves the style in which the persuasive material is communicated, for example, the message's clarity, forcefulness, literalness, or humorousness. Psychologists have studied forcefulness under the rubric of *vividness* (Taylor & Thompson, 1982). For example, arguing by factual examples versus abstract principles has had particularly rich implications (Reyes, Thompson, & Bower, 1980). Literal versus figurative language constitutes another style variable that deserves more investigation (McGuire, 2000).

Effects on Persuasion of Amount of Material

A number of variables having to do with quantitative aspects of persuasive communication are of considerable practical importance (e.g., length of commercials, number of showings). When a given audience is subjected to repetitions of an ad (even in varied form), diminishing returns set in quite early, by three to five repetitions (Calder & Sternthal, 1980), perhaps because, beyond the first few receptions, repetitive presentations of the ads tend to evoke increasing numbers of negative thoughts about the product (McCullough & Ostrom, 1974) or simple *wear out*. The elaboration–likelihood model (Petty & Cacioppo, 1986) indicates that repetition can, under certain conditions such as weak arguments, reduce persuasion.

Channel Variables That Increase Persuasive Impact

Media Use

Most persuasion campaigns are transmitted via the mass media (and increasingly through digital and online media—see Rice & Atkin, 2009) in the form of ads, PSAs, news, documentaries, or interview programs. Extensive commercial audience research identifies which target audiences prefer which media and which content at which times (Webster, 2005). For example, radio stations, cable channels, and social media followed by youth groups are likely to be more cost-effective than prime-time network television. Direct mail advertising addressed specifically to high-risk groups may deserve greater usage, as might word-of-mouth agitation through community groups, such as churches and workplaces, and through posters placed where members of high-risk groups meet.

Evidence for Intended Television Effects

McGuire (1986) reviewed evidence about proposed massive television effect and concluded that studies rarely show massive—or even substantial—effects, as can be illustrated in the effect of commercial advertising on purchasing behavior (or even on weaker criteria such as brand recognition or preference). Significant effects are sometimes found here, but the artificiality of these laboratory situations makes generalization to the natural world hazardous.

Evidence for Unintended Television Effects

The unintended persuasive effects of media content tend to involve material presented in the programs themselves, such as depiction of violence in programs affecting viewers' antisocial aggression. Laboratory studies yield an effect that often reaches the conventionally accepted levels of significance, at least in preangered viewers and with somewhat ambiguous measures of aggression (Comstock, 1982). In natural world studies, the effects tend to be rather small in size, accounting at most for only a few percent of the individual-difference variance in violence (Milavsky, Kessler, Stipp, & Rubens, 1982).

Arguments and Excuses for the Lack of Evidence of Effects

Five classes of excuses have been used to explain away the weakness of the evidence and to keep the faith in massive media effects (described and largely rejected by McGuire, 1986): 1) poor methodology, 2) accidental circumstances regarding media exposure, 3) emphasizing major effects obscures circumscribed effects, 4) effects are most likely on especially susceptible subgroups, or 5) they occur only indirectly (e.g., two-step flow theory, the agenda-setting hypothesis, the spiral of silence notion, the perception of what is normative in society, the "self-realizing prophesy" that the general belief in massive media effects, even if false, may produce its own truth).

Audience Variables That Affect Persuasive Impact

A persuasion campaign aimed at the general public should be able to influence all types of people, if necessary, including variant forms of the campaign to reach different high-risk subgroups who differ in susceptibility to various modes of influence.

A Mediational Theory of Susceptibility to Social Influence

McGuire's (1989a) general theory uses a half dozen postulates to predict and explain how people's individual differences in personality, abilities, and motivations affect their susceptibility to social influence by mass communication persuasion and conformity pressures, suggestion, and face-to-face discussion.

The first, *multiple mediator postulate*, asserts that how peoples' positions on individual-difference variables (e.g., their anxiety levels) will affect their ultimate behaviors (e.g., donating blood) will depend on how anxiety affects each of the 13 output mediators—attention, comprehension, agreement, and so on—shown in Table 9.1. Because each step is evoked only probabilistically by the preceding step, the ultimate payoff is a multiplication of probabilities well below 1.00, so that any one campaign will have only an attenuated impact. The second *compensatory principle* is that individual-difference variables, such as anxiety, tend to have opposite effects on different mediators. For example, anxiety would tend to lower persuasive impact by interfering with comprehension of the communication contents but would tend to increase persuasive impact by enhancing yielding to such arguments as they are comprehended.

A third, *nonmonotonic principle,* states that, because of this compensatory tendency, people with intermediate levels of anxiety (or any other individual-difference variable) will tend to be more influenceable than those very high or very low in anxiety. A fourth, *acute-chronic interaction principle,* calls attention to how variations in the level of fear arousal in the message will interact with the audience's chronic level of anxiety in affecting persuasive impact. For example, in a campaign to get parents to bring their preschoolers for immunizations, if the fear-arousing depiction of the dangers of noncompliance is raised in the persuasive message, this would tend to increase compliance in parents low in chronic anxiety but decrease compliance in parents whose chronic anxiety level is high.

A fifth, *situational weighting principle,* asserts that the parameters of the nonmonotonic relation between a personality variable such as anxiety and influenceability will vary across situations depending on the relative contributions to compliance made by each of the mediating steps. For example, because anxiety decreases influenceability by reducing comprehension, but increases influenceability by increasing agreement with whatever part of the message is comprehended, anxiety will increase susceptibility to a health campaign whose message is simple and decrease susceptibility to campaigns involving complex instructions.

A sixth, *confounded variable principle,* is that a person's chronic level on a characteristic such as anxiety will tend to become embedded in a syndrome of compensatory coping characteristics. For example, a person high in anxiety will tend to develop threat-avoiding coping habits that protect him or her from experiencing anxiety. Therefore, the campaign must be designed to take into account not only the effects of the personality characteristic of initial interest but also the effects of the other characteristics with which it will have become clustered. A seventh, *interaction* principle, is that any personal characteristic is likely to interact with other communication variables in its effect on influenceability. Thus, personal characteristics such as anxiety will interact with whether frightening or reassuring appeals are used in the message and whether it is being transmitted by face-to-face or mass media channels.

Special Target Groups

Public policy and epidemiological considerations make certain age, sex, and ethnic groups of special interest in one or another health campaigns. As people mature, their improving comprehension of persuasive messages makes them more susceptible to influence, but their decreasing tendency to agree with what they are told makes them less susceptible. It is also commonly assumed that, because more educated people have characteristics like being better informed, more critical, and more willing to maintain a deviant position, they will be less influenceable. However, education tends also to improve message comprehension, which tends to make better-educated audiences more persuadable.

Target Variables That Affect Persuasive Impact

Persuasive impact is affected by variables having to do with the kind of target attitudes or actions at which the campaign is aimed.

Beliefs Versus Attitudes Versus Behavior

Correlations between how a given communication affects knowledge about a topic, feeling regarding it, and behavior toward it tend to be modest (see McGuire, 1989c). There is some correlation among the three in that at any given time the person's information attitudes and behaviors tend to be positively correlated in regards to favorability to the topic at issue. Also, when a message produces a change in one, it tends to induce similar changes in the other two.

Persistence of Persuasive Impact

Both practitioners and basic researchers tend to assume that the attitude change induced by a persuasive communication is at a maximum immediately after the audience receives the message and then decays progressively as time passes. However, the slope and even direction of time curves vary greatly with diverse variables, such as source credibility, subtlety of argument, order of presentation, and channel (Cook & Flay, 1978; McGuire, 1985). Alternatively, persuasion effects may increase in the near term due to the discounting-cue sleeper effect, mutual postcommunication proselytizing, two-step flow, agenda-setting sensitization, the consistency reaction, reactance, and predispositional drift (McGuire, 1985; Pratkanis & Greenwald, 1985).

Inducing Resistance to Persuasion

Public health campaigns are usually designed to produce a change but sometimes are designed to confer resistance to persuasion, for example, campaigns to prepare children to resist peer pressure to smoke or do drugs (McGuire, 1964, 1985).

One approach to producing resistance to persuasion is to *use prior commitment,* such as having the person express publicly (or even just think privately about) his or her initial position. A second approach is to induce resistant motivational states, such as preangering the person or raising self-esteem or anxiety level. A third approach is to confer resistance by anchoring the person's initial stand on a given issue to the person's other beliefs or values or to esteemed reference groups. A fourth immunizing approach is to educate people in critical thinking, recognizing persuasion attempts, detecting weaknesses in the attacking arguments, and summoning up counterarguments. A fifth means of conferring resistance to persuasion is to show the person unyielding (resistant) models (Milgram, 1974). A sixth procedure is the inoculation approach, that is, preexposing the believer to weakened belief-threatening material, which stimulates belief defenses without overcoming them (McGuire, 1964).

PROMISING OUTPUT TOPICS ON HOW PERSUASION WORKS

The output side of the communication–persuasion matrix can be usefully represented as a series of sequential, mediating behavioral steps that persuasive communications tend to evoke and that culminate in the desired output behavior (e.g., adopting the more healthful lifestyles being urged in a health campaign) (see Table 9.1). The following sections summarize research on how people use the media, processes that mediate persuasive impact, and where attitudes fit in the persuasion process.

Insights Into How People Use the Media

[handwritten margin notes: in the show) alone]

Because a high percentage of watchers switches television channels at the beginning of a commercial break, PSAs, now shown in the commercial break, might more effectively be incorporated in the program itself (McGuire, 1984; Piotrow, Rimon, Winnard et al., 1990).

There is some evidence that people are more persuaded when exposed to a given message when they are alone (e.g., watching daytime soap operas and late-night movies) rather than with other people present (e.g., with prime-time viewing) (Keating & Latané, 1976), which may favor impacts of PSAs that are typically shown at hours that attract the sole viewer.

Mediators of the Persuasive Impact

Four research areas illustrate the range of mediator issues (multiple paths and mediating substeps) currently receiving deserved attention.

Multiple Paths to Persuasion

Useful proposals of alternative routes to persuasion include Chaiken's (1980) distinction between systematic versus heuristic processing and Petty and Cacioppo's (1986) proposed central versus peripheral paths (Chaiken, 1980). An audience uses the central route, involving a complex chain of behaviors such as those shown in Table 9.1, to the extent that the communication situation is important and deserving of careful scrutiny. Peripheral routes, involving much-abbreviated paths, are used in the more typical low-involvement situations. Petty and Cacioppo (1986) have confirmed that certain variables (such as argument strength) are important in central processing while other variables (such as source credibility) are more important in peripherally-processed persuasion.

Sequences of the Mediating Processes

The traditional, commonsensical output sequence shown in Table 9.1 is usually taken for granted by persuasion practitioners, such as those using the standard Health Belief Model. However, several reversals of the commonsense relations among the steps are likely. In perceptual distortion or selective exposure, Step 7 (attitude) precedes Step 4 (comprehension) or Step 2 (attending). The person may react affectively to the message content before he or she can report what that content is, reversing Step 3 and Step 4. This poses a challenge to health campaigns (e.g., against drug abuse) in that high-risk members of the public would be able to tune out the unpleasant advice before they have processed what the advice is.

Communication Recall as a Mediator of Persuasion

The two mediating processes that researchers and practitioners in marketing and advertising most often use to evaluate communications and predict their ultimate persuasive impact on buying behavior are recall and liking for the communication (Steps 2, 3, 4, and 9) rather than by the payoff (Step 11) of actually buying the advertised product (Beattie & Mitchell, 1985). A useful modification of the conventional Step 4 (comprehension) mediator deriving from the *cognitive responses* approach has served as a corrective to the classical *information processing* model of persuasion. The person may be persuaded, not simply by learning the new information presented in the message from the external source, but also by manipulating the salience of information already in the person's belief system (McGuire & McGuire, 1991).

Communication Liking as a Mediator of Persuasion

Ad liking (Step 3) is used almost as often as ad recall (Step 9) as an index of persuasive effectiveness in the advertising and marketing industry but is even more removed from taking action (Step 11). Any relation between enhanced liking and later action could be due to better attention to and learning of the message content, or to increased source attractiveness, which in turn leads to persuasive impact, or to a positive mood effect such that the humor or other inputs make the recipient more mellow and accepting.

The Decision Process Evoked by Persuasive Communications

This section reviews four topics about how the decision to comply is evoked by the persuasive communication and how it is related to the prior and subsequent persuasion steps listed in Table 9.1.

Cognitive Algebra in Making Judgments

Most early attitude theorists as well as advertising and marketing practitioners, took for granted the Expectancy × Value Rational–Choice Model (Feather, 1982). In its most common variant, the model assumes that a person, in choosing among health alternatives (e.g., a parent deciding what food to serve), generates (or abstracts from a persuasive message) a list of costs and benefits of each alternative food, then attaches a scale value to each cost or benefit, and then multiplies this value by the probability that a given food will lead to that cost or benefit. The person then sums (or averages) these algebraic products for each food and serves the food with the highest score (see Anderson, 1981). More realistically, the person may use some quick-and-dirty (but effective) approximation, such as using a sufficing rather than optimizing criterion, or using only the most salient costs or benefits, or using only the benefits or even related nonhealth benefits.

Shortcut Heuristics in Making Decisions

It seems likely that humans have developed heuristic biases that lead easily to behavioral choices similar to the choices that would have been yielded by an effortful consideration of the full information (Caverni, Fabre, & Gonzalez, 1990; McGuire & McGuire, 1991; Sherman & Corty, 1984; Tversky & Kahneman, 1974). There tends to be a positivity bias such that the public is more influenced by messages stressing health benefits gained than sickness dangers avoided (McGuire & McGuire, 1991). The *representativeness* heuristic leads people to misperceive the health danger of various behaviors unless considerations like base rates, regression, and sample size are vigorously stressed in the message. The *availability* prototype and *simulation* heuristics indicate that persuasive communication should take into account the ease with which people can bring to mind instances of the various alternatives. There is also the *anchoring-and-adjusting* heuristic such that people tend to begin with some reference value (which the health communicator should be aware of) and adjust it (perhaps only marginally) until the final judgment is reached. The operation of such oversimplifying heuristics is likely to be particularly pronounced in high-risk and high-uncertainty situations (Covello, von Winterfeldt, & Slovic, 1990), which often characterize decision making in matters of health.

Remote Ramifications of Persuasive Communications

Persuasive communications may have effects on topics and dimensions beyond those explicitly mentioned in the message (McGuire & McGuire, 1991; McGuire, 1991). For example, a message that is successful in its explicit urging to get one's children immunized may generalize to other topics (e.g., to taking one's children for dental checkups) and to other dimensions (e.g., proselytizing other parents to get their children immunized). Another asymmetry is that generalization tends to occur more vertically to antecedents and consequences of the explicit topic rather than to parallel topics.

The Decision Model and Supplementary Processes

A widely used broader model is the theory of reasoned action (Fishbein & Ajzen, 1975; and its descendent, the Theory of Planned Behavior, Ajzen, 1991) at whose core is the traditional additive Expectancy × Value Model. With regard to further processes hypothesized to contribute to evoking the Step 11 behavior, Fishbein's model adds a *subjective norm* term that behavior (or behavioral intentions) depends not only on one's belief about the consequences of the behavior but also on one's perception of how one's valued reference groups feel about the behavior. A health message to induce parents to get their children immunized should mention not only favorable consequences of immunization but also that the parents' valued reference groups favor getting children immunized. Another type of elaboration is to trace out alternative paths by which the attitudinal and decision processes relate to the other factors, for example, that beliefs can affect decisions via routes other than attitudes and that attitudes may affect behavior via paths other than behavioral intention (Bagozzi, 1982).

SOME BASIC IMPLICATIONS

The input analysis into source, message, channel, audience, and target variables, each with subdivisions, provides a resource checklist that allows campaign designers to review a wide range of communication variables that can be added or emphasized. Analyzing the output into successive mediational steps (exposure, attention, liking, etc.) provides the campaign designer with a diagnostic checklist that can be used to evaluate how capable a proposed campaign is to evoke each of the dependent-variable mediational steps leading to persuasion and to identify which steps need bolstering. The matrix also heightens attention to the interaction between input and output variables, the multiplicative nature of the persuasion process, and the possibility of opposing effects of communication variables by different mediating steps. McGuire (1985) provides a fuller discussion of the many uses of the communication and persuasion matrix and of its shortcomings and alternatives for constructing persuasion campaigns.

References

Abrams, D., & Hogg, M. A. (1990). Social identification, self-categorization, and social influence. In W. Stroebe & M. Hewstone (Eds.), *European Review of Social Psychology* (Vol. 1, pp. 195–228). London: Wiley.

Ajzen, K. (1991). The theory of planned behavior. *Organizational Behavior and Human Decision Processes, 50,* 179–211.

Anderson, N. H. (1981). *Foundations of information integration theory.* New York: Academic Press.

Bagozzi, R. P. (1982). A field investigation of causal relations among cognitions, affect, intentions, and behavior. *Journal of Marketing Research, 19,* 562–584.

Beattie, A. E., & Mitchell, A. A. (1985). The relationship between advertising recall and persuasion: An experimental investigation. In L. F. Alwitt & A. A. Mitchell (Eds.), *Psychological processes and advertising effects: Theory, research, and application* (pp. 129–155). Hillsdale, NJ: Lawrence Erlbaum.

Calder, B. J., & Sternthal, B. (1980). Television commercial wear-out: An information-processing view. *Journal of Marketing Research, 17,* 173–186.

Caverni, J. P., Fabre, J. M., & Gonzalez, M. (Eds.). (1990). *Cognitive biases.* Amsterdam: Elsevier.

Chaiken, S. (1980). Heuristic versus systematic information processing and the use of source versus message cues in persuasion. *Journal of Personality and Social Psychology, 39,* 752–766.

Cialdini, R. B. (2001). *Influence: Science and practice.* Needham Heights, MA: Allyn & Bacon.

Comstock, G. (1982). Violence in television content: An overview. In D. Pearl, L. Bouthilet, & J. Lazar (Eds.), *Television and behavior: Ten years of scientific progress and implications for the eighties* (Vol. 2, pp. 108–125). Washington, DC: U.S. Government Printing Office.

Cook, T. D., & Flay, B. R. (1978). The persistence of experimentally induced attitude change. In L. Berkowitz (Ed.), *Advances in experimental social psychology* (pp. 1–57). New York: Academic Press.

Covello, V. T., von Winterfeldt, D., & Slovic, P. (1990). *Risk communication: Research and action.* Cambridge, UK: Cambridge University Press.

Eagly, A. H., & Chaiken, S. (1993). *The psychology of attitudes.* San Diego, CA: Harcourt Brace Jovanovich.

Edwards, K. (1990). The interplay of affect and cognition in attitude formation and change. *Journal of Personality and Social Psychology, 59,* 202–216.

Feather, N. T. (Ed.). (1982). *Expectations and actions: Expectancy-value models in psychology.* Hillsdale, NJ: Lawrence Erlbaum.

Fishbein, M., & Ajzen, I. (1975). *Belief, attitude, intention, and behavior.* Reading, MA: Addison-Wesley.

Hatfield, E., & Sprecher, S. (1986). *Mirror, mirror: The importance of looks in everyday life.* Albany: State University of New York at Albany Press.

Keating, J. P., & Latané, B. (1976). Politicians on TV: The image is the message. *Journal of Social Issues, 32*(4), 116–132.

McCullough, J. L., & Ostrom, T. M. (1974). Repetition of highly similar messages and attitude change. *Journal of Applied Psychology, 59,* 395–397.

McGuire, W. J. (1960). A syullogistic analysis of cognitive relationships. In M. J. Rosenberg & C. I. Hovland (Eds.), *Attitude organization and change* (pp. 65–111). New Haven, CT: Yale University Press.

McGuire, W. J. (1964). Inducing resistance to persuasion. In L. Berkowitz (Ed.). *Advances in experimental social psychology* (Vol. 1, pp. 191–229). New York: Academic Press.

McGuire, W. J. (1983). A contextualist theory of knowledge: Its implications for innovation and reform in psychological research. In L. Berkowitz (Ed.), *Advances in experimental social psychology* (Vol. 16, pp. 1–47). New York: Academic Press.

McGuire, W. J. (1984). Public communication as a strategy for inducing health-promoting behavior change. *Preventive Medicine, 13,* 299–319.

McGuire, W. J. (1985). Attitudes and attitude change. In G. Lindzey & E. Aronson (Eds.), *Handbook of social psychology* (3rd ed., Vol. 2, pp. 233–346). New York: Random House.

McGuire, W. J. (1986). The myth of massive media impact: Savaging and salvagings. In G. Comstock (Ed.), *Public communication and behavior* (Vol. 1, pp. 173–257). New York: Academic Press.

McGuire, W. J. (1989a). A mediational theory of susceptibility to social influence. In V. Gheorghiu, P. Netter, H. J. Eysenck, & R. Rosenthal (Eds.), *Suggestibility: Theory and research* (pp. 305–322). Heidelberg, Germany: Springer-Verlag.

McGuire, W. J. (1989b). A perspectivist approach to the strategic planning of programmatic scientific research. In B. Gholson, W. R. Shadish, Jr., R. A. Neimeyer, & A. C. Houts (Eds.), *The psychology of science: Contributions to metascience* (pp. 214–245). New York: Cambridge University Press.

McGuire, W. J. (1989c). The structure of individual attitudes and attitude systems. In A. R. Pratkanis, S. J. Breckler, & A. G. Greenwald (Eds.), *Attitude structure and function* (pp. 37–69). Hillsdale, NJ: Lawrence Erlbaum.

McGuire, W. J. (1989d). Theoretical foundations of campaigns. In R. E. Rice & C. K. Atkin (Eds.), *Public communication campaigns* (2nd ed., pp. 43–65). Newbury Park, CA: Sage.

McGuire, W. J. (2000). Standing on the shoulders of ancients: Consumer research, persuasion, and figurative language. *Journal of Consumer Research, 27,* 1–23.

McGuire, W. J., & McGuire, C. V. (1991). The content, structure, and operation of thought systems. In R. S. Wyer, Jr., & T. K. Srull (Eds.), *Advances in social cognition* (Vol. 4., pp. 1–78). Hillsdale, NJ: Lawrence Erlbaum.

Metzger, M., Flanagin, A., Eyal, K., Lemus, D., & McCann, R. (2003). Credibility for the 21st century: Integrating perspectives on source, message, and media credibility in the contemporary media environment. In P. Kalbfleisch (Ed.), *Communication yearbook 27* (pp. 293–335). Mahwah, NJ: Lawrence Erlbaum.

Milavsky, J. R., Kessler, R. C., Stipp, H. H., & Rubens, W. S. (1982). *Television and aggression: Results of a panel study.* New York: Academic Press.

Milgram, S. (1974). *Obedience to authority: An experimental view.* London: Tavistock.

Millar, M. G., & Millar, K. U. (1990). Attitude change as a function of attitude type and argument type. *Journal of Personality and Social Psychology, 59,* 217–228.

Petty, R. E., & Cacioppo, J. T. (1986). *Communication and persuasion: Central and peripheral routes to attitude change.* New York: Springer-Verlag.

Piotrow, P. T., Rimon, J. G. II, Winnard, K., Kincaid, D. L., Huntington, D. & Convisser, J., et al. (1990). Mass media family planning promotion in three Nigerian cities. *Studies in Family Planning, 21*(5), 265–274.

Pratkanis, A. R., & Greenwald, A. G. (1985). A reliable sleeper effect in persuasion: Implications for opinion change theory and research. In L. F. Alwitt & A. A. Mitchell (Eds.), *Psychological processes and advertising effects: Theory, research, and application* (pp. 157–173). Hillsdale, NJ: Lawrence Erlbaum.

Reyes, R. M., Thompson, W. C., & Bower, G. H. (1980). Judgmental biases resulting from differing availabilities of arguments. *Journal of Personality and Social Psychology, 39,* 2–12.

Rice, R. E., & Atkin, C. K. (2009). Public communication campaigns: Theoretical principles and practical applications. In J. Bryant & M. B. Oliver (Eds.), *Media effects: Advances in theory and research* (3rd ed., pp. 436–468). Hillsdale, NJ: Lawrence Erlbaum.

Sherman, S. J., & Corty, E. (1984). Cognitive heuristics. In R. S. Wyer & T. K. Srull (Eds.), *Handbook of social cognition* (Vol. 1, pp. 189–286). Hillsdale, NJ: Lawrence Erlbaum.

Sidanius, J. (1993). The psychology of group conflict and the dynamics of oppression: A social dominance perspective. In S. Iyengar & W. J. McGuire (Eds.), *Explorations in political psychology* (pp. 183–224). Durham, NC: Duke University Press.

Tajfel, H. (Ed). (1982). *Social identity and intergroup relations.* Cambridge, UK: Cambridge University Press.

Taylor, S. E., & Thompson, S. C. (1982). Stalking the elusive "vividness" effect. *Psychological Review, 89,* 115–181.

Turner, J. C., & Oakes, P. J. (1989). Self-categorization theory and social influence. In P. B. Paulus (Ed.), *The psychology of group influence* (2nd ed.). Hillsdale, NJ: Lawrence Erlbaum.

Tversky, A., & Kahneman, D. (1974). Judgment under uncertainty: Heuristics and biases. *Science, 185,* 1124–1131.

Webster, J. (2005). *Ratings analysis: The theory and practice of audience research* (3rd ed.). Mahwah, NJ: Lawrence Erlbaum.

CHAPTER 10

Sense-Making Methodology as an Approach to Understanding and Designing for Campaign Audiences

A Turn to Communicating Communicatively

Brenda Dervin and Lois Foreman-Wernet

This chapter introduces Dervin's Sense-Making Methodology (SMM) as an alternative approach to conducting research for, designing, and implementing public communication campaigns. In positioning itself as an alternative approach, SMM starts with the assumption that what is commonly called a public communication campaign is more usefully defined as part of a broad and comprehensive communication approach designed to create lasting and viable intersections between institutions and internal and external constituencies. SMM is based on a theory of the practice and design of dialogue. Inherent to that theory is the assumption that all participants in communication processes always have potential freedoms to interpret and, thus, accept, resist, or reject "expertise" based on their own anchorings in material experiences. SMM assumes that the challenge of public communication is to design messages and practices that privilege these freedoms and, hence, engender potential for genuine dialogue. This chapter starts with a brief review of the idea of a public communication campaign—history, dominant approaches and assumptions, and contests and critiques. The purpose of this review is to provide a framework from which to examine SMM's approach as explicitly designed as an alternative.

HISTORICAL BACKGROUND

The idea of a public communication campaign has a long history in the United States (see also Paisley and Atkin, Chapter 2). Our historical review and critique of public communication campaigns rests in particular on these sources: Bauer, 1964; Bernays, 1947; Bishop, 2005;

Coffman, 2002; Creel, 1920; Ewen, 1996; Lazarsfeld, 1944; McLuskie, 1993; Merton, 1946; Morrison, 1978; Out of the question, 2011; Rona, 1982; Simpson, 1996; Sterne, 2005; and Tye, 1998. Even what exactly constitutes that history is contested. What origins, issues, events, factors, policy imperatives, and research traditions should be included vary depending on the vantage points that are adopted for historical reviews. Some of the extensive debates among campaign strategists over the past century are still being discussed in communication research today: How do we conceptualize audiences? How and to what end do we hear the voices of people? How should we study media? What is ethical communication research? Can campaigns based on marketing premises ever be ethical? Should research be based on quantitative scientific approaches or more humanistic narrative and qualitative approaches?

In historical retrospect, it is common to see these tensions reduced to polarizations (e.g., quantitative vs. qualitative, administrative vs. critical). On the one hand, the field encompasses discourse communities whose missions are to conduct research aimed at creating more effective communication campaigns that achieve specified campaign outcomes. At the same time, the field is home to critical antagonists who suggest that, no matter how carefully cloaked as attempts to "understand" and benevolently reach audiences, the intent of the campaign remains top-down social control—to entice audiences to comply with what "experts" deem appropriate.

The importance of this point for our purposes here is that SMM, as an alternative approach, is designed intentionally to fall in the cracks between these divides, as described more fully below. The most important of these divides can be most clearly articulated for purposes here in terms of Giddens' (1986) seminal distinctions between the structures of society and the agencies of actors in society. Essentially, what has gotten buried over time are deep, philosophical differences in how to position citizens vis-à-vis society.

Through the haze of time, it is difficult to understand that the proponents of public communication campaigns—whatever their backgrounds—did not conceptualize a time when informational expertise would be contested or indeed that well-meaning expert elites would be challenged. Few predicted a time when corporations and governments would have deleterious impacts on the trajectories of scientific research. Even the few who examined the idea of public communication campaigns through the lens of societal critique rarely called attention to citizenry agency per se. Yet, a kind of dialectical paradox permeated the history. On the one hand, we were presumably creating a nation of free-minded and educated citizens who were open to information from experts. On the other, we were designing communication efforts to get citizens to fall in line for their better good. This paradox continues to this day.

The idea of the public communication campaign emerged cleansed from its history in essentially the same form we find it today. By far, the dominant emphasis focuses on finding ways to reach audiences to achieve campaign objectives: Institutions are given primacy. Absent, for the most part, is systematic emphasis on how to create meaningful dialogic interfaces in which systems hear more often than they speak. The stream of arguments about the ethical considerations that need to be addressed for the most part disappeared from public communication campaign literatures, with a few exceptions (e.g., Guttman, 2001). Borrowing from Toulmin (1990), the enterprise marched forward with an emphasis on practical and instrumental agendas—and with the assumption of the authority of science as a source of knowledge—and left behind what Toulmin came to define as the necessary marriage of humanistic skepticism to modernist emphases on scientifically generated expertise.

THE COMMUNICATIVE PREMISES OF THE PUBLIC COMMUNICATION CAMPAIGN

Seen through the lens of history, a project that aims to fulfill the mandate called forth by the term *public communication campaign* is based on a central assumption about communication: We—the experts—have a job to do. We possess knowledge and expertise that has been deemed by society as important to societal health and well-being. We need to help citizens become aware of our expertise and, even more importantly, to act on that knowledge. Our goal is usually to gain compliance with that knowledge. Campaigns usually focus on mass distribution of intended messages via varied channels to audiences defined as specific groups. More often than not, the stated aims of campaigns are focused on helping specific population groups avoid risks. These social policy goals are usually based on evidence accepted as identifying that the reduction of these risks should yield life- and resource-saving outcomes.

The list of aims to which this essential public communication campaign mandate is applied is long and usually accepted as self-evidently admirable. Yet, across hundreds of studies, the record of successes is modest at best. It is commonly accepted that it is easier—given enough money and enough repetition of messages—to achieve awareness. Much harder to achieve is compliance, with studies more often than not showing low compliance outcomes (see Snyder & LaCroix, Chapter 8). It is generally accepted that achieving behavioral change outcomes is difficult and costly and rarely results from communication efforts alone. Interventions based on law and on economic leverages have generally proved most effective. If a campaign also is supported in some way by widespread public belief, this also predicts higher campaign success, although even then at high cost and with great repetition. Campaigns to reduce smoking, increase seat belt use, and most recently to curtail mobile phone use while driving serve as examples. In the case of smoking, increased taxation costs have also played an important role.

Despite the force of these findings, while public communication campaigns rarely achieve the levels of success funders hope for in a mass society, however conceptualized, the campaign is deemed as necessary even if successes are measured by small changes over time. Further, it is fair to say that the core idea—that the public communication campaign must implement expert-defined goals—still drives public policy with avalanches of research, entire journals, and massive increases in public funding still oriented to finding better and more efficient ways to achieve prescribed campaign outcomes. Efforts to achieve campaign outcomes have initiated a wide variety of approaches ranging from fine-tuning campaign messages to intensive forms of community involvement (e.g., see Bracht & Rice, Chapter 20). We set this variety within the context of SMM's alternative approach below.

THE COMMUNICATION THEORIES DRIVING PUBLIC COMMUNICATION CAMPAIGNS

It is important to distinguish the communicative goals of the public communication campaign from that of a marketing or advertising campaign even though one finds the distinctions too often collapsed in the literature. Both do measure success by a kind of compliance. Both are oriented to finding more successful avenues for reaching audiences. But marketing and advertising campaigns focus on introducing new products and behaviors that serve established functions or on changing brands. It is expected that costly marketing efforts can yield small-percentage outcomes yet, at the same time, huge gains in profits.

While what are commonly called advertising and marketing versus public communication campaigns face similar communication struggles in effectively reaching intended audiences, the public communication campaign faces the more arduous challenge of convincing audiences to comply with what often are entirely new or radically changed behaviors or adopting new ideas and inclinations that break with long-established modes of being and often move toward behaviors and ideas previously seen as alien personally and culturally. It is the arduousness of this challenge and the low levels of success that led Bauer to label audiences obstinate as early as 1964. The adjective is as applicable today as it was then. Despite the arduousness of the challenge, any cursory examination of communication field literature suggests that efforts to beat the challenge have redoubled over the years. Examination of the literature easily captures the quantity of creative, innovative, and well-meaning attentions brought to this effort.

For our purposes, we find it useful to abstract these attentions in terms of the essential theories of communication that guide them. In the beginning, it was assumed that self-evident argument would suffice. Then, it was assumed that one needed to perfect presentation of the argument with well-researched message designs. Then, it became evident that differences between people made a difference in receptivity, and a series of communication logics based on audience segmentations were introduced. Roughly in chronological order of their introduction, we find campaign messages and strategies constructed to target audiences in terms of segmentations based on 1) demographic and trait group memberships, 2) interests, styles, and life situations, 3) cultural and community memberships, needs, and values, and 4) most recently, an emphasis on narratives and metaphors relating to campaign objectives that are normatively used by different target audiences (Dervin, 2010b).

These different "theories" have not supplanted each other. While in general, we see more interest in understanding target audiences as cultural groups and communities, or as discourse communities with normative narrative practices, we still see emphasis on constructing more perfect messages and on streamlining campaigns for target audiences based on each of the different theoretical approaches. Further, cutting across the literature, it has become a truism that successful campaigns combine as many avenues of communication as possible—interpersonal, group, community, organizational, media, and now with the new technologies, digitally interactive and participatory (see Atkin &

Rice, Chapter 1; Lieberman, Chapter 19). This latter emergence is in itself a break with the top-down designs of the past and essentially allows the campaign message and intent to become both public tool and victim of participatory debate. Numerous scholarly attentions are being brought to bear on issues relating to what is feared to be misinformation sharing between nonexperts and the implications of this for expert practice. A particularly robust terrain that exemplifies this concern is that of health communication (Rice & Katz, 2001) and especially the contest between popular acceptance of alternative medicines and mainstream medical reluctance (see, e.g., American Medical Association, 1997).

CRITIQUES OF DOMINANT APPROACHES

In the face of what are usually lower compliance rates than hoped for, virtually every study reporting on a campaign has also critiqued its gaps and suggested potential improvements (see, e.g., Coffman, 2002, and Salmon & Murray-Johnson, Chapter 7). We see most of these critiques as falling into two major categories. The first focuses on critiquing campaign goals and the second on research methods.

Regarding campaign goals, critiques fall into these major groups: 1) While campaigns can sometimes increase awareness and knowledge, this is not always the case, 2) even when awareness is a positive outcome, compliance is usually low, 3) lack of compliance sometimes results from audience members simply rejecting campaign expertise, 4) communication alone is usually not enough, nor are incentives, prizes, fear appeals, and even strongly worded messages, 5) what is needed for some campaign goals is simply negative reinforcement and sanctions, and 6) some central assumptions about audience responses are contested in the empirical evidence—for example, focusing campaign messages on behavioral intentions when intentions alone may or may not lead to behavioral change.

Regarding research methods, we cluster the critiques into four major groups. One major thrust of criticism focuses on the dominant use of standardized polling methods and statistical approaches and how more qualitative research is needed. A second category of critique focuses on how so many targeted campaign audiences are from societally marginalized groups, and research too frequently neglects indigenous differences in perspectives and use of language. In short, campaigns are critiqued as being too often Westernized and Eurocentric in design. At a higher level of abstraction, a third critique addresses issues of how campaigns too frequently conceptualize their target audiences as illiterate—in, for example, reading, math, computer skills, or knowledge of specific topical areas. As a result, the critique suggests target audiences are unfairly blamed for lack of compliance without accounting for real-life conditions and constraints (for an explicit emphasis on these questions, see Dorfman & Wallack, Chapter 23). A fourth critique suggests that the yawning gap between experts and nonexperts is a far greater problem than the differences expected in terms of traditional approaches to target audience segmentation.

WHAT IS DIFFERENT ABOUT SENSE-MAKING METHODOLOGY: FUNDAMENTAL ASSUMPTIONS

While the term *sense-making* is being widely used for a host of research applications, both systematic (see Dervin & Naumer, 2010) as well as capricious, Dervin's SMM differs in that it is a metatheoretically guided approach for the design of dialogue (Dervin & Foreman-Wernet, 2003). It sets out to establish foundation from which we can design dialogue communicatively by encompassing a set of fundamental assumptions about the nature of human communication drawn from a large number of North American, European, and South American philosophers and theorists (see Carter, 2003; Dervin, 2010a, b). Among these fundamental assumptions are the following:

1. Individual human beings change as they move across time–space. They are in constant intrapersonal communication with the self—how they think, feel, question, and experience changes as they move from time to time and situation to situation.

2. The outcomes that we usually call communication (i.e., compliance, agreement) are in fact only outcomes and not communication processes—and are relatively rare outcomes of highly complex communicatings inside people and between people.

3. When it comes to communication, the receiver—the intended audience member—controls all the gates. It is the inside communicatings that matter—the internal, phenomenological sense-makings of interior life and material circumstances. While indeed there are some constancies in these internal sense-makings across time, in actuality, very little variance in reception of messages has been accounted for with traditional attempts to predict.

4. Perhaps ironically, audience segmentation approaches work best only for habitual sense-makings and behaviors—the very kind that campaigns and education seek to change.

5. While humans are born into and live in community, cultural, and societal groups, only small subsets of what can be called communication behaviors are predicted by these segmented memberships. The reason for this is that the collective memberships to which humans are assigned by society do not well represent variations in human life facing. There is often more variance within groups than between. The behaviors best predicted by segmentation are those that are externally controlled. Hence, for example, higher-income persons are more likely to invest in more costly means of protecting their privacy (Shields & Dervin, 1998), but they are far less likely to differ in terms of how they want privacy protection to help. Likewise, higher-educated persons are more likely to interpret artworks in ways similar to art experts but only at shallow-meaning levels. At the deeper levels of sense-making, education differences are much diminished (Foreman-Wernet & Dervin, 2010, 2011).

6. What makes individuals more alike in their internal communicatings has been shown repeatedly in SMM studies to not be individual traits and characteristics but what

SMM calls *person-in-situation* characteristics—in particular how people see themselves as struggling with and attempting to make sense of changing circumstances.

7. It is a truism that, of almost all efforts to reach audiences, these efforts succeed best with those people who are most like the experts themselves. The largest gaps between "expert" systems and their mandated constituencies or audiences are the *noun* worlds of expertise that are imposed on targeted audiences. SMM explicitly calls for moving from noun approaches to *verbing* approaches. This idea is developed more fully below.

8. Expertise gained from the everyday experiences of living is not systematically acknowledged in the modern constructions of our expertise systems.

9. Primary sources of input that people turn to in facing everyday life challenges are, first of all, self and, second, family, friends, coworkers, and peers. This is true across demographic and other trait characteristics. In the context of a global media environment where, for example, the science behind expertise is more shallowly built and more frequently contested, there is evidence that reliance on trusted close and homogeneous others necessarily increases. The traditional emphasis on opinion leaders that grew out of diffusion of innovations research gives nod to this truism (Rogers, 2003). Campaign designers frequently turn to those who share community and culture with target audience members. Yet, it has been documented that opinion leaders wear out when used as tools by those imposing change from above. In short, audiences may be more willing to hear messages from those in peer-kin-community networks, but that willingness is not a guarantee of acceptance.

10. Unless individuals are willing to open their sense-making gates, no amount of expertise, however exquisitely packaged, will be welcomed. Communication is ultimately a process of quid pro quo. People are willing to listen to that which collides with or is new to their worlds when those communicating at them change to communicating with them. This requires respecting individual rights to reject our expertise or raise doubts about it—what physicist Richard Feynman (1999) called for: acknowledging that expertise (i.e., knowledge) is always surrounded by doubt. SMM adheres to this premise by focusing on humans as moving through situations where they are sometimes in conflict, sometimes in confusion and doubt, and sometimes journeying ahead with confidence. When fully implemented, SMM attempts to provide tools for gap bridging between institutions and possible audiences built on genuine two-way dialogue that acknowledge the struggles all humans share—to bridge gaps across continuities and discontinuities of existence.

SENSE-MAKING METHODOLOGY: THE CENTRAL METAPHOR THAT DRIVES PRACTICE

Numerous studies over a 40-year period support the utility of applying these assumptions as an alternative approach to public communication. SMM has been used since 1972 as an approach to research, design, and practice for numerous institutions whose mandates involve bridging gaps with one or more constituency audiences. Research has been conducted to extract (and in some cases apply) recommendations to actual communication practice. Hence, SMM has been used to conduct research relevant to the design of systems, procedures, and outreach programs of—as examples—libraries, information systems, websites, media systems, health institutions, museums and performing arts organizations, nursing practice, knowledge management, citizen participation in policy discussions, journalism practice, disability services, environmental agencies, science education, and literacy programs. Intended audiences have ranged from general population citizens to specific, presumably hard-to-reach subgroups (e.g., the poor, culturally silenced, ethnic minorities). Research has been funded by numerous governmental agencies, both state and federal (e.g., National Cancer Institute, U.S. Office of Education, Institute of Museum and Library Services, California State Library, California Public Utilities Commission, Ohio Environmental Protection Agency). Some private funding has supported the work, focusing on design of communication programs for internal and external constituencies. The most recent of such applications have been to knowledge management systems.

The wide range of these applications is one way in which SMM is not normative as an approach to campaign research. Because SMM focuses on what is communicative as *essence,* it has not been concerned about the particular noun world of expertise to which it has been applied. In SMM terms, the mandated move to verbing approaches can be usefully applied in any communicative context because SMM mandates refocusing communication attention on dialogue rather than transmission.

While SMM is best described as a methodological framework, it is one that for the most part falls between the cracks. The bedrock edifice of SMM rests on a systematic theory of interviewing and dialogue that is primarily qualitative, but in application, SMM has been applied using a wide range of research approaches focusing on a wide range of policy issues. In practice, SMM has been used in both quantitative and qualitative studies advanced by virtually every form of listening to and understanding others—focus groups, surveys, in-depth interviews, guided participant observation—implemented in person, by phone, in groups, on the web, and in observational field settings. In all cases, the purpose of SMM has been to guide research question design, data collection (both observing and interviewing), and data analysis. Further, the purpose has been to communicatively design recommendations for programs and practices.

Communicatively is defined explicitly in SMM as an implementation of the assumptions listed in the preceding section. In design of practical programs, SMM mandates that dialogue be addressed communicatively. This means that it is not assumed that expertise flows only from the top down, nor is it assumed that the goal is to achieve compliance or agreement. Rather, it is assumed that participants (either mediated audience members or persons directly participating in group or individual contact) are in the process of becoming—what SMM calls *verbing* across time–space.

Regardless of whether SMM is applied in one-on-one interviewing, or in focus groups, or in mass and electronic media designs, it mandates continued attention to how people move through time and space, sometimes with confidence and sometimes in confusion. As an example, an SMM group or organizational dialogue—including the SMM approach to the focus group—would ask participants (including those whom the system names as appointed experts) to share orally their sense-makings, for example: what did you hear that you agreed with; that confused you; that you disagreed with; how does this relate to your experience; and how have things changed (across time and across situations)? At the same time, participants would be asked to participate simultaneously in intrapersonal communicatings—what SMM calls *Sense-Making Journalings*—in which they privately write down their reactions using the same array of queries, but now they focus on what others in the room said. In this way, SMM systematically attempts to procedurally partition interpersonal communicating from intrapersonal because evidence from SMM studies has shown that reflective communicatings with self are suppressed by interpersonal and group communicatings that too often stress agreement, compliance, and consensus (e.g., Schaefer & Dervin, 2009). Unlike most approaches to group communication, in SMM, spontaneous communicatings are deliberately curtailed so that all participants share time, and space is opened for what is usually left unsaid.

A fundamental assumption of SMM is that most of the normatively used approaches that attempt to hear others, whether qualitative or quantitative, are in actuality driven by noun-based worlds of expertise, and the result is that sharings end up replicating stereotypes (and societally driven habits—hegemony and habitus) rather than genuinely opening up avenues for hearing differences. SMM further assumes that it is as hard to hear differences from populations homogeneous with experts guiding the research as it is to hear differences from those exhibiting wide diversities. In the former case, too ready agreement and acceptance of the nouns of expertise cloaks differences; in the latter, the nouns of expertise are quite simply alien.

There is behind the explanations above a systematic theory of communication drawn from multiple philosophic sources. This theory implements what SMM calls its *verbing* approach, as captured in Figure 10.1, the central Metaphor of Sense-Making Methodology. In this metaphor, a squiggly human (intended to represent how we humans are both orderly and disorderly) moves through situations with history and past experience, across gaps—discontinuities defined as ever-present in the human condition—forging bridges (which may be newly invented, borrowed from sources of input, copied from the past, or implemented mindlessly), moving to outcomes. In the metaphor, sources are the bricks of the bridge, and relevances are the criteria actors use to evaluate how sources help or hinder. Actors are assumed to be both making and unmaking sense as they move. The roads traveled, the outcomes, even the bricks of the bridge are pictured as *gappy*. The umbrellas actors carry are also gappy, indicating that the structural conditions that actors are born into and live within are assumed to be constraining but not absolutely so. SMM assumes humans are constantly making and unmaking sense as they navigate with their agencies the structural constraints of their situations.

From this metaphor is drawn the core set of foundational concepts emphasized in SMM studies and SMM-guided implementations of communication: time, space, movement, gap, horizon, energy, power, history, experience, constraint, change, flexibility, caprice, chaos, habit, inflexibility, rigidity, and constancy. These concepts—all focusing on universals of human movement through time–space—are the foundation from which SMM draws its core set of queries used in all dialogues, both research and practice directed. These core questions, stated in abbreviated form, focus on the following: What happened? How does it connect with your life or past? What questions or muddles have you had? What ideas or conclusions have you come to? What emotions or feelings have you experienced? What has helped or hindered? How do you see this as connecting to how power operates in this context or to your sense of self? If you could wave a magic wand, what would have helped?

FIGURE 10.1   SMM's central metaphor: Bridging the gap.

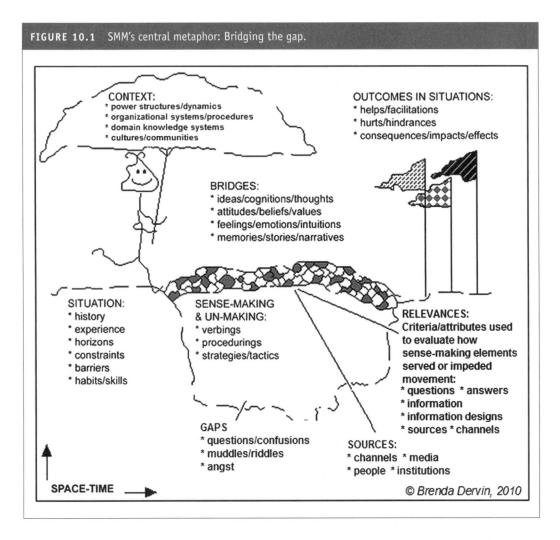

CONTEXT:
* power structures/dynamics
* organizational systems/procedures
* domain knowledge systems
* cultures/communities

OUTCOMES IN SITUATIONS:
* helps/facilitations
* hurts/hindrances
* consequences/impacts/effects

BRIDGES:
* ideas/cognitions/thoughts
* attitudes/beliefs/values
* feelings/emotions/intuitions
* memories/stories/narratives

SITUATION:
* history
* experience
* horizons
* constraints
* barriers
* habits/skills

SENSE-MAKING
& UN-MAKING:
* verbings
* procedurings
* strategies/tactics

RELEVANCES:
Criteria/attributes used
to evaluate how
sense-making elements
served or impeded
movement:
* questions * answers
* information
* information designs
* sources * channels

GAPS
* questions/confusions
* muddles/riddles
* angst

SOURCES:
* channels * media
* people * institutions

SPACE-TIME

© Brenda Dervin, 2010

In SMM interviewing practice, these core questions constitute 90% or more of the utterances SMM interviewers are allowed to speak. Sometimes, wrapped around these queries are various quantitative scales, all themselves defined as focusing not on nouns but on forces and movement. For example, informants might be asked to evaluate troublesome situations they have faced in terms of level of importance, extent of barriers faced, or intensity of emotion.

Implementation of Questions

Figure 10.2 illustrates some of the ways in which these mandated questions are implemented, for purposes here, all presented in past tense (Dervin, 2008). Adaptations must be made, of course, to critical entries that focus on the particular gaps institutions aim to

FIGURE 10.2 The core SMM queries with example questions.

TO TAP SITUATIONS:
What happened?
What stood in the way?
What were you trying to deal with?
How did that connect with past events?
How did it connect to forces of power in family, community, society?

TO TAP GAPS:
What were your big questions?
What were you trying to unconfuse, figure out, learn about?
What did you struggle with?

TO TAP BRIDGES:
What conclusions/ideas did you come to?
What emotions/feelings did you come to?
What led you to that conclusion/idea/emotion/feeling?

TO TAP OUTCOMES SOUGHT AND/OR OBTAINED:
How did that [name that] help/facilitate? [...and, how did that help?...and, how did that help?]
How did that [name that] hinder? [...and, how did that hinder?...and, how did that hinder?]
Taking what happened as given, if you could wave a magic wand, what would have helped?

TO DIG DEEPER INTO GAPS AND STRUGGLES:
What was missing?
How did that stand in the way?
And, how did that prevent you getting more help?

TO DIG DEEPER INTO WHAT LED TO AN EVALUATION:
What led you to that assessment?
How did that evaluation connect with your situation?
What was limited or incomplete about that?

TO DIG DEEPER INTO HOW THINGS HELP:
And, how did that help?
What did that allow you to do/achieve/think?

© Brenda Dervin, 2010

bridge with one or more constituencies. In addition, a must in all qualitative interviewing is to adapt to the cultural forms and normative narratives of expected informants (Briggs, 1986). However, unlike the challenges of, for example, most accepted ethnographic interviewing practices, where researchers are mandated to be deeply immersed in the noun worlds of informants, in SMM, it is informants who are invited to describe these noun worlds to interviewers. The SMM interviewing instrument needs to translate the time–space–movement emphases mandated by SMM theory into words and phrases that capture these images for informants.

The first absolute mandate of the SMM interview is to keep the interviewers' and institutions' nouns off the interviewing interface. The second is to focus on verbing-oriented queries—the set of questions that allows informants to piece together on their own terms and in the contexts of their own phenomenological and material worlds the connections and disconnections they see between past, present, and future; between themselves and others; between their internal worlds and external circumstances; and between the structures within which they live and their private dreams and visions.

Fundamentally, in SMM, informants are positioned as "theorists" of their own worlds, and it is expected that there will emerge a variety of "theories," some of which may or may not agree with expert theories. It is expected as well that, even when the expert theories being advanced are supported by the "truth" values of science, space must be made for lay disagreement. It has been documented that average citizens are sometimes better able to break through the confines of expert nouns than are the very experts who espouse them. Every SMM encounter hinges on this possibility—the necessity to humble expert knowledge and information.

This core approach to SMM questioning forms the bedrock foundation for all SMM-guided projects whether they focus on one-shot research studies designed to produce recommendations for practice or on ongoing dialogues constructed between institutions and constituencies. While the term *public communication campaign* is traditionally applied to the sometimes brief, sometimes sustained efforts to gain awareness and involvement as mandated by a specific terrain of expertise, in SMM, the term is redirected to the entire set of communication intersections between an organization and its constituencies and always to the goal to establishing two-way dialogue.

SENSE-MAKING METHODOLOGY APPLICATIONS

For SMM, the term *public communication campaign* is repositioned as *public communication*. This section includes examples of two different applications.

One type of example is how SMM is used as interviewing approaches for what could have been designed as traditionally conceptualized *audience campaign* studies but were instead designed with SMM's approach to interviewing. The Ohio Department of Health wanted to respond to citizen concerns about a toxic waste site in a small (roughly 3,000 residents) community. In all, 189 interviews averaging 23 minutes were conducted, asking informants about problems experienced, conclusions reached, solutions they or others tried, and what they thought would help. Interview queries asked included the following: What problems relating to the waste site had impacted the informant, personally, your family, neighbors, community, and so on? For the most important impacting situation, what happened? What did this lead you to conclude? Did the situation lead you to be confused or uncertain? How? Did the situation constrain, bother, upset, or hurt you? How? What alternative solutions do you think there are? What ought to be done? Have some solutions already been tried? Did they help or hinder? How? What actions have you, friends, or neighbors taken? Did they help or hinder? How? What sources of information helped? How? Which hindered? How? Who was seen as most knowledgeable? The study led to a commitment for action from the state health department to consider further scientific investigation to answer citizen concerns, and particular emphasis was placed on improving communication with community residents to increase information available and reduce uncertainty (Dervin, Waldron, Shields, Hariharan, Albarran, Teboul, et al., 1988; Mortensen, 1988).

In the second type of application, SMM's approach to questioning is designed as a way of informing all intersections between institutions and their publics—in person, in groups, or mediated; and not just as one-shot attempts to hear constituency voices but as continuing iterative flows of institutional contacts with constituencies; not just for getting "those people" to come to us, accept us, or comply with us; but for them to help us serve them and change us for the better; and for us to establish with them continuing instructive and productive relationships. We use one example here to encapsulate the essential characteristics of applications of SMM to these kinds of dialogic designs. Knowledge Management Specialist Bonnie Cheuk sought widespread involvement in a corporate program. Cheuk ran an internal public communication program for her prior employer, ERM (Environmental Resources Management, the world's largest, all-environmental consulting firm) to invite staff to provide insights and ideas to help shape the future of company strategies. Instead of encouraging only spontaneous dialogue (by usual online forums, tweets, and focus groups) within an 8-week period, she designed a way to allow minority voices to be heard using anonymous e-mail contributions and asking managers to have individual or small group dialogues with shy colleagues. It was made very clear from the start that ERM was inviting both positive and negative reflections about current practices. The latter was emphasized and ritualized, so colleagues felt comfortable that this was what leaders were asking for. Cheuk reported that SMM helped because it illuminated how power issues were locked in existing structures. As one example, a staff member from Mexico mentioned that she could not voice her opinion in an open forum because her ideas pointed out the poor management style of her line manager. She sent an anonymous posting by e-mail (Cheuk, personal communication, December 29, 2010; Cheuk & Dervin, 2011).

SENSE-MAKING METHODOLOGY: BETWEEN THE CRACKS AND AGAINST THE GRAIN

The intent of the above has been to show how SMM, as an alternative approach to understanding and designing for campaign audiences, has been, in fact, developed as an interruption to the usual assumptions of public communication campaigns as enterprise. SMM does not target audiences in audience segmentations; it does not seek compliance or assent. Rather, its intent is to serve as dialogic interface that builds upon the essential communicative nature of communication. What this means is that it is assumed that, in communication, intended recipients control the interpretive gates, and there is but one way to open up avenues for more effective communicating. That is to establish the quid pro quo that is a communication essential: You listen to me, and I will listen to you; you learn from me, and I will learn from you; you trust my narratives about my material circumstances, and I may listen to the narratives within which you wrap your expertise. But, you will also have to listen to my expertise.

SMM is between the cracks because it stands between the usual assumptions of research polarities. It is critical and administrative, qualitative and quantitative, focused on the material as well as the interpretive, and focused on source-receivers as well as receiver-sources. SMM is against the grain because it intends to humble and challenge expertise in order to open a space where expertise can be viable. In a world where science is no longer the sole anchor for judging the correctness of expertise and where science has become tool of media, government, and corporate manipulation, well-meaning experts need to humble their knowledge and themselves in order to be heard. SMM assumes that communication is always dialogic—and always has been—even if experts and institutions have not designed and do not design it that way.

What SMM ultimately interrupts in the dominant positions regarding implementing public communication campaigns is the idea that the goal of the campaign should be to transmit expert information to target audiences because it is assumed that expertise is of value, useful, even lifesaving. This well-meaning assumption usually guides campaign research and design and sets the bounds with which campaigns are critiqued. The problem is reduced to a failure to communicate. Even when concerted effort is directed to understanding audience needs, values, and experiences, these efforts are usually focused on finding ways to use these understandings to improve successful transmission of expertise. The focus is not one of engendering public dialogue in open democratic forms but one of top-down persuasion.

What makes SMM fundamentally different is its emphasis on the idea that both organizations and constituencies have expertise to share, common struggles to ponder, and capacities to teach and learn from each other. Thus, in SMM public communication is defined as the means to not merely change constituencies but to change organizations as well. Primary emphasis in the four decades of SMM's evolution has been placed on developing and testing systematic approaches to theory, research, dialogue, and design for making these outcomes possible. The ultimate goal is to build and sustain genuinely and iteratively responsive communication systems.

References

American Medical Association. (1997). *Report 12 of the Council on Scientific Affairs (A-97—Alternative medicine.* Retrieved March 3, 2011, from http://www.ama-assn.org/ama/no-index/about-ama/13638.shtml

Bauer, R. A. (1964). The obstinate audience: The influence process from the point of view of social communication. *American Psychologist, 19,* 319–328.

Bernays, E. L. (1947). The engineering of consent. *The Annals of the American Academy of Political and Social Science, 250,* 113–120.

Bishop, G. F. (2005). *The illusion of public opinion: Fact and artifact in American public opinion polls.* Lanham, MD: Rowman & Littlefield.

Briggs, C. (1986). *Learning how to ask.* Cambridge, UK: Cambridge University Press.

Carter, R. F. (2003). Communication, a harder science. In B. Dervin & S. H. Chaffee, with L. Foreman-Wernet (Eds.), *Communication, a different kind of horserace: Essays honoring Richard F. Carter* (pp. 369–376). Cresskill, NJ: Hampton Press.

Cheuk, B. W., & Dervin, B. (2011). Leadership 2.0 in ACTION: A journey from knowledge management to "Knowledging." *Knowledge Management & E-Learning: An International Journal, 3*(2). Retrieved March 3, 2011, from http://www.kmel-journal.org/ojs/index.php/online-publication/article/viewArticle/107

Coffman, J. (2002). *Public communication campaign evaluation: An environmental scan of challenges, criticisms, practice, and opportunities.* (Report prepared for the Communications Consortium Media Center). Cambridge, MA: Harvard Family Research Project. Retrieved March 3, 2011, from http://www.hfrp.org/evaluation/publications-resources

Creel, G. (1920). *How we advertised America.* New York: Harper & Brothers.

Dervin, B. (2008). *Interviewing as dialectical practice: Sense-Making Methodology as exemplar.* Paper delivered at International Association of Media and Communication Research annual meeting, Stockholm, Sweden.

Dervin, B. (2010a). Clear . . . unclear? Accurate . . . inaccurate? Objective . . . subjective? Research . . . practice? Why polarities impede the research, practice, and design of information systems and how Sense-Making Methodology attempts to bridge the gaps, parts 1 and 2. *Journal of Evaluation in Clinical Practice, 16*(5), 994–1001.

Dervin, B. (2010b). Hidden passions, burning questions: The other side of so-called mass audiences. In L. Foreman-Wernet & B. Dervin (Eds.), *Audiences and the arts: Communication perspectives* (Chap. 14, pp. 243–254). Cresskill, NJ: Hampton Press.

Dervin, B., & Foreman-Wernet, L. (with Lauterbach, E.). (Eds.). (2003). *Sense-Making Methodology reader: Selected writings of Brenda Dervin.* Cresskill, NJ: Hampton Press.

Dervin, B., & Naumer, C. M. (2010). Sense-Making. *Encyclopedia of Library and Information Science* (3rd ed., Vol. 1, pp. 4696–4707).

Dervin, B., Waldron, V., Shields, V., Hariharan, U., Albarran, A., Teboul, B., et al. (1988). *Report #2: Final report: Citizen communication needs and perceptions of risk relating to the Union Town toxic waste site.* (Report presented to Dr. Kim Mortensen, Chief, Division of Epidemiology, Bureau of Preventive Medicine). Columbus: Ohio Department of Health.

Ewen, S. (1996). *PR! A social history of spin.* New York: HarperCollins.

Feynman, R. F. (1999). *The pleasure of finding things out.* Cambridge, MA: Perseus.

Foreman-Wernet, L., & Dervin, B. (Eds.). (2010). *Audiences and the arts: Communication perspectives.* Cresskill, NJ: Hampton Press.

Foreman-Wernet, L., & Dervin, B. (2011). Cultural experience in context: Sense-Making the arts. *Journal of Arts Management, Law, and Society, 41*(1), 1–37.

Giddens, A. (1986). *The constitution of society: Outline of the theory of structuration.* Berkeley: University of California Press.

Guttman, N. (2001). *Public health communication interventions: Values and ethical dilemmas.* Thousand Oaks, CA: Sage.

Lazarsfeld, P. F. (1944). The controversy over detailed interviews—an offer for negotiation. *The Public Opinion Quarterly, 8*(1), 38–60.

McLuskie, E. (1993). Founding U.S. communication research in the Viennese tradition: Lazarsfeld's silent suppression of critical theory. *Medien und Zeit, 8*(2), 3–13.

Merton, R. (1946). The focused interview. *American Journal of Sociology, 51,* 541–557.

Morrison, D. E. (1978). Kultur and culture: The case of Theodor W. Adorno and Paul F. Lazarsfeld. *Social Research, 44,* 331–355.

Mortensen, K. (1988). *Citizens' communication needs and perceptions of risk relating to industrial excess landfill.* (Final report and recommendations, Division of Epidemiology and Toxicology). Columbus: Ohio Department of Health.

Out of the question: Women, media, and the art of inquiry [Documentary film]. Retrieved March 3, 2011, from www.outofthequestion.org

Rice, R. E., & Katz, J. E. (Eds.). (2001). *The Internet and health communication: Expectations and experiences.* Thousand Oaks, CA: Sage.

Rogers, E. M. (2003). *Diffusion of innovations* (5th ed.). New York: Free Press.

Rona, T. (1982). *Our changing geo-political premises.* New Brunswick, NJ: Transaction Publishers.

Schaefer, D. J., & Dervin, B. (2009). From the dialogic to the contemplative: A conceptual and empirical rethinking of online communication outcomes as verbing micro-practices. *Ethics and Information Technology, 11,* 265–278.

Shields, P., & Dervin, B. (1998). Telephone privacy: Residential user perspectives and strategies. *Media International Australia, 87,* 95–113.

Simpson, C. (1996). *The science of coercion: Communication research and psychological warfare. 1945–1960.* New York: Oxford University Press.

Sterne, J. (2005). C. Wright Mills, the Bureau of Applied Social Research, and the meaning of critical scholarship. *Cultural Studies←→Cultural Methodologies, 5*(1), 65–94.

Toulmin, S. E. (1990). *Cosmopolis: The hidden agenda of modernity.* New York: The Free Press.

Tye, L. (1998). *The father of spin: Edward L. Bernays and the birth of public relations.* New York: Henry Holt.

CHAPTER 11

Inducing Fear as a Public Communication Campaign Strategy

Marco C. Yzer, Brian G. Southwell, and Michael T. Stephenson

Inducing fear is a popular strategy for many types of public communication efforts. Fear appeal messages "refer to those contents of a persuasive communication which allude to or describe unfavorable consequences that are alleged to result from failure to adopt and adhere to the communicator's conclusions" (Hovland, Janis, & Kelley, 1953, p. 60) and "attempt to change our attitudes by appealing to [the] unpleasant emotion of fear" (Rogers, 1983, p. 153). Simply put, the logic of a fear appeal strategy is to get people's attention and emphasize the dangers of risky behaviors, thereby increasing the likelihood that people will engage in less risky behaviors.

The idea that fear can motivate action is intuitively compelling and, in fact, has been a central tenet of emotion theory (Frijda, Kuipers, & ter Schure, 1989; Roseman, Wiest, & Swartz, 1994), as we will discuss. However, decades of scholarship also suggest a complex picture in which exposure to fear appeals sometimes reduces risky behavior but only under certain circumstances. Here, we review relevant scholarship to understand what those circumstances are and describe paths for future research. Because fear is particularly widely solicited by public health and medical communication practitioners, we draw on health communication research for many of our examples. Note, however, that our discussion should be relevant for many other domains, such as threats having to do with the environment, personal safety, or political choices.

Our objectives are to describe theoretical perspectives most pertinent to fear appeal effects and highlight that these theories produce different predictions. We additionally stress that although fear appeal research appears dominantly in the communication literature, theoretical accounts primarily take a psychological perspective. There is good reason for this, as fear appeal effects, in essence, are about how people regulate fear in response to threatening information. Importantly, however, the extensive attention on the psychology of fear has not been matched by attention to public communication perspectives. We will therefore also address critical issues about fear as a communication strategy in public campaigns.

THE FUNCTION OF FEAR

Our propositions regarding the utility of fear in public communication campaigns rest in part on two fundamental notions that are not without controversy, namely that 1) an affective state of fear is a discrete emotion with characteristics distinct from other emotions, and 2) fear has served a function for humans over time. Regarding the discrete nature of emotion, a host of researchers have argued that we should see our various affective states not simply in terms of positive or negative valence but in terms of distinct signal values and action tendencies (Dillard & Nabi, 2006; Nabi, 1999). From this perspective, fear propels people to protective action in response to perceived danger, whereas other emotions function differently; for example, happiness invites behavioral maintenance, and anger invites active attack to remove perceived obstacles. As Dillard and Nabi (2006) suggest, fear seems to be particularly tied to situations that emphasize susceptibility to threat, combining both the existence of danger and one's own vulnerability to it. What is not necessarily guaranteed in response to fear, however, is compliance with a specific behavioral recommendation, per se; there are various ways people can attempt to protect themselves, or withdraw from the presence of danger.

This discrete and functional perspective on emotions resonates quite well with the campaign evaluation and health promotion literatures. Dillard, Plotnick, Godbold, Freimuth, and Edgar (1996) studied public service announcements intended to arouse fear and found not only that a substantial proportion of such messages failed to arouse fear but also that some messages intended to induce fear actually invited other types of emotional responses, such as anger. Similarly, Williams-Piehota, Pizarro, Schneider, Mowad, and Salovey (2005) observed that a cancer screening message can produce not only anxiety but also hope and reassurance. Before turning to fear as our focus of attention, we therefore offer as a precautionary note that researchers must not operate under the assumption that all emotional appeals intended to elicit fear actually do so. Likewise, fear reactions are importantly distinct from other types of affective responses.

PERCEIVED RISK AND FEAR

Risk represents the possibility of danger, and danger indicates a possible loss, injury, or other negative outcome. When we consider that behaviors are causally related to risk for many individuals, we see the relevance of risk for communication purposes. That is, if a persuasive message makes people aware of how much their behavior puts them at risk, is it not reasonable then to expect people to change their behavior to reduce their risk? Such seemingly logical behavior change, however, is not always the most likely response to risk information.

One important explanation for why exposure to risk information does not uniformly translate into behavior change lies in the lack of uniformity among people in the perception and interpretation of risk. There often is a gap between real and perceived risk because, for example, many people lack the numeracy skills necessary to accurately interpret risk information (such as likelihood) regarding a particular danger (Reyna & Brainerd,

2007). In addition, and of particular importance for the purposes of this chapter, a key reason for the gap between real and perceived risk perception may be motivational. The motivational explanation for biased risk perceptions holds that information about being at risk for a significant danger induces an unpleasant emotional state and that thinking that one in fact is not at risk, or not as much as others, is a useful way to reduce the unpleasant emotion. If fear is a negative emotion that perceptions of risk can induce, rather than an automatically triggered alert as to objective danger, then objective risk will not always produce fear.

Regardless of whether it is a perception or a motivation issue (or both), research shows that individuals consistently underestimate their risk to hazards that occur relatively frequently in the general population, including contracting a sexually transmitted disease or getting a divorce (Rothman, Klein, & Weinstein, 1996). Further, people "consistently and substantially" overestimate risks to others (e.g., the "third person" effect), particularly when making comparisons to their own vulnerability (Rothman et al., 1996, p. 1231). Such self-serving beliefs about superiority over others help to maintain a relative optimistic bias (Rothman et al., 1996; Salovey, Rothman, Detweiler, & Steward, 2000; Weinstein, 1984). In a striking example, Klein and Kunda (1993) found that individuals even modified reports of their own behavior, such as drinking alcohol, to distinguish their own behavior as being more acceptable than that of others.

Overall, then, risk information very often is not processed objectively but in a manner that serves to reduce, control, or deny the presence of negative emotions—an assumption that, in varying degrees, has informed theoretical thinking about fear appeals.

FEAR APPEAL THEORIES

Four theoretical perspectives have dominated fear appeal research to date: *a fear-as-drive model, the parallel process model, the protection motivation theory,* and the *extended parallel processing model.* We will briefly discuss each of these and then discuss two additional perspectives that are relevant for our discussion yet not commonly included in discussions of fear appeal processes and effects—*information processing* and *fear and self-esteem regulation.*

Fear as a Drive

Some of the earliest scientific work on fear appeals by Hovland and colleagues (1953) rested on the assumption that intense and disturbing emotions, including fear, are functionally similar to a drive. A drive is a state of tension that motivates people to find ways to reduce this tension. Thus, when people experience intensely unpleasant emotions, they are motivated to find a way to reduce the unpleasantness of their emotional state. Hovland and colleagues proposed that responses that successfully reduce fear induced by a particular threat will become the preferred, habitual response to that threat because it is rewarding to eliminate the negative drive. Importantly, though, responses will tend to center on reducing unpleasant emotions and not necessarily on averting an objective threat, per se. In this regard, cognitive risk reappraisal, such as denial of personal risk, can work to reduce unpleasant emotions as well as, or better than, would adopting less risky behavior.

Hovland and colleagues (1953) therefore proposed that to increase control over responses to a fear appeal, a message should not only include a fear-inducing component but also reassuring recommendations. Consistent with learning theories, recommendations for how a person can avert threat reduce emotional distress, which in turn reinforces the behavioral recommendations whenever similar cues to the threat are present. However, if these recommendations do not work to reduce the unpleasant emotional state, people revert to more maladaptive strategies, such as defensive avoidance (i.e., not thinking about the threat) or perceived manipulation (i.e., feeling angry because of a perception of being manipulated). Whichever method works best to reduce fear, either adhering to the recommendation or evading the threat, becomes the preferred and habitual response to the threat. Ultimately, Janis (1967) proposed a curvilinear interpretation where increased fear produces adaptive responses up to the point where fear becomes too strong, after which adaptive responses should decrease. In this view, moderate fear appeals should be most effective in motivating adaptive action.

Parallel Response Model

Despite the empirical evidence in support of the fear-as-drive curvilinear model, Leventhal's research (Leventhal & Watts, 1966) began to suggest that increased fear produced gains in protective responses. In introducing his parallel response model, Leventhal (1970) challenged the assumptions of the drive models that "fear arousal instigates the cognitive processes that mediate acceptance of fear appeals' recommendations" (Eagly & Chaiken, 1993, p. 440). Instead, he proposed that a threat is cognitively evaluated, which in turn triggers one or both of two distinct processes. One is primarily a cognitive process, called danger control, and occurs when people think about the threat and ways to avert it. The focus of danger control is on controlling the threat. The second process, called fear control, is primarily affective and occurs when people engage in strategies to control their fear because it is an undesirable emotion.

The major difference with fear-as-drive models is that the parallel response model is open to the possibility that fear is not the only possible immediate response to risk information. Unfortunately, however, Leventhal's parallel response model does not specify when people engage in danger control, fear control, or both, and how these processes interact.

Protection Motivation Theory

In response to the lack of specificity in Leventhal's model, Rogers (1975, 1983) introduced the protection motivation theory, which focuses solely on the danger control side of the parallel response model. Protection motivation theory claims that four components are needed in a fear appeal: *perceived vulnerability*, which is the perceived probability that a threat will occur; *perceived severity*, which is the perceived magnitude of noxiousness of a threat; *response efficacy*, which is the perceived effectiveness of the recommended response; and *self-efficacy,* which is the degree to which one feels capable of performing the recommended response. Protection motivation theory suggests that these components produce two cognitive mediating processes—*threat appraisal* and *coping appraisal.* Perceptions of vulnerability and severity elicit a threat appraisal process, whereas response efficacy and self-efficacy facilitate a coping appraisal process. If both processes are positive, then the maximum amount of protection motivation (and thus attitude or behavior change) would be elicited, but if one or both are negative, then maladaptive responses are more likely. Yzer, Fisher, Bakker, Siero, and Misovich (1998), for example, tested interactions between perceived risk and self-efficacy in a sample of young women. They found that intention to use condoms was highest among women who had received information that their risk of getting infected with HIV was high and who had relatively high self-efficacy. These women also were least likely to engage in denial of their risk of HIV infection.

Protection motivation theory's explication of the nature of threat and coping message components has importantly advanced understanding of risk communication. The theory's focus, however, primarily involves cognitive processes and does not explicate the possible explanatory role of fear as an emotion.

The Extended Parallel Process Model

Witte (1992) reintegrated the affective process with the cognitive framework advanced by Rogers (1975, 1983) and built on the parallel danger and fear control framework established by Leventhal (1970) to introduce the extended parallel process model. According to the extended parallel process model, exposure to a fear appeal initiates two appraisals of the message. First, information in the message is used to appraise the threat of the hazard, based on perceptions about the severity of the threat as well as how susceptible individuals believe themselves to be to the threat. The more individuals believe the threat is severe and that they are susceptible to serious danger, the more motivated they are to begin the second appraisal, which is an evaluation of the efficacy of the recommended response. More specifically, individuals gauge the perceived effectiveness of the response (response efficacy) to avert the threat as well as their beliefs about their own ability to effectively avoid the hazard (self-efficacy). If no information regarding the efficacy of the recommended response is given, individuals will rely on past experiences and prior beliefs to determine perceived efficacy.

The extended parallel process model maintains that individuals do one of three things following the appraisals of a fear appeal. People are likely to ignore the message if the threat is perceived as irrelevant or insignificant, leaving no motivation to process the message at all. Alternatively, people may engage in danger control, where they cognitively process the message and take action to avoid the threat. Danger control processes dominate when people realize they are susceptible to a serious threat and believe they can successfully avert it. A combination of high threat (e.g., "Your age and diet make colon cancer a real risk for you") and high efficacy (e.g., "If detected early, colon cancer in many cases is treatable. Screening tests are available to you") in a message can encourage this realization of danger control as an appropriate path. As a third possible response, people engage in fear control upon exposure to a serious threat when they believe themselves to be susceptible but do not believe they can successfully avoid the threat. Such beliefs emerge from exposure to a high-threat, low-efficacy message. In contrast to the cognitive danger control processes, fear control processes are largely focused on emotion, where people respond to and cope with their fear and not the danger. Under fear control, heightened fear arousal leads people to defensive avoidance (e.g., "I'm just not going to think about colon cancer because it scares me too much"), denial (e.g., "I'm not going to get colon cancer; no one else I know has it"), or message manipulation (e.g., "They are just trying to scare me, but it won't work on me").

Information Processing Perspectives on Fear

Whereas fear appeal theories developed clear predictions about outcomes of exposure to particular message configurations, they have been less clear on the message processing mechanisms that explain those outcomes. In recent discussions, scholars have argued for the usefulness of information processing theory for expanding our understanding of fear appeals (de Hoog, Stroebe, & de Wit, 2007; Ruiter, Abraham, & Kok, 2001). Particularly useful are ideas about the roles of motivation for information processing developed in the heuristic–systematic model (Chaiken, 1980, 1987). Briefly, the heuristic–systematic model describes the nature of information processing in terms of cognitive effort. The heuristic–systematic model allows for two main types of processing, which might co-occur but which nonetheless highlight different information engagement strategies. People sometimes process information with minimal cognitive effort *(heuristic)*, that is, by relying on heuristic decision rules. Sometimes, people process information in a relatively more cognitively effortful manner *(systematic)*, that is, by deeply considering arguments put forth in the message.

The model proposes accuracy and defense motives as primary influences on the nature of information processing. *Accuracy-motivated processing* involves unbiased information use in order to attain an objective, well-founded judgment. In contrast, *defense-motivated processing* is biased in the sense that it uses information in such a way that it is "congruent with one's perceived . . . self-definitional beliefs" (Chen, Duckworth, & Chaiken, 1999, p. 45). The stronger either accuracy motivation or defense motivation, the more systematically information will be processed.

There have been efforts to apply these ideas to understand fear appeal effects. For example, de Hoog and colleagues (2007; see also Das, de Wit, & Stroebe, 2003) interpret the likelihood of processing mode (heuristic or systematic) and goal (accuracy or defense motive) as a function of the levels of perceived risk and severity of the threat. According to this reasoning, self-defining beliefs (e.g., about being a healthy person) are challenged when people feel at risk for a severe threat. As a result, information is processed systematically and defensively, such that high effort is expended to find validation for one's belief of being a healthy person. High risk to a nonsevere threat or low risk to a severe threat are hypothesized to pose lesser challenge to self-defining beliefs, yet indicate relevance, and thus induce systematic processing activated by an accuracy motive. Last, low risk to a nonsevere threat indicates neither relevance nor challenged self-definitions, and information therefore is processed with minimal effort if at all.

These recent contributions usefully qualify predictions from previous fear appeal theories about optimal fear appeal configurations. Similar to previous theories, however, the explanatory role of fear remains underdeveloped, and "the specific role of fear is still not clear in any of these models" (Ordoñana, González, Espín-López, & Gómez-Amor, 2009, p. 196). More specifically, many theories that propose to account for effects of induced fear work on the assumption that the emotion of fear is a function of cognitions regarding risk and severity of the threat and therefore elaborate on these cognitive determinants of fear but not explicitly on fear itself, which is the factor that theoretically should explain effects (Dillard, 1994).

Fear and Self-Esteem Regulation

The emotion literature provides more explicit considerations of the explanatory role of fear. Not unlike traditional drive models, the emotion literature generally maintains that induced positive and negative emotions activate motivated response sets (Chen & Bargh, 1999). According to this perspective, intense positive emotions activate an approach system, and intense negative emotions, including fear, activate a defensive system (Bradley, Codispoti, Cuthbert, & Lang, 2001). Approach activation involves consideration of all available information, whereas defense activation leads people to quickly fall back on internalized responses (Lang, 2006). This implies that when a threatening message induces fear, people are less inclined to fully process the message than when it does not induce fear.

One explanation for the activation of defensive responses in response to fear has to do with the core human motive of maintaining positive self-esteem. Whereas many different mechanisms can be employed to regulate self-esteem, they all serve the purpose to defend the integrity of the self (Tesser, 2000). Integrity is one's sense that one is a good person—for example, competent, rational, and stable—and that one's beliefs and thoughts are socially appropriate (Sherman & Cohen, 2006; Steele, 1988).

People respond in one of three ways to threats to their self-integrity (in this case, a fear appeal message). First, individuals can accept the threat and accept necessary belief and behavioral change when the threat is not central to their self-defining beliefs. It will be more difficult to maintain self-integrity when the threat is important to people's sense of self, however, because the message that people's beliefs or behavior put them at risk for—for example, sexually transmitted disease infection—contravenes one's sense of self as a responsible and healthy person. Under such circumstances, we would be forced to uncomfortably confront the possibility that we have made past behavioral mistakes. Rather than accept this change in self-definition, and out of a desire to protect a self-image of oneself as rational and healthy, people may define the behavior as rational and healthy and, as a consequence, ultimately persevere in what others would deem irrational and unhealthful behavior (Sherman & Cohen, 2006, p. 194). For example, Jessop and colleagues showed that information about mortality-related risks of drinking increased intentions to binge drink among people for whom drinking is important to the self (Jessop & Wade, 2008) and increased intended and actual reckless driving among people for whom driving fast was important to their sense of self (Jessop, Albery, Rutter, & Garrod, 2008; see also Greenberg, Solomon, & Pyszcynski, 1997).

Do self-integrity motives always undermine messages that threaten self-definitional beliefs? Not necessarily. According to self-affirmation theory, reflection on an alternative part of people's sense of self that is unrelated to the threat protects people's overall sense of self-integrity. Having secured the sense that, overall, one is a good person, threatening information no longer necessarily challenges a person's global self-integrity. A message recipient then can consider the message for its information value and not as a challenge to self-integrity. Consequently, people will not feel the need to employ defensive biases and in fact are more likely to accept the personal relevance of the message (Harris & Napper, 2005; Klein & Harris, 2009; van Koningsbruggen & Das, 2009). Consistent with this, research has demonstrated that self-affirmation in domains other than the threatened information leads to more systematic, unbiased information processing (Correll, Spencer, & Zanna, 2004) and increases accessibility of threat-relevant cognitions (van Koningsbruggen, Das, & Roskos-Ewoldsen, 2009). This results in deep and unbiased processing of the message and increases message acceptance (Sherman & Cohen, 2006), particularly in response to messages framed in terms of the unfavorable consequences of the risky behavior (Zhao & Nan, 2010).

Conversely, people are more likely to resist the message when self-affirmation occurs in the same domain as the threat because this makes clear the discrepancy between what one believes to be and what a message asks them to be. The implied challenge for campaign developers thus is to design messages that do not affirm message recipients in threat-related domains but instead affirm in domains unrelated to the threat (Sherman & Cohen, 2006). This advice actually appears to run somewhat counter to recommendations some have drawn from fear appeal theories to affirm people's ability to effectively cope with a threat directly (which necessarily directs attention to the domain of the specific threat).

RESEARCH EVIDENCE FOR FEAR APPEAL EFFECTS

Before examining research support for the aforementioned theoretical frameworks, we first assess the nature of extant research in terms of its design. The experiment is the quintessential fear appeal study design, and only a few field tests of fear appeals have been published. In terms of theoretical foundations, most empirical fear appeal research draws on parallel response theory, such as the extended parallel response model. (Note that there is extensive research in the self-esteem regulation literature that also bears on fear appeal effects, but only a limited number of studies directly apply this literature to fear appeal effects; for example, see van Koningsbruggen et al., 2009.) Parallel process research typically examines message effects on danger control and fear control. Danger control is conceptualized as message acceptance and is typically operationalized as effects on self-reported attitude, intention, and behavior. Operationalization of fear control is much more diverse and includes, for example, effects on self-reported message avoidance, religiosity, or even absence of message acceptance (for an overview see Good & Abraham, 2007). Induced fear also typically is assessed with self-report measures, although research is emerging that employs arguably more internally valid psychophysiological measures of fear (Kessels, Ruiter, & Jansma, 2010; Ordoñana et al., 2009).

Beyond experimental research, reviews and meta-analytical tests of predictions developed in fear appeal theories also permit a number of conclusions. First, linear effects of fear appeals on message acceptance are more likely than curvilinear effects (Boster & Mongeau, 1984; Witte & Allen, 2000). In addition, fear appeal components (i.e., perceived risk, perceived severity, response efficacy and self-efficacy) each contribute to message acceptance, but their interaction has not received strong meta-analytical support (de Hoog, Stroebe & de Wit, 2007; Witte & Allen, 2000). A threat is more likely to trigger self-defensive responses when personal relevance of the threat is high than when it is low (Good & Abraham, 2007). However, threat-irrelevant self-affirmation and self-efficacy message manipulations reduce the need for defensive responses and increase message acceptance even if the threat is personally relevant (Good & Abraham, 2007; Sherman & Cohen, 2006).

Although these findings have potentially important implications for campaign message design, extant research does not conclusively point at one prediction as superior to others. This contention is informed by a number of observations. To begin, because original research predominantly tested hypotheses within the context of a single fear appeal framework, comparative inferences are difficult to make. Because meta-analysis can estimate effect sizes as a function of systematic differences between studies, meta-analytical work has been useful in this regard. There are no published meta-analyses, however, that systematically compare predictions from the major classes of theory that we discussed in this chapter, that is, parallel process models, information processing, and self-esteem regulation. For example, it is not yet clear how self-affirmation interacts with varying levels of threat and efficacy message components. In the absence of threat-irrelevant self-affirmation, are defensive responses likely even if a message contains both threat and efficacy information?

Understanding of the role of fear also is hampered by a shortage of optimal tests of the theorized roles of fear. Consider, for example, Boster and Mongeau's (1984) claim that many studies actually might not elicit fear adequately. These authors used meta-analysis to examine 40 fear appeal studies and found a mean correlation between fear manipulation and perceived fear of $r = .36$. Witte and Allen (2000) reported similar results from 51 studies. De Hoog and colleagues (2007) examined vulnerability (23 studies) and severity manipulations (39 studies) separately. The Cohen d values that de Hoog and colleagues report translate into a vulnerability manipulation–perceived fear correlation of $r = .16$ and a severity manipulation–perceived fear correlation of $r = .28$. If we accept for sake of discussion that the measures in the studies submitted to these three meta-analyses validly gauged induced fear, then the observed correlations suggest that, on average, fear appeal research has not been able to produce very strong levels of fear (O'Keefe, 2002). Put differently, much of what we think we know about fear as a mechanism is based on a comparison between low and moderate levels of fear.

We therefore should pay careful attention to interpretations of fear appeal effects and, in particular, of null findings. For example, some research failed to find support for fear appeal effects on message acceptance (e.g., Earl & Albarracin, 2007). A common interpretation of such findings is that they demonstrate that fear appeal messages do not produce desired effects. If induced fear mediates message effects as theorized, however, then a message that does not produce very high levels of fear should be expected to produce only small effects on message acceptance (Boster & Mongeau, 1984). That is, the low effects are not necessarily due to lack of relationship but to a lack of treatment.

As the fear appeal definitions quoted in the opening paragraph of this chapter illustrate, fear appeals have been interpreted both in terms of message components and as the level of fear induced in an audience (O'Keefe, 2002). As a result, much research examined direct effects of fear appeal message components or perceived fear on attitude, intention, and behavior. Such analytical strategies are not optimal tests of the theorized role of fear. More specifically, multiple fear appeal theories propose a mediation process by which a message induces fear, and fear in turn affects attitude, intention, and behavior. Tests of the direct effects of exposure of fear appeal messages on attitude, intention, and behavior are not appropriate mediation tests, per se, meaning such studies typically leave claims about fear as an explanatory mechanism unsubstantiated (Stephenson, Southwell, & Yzer, 2011).

FEAR APPEALS IN A PUBLIC COMMUNICATION CONTEXT

There is good reason why our discussion thus far has focused on theoretical explanations for fear appeal effects. As just summarized, however, development of these theories for the most part has relied on experimental or quasi-experimental research. What does this mean for our interest in fear induction as a public communication campaign strategy? Hastings, Stead, and Webb (2004) argue that "the crucial question is not 'can fear messages change behavior in the laboratory' but, rather, 'can fear appeals change behavior in the sophisticated and overcrowded clutter of the real-world communications environment?'" (p. 963).

Indeed, the complex information environment in which public communication campaigns operate have little resemblance with laboratory settings in which all possibly competing or reinforcing sources of influence are controlled (Hornik, 2002). "We have no idea, for example, whether the average television viewer actually watches a fear appeal if exposed, or whether she or he immediately changes the channel" (Witte & Allen, 2000, p. 605), or for that matter, perceives the fear content at all.

Hastings and colleagues (2004) report that the few evaluations of explicit fear appeal campaigns that have been published generally demonstrate smaller fear appeal effects than lab studies. In addition, Earl and Albarracin's (2007) meta-analysis of 76 HIV prevention intervention studies found that fear induction was associated with decreased short- and longer-term HIV-relevant knowledge and behavior. Although there remains a very clear need for more field-based fear appeal research, these studies call for careful interpretation of the generalizability of results from lab studies on fear appeals.

The possibility that, in a public communication context messages can have both direct and indirect effects is another important idea that has been around for over 50 years (for review, see Southwell & Yzer, 2007). Curiously, however, it has been absent in fear appeal research. Current fear appeal research and theory uniformly focus on individual and direct processes to account for how fear appeal messages affect message recipients. In contrast, a campaign can induce talk with members from social networks about both message format and message topic, and this talk can subsequently affect people. Fear appeal messages with intense depictions of negative consequences are particularly likely fodder for talk (Hoeken, Swanepoel, Saal, & Jansen, 2009), and yet we know little about the indirect effects of fear appeal exposure that may ripple through social networks in all sorts of ways. Whereas a person may turn away upon direct exposure to a gruesome message, later conversation with someone else about the message and its topic likely will not be as immediately fearful (and in fact might be engaged as something of a self-soothing strategy). A more balanced discussion of the threat may thus be possible, meaning that conversational partners actually get exposed to a less threatening and possibly more accurate message than did the original fear appeal audience.

Danger response or fear response?

Conclusion

Despite a cumulative science of fear appeals, some questions are yet to be answered. For example, there remains a need for systematic inquiry into message components and individual differences among receivers to understand when fear is most likely to produce desired effects. Promising examples are Stephenson and Witte's (1998) work on the vividness of fear appeals, and de Hoog and colleagues' (2007) comparative analysis of visual and written threat severity information. Also, despite theoretical recognition that a fear appeal can be assessed both in terms of message component differences and in terms of actual emotional and physiological responses, extant research still primarily focuses on message components and cognitions in response to those components.

Importantly, developments in research on fear appeal messages have also spurred a number of new questions. What about simultaneous effects of theoretically distinct message elements, for example? Can we detect whether public campaign messages both tell an audience that they are at risk for a particular danger while at the same time help the audience maintain (or boost) their self-esteem? At issue here is the larger question of theoretical integration; much work in the fear appeal literature contrasts theoretical approaches. However, there is not enough work that systematically examines how parallel process models, information processing theory, and self-esteem regulation theory provide complementary insights as to how fear appeal messages work. Lastly, we need field studies to further examine the usefulness of fear appeal messages as a public campaign tool to examine fear appeals in more natural settings. Such natural settings matter as real-world messages do not exist in a vacuum, and we need to better understand the social and physical context of fear appeal engagement. Rather than directly and immediately transforming an audience's belief system, fear-inducing messages may also instigate conversation about message and message topics that may act as a catalyst for change, both for the individuals involved as well as for larger society. Field work could help us understand that process better.

Despite these future opportunities, we should recognize that advances in research on fear appeals already have valuable implications for the development of effective messages. We know that messages that emphasize the severity of a risky behavior and the vulnerability of a specific target group that engages in such behavior are successful, provided a strong efficacy component is also part of the message. More recent work further contends that the degree to which a message is central to a person's self-definition regulates the cognitive effort afforded to processing the message and that self-relevant fear appeal messages are successful when they allow an audience to maintain their self-esteem. Thus, messages that frame severity, vulnerability, and efficacy information to suggest that a recommended behavior both fits with one's sense of self and does not drastically depart from it are most likely to be effective as we seek to change behavior.

References

Boster, F. J., & Mongeau, P. A. (1984). Fear-arousing persuasive messages. In R. Bostrom (Ed.), *Communication yearbook 8* (pp. 330–375). Newbury Park, CA: Sage.

Bradley, M. M., Codispoti, M., Cuthbert, B. N., & Lang, P. J. (2001). Emotion and motivation I: Defensive and appetitive reactions in picture processing. *Emotion, 1,* 276–298.

Chaiken, S. (1980). Heuristic versus systematic information processing and the use of source versus message cues in persuasion. *Journal of Personality and Social Psychology, 39,* 752–766.

Chaiken, S. (1987). The heuristic model of persuasion. In M. P. Zanna, J. M. Olson, & C. P. Herman (Eds.), *Social influence: The Ontario Symposium* (Vol. 5, pp. 3–39). Hillsdale, NJ: Lawrence Erlbaum.

Chen, M., & Bargh, J. A. (1999). Consequences of automatic evaluation: Immediate behavioral predispositions to approach or avoid the stimulus. *Personality and Social Psychology Bulletin, 25,* 215–224.

Chen, S., Duckworth, K., & Chaiken, S. (1999). Motivated heuristic and systematic processing. *Psychological Inquiry, 10,* 44–49.

Correll, J., Spencer, S. J., & Zanna, M. P. (2004). An affirmed self and an open mind: Self-affirmation and sensitivity to argument strength. *Journal of Experimental Social Psychology, 40,* 350–356.

Das, E. H. H. J., de Wit, J. B. F., & Stroebe, W. (2003). Fear appeals motivate acceptance of action recommendations: Evidence for a positive bias in the processing of persuasive messages. *Personality and Social Psychology Bulletin, 29,* 650–664.

de Hoog, N., Stroebe, W., & de Wit, J. B. F. (2007). The impact of vulnerability to and severity of a health risk on processing and acceptance of fear-arousing communications: A meta-analysis. *Review of General Psychology, 11,* 258–285.

Dillard, J. P. (1994). Rethinking the study of fear appeals. *Communication Theory, 4,* 295–323.

Dillard, J. P., & Nabi, R. L. (2006). The persuasive influence of emotion in cancer prevention and detection messages. *Journal of Communication, 56,* s123–s139.

Dillard, J. P., Plotnick, C. A., Godbold, L. C., Freimuth, V. S., & Edgar, T. (1996). The multiple affective outcomes of AIDS PSAs: Fear appeals do more than scare people. *Communication Research, 23,* 44–72.

Eagly, A. H., & Chaiken, S. (1993). *The psychology of attitudes.* Orlando, FL: Harcourt Brace.

Earl, A., & Albarracin, D. (2007). Nature, decay, and spiraling of the effects of fear-inducing arguments and HIV counseling and testing: A meta-analysis of the short and long-term outcomes of HIV-prevention interventions. *Health Psychology, 26,* 496–506.

Frijda, N., Kuipers, P., & ter Schure, E. (1989). Relations among emotion, appraisal, and emotional action readiness. *Journal of Personality and Social Psychology, 57,* 212–228.

Good, A., & Abraham, C. (2007). Measuring defensive responses to threatening messages: A meta-analysis of measures. *Health Psychology Review, 1,* 208–229.

Greenberg, J., Solomon, S., & Pyszczynski, T. (1997). Terror management theory of self-esteem and cultural worldviews: Empirical assessments and conceptual refinements. In M. P. Zanna (Ed.), *Advances in experimental social psychology* (Vol. 29, pp. 61–141). San Diego, CA: Academic Press.

Harris, P. R., & Napper, L. (2005). Self-affirmation and the biased processing of threatening health-risk information. *Personality and Social Psychology Bulletin, 31,* 1250–1263.

Hastings, G., Stead, M., & Webb, J. (2004). Fear appeals in social marketing: Strategic and ethical reasons for concern. *Psychology & Marketing, 21,* 961–986.

Hoeken, H., Swanepoel, P., Saal, E. O., & Jansen, C. J. M. (2009). Using message form to stimulate conversations: The case of tropes. *Communication Theory, 19,* 49–65.

Hornik, R. C. (2002). Exposure: Theory and evidence about all the ways it matters. *Social Marketing Quarterly, 8,* 30–37.

Hovland, C., Janis, I., & Kelly, H. (1953). *Communication and persuasion.* New Haven, CT: Yale University Press.

Janis, I. L. (1967). Effects of fear arousal on attitude change: Recent developments in theory and experimental research. *Advances in Experimental Social Psychology, 3,* 167–225.

Jessop, D. C., Albery, I. P., Rutter, J., & Garrod, H. (2008). Understanding the impact of mortality-related health-risk information: A terror management perspective. *Personality and Social Psychology Bulletin, 34,* 951–964.

Jessop, D. C., & Wade, J. (2008). Fear appeals and binge drinking: A terror management theory perspective. *British Journal of Health Psychology, 13,* 773–788.

Kessels, L. T. E., Ruiter, R. A. C., & Jansma, B. M. (2010). Increased attention but more efficient disengagement: Neuroscientific evidence for defensive processing of threatening health information. *Health Psychology, 29,* 346–354.

Klein, W. M., & Kunda, Z. (1993). Maintaining self-serving social comparisons: Biased reconstruction of one's past behaviors. *Personality and Social Psychology Bulletin, 19,* 732–739.

Klein, W. M. P., & Harris, P. R. (2009). Self-affirmation enhances attentional bias toward threatening components of a persuasive message. *Psychological Science, 20,* 1463–1467.

Lang, A. (2006). Using the Limited Capacity Model of Motivated Mediated Message Processing to design effective cancer communication messages. *Journal of Communication, 56,* S57–S80.

Leventhal, H. (1970). Findings and theory in the study of fear communications. In L. Berkowitz (Ed.), *Advances in experimental social psychology* (Vol. 5, pp. 119–186). New York: Academic Press.

Leventhal, H., & Watts, J. C. (1966). Sources of resistance to fear-arousing communications on smoking and lung cancer. *Journal of Personality, 34,* 155–175.

Nabi, R. L. (1999). A cognitive-functional model for the effects of discrete negative emotions on information processing, attitude change, and recall. *Communication Theory, 9,* 292–320.

O'Keefe, D. J. (2002). *Persuasion: Theory and research* (2nd ed.). Thousand Oaks, CA: Sage.

Ordoñana, J. R., González, F., Espín-López, L., & Gómez-Amor, J. (2009). Self-report and psychophysiological responses to fear appeals. *Human Communication Research, 35,* 195–220.

Reyna, V. F., & Brainerd, C. J. (2007). The importance of mathematics in health and human judgment: Numeracy, risk communication, and medical decision making. *Learning and Individual Differences, 17,* 147–159.

Rogers, R. W. (1975). A protection motivation theory of fear appeals and attitude change. *Journal of Psychology, 91,* 93–114.

Rogers, R. W. (1983). Cognitive and physiological processes in fear appeals and attitude change: A revised theory of protection motivation. In J. Cacioppo & R. E. Petty (Eds.), *Social psychophysiology* (pp. 153–176). New York: Guilford Press.

Roseman, I. J., Wiest, C., & Swartz, T. S. (1994). Phenomenology, behaviors, and goals differentiate discrete emotions. *Journal of Personality and Social Psychology, 67,* 206–221.

Rothman, A. J., Klein, W. M., & Weinstein, N. D. (1996). Absolute and relative biases in estimations of personal risk. *Journal of Applied Social Psychology, 26,* 1213–1236.

Ruiter, R. A. C., Abraham, C., & Kok, G. (2001). Scary warnings and rational precautions: A review of the psychology of fear appeals. *Psychology and Health, 16,* 613–630.

Salovey, P., Rothman, A. J., Detweiler, J. B., & Steward, W. T. (2000). Emotional states and physical health. *American Psychologist, 55,* 110–121.

Sherman, D. K., & Cohen, G. L. (2006). The psychology of self-defense: Self-affirmation theory. In M. P. Zanna (Ed.), *Advances in experimental social psychology* (Vol. 38, pp. 183–242). San Diego, CA: Academic Press.

Steele, C. M. (1988). The psychology of self-affirmation: Sustaining the integrity of the self. In L. Berkowitz (Ed.), *Advances in experimental social psychology* (Vol. 21, pp. 261–302). New York: Academic Press.

Stephenson, M. T., & Witte, K. (1998). Fear, threat, and perceptions of efficacy from frightening skin cancer messages. *Public Health Reviews, 26,* 147–174.

Stephenson, M. T., Southwell, B., & Yzer, M. C. (2011). Advancing health communication research to the next level: Issues and controversies in experimental design and data analysis. In T. L. Thompson, R. L. Parrott, & J. Nussbaum (Eds.), *Handbook of health communication* (Vol. 2, pp. 560–577). New York: Routledge.

Southwell, B. G., & Yzer, M. C. (2007). The roles of interpersonal communication in mass media campaigns. In C. Beck (Ed.), *Communication yearbook 31* (pp. 419–462). New York: Lawrence Erlbaum Associates.

Tesser, A. (2000). On the confluence of self-esteem maintenance mechanisms. *Personality and Social Psychology Review, 4,* 290–299.

van Koningsbruggen, G. M., & Das, E. (2009). Don't derogate this message! Self-affirmation promotes online type 2 diabetes risk test taking. *Psychology and Health, 24,* 635–649.

van Koningsbruggen, G. M., Das, E., & Roskos-Ewoldsen, D. R. (2009). How self-affirmation reduces defensive processing of threatening health information: Evidence at the implicit level. *Health Psychology, 28,* 563–568.

Weinstein, N. D. (1984). Why it won't happen to me: Perceptions of risk factors and susceptibility. *Health Psychology, 3,* 431–457.

Williams-Piehota, P., Pizarro, J., Schneider, T. R., Mowad, L., & Salovey, P. (2005). Matching health messages to monitor-blunter coping styles to motivate screening mammography. *Health Psychology, 24,* 58–67.

Witte, K. (1992). Putting the fear back into fear appeals: The extended parallel process model. *Communication Monographs, 59,* 329–349.

Witte, K., & Allen, M. (2000). A meta-analysis of fear appeals: Implications for effective public health campaigns. *Health Education & Behavior, 27,* 591–615.

Yzer, M. C., Fisher, J. D., Bakker, A. B., Siero, F. W., & Misovich, S. J. (1998). The effects of information about AIDS risk and self-efficacy on women's intentions to engage in AIDS preventive behavior. *Journal of Applied Social Psychology, 28,* 1837–1852.

Zhao, X., & Nan, X. (2010). Influence of self-affirmation on responses to gain- versus loss-framed antismoking messages. *Human Communication Research, 36,* 493–511.

CHAPTER 12

Truth in Advertising

*Social Norms Marketing Campaigns to Reduce College
Student Drinking*

William DeJong and Sandi W. Smith

Several studies have demonstrated that most college students believe their peers are drinking much more alcohol on average than is actually the case (Borsari & Carey, 2003; Perkins, Meilman, Leichliter, Cashin, & Presley, 1999). That so many students misperceive campus drinking norms should not be a surprise. Beginning with the film *Animal House* in 1978, several Hollywood comedies have glorified high-risk drinking on campus and made light of alcohol-related problems. Televised college football and basketball games feature advertising by breweries and other alcohol producers. Even television news reports, which often show images of students doing shots or using beer funnels, inadvertently convey the mistaken idea that most college students drink frequently and heavily when, in fact, the majority are drinking moderately or not at all.

A major concern is that misperceptions of student drinking norms are likely to drive up actual student alcohol consumption (Perkins & Craig, 2003). This viewpoint is bolstered by the Theory of Planned Behavior. According to this theory, perceived *subjective norms*— beliefs about what important others expect a person to do in a given situation—are a major determinant of social behavior (Ajzen, 1985; Fishbein & Ajzen, 1975). In turn, perceptions of subjective norms are shaped by 1) *descriptive norms*—beliefs about what most people do in a given situation and 2) *injunctive norms*—beliefs about which behaviors have social approval (Park, Klein, Smith, & Martell, 2009). The process of collecting, analyzing, storing, and recalling this social information is highly prone to error (Nisbett & Ross, 1980). Even so, subjective norms derived from inaccurate assessments of what people are doing and approve of are nonetheless important influences on behavior (Ajzen, 1985).

Perkins and Berkowitz (1986) speculated that a communication campaign that provides accurate information about student alcohol use would reduce misperceptions of campus drinking norms, diminish normative pressure to drink, and thereby reduce student alcohol consumption. This type of campaign has become known as *social norms marketing* (SNM). These campaigns, they argued, should result in less drinking behavior after the true norm is publicized widely, providing that the true norm is believable to students and does not fall into their *latitude of rejection* (Glazer, Smith, Atkin, & Hamel, 2010; Park, Smith, & Klein, 2011; Smith, Atkin, Martell, Allen, & Hembroff, 2006).

OVERVIEW OF SOCIAL NORMS AND COLLEGE DRINKING

Early Research on Social Norms Marketing

Campus administrators at a handful of colleges were the first to try this innovative approach, beginning with Northern Illinois University in 1989 (Haines & Barker, 2003). At the University of Arizona, the percentage of students who reported in anonymous surveys that they had five or more drinks in a row in the past two weeks decreased from 40% to 31% (Johannessen & Glider, 2003). At Hobart and William Smith Colleges, the percentage of students who reported drinking at that level of three or more times in the past two weeks decreased from 41% to 28% (Perkins & Craig, 2003).

These investigations were preexperiments—that is, simple before–after comparisons without a control group. Even so, advocates of this approach presented SNM as the best solution to college drinking. Officials at several colleges, eager to try something new, began to replicate SNM on their campuses despite the absence of rigorous research. Those who used extensive formative research to create their campaigns and then make midcourse corrections and also maintained the campaigns over several years also reported progress in changing students' alcohol-related attitudes and behaviors (Lederman, Stewart, Barr, Powell, Laitman, & Goodhart, 2011; Lederman & Stewart, 2005).

In 2002 the National Institute on Alcohol Abuse and Alcoholism (NIAAA) Task Force on College Drinking classified this approach as a Tier 3 strategy—meaning that it was a promising approach. There were both logical and theoretical reasons for thinking that SNM campaigns might work, but the absence of rigorous evaluations involving control groups left the matter in doubt.

At this time, critics expressed concern that SNM campaigns would play into the hands of the alcohol industry by appearing to minimize the scope of the campus drinking problem and thus undermine support for stricter campus policies, tougher law enforcement, and higher alcohol excise taxes that would decrease student access to alcohol and reduce consumption (Wechsler & Wuethrich, 2002). Indeed, a few campus SNM campaigns were sponsored by Anheuser-Busch, the nation's largest beer producer.

To investigate the impact of SNM campaigns, Wechsler, Nelson, Lee, Seibring, Lewis, & Keeling (2003) asked a senior administrator at each of 98 institutions whether their campus used *social norms marketing*. A comparison of colleges with versus without a campaign showed that SNM had no effect on student drinking. Unfortunately, the researchers failed to look into the scope, intensity, or quality of the campaigns to make sure that they were well executed. In fact, one of the included campaigns was the subject of a critical case study report that analyzed its several design and implementation flaws (Russell, Clapp, & DeJong, 2005).

Social Norms Marketing Research Project

DeJong, Schneider, Towvim, Murphy, Doerr, Simonsen, and colleagues (2006, 2009) conducted two randomized control trials as part of the Social Norms Marketing Research Project, each with matched four-year colleges and universities randomly assigned to either a treatment group or a nonintervention control group. Project staff trained campus officials on how to conduct a campaign following the University of Arizona model (Johannessen & Glider, 2003) and vetted all draft materials to ensure that they met program guidelines. The campaigns used a variety of media channels, including posters, fliers, newspaper ads, radio and television ads, table tents, staged public events, talks and presentations, and item giveaways. Each campaign ran for three years.

The social norms messages had to be targeted to the entire undergraduate population; convey factual information about a behavior typical of a majority of students, as documented by a random-sample, preintervention survey; correct social norms that were misperceived, again documented by a survey; and avoid a judgmental or moralistic tone. Campaign materials also had to include the campaign logo ("Just the Facts"), describe the random-sample survey, and present the definition of a *drink* used in the survey (i.e., 1 drink = 12 oz. beer = 4 oz. wine = 1 oz. liquor). Print ads had to include an eye-catching photograph of students.

It is important to understand that students who are abstainers or light drinkers are unlikely to start drinking more alcohol after an SNM campaign informs them that the majority norm is for students to have, for example, zero to four drinks when partying. These students had already decided whether and how they would use alcohol when believing that the true drinking norm was higher than the level announced by the campaign, despite whatever normative pressure to conform that their misperception might have created. Now knowing that the true drinking norm is less than they believed should result in their feeling even less pressure and not more.

The first study, involving 18 institutions, showed that the SNM campaigns had been effective. Across several survey measures, the level of drinking at the control group schools went up significantly, matching national trends reported by the Core Institute, while the intervention group schools remained stable and showed no such increase (DeJong et al., 2006). Surprisingly, the second study, involving 14 institutions, showed no differences between the treatment and control group schools, even though the second round of campaigns was better executed (DeJong et al., 2009).

Scribner and colleagues (2011) reanalyzed the combined data from the two studies, taking into account the density of on-premise alcohol outlets (bars, taverns, restaurants) within a three-mile radius of each of the 32 campuses. Specifically, the investigators compared how well the SNM campaigns did when outlet density was at or above the median (10.78 outlets per 1,000 students) versus below the median. They found that the SNM campaigns did make a difference at institutions located in communities with low outlet density but failed to have an effect in communities with high density.

This finding explained the differing results for two studies. In the first, which showed that social norms campaigns can be effective, 13 of the 18 institutions were located in low-density communities. In the second study, a replication failure, 11 of the 14 institutions were located in high-density communities.

A possible explanation for these results is that the alcohol outlets—by their mere presence but also because of their promotional advertising—communicated messages about the campus drinking culture that competed with the SNM campaigns and reinforced student misperceptions of campus drinking norms. The DeJong and colleagues studies provided each campus with start-up funds of only $2,000 per year, with supplemental funds of $300 to $1,650 per campus awarded for the second and third years. The colleges in high-density communities may have had insufficient resources to mount effective campaigns given the extent of the proalcohol messaging found there.

The small budgets for the two studies' SNM campaigns and the relatively limited message dissemination that resulted suggest a more basic explanation for their restricted impact: They failed to achieve the high volume of message repetition that is necessary to attain large audience exposure and promote learning, both crucial determinants of a health campaign's effectiveness (Atkin, 2001; Atkin & Salmon, 2010).

The remainder of this chapter underscores the importance of message repetition—and message quality—by reviewing two major case studies at universities with leading social norms campaigns.

UNIVERSITY OF VIRGINIA CASE STUDY

A case study conducted at the University of Virginia showed that a large, well-funded, and highly visible social norms campaign can counteract an entrenched drinking culture and reduce alcohol-related problems (Turner, Perkins, & Bauerle, 2008). The university's campaign began in 1999 with a focus on first-year students and then expanded in 2002 to include all undergraduates. The campaign messages corrected misperceptions about the quantity and frequency of alcohol use while also communicating that most students practiced protective behaviors, such as asking friends to slow down if they were drinking excessively, tending to a friend who had passed out, not allowing an intoxicated friend to drive, and using a designated driver or alternative transportation.

The campaign grew over time. In 1999, staff introduced the campaign through a monthly series of posters. In 2002, the campus-wide campaign was introduced with weekly campus posters, e-mails, and newspaper ads and articles, plus staff and peer presentations in residence halls, Greek residences, and classrooms. In 2003, the staff organized small group sessions for fraternity and sorority members and athletes. In 2004, the campaign began to host an annual music event. Facebook ads commenced in 2005. Parent orientation sessions started before the 2002–2003 academic year.

The study did not include any control group institutions. Nonetheless, the University of Virginia study has two strengths. First, survey data were collected annually from 2001 through 2006. Second, no new policies or programs to address student drinking were launched at the institutional, community, or state level during this time. This convenient fact increases the likelihood that any observed changes were due to the SNM campaign and not to other initiatives. That noted, alternative explanations—having nothing to do with the campaign, such as changes in the composition of the student body—cannot be completely ruled out.

The changes in student behavior reported over the course of this intensive SNM campaign were dramatic. According to annual survey data, in 2001 only 33% of undergraduates reported experiencing none of 10 negative consequences due to alcohol use compared to 51% in 2006, and while 44% experienced multiple negative consequences in 2001, only 26% did so in 2006. Nationally, alcohol-impaired driving is the primary cause of alcohol-related student deaths. In 2001, 27% of University of Virginia undergraduates said they had driven under the influence of alcohol, but in 2006, only 15% indicated this was the case.

As Turner and his colleagues (2008) point out, national surveys of college students showed no decrease or even slight increases in several self-reported negative consequences between 2001 and 2005. The University of Virginia's experience stands in stark contrast, as does Michigan State University's (MSU's) experience.

MICHIGAN STATE UNIVERSITY CASE STUDY

MSU's social norms marketing campaign is frequently cited as one of the better campaigns. The campaign is grounded in basic communication principles and practices but also illustrates how informative prevention messages about student drinking can be introduced in a creative and lighthearted way that draws student attention, stimulates interpersonal communication, and changes the campus culture.

In the late 1990s and early 2000s, MSU had a student culture fueled by alcohol. The campus was named regularly on the "Top 10 Party School" lists, and several riots had occurred, one of which was over the perceived "right" to consume alcohol on a certain spot on campus when tailgating before football games. An action team made up of campus and community members was formed to change MSU's high-risk drinking culture. Implementation of an SNM campaign was one of the key recommendations that followed. Since that time, a multidisciplinary team from the Olin Health Center, the Office for Survey Research, and the Department of Communication has worked on the social norms campaign with the approval of the university's senior administrators.

Early Campaign Development

As noted, the first step in an SNM campaign is to determine misperceptions of the behavior in question—in this case, alcohol consumption. MSU accomplished this through a large-scale, random-sample survey conducted in 2000, which was repeated in subsequent years. In 2000, students perceived that the typical MSU student drank an average of 6.1 drinks the last time they partied. In actuality, the average student reported drinking 5.4 drinks, showing that the descriptive norm, as expected, was higher than the actual level of alcohol consumed.

Using these data, MSU created and frequently disseminated campaign materials that highlighted the actual level of alcohol consumption. Representative ads are presented in Figure 12.1. A wide variety of communication channels were used, including print and electronic newspaper ads, Facebook ads, tabletop displays, posters, flyers, billboards, coasters, BAC cards, T-shirts, academic orientation sessions, and classroom presentations. In addition, web-based alcohol education programs that incorporated normative feedback were used for all incoming freshmen and judicially referred students (Paschall, Antin, Ringwalt, & Saltz, 2011), while counseling, judicial, clinical, and residence hall staff received training to provide individualized normative feedback to students during one-on-one meetings.

FIGURE 12.1   Examples of MSU's SNM campaign ads.

Findings from subsequent annual surveys have been used to guide new message development, inform campaign management, and evaluate overall success in meeting project goals and objectives. In this way, the MSU campaign is a cyclical process with evaluation data feeding back to inform new and revised campaign materials (see Atkin & Freimuth, Chapter 4; Valente & Kwan, Chapter 6).

Recent Findings Show Promising Impact

MSU's 2010 survey showed that students perceived that the typical MSU student drank 5.3 drinks the last time that they partied, when in actuality, they reported drinking an average of 4.2 drinks. Clearly, much progress has been made on the MSU campus, with misperceptions reduced from an average of 6.1 drinks in 2000 to 5.3 in 2010 and with alcohol consumption reduced from an average of 5.4 drinks in 2000 to 4.2 in 2010. These data also reveal, however, that the new norms still involve a misperception, thus setting the stage for the campaign's next phase. The strategy at MSU and for other long-running SNM campaigns is to ratchet down the levels of alcohol consumption and the attendant misperceptions by providing updated normative information at the beginning of each new campaign cycle.

Keys to Success in Michigan State University Campaign

Several campaign features and milestones explain the MSU campaign's success. The first feature of the MSU campaign is that both descriptive and injunctive norms are measured and presented in the messages. The messages in Figure 12.1 illustrate both types of norms. Descriptive norms are featured in all three advertisements. For example, "What Spartans Do" shows the percentage of MSU students who reported engaging in each behavior according to the preceding survey. Injunctive norms are the focus of the third panel of the Halloween advertisement, sometimes referred to as the "Puking Pumpkin" ad. This panel shows the percentage of MSU students who reported disapproval of certain behaviors in the survey preceding the ad.

A second important feature of the campaign is that it focuses on two different types of alcohol consumption: *celebration* drinking versus *global* (or everyday) drinking patterns (Atkin, Martell, Smith, & Greenamyer, 2004; Martell, Atkin, Hembroff, Smith, Baumer, & Greenamyer, 2006). The celebratory events included in the campaign are tailgating, Halloween, St. Patrick's Day, and spring break. Research at MSU discovered that students perceive a higher descriptive norm and a lower injunctive norm for celebration drinking— that is, they think that other students drink more during celebration events and disapprove of this behavior less than they do everyday drinking. The three advertisements shown in Figure 12.1 provide examples of both global and event-specific messages.

The third key feature of the MSU campaign is the encouragement of protective behaviors (Atkin, Smith, Klein, Glazer, & Martell, 2008; Smith et al., 2011). For example, the first two panels of the Halloween ad focus on the descriptive norms for two protective behaviors—staying with the same group of friends and eating before or during drinking. These and many other protective behaviors, coupled with an overall reduction in alcohol consumption, have been shown to reduce the negative consequences that students can experience from drinking, including doing something that they later regretted, blacking out (drinking to the point of not remembering where they were or what they did), injuring themselves or someone else, having unprotected sex, and experiencing academic harm.

Three milestones occurred during the campaign. The first milestone occurred in 2005 when, for the first time, a majority of MSU students (57%) reported that they drank zero to four drinks (rather than zero to five drinks) the last time they partied. This lower consumption level has been maintained since that time, making it possible to create messages using the more restrictive zero to four drink guideline. Figure 12.1 advertisements show this change, with the second ad showing zero to five drinks and the third ad showing zero to four drinks.

The second milestone is that the campaign was chosen as a Model Program by the U.S. Department of Education in 2007. The grant funds that came with this honor were used in part for website development; campaign materials can be found at socialnorms@msu.edu. The grant funds were also used to allow members of the MSU team to serve as resources for other schools as they developed their own SNM campaigns.

The third milestone occurred when an engaging new creative symbol was developed by members of a project team in an MSU advertising class, who were working with Olin Health Center campaign personnel. The award-winning "Duck Campaign" was thus born. The third ad in Figure 12.1 is an example of one of the "Duck" ads. Students report that they find the iconic duck to be highly likeable and a trustworthy source of information. MSU now has educational events called "It's Your Ducky Day" to educate students about social norms through interactive games, messages, and campaign giveaways such as T-shirts, posters, and bookmarks. These events, staffed by a volunteer group called the "Quack Pack," are popular with students.

Evaluation of the campaign over its 10-year history has shown a consistent downward trend in misperceptions, alcohol consumption, and associated harms and a corresponding upward trend in the use of several protective behaviors. This success is due to a highly committed multidisciplinary team acting with upper administration approval, adherence to the principles of SNM, and the ongoing use of formative and summative evaluation to inform the campaign's development and later refinement.

LESSONS LEARNED FROM RECENT RESEARCH

There are several important lessons to be learned from past research on SNM. First, it is especially important for the campaign to have a high level of activity with frequent message repetition. Occasional messages are insufficient. There should be a variety of supportive messages and media executions to keep the campaign fresh and avoid message fatigue.

Second, not all students are exposed to the same communication channels. As a result, reaching the broadest cross-section of students requires using multiple venues (see Atkin & Freimuth, Chapter 4). Special consideration needs to be given to commuter students, who tend to be less engaged with campus life and therefore view student newspapers or other traditional student media less frequently.

Third, students have grown up with the idea that most college students drink heavily and therefore may greet an SNM campaign with skepticism, especially at first. Campaign organizers need to anticipate and prepare for this possibility. Early messaging that explains how the student surveys were conducted and why drinking norms are so often misperceived can help persuade students to trust the data.

Another method for building trust in the campaign is to begin with messages that focus on other normative behaviors that are uncontroversial and therefore unlikely to raise doubts about the information source (e.g., percentage of students involved in community service, average time spent sleeping) and then to weave in the alcohol-related messages later on (Perkins & Craig, 2003).

Fourth, students will not be moved to change their behavior if they do not identify with the student body as a whole (Neighbors, O'Connor, Lewis, Chawla, Lee, & Fossos, 2008). To mitigate this possibility, campaign materials can include supportive messages that emphasize campus traditions and themes and student spirit and that remind students of what they have in common as members of the same academic community.

The research has shown that campaigns with general messages about all undergraduates can be effective, yet there is always the possibility that some subgroups of students will not see the larger student body as a salient comparison group and therefore be unmoved by the campaign. For example, student athletes and fraternity and sorority members—who drink more on average than other students (Wechsler & Nelson, 2008)—may be more influenced by group norms than campus-wide norms. Members of these groups tend to hold exaggerated perceptions of drinking norms within their own groups (Perkins & Craig, 2006). For that reason, researchers have explored whether targeted messages with these students that highlight salient group norms might be a more effective way of reducing their alcohol consumption (e.g., Bruce & Keller, 2007; Far & Miller, 2003; Perkins & Craig, 2006).

Conclusion

Over time, both practitioners and researchers have learned how to create effective SNM campaigns, as illustrated by the long-term campaigns conducted at the University of Virginia and MSU. As a result, these campaigns are an increasingly accepted strategy for reducing college student drinking and related harms. Accordingly, college administrators are now experimenting with SNM campaigns directed at other student health issues, including sexual violence, tobacco and other drug use, nutrition, and physical exercise. Future research will show whether this approach will work as well in addressing those areas of concern.

References

Ajzen, I. (1985). From intentions to actions: A Theory of Planned Behaviour. In J. Kuhl & J. Beckman (Eds.), *Action-control: From cognition to behaviour* (pp. 11–39). New York: Springer.

Atkin, C. K. (2001). Theory and principles of media health campaigns. In R. Rice & C. K. Atkin (Eds.), *Public communication campaigns* (3rd ed., pp. 49–68). Thousand Oaks, CA: Sage.

Atkin, C. K., Martell, D., Smith, S. W., & Greenamyer, J. (2004). Specialized social norm message strategies focusing on celebratory drinking. *Report on Social Norms, 3,* 4–5.

Atkin, C. K., & Salmon, C. (2010). Communication campaigns. In C. Berger, M. Roloff, & D. Roskos-Ewoldsen (Eds.), *Handbook of communication science* (2nd ed., pp. 419–435). Thousand Oaks, CA: Sage.

Atkin, C. K., Smith, S. W., Klein, K., Glazer, E., & Martell, D. (2008). In their own words: Student characterizations of protective behaviors to prevent alcohol harm. *Most of us: Report on social norms.* Retrieved March 14, 2011, from http://mostofus.org/newsletter/article.php?newsletterID = 22& articleID=78

Borsari, B. B., & Carey, K. B. (2003). Descriptive and injunctive norms in college drinking: A meta-analytic integration. *Journal of Studies on Alcohol, 64,* 331–341.

Bruce, S., & Keller, A. (2007). Applying social norms theory within affiliation groups: Promising intervention for high-risk drinking. *NASPA Journal, 44,* 101–122.

DeJong, W., Schneider, S. K., Towvim, L. G., Murphy, M. J., Doerr, E. E., Simonsen, N. R., et al. (2006). A multisite randomized trial of social norms marketing campaigns to reduce college student drinking. *Journal of Studies on Alcohol, 67,* 868–879.

DeJong, W., Schneider, S. K., Towvim, L. G., Murphy, M. J., Doerr, E. E., Simonsen, N. R., et al. (2009). A multisite randomized trial of social norms marketing campaigns to reduce college student drinking: A replication study. *Substance Abuse, 30,* 127–140.

Far, J. M., & Miller, J. A. (2003). The small groups norms-challenging model: Social norms interventions with targeted high-risk groups. In H. W. Perkins (Ed.), *The social norms approach to preventing school and college age substance abuse: A handbook for educators, counselors, and clinicians* (pp. 111–132). San Francisco: Jossey-Bass.

Fishbein, M., & Ajzen, I. (1975). *Belief, attitude, intention, and behavior: An introduction to theory and research.* Reading, MA: Addison-Wesley.

Glazer, E. L., Smith, S. W., Atkin, C. K., & Hamel, L. M. (2010). The effects of sensation seeking, misperceptions of peer consumption, and believability of social norms messages on alcohol consumption. *Journal of Health Communication, 15,* 825–839.

Haines, M. P., & Barker, G. P. (2003). The Northern Illinois University experiment: A longitudinal case study of the social norms approach. In H. W. Perkins (Ed.), *The social norms approach to preventing school and college age substance abuse: A handbook for educators, counselors, and clinicians* (pp. 21–34). San Francisco: Jossey-Bass.

Johannessen, K., & Glider, P. (2003). The University of Arizona's campus health social norms media campaign. In H. W. Perkins (Ed.), *The social norms approach to preventing school and college age substance abuse: A handbook for educators, counselors, and clinicians* (pp. 65–82). San Francisco: Jossey-Bass.

Lederman, L. C., Stewart, L. P., Barr, S. L., Powell, R. L., Laitman, L., & Goodhart, F. W. (2001). RU SURE? Using communication theory to reduce dangerous drinking on a college campus. In R. E. Rice & C. K. Atkin (Eds.), *Public communication campaigns* (3rd ed., pp. 295–299). Thousand Oaks, CA: Sage.

Lederman, L. C., & Stewart, L. P. (2005). *Changing the culture of college drinking: A socially situated health communication campaign.* Cresskill, NJ: Hampton Press.

Martell, D., Atkin, C. K., Hembroff, L. A., Smith, S. W., Baumer, A. J., & Greenamyer, J. (2006). College students and "celebration drinking." *Social Norms Review, 1,* 10–17.

Neighbors, C., O'Connor, R. M., Lewis, M. A., Chawla, N., Lee, C. M., & Fossos, N. (2008). The relative impact of descriptive and injunctive norms on college student drinking: The role of reference group. *Psychology of Addictive Behaviors, 22,* 576–581.

Nisbett, R. E., & Ross, L. (1980). *Human inference: Strategies and shortcomings in social judgment.* Englewood Cliffs, NJ: Prentice Hall.

Park, H. S., Klein, K. A., Smith, S. W., & Martell, D. (2009). Separating subjective norms, university descriptive and injunctive norms, and U.S. descriptive and injunctive norms for drinking behavior intentions. *Health Communication, 24,* 746–751.

Park, H. S., Smith, S. W., & Klein, K. A. (2011). The effects of drinking status and believability of ads featured in a social norms campaign on college students' estimation and accuracy of other students celebratory drinking. *Journal of Health Communication, 15,* 504–518.

Paschall, M. J., Antin, T., Ringwalt, C. L., & Saltz, R. F. (2011). Effects of AlcoholEdu for college on alcohol-related problems among freshmen: A randomized multicampus trial. *Journal of Studies on Alcohol and Drugs, 72,* 642–650.

Perkins, H. W., & Berkowitz, A. D. (1986). Perceiving the community norms of alcohol use among students: Some research implications for campus alcohol education programming. *International Journal of the Addictions, 21,* 961–976.

Perkins, H. W., & Craig, D. W. (2003). The Hobart and William Smith Colleges experiment: A synergistic social norms approach using print, electronic media, and curriculum infusion to reduce collegiate problem drinking. In H. W. Perkins (Ed.), *The social norms approach to preventing school and college age substance abuse: A handbook for educators, counselors, and clinicians* (pp. 35–64). San Francisco: Jossey-Bass.

Perkins, H. W., & Craig, D. W. (2006). A successful social norms campaign to reduce alcohol misuse among college student-athletes. *Journal of Studies on Alcohol, 67,* 880–889.

Perkins, H. W., Meilman, P., Leichliter, J. S., Cashin, J. R., & Presley, C. (1999). Misperceptions of the norms for the frequency of alcohol and other drug use on college campuses. *Journal of American College Health, 47,* 253–258.

Russell, C., Clapp, J. C., & DeJong, W. (2005). "Done 4": Analysis of a failed social norms marketing campaign. *Health Communication, 17,* 57–65.

Scribner, R., Theall, K., Mason, K., Simonsen, N., Schneider, S. K., Towvim, L. G., & DeJong, W. (2011). Alcohol prevention on college campuses: The moderating effect of the alcohol environment on the effectiveness of social norms marketing campaigns. *Journal of Studies on Alcohol and Drugs, 72,* 232–239.

Smith, S. W., Atkin, C. K., Martell, D., Allen, R., & Hembroff, L. (2006). A social judgment theory approach to conducting formative research in a social norms campaign. *Communication Theory, 16,* 141–152.

Smith, S. W., LaPlante, C., Wibert, W. N., Mayer, A., Atkin, C. K., Klein, K., et al. (2011). Student generated protective behaviors to avert severe harm due to high-risk alcohol consumption. *Journal of College Student Development, 52,* 101–114.

Turner, J., Perkins, H. W., & Bauerle, J. (2008). Declining negative consequences related to alcohol misuse among students exposed to a social norms marketing intervention on a college campus. *Journal of American College Health, 57,* 85–93.

Wechsler, H., & Nelson T. F. (2008). What we have learned from the Harvard School of Public Health College Alcohol Study: Focusing attention on college student alcohol consumption and the environmental conditions that promote it. *Journal of Studies on Alcohol and Drugs, 69,* 481–490.

Wechsler, H., Nelson, T. F., Lee, J. E., Seibring, M., Lewis, C., & Keeling, R. P. (2003). Perception and reality: A national evaluation of social norms marketing interventions to reduce college students' heavy alcohol use. *Journal of Studies on Alcohol, 64,* 484–494.

Wechsler, H., & Wuethrich, B. (2002). *Dying to drink: Confronting binge drinking on college campuses.* Emmaus, PA: Rodale Books.

Applying Theory and Evaluation

The Go Sun Smart Campaign

*Achieving Individual and Organizational Change
for Occupational Sun Protection*

David B. Buller, Barbara J. Walkosz, Peter A. Andersen, Michael D. Scott,
Mark B. Dignan, and Gary R. Cutter

Authors' Note: The research reported here was supported by grants from the National Cancer Institute (CA81028 and CA104876). The design, conduct of the study, interpretation of the data, and preparation of this chapter was performed solely by the authors.

Skin cancer prevention is a national priority. More than 2 million cases of basal and squamous cell carcinomas, as well as thousands of potentially deadly melanomas, are diagnosed annually in the United States. Few populations are at as much risk of developing skin cancer as the nearly 10% of American workers who regularly perform jobs outdoors but practice inadequate sun protection, despite their chronic exposure to the sun's ultraviolet (UV) rays, a primary but easily reduced risk factor for skin cancer (Armstrong & English, 1996; Kricker, Armstrong, English, & Heenan, 1995). As a result, outdoor workers evidence a higher prevalence of skin cancer, especially nonmelanoma skin cancer (NMSC)—although to a lesser extent melanoma—than the population as a whole (Lear, Tan, Smith, Jones, Heagerty, Strange et al., 1998; Woodward & Boffetta, 1997).

U.S., Australian, and Canadian authorities recommend comprehensive workplace sun protection interventions, including policies that mandate environmental and administrative controls as well as communication that motivate personal protection by employees (see Figure 13.1). While a number of interventions have successfully improved sun protection in schools and communities (Centers for Disease Control and Prevention, 2003), health communication designed to increase sun protection among outdoor workers has received comparatively little attention (Glanz, Buller, & Saraiya, 2007).

Our team has spent the past 10 years developing and testing a communication theory-based occupational sun protection program that was successfully applied in the field (Scott, Buller, Walkosz, Andersen, Cutter, & Dignan, 2008). Supported by a series of research grants from the National Cancer Institute (NCI), our initial efforts created the *Go Sun Smart* (GSS) campaign. This is a multichannel workplace campaign promoting personal

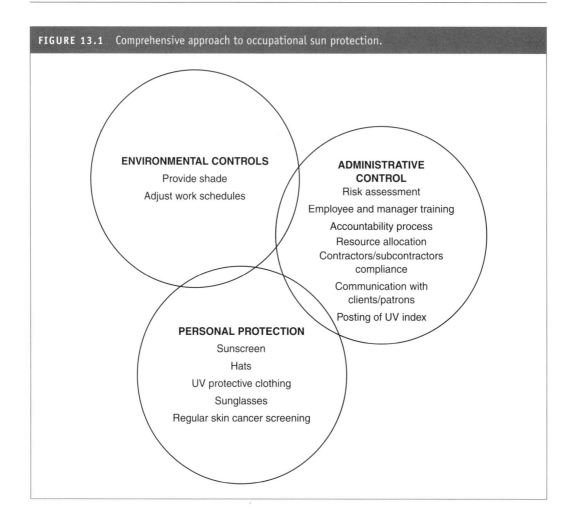

FIGURE 13.1   Comprehensive approach to occupational sun protection.

ENVIRONMENTAL CONTROLS
Provide shade
Adjust work schedules

ADMINISTRATIVE CONTROL
Risk assessment
Employee and manager training
Accountability process
Resource allocation
Contractors/subcontractors compliance
Communication with clients/patrons
Posting of UV index

PERSONAL PROTECTION
Sunscreen
Hats
UV protective clothing
Sunglasses
Regular skin cancer screening

sun protection among employees working at high elevation, who were particularly at risk for developing skin cancer. Evaluation research showed that the campaign was highly effective in the near term (Andersen, Buller, Voeks, Walkosz, Scott, & Cutter, 2008; Buller, Andersen, Walkosz, Scott, Cutter, Dignan et al., 2005), and our team is currently seeking to assess sustainability of program use and effects. This chapter focuses on the conceptual and operational features of GSS and describes how we developed, applied, and tested the occupational sun protection campaign. Our discussion includes lessons we learned in the process and how we are using these lessons in our current research.

We begin our discussion with perhaps the most important lesson of all: The success of workplace health communication depends on the cooperation and collaboration of stakeholders (see also Morgan, Chapter 15). GSS was developed and conducted with the cooperation of the North American ski industry—primarily, the National Ski Areas Association

(NSAA) and also professional associations for ski and snowboard instructors and ski patrollers. A key mission of these organizations is to identify emerging health and safety issues and locate effective solutions. These organizations not only saw the value of GSS in this regard, but their support conveyed the importance of occupational sun protection to their industry and membership. This led to senior and middle-level managers at more than 100 U.S. and Canadian ski areas providing us access to their operations and workforce for our research and facilitated their needed input on the design and implementation of GSS (an example of community-based campaigns—see Bracht & Rice, Chapter 20).

CONCEPTUAL BASIS OF GO SUN SMART

Based on formative research in which we surveyed and conducted focus groups with workers, a multitheoretical model was created to guide GSS. Diffusion of innovations (DIT) (Rogers, 2003) served as the overarching theoretic framework. According to DIT, as individuals adopt a new behavior, they predictably pass through five stages: 1) acquisition of knowledge of an innovation, 2) attitude formation around the innovation, 3) decision to adopt or reject the innovation, 4) implementation of the new idea, and 5) confirmation of this decision. GSS was designed to influence employees at each of these stages specifically by demonstrating the need for sun safety on the job, teaching sun safety skills, showing that it can be easily integrated with work, and describing the personal benefit of sun safety.

Our formative research revealed that persuading workers to be sun safe would be no easy task (Buller, Andersen, Walkosz, Scott, Maloy, Dignan, et al., 2005). Ski areas are saturated with employer and commercial messages competing for employee attention. Commonly, employees are attracted to the work because they enjoy skiing themselves and are high sensation seekers, meaning they can be difficult to reach with standard messages (see Palmgreen, Noar, & Zimmerman, Chapter 14). Many employees acknowledged the importance of sun protection but also believed it was unrealistic to expect them to always remember it. Likewise, they felt that it was unrealistic to expect them to avoid all tanning but that they could realistically prevent sunburns. Tanning differs from sunburn in that tanning leads to darkened skin as a result of chronic exposure to the sun, while sunburns are the result of single severe exposures that produce red, painful, and sometimes blistered skin.

We incorporated several specific campaign strategies to address these barriers to adoption. Recognizing that our information needed to penetrate an environment saturated with commercial and job-related messages, it contained messages with very high production value. We also used a high degree of novelty and vividness to increase the messages' sensation value (Donohew, Lorch, & Palmgreen, 1998) and targeted these messages to employees and guests who were high in sensation-seeking characteristics. Based on agenda-setting theory (Dearing & Rogers, 1996), we repeatedly placed messages in prominent workplace channels and venues to elevate the importance of sun protection on the organization's overall safety agenda. To adapt to employee beliefs, messages did not mention tanning and instead emphasized avoiding sunburns, which are clear, observable, and memorable indicators of excessive sun exposure owing to inadequate precautionary behaviors (Shoveller & Lovato, 2001). Messages advocating sunburn avoidance were

FIGURE 13.2   Theory-based Go Sun Smart messages: a) high sensation value message for young males, b) risk message in fear appeal.

designed to be sufficiently credible to avoid being dismissed by employees and to reinforce their self-efficacy (Bandura, 1986) for occupational sun safety.

     With employees' attention captured, theory-driven persuasive appeals were embedded in GSS messages to create attitudes supporting occupational sun safety as well as to reinforce the perception that occupational sun safety was normative in the workplace. Several appeals were based on principles of Bem's (1972) self-perception theory, such as talking about sun protection with coworkers and guests should influence employees themselves, and Bandura's (1986) social cognitive theory, such as the use of sun protection displayed by attractive, similar models should create positive outcome expectations. The extended parallel process model (Witte, 1992; see Yzer, Southwell, & Stephenson, Chapter 11) guided fear appeal messages that highlighted employee risk from excessive sun exposure while also telling them that it could be reduced by simple and effective sun safety behaviors such as wearing sunscreen, sunglasses, and a hat (Figure 13.2b). In response to questions asked by employees, we created factual messages about UV exposure and sun safety on risk and risk reduction. Consistent with DIT, many GSS messages emphasized that sun protection was easy to implement, personally advantageous, and compatible with current work site safety procedures.

A few messages were designed that specifically appealed to employee subgroups to overcome barriers to message reception or resistance to appeals for sun safety, including graphic messages for low-literate groups and messages incorporating role models depicting behaviors counter to gender-related sun safety practices uncovered in formative research. For example, messages addressed male employees' hesitancy to wear sunscreen (a photograph and text arguing that sunscreen is easy compared to snowboarding; Figure 13.2a) and female employees' avoidance of hats (attractive woman modeling a wide-brimmed hat).

GSS also drew heavily from the research on opinion leadership, a core concept in DIT (Rogers, 2003). Influential employees (e.g., ski patrollers) were identified by coworkers as key opinion leaders on matters of mountain safety. We produced messages encouraging opinion leaders to advocate sun protection among employees with whom they came into contact.

THE GO SUN SMART PROGRAM

The GSS health communication campaign relied on written, electronic, visual, and interpersonal channels of communication in the workplace to promote sun safety to employees. A logo and tag line for GSS, "Wear sunscreen, sunglasses, and a hat," pretested positively in employee focus groups and branded all materials for message consistency. We incorporated variety into the design of campaign materials so they could be placed in multiple workplace channels to increase prominence (Dearing & Rogers, 1996), including the following: large and small posters for posting inside buildings; signs and displays at chairlifts; brief messages for whiteboards and electronic signs used inside and outside buildings; logo art on magnets, buttons, window decals, and water bottles; table tents for use in food service areas; a banner; signs designed to be attached to windows and mirrors; articles and sun safety messages for newsletters, meetings, and other communication; and an employee training program.

The sun safety employee training program was designed for managers to deliver in formal or informal meetings. The six-unit program, featuring an instructor's guide, slides, and brochures, served multiple goals, including making sun safety a routine agenda item for managers, helping employees recognize their personal risk for skin cancer, and providing them with step-by-step instructions to reduce this risk. The last unit described techniques for discussing sun safety with other coworkers and guests to generate self-persuasion, create a workplace norm, and stimulate opinion leadership for sun protection.

A unique feature of outdoor recreation industries, such as the ski industry, is that employees interact directly with clients in the workplace (i.e., guests). To reach the guests at ski areas, we used some of the campaign materials previously discussed, as well as a brochure for guests, posters for use in ski and snowboard schools, and a brochure featuring games and puzzles for children's facilities. The ski and snowboard school messages were designed to appeal to both children and parents (e.g., reminder to provide children with sunscreen, facts on the importance of sun protection during childhood). To appeal to young children, cartoon figures—Willey Widebrim, Susie Sunscreen, and Gary Goggles—were included in a poster and the brochure.

The GSS website (www.gosunsmart.org) was launched with online information for employees and guests. There were descriptions of simple sun safety strategies, details of risk for skin damage due to being outdoors at high elevations in snow-covered environments, facts on UV and sun safety practices, answers to frequently asked questions, and links to other online resources about skin cancer prevention. This online content was intended to show that sun safety was easy, advantageous, and compatible with mountain safety procedures (Rogers, 2003).

To increase the prominence and novelty of the sun protection promotion, a new set of GSS materials was released every six weeks during the ski season. Managers received a program guide with instructions for implementing GSS. Also, researchers visited ski areas at the beginning of the ski season and reviewed plans for using GSS with managers.

Thus, GSS was a full-featured occupational sun protection program based on communication theories. Messages were placed in many workplace channels from signage to print to training to online so as to ensure that occupational sun safety messages reached a large proportion of workers several times in a variety of settings on the job.

THE GO SUN SMART EFFECTIVENESS TRIAL

Research Design

The effectiveness of GSS was evaluated in a group-randomized pretest–posttest controlled trial (Andersen et al., 2008; Buller et al., 2005). Twenty-six ski areas in Western North America from Alaska to New Mexico were randomized to either implement GSS or serve as untreated control groups. Initially, on-mountain employees completed pretest surveys at the GSS ski areas at the beginning of the ski season in venues from hiring fairs to orientation sessions to staff meetings. In order to obtain a high proportion of employees who worked at least part time outdoors, GSS was implemented for five months of the prime ski season, and samples of pretested employees at each ski area were posttested by telephone and mail at the end of the season. Employees were posttested a second time at the end of the following summer to explore long-term campaign effects.

Process evaluation showed that the level of GSS implementation varied across ski areas (Buller et al., 2005). We visually inspected each of the 13 ski areas in the intervention condition and found that five areas implemented 40% or less of GSS materials, four areas used 60% of the materials, and four areas used 80% or more of them. This variation in program implementation shows a weakness of field trials that rely on third parties (i.e., managers) to implement the treatment (see Rice & Foote, Chapter 5, for further discussion of this issue of planned vs. engaged inputs).

Results

Positive Effects on Employees

GSS improved employees' sun protection during the ski season, and its benefits actually carried over into their summer work. GSS reduced the occurrence and number of sunburns during the ski season (Buller et al., 2005) and summer (Andersen et al., 2008). Specifically, in the 2002 ski season, employees in the intervention ski areas reported a 14% reduction in sunburns (from 46% in 2001 to 32%), and this decline was significantly larger than the 8% decline observed in control ski areas (49% in 2001 to 41%). Further, the prevalence of sunburns was lowest at ski areas that used the most GSS materials, suggesting a strong campaign exposure effect. The effect of the winter GSS program was even stronger the following summer, suggesting a long-term effect of the program (potentially boosted by summer population reminders about sun safety, warm temperatures, and more exposed skin). Again, fewer employees who worked at intervention ski areas (50% vs. 53%) reported sunburns in the previous three months in the summer than employees who worked at control ski areas and more frequently wore protective clothing, sunglasses, and sunscreen and limited their time in the sun while working in the summer. Employees at the GSS ski areas also were more likely to report discussing sun safety with their families, implying diffusion effects of campaign messages.

Positive Effects on Guests (Including Ski and Snowboard School)

As mentioned earlier, some of the GSS materials were used to promote sun protection to guests, and we created messages that encouraged employees to advise guests to be sun safe. However, because guests visit ski areas sporadically and for short periods, we expected that GSS might affect guests less than employees. To measure this possible effect, we surveyed guests face-to-face while riding chairlifts up the mountain and when picking up children from ski and snowboard school. Pretest and posttest surveys were conducted with separate cross-sectional samples of guests on chairlifts and posttest surveys only with parents.

We were pleased to learn that GSS had positive effects on sun safety by guests during their ski area visits (Andersen, Buller, Walkosz, Maloy, Scott, Cutter et al., 2009; Walkosz, Voeks, Andersen, Scott, Buller, Cutter et al., 2007; Walkosz, Buller, Andersen, Scott, Dignan, Cutter et al., 2008). However, its influence was not the result of mere general program implementation but rather was confined primarily to guests who were exposed to its messages, measured by their ability to recall seeing or hearing sun safety messages while at the ski area (primarily from signage). Interestingly, recall of sun safety messages (60% vs. 36%) and the GSS logo (37% vs. 6%) at posttest only by adult guests was significantly higher at the intervention than control ski areas and was associated with improved guest sun protection at ski areas using GSS but not at control ski areas. In particular, sunscreen and sunscreen lip balm were used most by guests at intervention resorts who reported seeing a message (1.01 [adjusted proportion]) compared to intervention resort guests who did not see a message (0.83) and to guests in control resorts who saw (0.89) or did not see (0.89) a sun safety message. Similarly, parents with children in ski and snowboard schools at intervention ski areas recalled more sun safety messages than at control ski areas (46% vs. 32%). However, for parents, sunscreen use was higher at intervention ski areas (compared to controls) (OR 2.72, 95% CI, 1.24, 5.95) only in northwestern North America.

Conclusions on Program Effectiveness

The messages in GSS appeared to have meaningful and sustained impact on employees' occupational sun protection; sunburn was substantially reduced by GSS. Further, the campaign appeared to instill a long-term commitment to occupational sun safety, for employees exposed to it continued to take more precautions as they moved into their summer jobs.

The analyses on guests also illustrated the value of basing health communication on well-established communication theory. Existing messages regarding sun protection in the ski industry (e.g., ads for sunscreen or hats) were not effective at influencing sun protection. Sun protection increased when they recalled sun safety messages only at ski areas using GSS, where messages were built based on sound theoretical communication principles.

Sun protection for children enrolled in ski and snowboard schools increased only at the intervention ski areas in the northwestern region. With lower UV levels and more cloud cover in this region, sunscreen use may be less normative in that region; plus, a large majority of the parents in the central and southwest regions in both conditions already used sunscreen on their children (representing a ceiling effect). Thus, exposure to the GSS messages in the northwest was associated with parents becoming engaged in sun protection for their children.

THE INDUSTRY-WIDE DISSEMINATION TRIAL ON GO SUN SMART

Researchers who experience the success we did with GSS might be tempted to "declare victory" and move on to the next health campaign. However, the GSS trial was limited to a demonstration of intervention efficacy at certain study sites. The next step was to investigate whether GSS was also effective when applied beyond the original research context. In other words, can GSS be disseminated and adopted by employers and improve occupational sun safety of employees throughout the industry? The partnership with NSAA presented a unique opportunity to study GSS's dissemination to the entire membership of 350 ski areas.

In this second project, also funded by NCI, we evaluated communication theory-based strategies for ensuring that GSS was implemented with sufficient fidelity to be effective as it was rolled out to the industry. In the parlance of a comprehensive approach to occupational sun safety (Figure 13.1), dissemination of GSS represented an attempt to change administrative procedures, that is, adoption and implementation of a new program. We studied the basic dissemination strategy used by NSAA to distribute partner programs and designed an enhanced dissemination strategy to elevate the effectiveness of dissemination, a method classified as an expert specialist purveyor strategy (Fixsen, Blase, Naoom, & Wallace, 2009).

Once again, we applied DIT (Rogers, 2003) and principles of persuasive communication to construct the enhanced strategy aimed at maximizing adoption and use of GSS. In this project, the primary goal was to achieve organizational change (i.e., increased use of GSS at ski areas) rather than individual sun protection, although we did assess employees and guests. DIT explains that organizational diffusion is more complicated than individual adoption. Organizational diffusion has two phases—adoption and implementation (Rogers, 2003). Adoption includes agenda setting (recognition of a problem and a search for innovations to solve it), matching (evaluating fit between problem and innovation), and an adoption decision. Once the adoption decision occurs, organizations engage in the stages of redefining and restructuring (adapting the innovation or changing the organization to improve the innovation's fit), clarifying (communicating changes to employees), and routinizing (making innovation part of the organization's regular activities, i.e., institutionalizing it). Through organized efforts, external change agents have successfully promoted adoption of disease prevention programs to diverse organizations (Rogers, 2003). We expected a professional association, such as NSAA, to be an influential change agent partner because it linked together, in a communication sense, a set of similar employers.

Dissemination Strategies

Basic Strategy

Partner programs on education and safety are disseminated by NSAA by 1) promoting them at informational booths at annual and regional trade shows and 2) distributing starter kits of free program materials to member ski areas. We used these practices as the basic dissemination strategy (BDS) for GSS with NSAA. We also distributed a guidebook, catalog of GSS materials, letter from the NSAA president, informational tip sheets, and packing lists. These additional pieces were intended to highlight the need for occupational sun safety and fit of GSS with ski area operations.

Enhanced Strategy

To create the enhanced dissemination strategy (EDS), NSAA's BDS was supplemented with a series of personal contacts and communication with ski area managers designed to promote program adoption and implementation by providing training, ongoing coaching, and support (Fixsen et al., 2009). The communication tactics included a personal visit to the ski area where project staff presented GSS to managers and employees (upon request), distributed theoretically based print materials promoting GSS use, sought commitment to use GSS from managers, helped them formulate plans to use GSS, and tried to identify internal champions to ensure the use of GSS. Also, project staff continued to support managers by e-mail and telephone. The theoretically based print materials addressed methods for implementing GSS and overcoming resistance from other managers and employees. Through this communication, research staff tried to 1) reduce uncertainty about GSS, 2) build credibility for GSS, 3) achieve public commitment to use it, 4) coach managers to implement GSS, and 5) engender reciprocity within the interpersonal relationships between research staff and managers.

Research Design

The two dissemination strategies (BDS and EDS) were compared in a two-group randomized design. All ski areas that were members of NSAA received GSS through the BDS over three ski seasons from 2005–2008. Given the benefits of GSS in the effectiveness trial, it could have been considered unethical to withhold it from any ski areas, so NSAA offered it to all members. To evaluate the dissemination strategies, we recruited 69 ski areas and randomly assigned half of them to receive GSS through the EDS while the other half received it through the BDS. We assessed program adoption and implementation at posttest by visiting each ski area and recording all GSS materials in use. Ski area managers were surveyed at pretest and posttest online or by telephone. Employees completed self-administered surveys and guests were interviewed face-to-face on chairlifts or when picking up children from ski and snowboard schools at posttest.

Preliminary Results and Conclusions

Emerging data from this trial confirmed that the BDS achieved widespread adoption of GSS by nearly all ski areas, confirming the important linkage function performed by professional associations in industry networks. However, once again, there was considerable variability in the extent to which each ski area used the campaign (Buller, Andersen, Walkosz, Scott, Cutter, Dignan et al., in press).

With its foundation in communication theory, the EDS significantly boosted use of the GSS program. Several factors may explain its success, including calling the attention of managers to GSS and the need for sun safety, obtaining their commitment to use GSS, correcting misperceptions about the need for occupational sun safety and the fit of GSS, helping managers translate the need for occupational sun safety into real action (Morgan, 2009; Chapter 15), and creating pressure on managers to reciprocate the efforts of the research staff by using GSS. The success of enhancement was important: Both employees and guests elevated their sun protection after they were exposed to the GSS messages, which was more likely when more GSS materials were used by the ski areas (Andersen, Buller, Walkosz, Scott, Kane, Cutter et al., 2011).

General Conclusions and Next Steps

The GSS approach to meeting the challenge of increasing occupational sun protection showcases the value of communication theory for creating high-quality and effective health communication campaigns. It also emphasizes the advantages of blending multiple theories to address problems such as skin cancer prevention. The results add to the evidence that significant behavior change (in areas such as smoking, blood pressure control, or cholesterol consumption) has occurred as the result of major public communication efforts (Hornik, 2002; see Snyder & LaCroix, Chapter 8). Granted, much remains to be learned about the contributions of communication programs to public health (Hornik, 2002), but our findings on message exposure and design offer insights into how health communication programs can effectively reach their target audiences.

This GSS investigative effort also demonstrates the value of programmatic research that explores not only the creation of effective health communication but also continues to examine important aspects of its wide-scale implementation. Our research focusing on health communication for occupational sun protection continues. We are currently conducting a study in which we hope to show further how health communication can achieve adoption of formal workplace policies on occupational sun safety. Policy development in all sectors, including workplaces, is identified as a crucial strategy for improving health outcomes for individuals (Bauer, Hyland, Quiang, Steger, & Cummings, 2005; Suminski, Poston, & Hyder, 2006) and the public's health (e.g., smoke-free schools, hospitals, and work sites). Called *Sun Safe Colorado,* this campaign, too, is based on DIT, combines personal contacts and communication with web-based resources, and recommends environmental and administrative changes in workplaces that motivate, support, and monitor sun protection.

Future studies will examine the sustained implementation of GSS by the ski areas to record GSS use, interview managers and employees, and explore whether organizational culture has changed in ways that institutionalized occupational sun safety. We will also explore whether organizations implement and maintain GSS as we created it or modify it or implement some principles for promoting occupational sun protection (i.e., evidence-based practices) but not all GSS components (i.e., evidence-based program) (Fixsen et al., 2009). This later practice is often called the maintenance of theoretic fidelity (Rovniak, Hovell, Wojcik, Winett, & Martinez-Donate, 2005) or reinvention (Rogers, 2003); these practices again raise process evaluation issues.

We will expand our focus on sun safety from the winter to summer, from employees to guests, and to more complete protection behaviors. Many adults seem to practice sun safety when at home but engage in high-risk sun exposure during vacations (O'Riordan, Steffen, Lunde, & Gies, 2008). As a result, precancerous skin lesions and skin cancer have been associated with vacations in warm, sunny locations and by the water (Pettijohn, Asdigian, Aalborg, Morelli, Mokrohisky, Dellavalle, et al., 2009). When studying GSS, we found that people at resorts do not use sunscreen in ways that maximize its protective value (Buller, Andersen, Walkosz, Scott, Maloy, Dignan, et al., 2011); use protective clothing, hats, and shade infrequently; and rely on unreliable cues to when UV is high and protection is warranted (Andersen, Buller, Walkosz, Scott, Maloy, Cutter, et al., 2010).

To approach these issues, we use not only principles from the multitheoretic model on which we based GSS but couple it with narrative persuasive message formats based on transportation theory (Green & Brock, 2000) to achieve messages' acceptance and identification, shift normative beliefs about sun safety on vacation, reduce counterarguing (Green, 2006), and convince vacationers to practice sun safety. Transportation theory suggests that persuasion may occur via narrative transportation (i.e., immersion in the narrative world), where thoughts are focused on following the storyline and less effort is expended on counterarguing persuasive appeals, in this case, for sun safety (Green, 2006).

Health communication researchers should consider the multitheoretical approach we used to create large-scale campaigns that reach multiple audiences through multiple channels with multiple messages (also as applied in the Stanford Three Community and Five City cardiovascular health campaigns; Flora, 2001). We believe that GSS has been effective in increasing sun safety and preventing sunburns, which downstream should possibly reduce treatment, save lives, and lower our burgeoning national health bill. As the communication discipline intersects with public health, we concur with Hornik (2002) that there is nothing as practical as a good theory, especially for effective health communication.

References

Andersen, P. A., Buller, D. B., Voeks, J. H., Walkosz, B. J., Scott, M. D., & Cutter, G. R. (2008). Testing the long-term effects of the Go Sun Smart worksite sun protection program: A group-randomized experimental study. *Journal of Communication, 68,* 447–471.

Andersen, P. A., Buller, D. B., Walkosz, B. J., Maloy, J., Scott, M. D., Cutter, G. R., et al. (2009). Testing a theory-based health communication program: A replication of Go Sun Smart in outdoor winter recreation. *Journal of Health Communication, 14,* 346–365.

Andersen, P. A., Buller, D. B., Walkosz, B. J., Scott, M. D., Kane, I. L., Cutter, G. R., Dignan, M. B., & Liu, X. (2011, December 10). Expanding occupational sun safety to an outdoor recreation industry: a translational study of the Go Sun Smart program. *Translational Behavioral Medicine.* Retrieved December 21, 2011 from http://www.springerlink.com/openurl.asp?genre=article&id=doi:10.1007/s13142-011-0101-8

Andersen, P. A., Buller, D. B., Walkosz, B. J., Scott, M. D., Maloy, J. A., Cutter, G. R., et al. (2010). Environmental cues to ultraviolet radiation and personal sun protection in outdoor winter recreation. *Archives of Dermatology, 146,* 1241–1247.

Armstrong, B. K., & English, D. R. (1996). Cutaneous malignant melanoma. In D. Schottenfeld & J. F. Franmeni (Eds.), *Cancer epidemiology and prevention* (2nd ed., pp. 1282–1312). New York: Oxford University Press.

Bandura, A. (1986). *Social foundations of thought and action: A social cognitive theory.* Englewood Cliffs, NJ: Prentice Hall.

Bauer, J., Hyland, A., Quiang, L., Steger, C., & Cummings, K. (2005). A longitudinal assessment of the impact of smoke-free worksite policies on tobacco use. *American Journal of Public Health, 95,* 1024–1029.

Bem, D. J. (1972). Self-perception theory. In L. Berkowitz (Ed.), *Advances in experimental social psychology* (6th ed., pp. 1–62). New York: Academic Press.

Buller, D. B., Andersen, P. A., Walkosz, B. J., Scott, M. D., Cutter, G. R., Dignan, M. B., Kane, I. L., & Zhang, X. (in press). Enhancing industry-based dissemination of an occupational sun protection program with theory-based strategies employing personal contact. *American Journal of Health Promotion.*

Buller, D. B., Andersen, P., Walkosz, B. J., Scott, M. D., Maloy, J. A., Dignan, M. B., et al. (2012). Compliance with sunscreen advice in a survey of adults engaged in outdoor winter recreation at high elevation ski areas. *Journal of the American Academy of Dermatology, 66,* 63-70.

Buller, D. B., Andersen, P. A., Walkosz, B. J., Scott, M. D., Cutter, G. R., Dignan, M. B., et al. (2005). Randomized trial testing a worksite sun protection program in an outdoor recreation industry. *Health Education & Behavior, 32,* 514–535.

Centers for Disease Control and Prevention. (2003). *Preventing skin cancer: Findings of the task force on community preventive services on reducing exposure to ultraviolet light.* Atlanta, GA: Centers for Disease Control and Prevention. Retrieved October 18, 2011, from http://www.cdc.gov/mmwr/preview/mmwrhtml/rr5215a1.htm

Dearing, J., & Rogers, E. (1996). *Agenda setting.* Thousand Oaks, CA: Sage.

Donohew, L., Lorch, E. P., & Palmgreen, P. (1998). Applications of a theoretic model of information exposure to health interventions. *Human Communication Research, 24,* 454–468.

Fixsen, D. L., Blase, K. A., Naoom, S. F., & Wallace, F. (2009). Core implementation components. *Research on Social Work Practice, 19,* 531–540.

Flora, J. (2001). The Stanford community studies: Campaigns to reduce cardiovascular disease. In R. E. Rice & C. K. Atkin (Eds.), *Public communication campaigns* (3rd ed., pp. 193–213). Thousand Oaks, CA: Sage.

Glanz, K., Buller, D. B., & Saraiya, M. (2007). Reducing ultraviolet radiation exposure among outdoor workers: State of the evidence and recommendations. *Environmental Health, 6,* 22.

Green, M. C. (2006). Narratives and cancer communication. *Journal of Communication, 56*(Suppl. 1), S163–S183.

Green, M. C., & Brock, T. C. (2000). The role of transportation in the persuasiveness of public narratives. *Journal of Personality and Social Psychology, 79,* 701–721.

Hornik, R. C. (2002). Public health communication: Making sense of contradictory evidence. In R.C. Hornik (Ed.), *Public health communication* (pp. 1–21). Mahwah, NJ: Lawrence Erlbaum.

Kricker, A., Armstrong, B. K., English, D. R., & Heenan, P. J. (1995). Does intermittent sun exposure cause basal cell carcinoma? A case-control study in Western Australia. *International Journal of Cancer, 60,* 489–494.

Lear, J. T., Tan, B. B., Smith, A. G., Jones, P. W., Heagerty, A. H., Strange, R. C., et al. (1998). A comparison of risk factors for malignant melanoma, squamous cell carcinoma and basal cell carcinoma in the UK. *International Journal of Clinical Practice, 52,* 145–149.

Morgan, S. (2009). The interaction of conversation, cognitions, and campaigns: The social representation of organ donation. *Communication Theory, 19,* 29–48.

O'Riordan, D. L., Steffen, A. D., Lunde, K. B., & Gies, P. (2008). A day at the beach while on tropical vacation: Sun protection practices in a high-risk setting for UV radiation exposure. *Archives of Dermatology, 144,* 1449–1455.

Pettijohn, K. J., Asdigian, N. L., Aalborg, J., Morelli, J. G., Mokrohisky, S. T., Dellavalle, R. P., et al. (2009). Vacations to waterside locations result in nevus development in Colorado children. *Cancer, Epidemiology, Biomarkers and Prevention, 18,* 454–463.

Rogers, E. M. (2003). *Diffusion of innovations* (5th ed.). New York: Free Press.

Rovniak, L. S., Hovell, M. F., Wojcik, J. R., Winett, R. A., & Martinez-Donate, A. P. (2005). Enhancing theoretical fidelity: An e-mail-based walking program demonstration. *American Journal of Health Promotion, 20,* 85–95.

Scott, M. D., Buller, D. B., Walkosz, B. J., Andersen, P. A., Cutter, G. R., & Dignan, M. B. (2008). Go sun smart. *Communication Education, 57,* 423–433.

Shoveller, J. A., & Lovato, C. Y. (2001). Measuring self-reported sunburn: Challenges and recommendations. *Chronic Diseases in Canada, 22,* 83–98.

Suminski, R. R., Poston, W. S. C., & Hyder, M. L. (2006). Small business policies toward employee and community promotion of physical activity. *Journal of Physical Activity & Health, 4,* 405–414.

Walkosz, B. J., Buller, D. B., Andersen, P. A., Scott, M. D., Dignan, M. B., Cutter, G. R., et al. (2008). Increasing sun protection in winter outdoor recreation: A theory-based health communication program. *American Journal of Preventive Medicine, 34,* 502–509.

Walkosz, B. J., Voeks, J., Andersen, P., Scott, M., Buller, D., Cutter, G., et al. (2007). Randomized trial on sun safety education at ski and snowboard schools in western North America. *Pediatric Dermatology, 24,* 222–229.

Witte, K. (1992). Putting the fear back in fear appeals: The extended parallel process model. *Communication Monographs, 59,* 329–349.

Woodward, A., & Boffetta, P. (1997). Environmental exposure, social class, and cancer risk. *IARC Scientific Publications, 138,* 361–367.

CHAPTER 14

A Mass Media Campaign to Increase Condom Use Among High Sensation-Seeking and Impulsive Decision-Making Young Adults

Philip C. Palmgreen, Seth M. Noar, and Rick S. Zimmerman

Authors' Note: Preparation of this chapter was funded in part by grant R01-MH63705 from the National Institute of Mental Health (Principal Investigator: Rick S. Zimmerman).

HIV prevention intervention research over the past 15 years has begun to show impressive results. A number of programs have produced delay of onset of sexual initiation (Coyle, Kirby, Marin, Gomez, & Gregorich, 2004; Zimmerman, Cupp, Donohew, Sionean, Feist-Price, & Helme, 2008), while other programs have led to significant increases in condom use in populations including heterosexually active individuals (Albarracin, Gillette, Earl, Glasman, Durantini, & Ho, 2005; Noar, 2008). Most of these interventions have been implemented in small group, school, or individual-level clinical settings rather than via media dissemination.

Mass media campaigns such as televised PSA campaigns have recently been shown to be effective in changing a variety of behaviors (Hornik, 2002; Noar, 2006) including marijuana use in at-risk adolescents (Palmgreen, Donohew, Lorch, Hoyle, & Stephenson, 2001). For a number of reasons, however, including failing to utilize many of the campaign design principles discussed in this book, the full potential of these types of media campaigns in the HIV prevention arena has not yet been realized (Myhre & Flora, 2000; Noar, 2009). In fact, many campaigns focused on safer sexual behavior to date have tended to yield null or small campaign effects (Bertrand, O'Reilly, Denison, Anhang, & Sweat, 2006; Snyder, Hamilton, Mitchell, Kiwanuka-Tondo, Fleming-Milici, & Proctor, 2004).

SAFER SEX CAMPAIGN STUDY

This chapter describes a well-funded (by NIH) safer sex mass media campaign effort that applied many major campaign design principles (Atkin, 2001). The purpose was to rigorously and empirically test whether a televised HIV/AIDS media-only campaign embodying these principles could impact safer sexual beliefs and behavior (i.e., condom use) among at-risk young adults. The Safer Sex Campaign (SSC) study employed formative research, theory, audience segmentation, message design and targeting techniques, and channel selection procedures tied to the *sensation-seeking targeting approach* (SENTAR) (Palmgreen & Donohew, 2003; Palmgreen, Donohew, & Harrington, 2001). The SENTAR approach revolves around the personality variable sensation seeking as a particularly potent targeting factor in campaigns addressing unsafe sex, drug use, and other risky behaviors.

Sensation Seeking

Zuckerman (1994) defines sensation seeking as "the seeking of varied, novel, complex, and intense sensations and experiences, and the willingness to take physical, social, legal, and financial risks for the sake of such experience" (p. 27). Sensation seeking is a moderate to strong predictor of a variety of risky behaviors including drug use, unsafe sex, crime, delinquency, drinking and driving, and speeding, according to scores of studies spanning four decades across different cultures (Donohew, Zimmerman, Cupp, Novak, Colon, & Abell, 2000; Romer & Hennessy, 2007; Zuckerman, 1994). Hoyle, Fejfar, and Miller (2000) found sensation seeking to be the personality trait with the strongest and most consistent relationships with risky sexual behaviors including numbers of sexual partners, unprotected intercourse, and various high-risk sexual encounters.

Especially important from a campaign targeting perspective, however, is that high sensation seekers (HSS) also have distinct and consistent preferences for particular kinds of messages based on their needs for the novel, the unusual, and the intense (Donohew, Lorch, & Palmgreen, 1991; Palmgreen & Donohew, 2003). HSS prefer messages that are high in *sensation value* (HSV messages), that is, messages whose content and formal features elicit strong sensory, affective, and arousal responses (Palmgreen, Donohew, Lorch, Rogus, Helm, & Grant, 1991). Low sensation seekers (LSS) generally prefer lower levels of message sensation value (i.e., LSV messages). Experimental studies have demonstrated that HSV messages are more effective than LSV messages with HSS, while LSV messages are more effective with LSS in eliciting changes in drug use attitudes and intentions as well as greater liking for, attention to, and processing of prevention messages (Everett & Palmgreen, 1995; Lorch & Palmgreen, 1994; Palmgreen et al., 1991; Palmgreen, Stephenson, Everett, Baseheart, & Francies, 2002).

This research led to the development of the SENTAR approach to the prevention of a variety of risk-related behaviors. The approach is based on four major principles (Palmgreen & Donohew, 2003; Palmgreen et al., 2001): 1) Use sensation seeking as a major segmentation variable, 2) conduct formative research with HSS members of the target audience, 3) design HSV prevention messages to reach HSS, and 4) place campaign messages in HSV contexts (e.g., dramatic, novel, and often unconventional TV programs shown by formative research to be preferred by HSS). A drug abuse prevention campaign study, employing a SENTAR-based design and a controlled time-series evaluation similar to that used in the SSC study described here, showed that all three televised PSA campaigns in two moderate-sized cities resulted in large reductions in marijuana use among HSS teens (Palmgreen, Donohew, Lorch, et al., 2001). Another time-series study demonstrated that a major portion of the ongoing Office of National Drug Control Policy's antidrug campaign, the so-called Marijuana Initiative, using hard-hitting HSV messages, resulted in a large and significant drop in marijuana use among a large sample of HSS teens in two cities (Palmgreen, Lorch, Stephenson, Hoyle, & Donohew, 2007).

Impulsive Decision Making

Decision making can range from a highly rational style involving careful consideration of cognitive cues to a very impulsive act-without-thinking process that relies primarily on affective and physiological cues. Donohew and colleagues (2000) showed that impulsive decision makers (IDMs) were significantly more likely than rational decision makers (RDMs) to have had sex, to have ever used alcohol or marijuana, and to have had unwanted sex under pressure while drunk. The same study showed a moderate positive relationship between sensation seeking and impulsive decision making and also demonstrated that those high on both variables took greater sexual risks than those high on only one or none of the variables. Noar, Zimmerman, Palmgreen, Lustria, and Horosewski (2006) found, through structural equation modeling, that sensation seeking and impulsive decision making were negatively related to condom attitudes, social norms, and condom self-efficacy, which were in turn positively related to condom use. Finally, Zimmerman, Noar, Feist-Price, Dekthar, Cupp, Anderman et al.,(2007) tested an integrative model of condom use among male and female adolescents using structural equation modeling with longitudinal data. They found that impulsive decision making was significantly related to negative condom attitudes and social norms as well as low condom self-efficacy, which were in turn significantly associated with intentions to use condoms and condom use.

STUDY DESIGN

The SSC study involved a 21-month controlled time-series design (Palmgreen, 2009). Safer sex PSAs were aired from January through March, 2003, in Lexington, Kentucky, while no campaign took place in the comparison city, Knoxville, Tennessee. These two cities had similar demographics and nonoverlapping media systems. Data were collected May 2002—January 2004—that is, eight months prior to the onset of the Lexington campaign, three months during the campaign (January to March, 2003), and ten months postcampaign.

Formative Research and Public Service Announcement Development

The PSAs developed for the campaign were the product of formative research consisting of three waves of focus groups drawn from the target audience (Noar, Palmgreen,

Zimmerman, & Cupp, 2008). More than 40 focus groups consisting of high sensation-seeking or impulsive decision-making (i.e., above the median on one or the other variable) young-adult males or females were aimed at 1) gaining a better understanding of sexual risk taking, 2) pretesting existing safer sex TV PSAs with the target audience, and 3) testing scripts for campaign PSAs developed by the research team according to SENTAR principles. This led to the production (by a professional producer) of five original 30-second televised PSAs targeted at HSS-IDM young adults. All five PSAs used different combinations of characteristics known to increase the sensation value of messages (e.g., novelty, drama, strong emotion, unexpected visual and audio formats, loud music, unusual sound effects) (Noar, Palmgreen, Zimmerman, Lustria, & Lu, 2010; Palmgreen & Donohew, 2003). For example, the ad "Translation" begins with people dancing to loud music, while the text "Believe everything you hear?" is superimposed. Rapid-cut close-ups of young adults using pickup lines are featured, such as "I can give you everything you've ever dreamed of," followed by big, bold letters on the screen depicting negative consequences of unsafe sex (e.g., DIRTY DIAPERS, SCREAMING BABIES). These words are accompanied by a loud, jarring sound. The ad ends with a male saying, "I can put a smile on your face for weeks," followed by the superimposed words: "HE'S RIGHT . . . HE USES CONDOMS." The ad ends with the campaign slogan used with all five ads: "Use a condom. Every partner. Every time." Permission from the Kaiser Family Foundation was also secured to use some of their safer sex PSAs in the campaign. All five employed had been rated highly in formative research conducted for this study.

Theoretical Frameworks

In addition to the SENTAR approach, several concepts common to health behavior theories were used to guide message content and campaign evaluation. Messages encouraged positive attitudes toward condom use by featuring benefits of condom use and negative consequences of nonuse, promoted positive safer sex norms, emphasized increased condom use self-efficacy, encouraged discussion and negotiation of safer sex practices, and emphasized and modeled commitment to and planning ahead for safe sex (Noar, 2007). In addition, campaign messages focused on increasing perceived general and personal HIV/STD susceptibility and on dispelling the myth that intimate relationships protect against STDs (Noar, Zimmerman, & Atwood, 2004). Theoretical factors thought to be strong mediators of condom use, such as self-efficacy and intentions to use condoms, were used in the evaluation of the campaign. Across the 12-week campaign, messages were staged to focus on 1) perceived threat of HIV and other STDs (Weeks 1 to 3), 2) personalization of HIV/STD risk (Weeks 4 to 6), 3) benefits of condom use and negative consequences of nonuse (Weeks 7 to 9), and 4) skills necessary to enact condom use (Weeks 10 to 12).

The Televised Campaign

The campaign used television as its only channel for three reasons. First, television was chosen in order to test whether a single-channel, mass media-only campaign could be effective. Secondly, television was selected because members of this target audience still watch a significant amount of television each day (M = 2.44 hours per day in this study), despite increased use of new communication technologies. Finally, spots developed for TV can include various sound and music features, intense images, and other features that allow the sensation value of campaign messages to be maximized.

The campaign took place (using a 50/50 combination of paid and donated time) from January to March, 2003, in Lexington, Kentucky. A professional media buyer placed the paid PSAs in programming (especially in narrowly targeted cable programs) popular with the target audience, as determined by TV and cable ratings data and by precampaign survey data on the preferences of HSS and IDM respondents. Most pro-bono PSAs were placed in the same programs as the paid ads. Standard industry formulas estimated that 80% of the target audience would be exposed to an average of 33 campaign messages, considered high exposure for a three-month TV ad campaign.

Sampling, Participants, and Interviewing Methods

Beginning eight months before the campaign, interviews were conducted with independent cross-sectional samples (one interview per respondent) of approximately 100 randomly selected young adults each month in each community. The population cohort followed in each community was initially ages 18 years and 0 months to 23 years and 11 months, and they aged 20 months as the cohort was followed to the end of the study. This was accomplished by continuously adjusting the minimum and maximum ages for eligibility upward one month at the start of each month. Two sampling methods were used to recruit participants monthly: random digit dialing of the general population and the calling of random samples of undergraduate and graduate students at the University of Kentucky (Lexington) and the University of Tennessee (Knoxville). Of those contacted, 60% agreed to complete a brief screener over the phone. To be eligible, participants had to be: 1) in the appropriate age span for the particular study month, 2) heterosexually active (had sex with an opposite-sex partner) in the past three months, 3) not married or engaged, and 4) a U.S. citizen (because of logistical factors related to paying participants the incentive). Of those screened and determined to be eligible (N = 4,989), 82% completed interviews for the project (N = 4,032 individuals interviewed across 21 months in the two cities).

The majority of the private 40- to 45-minute interview was self-administered to all respondents via a laptop computer, which increased confidentiality and anonymity and also improved assessment of message exposure because participants actually viewed the PSAs on the laptop. Most interviews took place in the respondent's home, while some respondents chose to be interviewed at the survey research center or a nearby library. Interviewees were paid $30 for their participation in the study. This incentive increased approximately $5 every six months in order to keep the incentive payment competitive over time.

Measures

Measures included demographics, personality characteristics, sexual characteristics, condom self-efficacy, condom use intentions, condom use (in the past three months), program preferences, and PSA exposure (Zimmerman, Palmgreen, Noar, Lustria, Lu, & Horosewski, 2007). All multiple-item scales used five-point Likert response formats. Two particularly important measures are described here.

Sensation Seeking and Impulsive Decision Making

A composite risk variable called sensation seeking and impulsive decision making (SSIDM) was created as the product of two scales: sensation seeking and impulsive decision making. Sensation seeking was assessed using Hoyle, Stephenson, Palmgreen, Lorch, and Donehew's (2002) eight-item Brief Sensation Seeking Scale (BSSS), while impulsive decision making was measured with 12-item, decision-making-style scale (Donohew et al., 2000). Individuals above the median on the composite scale, within race by gender categories (to control for differences on these variables), were classified as high sensation seekers and impulsive decision makers (HSSIDMs), with those below the median classified as low sensation seekers and rational decision makers (LSSRDMs).

Cued PSA Exposure Measure

Respondents in both cities were shown the five PSAs developed by our team for the campaign. Respondents indicated how often they had seen each PSA using five categories ranging from "have not seen" to "more than 10 times."

RESULTS

Lexington and Knoxville samples matched closely on most demographic variables, which generally paralleled census and university figures for each city. With the first number in parentheses indicating the Lexington sample and the second number indicating the Knoxville sample, the samples were (57.4%; 55.7%) female, (80.7%; 86.9%) white, (69.3%; 68.9%) some college graduate degree, and (21.9; 21.7) years old. The samples matched closely on sensation seeking (M = 3.40; 3.43) and impulsive decision making (M = 2.59; 2.64), and on all variables related to sexual behavior: for example, currently in a relationship (72.0%; 73.3%), age at first intercourse (16.4; 16.7), condom use in past three months—sometimes or every time (68.9%; 69.2%), frequency of intercourse in past 30 days—males (11.6 times; 11.6 times), frequency of intercourse past 30 days—females (10.4 times; 10.9 times), median number of sexual partners in past year—males (2; 2), median number of sexual partners in past year—females (1; 1).

Process Evaluation and Campaign Exposure (Recall)

Process evaluation included a major focus on implementation of the televised campaign, with continuous reports provided by the television stations to our media buyer and the research team to monitor implementation (see Rice & Foote, Chapter 5; Valente & Kwan, Chapter 6). All indications were that the PSA spots actually aired as planned, including targeted placements made in programs related to gender and HSSIDM preferences. Figure 14.1 plots campaign message recall as reported by Lexington HSSIDMs from January

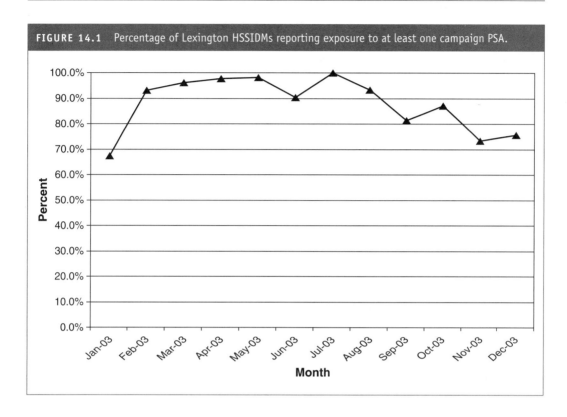

FIGURE 14.1   Percentage of Lexington HSSIDMs reporting exposure to at least one campaign PSA.

(the start of the campaign) through the end of the study. This figure shows the percentages that recalled seeing any one of the five original campaign PSAs (which received the greatest air time). As expected, recall was lower in the first month of the campaign (67%) and greatly increased to between 93% and 100% recall through August (i.e., four to five months after the end of the campaign). During the peak period of the campaign (February, March), we estimate that 96% of the target audience recalled seeing at least one of the original PSAs, 88% at least two different PSAs, 75% at least three, and 58% recalled four or more of the five PSAs. Regarding frequency of exposure, it was estimated conservatively (because the category "10 or more times" was coded as "11") that the target audience recalled seeing the five original PSAs 22 times on average during the campaign. Given that exposure to the Kaiser PSAs was not measured, it is likely that total exposure to all PSAs was higher than that estimated here (i.e., 22 times).

Lexington Time-Series Regression Analyses

Monthly means for all dependent variables were calculated separately by city for HSSIDMs and LSSRDMs, and the means for each category of respondents were analyzed separately with a regression-based, interrupted time-series procedure appropriate for data sets with fewer than 50 data points (Lewis-Beck, 1986). The procedure employs dummy variables to model slopes as well as intercept and slope changes due to the intervention. A series of different analyses using various models was run to clarify a complex pattern of results due to an apparent (but typical) wearing off of campaign effects a few months after the campaign ended.

Results for HSSIDMs

For those high on the composite risk variable (HSSIDMs), initial time-series analyses for all dependent variables were run using five dummy variables: one for the slope prior to the Lexington campaign, slope and intercept change variables for the Lexington campaign "interruption," and slope and intercept change variables for an expected downward change observed for each dependent variable two to three months after the campaign, apparently caused by campaign effects eventually wearing off.

A Lexington reduced-model analysis (which dropped nonsignificant intercept change terms) indicated the campaign produced a significant immediate upward slope change ($p < .05$) in frequency of condom use in the past month among HSSIDMs (five-point frequency scale), which lasted for three months after the campaign ended, after which the Lexington sample resumed its precampaign downward trend in condom use ($p < .05$ for this slope change—see Figure 14.2). Comparison of the postcampaign trend line (in bold) with projected condom use levels (thin line) in the absence of a campaign indicates that, despite the campaign wear out, participants had 12% higher condom use as measured by the five-point frequency scale (regression estimate $= 2.60$) at the end of data collection (nine months after the end of the campaign) than the level projected in the absence of a campaign (regression estimate $= 2.32$). This difference is significant at $p < .01$. Analyses for condom self-efficacy and condom use intentions as dependent variables produced almost identical results and thus are not presented. The conclusion that the effects observed were due to the campaign and not to history factors is strengthened by monthly online content analyses conducted as the data gathering proceeded for the major newspapers in each community, which revealed no programs or events that could plausibly have affected the dependent variables. National safer sex campaigns like the Kaiser Family Foundation's campaign were common to both cities, making it highly unlikely that they could account for the differential patterns observed.

Results for LSSRDMs

As expected, HSSIDMs were considerably and significantly higher than LSSRDMs on sexual risk variables across both cities prior to the campaign in Lexington. Also, as expected (as LSSRDMs were not targeted), various Lewis-Beck analyses (including both full and reduced models) involving LSSRDMs showed no campaign effects in Lexington on condom use, condom self-efficacy, or condom use intentions.

Knoxville Time-Series Regression Analyses

In order to test whether the respondents in the comparison (no-campaign) city exhibited any patterns similar to those in Lexington on the dependent variables, a series of Knoxville

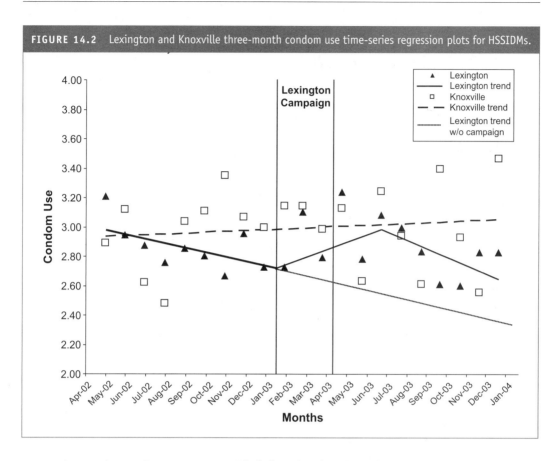

FIGURE 14.2   Lexington and Knoxville three-month condom use time-series regression plots for HSSIDMs.

time-series analyses was run with full and reduced models and employing the same campaign interruption points as Lexington. As expected, these analyses showed no significant slope changes for either HSSIDMs or LSSRDMs on any of the dependent variables.

Campaign Impact

An effect size for the Lexington campaign was calculated using Cohen's d, comparing condom use precampaign with postcampaign means and standard deviations and taking into account the secular trend in Knoxville, in this case, $d = .26$ (or $r = .13$), or slightly greater than a small effect size (Cohen, 1988). However, the campaign was considerably more effective than other safer sex campaigns. Snyder and colleagues (2004; see also Snyder & LaCroix, Chapter 8) reported the following effect sizes for safer sex campaigns: AIDS Community Demonstration Projects ($r = .03$), AIDS Prevention for Pediatric Life ($r = .05$), and America Responds to AIDS ($r = .01$).

Using the number of occasions of unprotected intercourse in the past 30 days as a second indicator of campaign impact, estimates derived from regression lines (similar to those in Figure 14.2), computed both with and without the impact of the Lexington campaign, were compared. On average, HSSIDMs engaged in a total of 10.49 fewer occasions of unprotected intercourse during the 12 months after the campaign began than would have been expected if the precampaign pattern of use had simply continued. The 2000 census estimate of the number of 18- to 26-year-olds (the target age range) in Lexington was divided by 2 to yield an estimated number of HSSIDMs (N = 20,649). Multiplying by those estimated in the SSC data to be sexually active in a 30-day period (84.4%) yielded 17,276 individuals. Multiplying this figure by the mean number of unprotected intercourse occasions averted as a result of the campaign (10.49) yields an estimate of 181,224 fewer such occasions among HSSIDMs between January and December, 2003 (out of a total of an estimated 1,688,382 total occasions of unprotected intercourse estimated to have occurred in the population without the intervention).

Discussion

Although the campaign appears to have been quite effective, as expected, its impact was relatively short term. This suggests that a continuing campaign presence is necessary to reinforce and sustain a behavior such as condom use, utilizing a constant supply of novel messages to maintain attention. In fact, reinforcement messages that might come in the form of booster campaigns are likely needed to overcome the dissipation of persuasive influence of the PSAs and the constant addition of new cohorts of young adults. Such reinforcement messages have been widely recommended for other behaviors (Randolph & Viswanath, 2004). Alternatively, it may be unrealistic to expect that media campaigns alone will have the kind of impact needed to sustain behavioral changes over the long term. Thus, combining media campaigns with other behavioral interventions such as school-based or community programs may be a manner in which to increase the efficacy and ultimate impact and sustainability of intervention efforts. Although some health campaigns have done this effectively (e.g., Slater, Kelly, Edwards, Thurman, Plested, Keefe et al., 2006; Worden, Flynn, & Hornik, 2002), additional research on synergistic links between health media campaigns and other behavioral interventions, including computer-based interventions (Noar, 2009), is needed. Indeed, many HIV prevention researchers have recently called for more mass media campaigns as a complement to individual-level approaches such as counseling and small group interventions (Romer, Sznitman, DiClemente, Salazar, Vanable, Carey et al., 2009).

Overall, the SSC study suggests that mass media campaigns alone can be effective in changing sexual risk behavior and related variables if well-documented principles of campaign design are followed. In this study, these principles included careful audience segmentation and targeting, as well as extensive formative research to design, test, and select campaign messages. Multiple theoretical perspectives, particularly SENTAR, were employed to inform these tasks. HSSIDMs are particularly relevant groups to target because of their proclivity for engaging in risky sexual behaviors. Evaluation of target audience program preferences immediately prior to the campaign allowed more precise placement of the campaign messages and helped in achieving the high reported exposure levels. Finally, a rigorous independent-sample, interrupted time-series design with a control community greatly strengthened causal inferences about campaign effects.

In terms of the scientific literature on HIV/AIDS campaigns, additional efforts are urgently needed that utilize numerous well-documented campaign design principles and that are rigorously evaluated so that campaign effects can be documented. While the literature in this area has continued to grow in recent years, with improvements in use of theory, message design, message exposure, and evaluation design (Noar, Palmgreen, Chabot, Dobransky, & Zimmerman, 2009), there are still too many campaign studies that are conducted with weak evaluation designs (as noted in Rice & Robinson, Chapter 16; Valente & Kwan, Chapter 6). In fact, while some studies use some campaign principles some of the time, there appears to be a dearth of studies that use numerous effective principles together in the design, implementation, and evaluation of campaigns. This may reflect a lack of appreciation for how campaign principles work synergistically or, in other cases, a lack of resources. Failure to attend to just one crucial principle, such as careful placement of messages (or other stages along the hierarchy of effects—see McGuire, Chapter 9), can easily lead to a failed campaign (i.e., due to inadequate message exposure). In addition, lack of attention to certain principles (i.e., audience segmentation) can affect the ability of campaign designers to effectively use other principles (i.e., message design and targeting) (Noar, in press). Until additional, carefully designed and evaluated media campaigns are undertaken in this area, the great potential of such efforts to effectively reach numerous populations at risk for HIV/AIDS and other STDs will not be realized. Finally, a potential limitation of HIV/AIDS prevention media campaigns may be that, as seen here, the effects of a campaign may only last for a total of five or six months, a shorter time period than that for some of the more intensive interpersonal interventions, which appear to have more lasting effects. However, mass media campaigns reach far more people than do interpersonal-oriented interventions. In order to better compare the two types of interventions, more rigorous cost-effectiveness comparisons need to be conducted between these different types of health interventions.

References

Albarracin, D., Gillette, J. C., Earl, A. N., Glasman, L. R., Durantini, M. R., & Ho, M. H. (2005). A test of major assumptions about behavior change: A comprehensive look at the effects of passive and active HIV-prevention interventions since the beginning of the epidemic. *Psychological Bulletin, 131*(6), 856–897.

Atkin, C. K. (2001). Theory and principles of media health campaigns. In R. E. Rice & C. K. Atkin (Eds.), *Public communication campaigns* (3rd ed., pp. 49–68). Thousand Oaks, CA: Sage.

Bertrand, J. T., O'Reilly, K., Denison, J., Anhang, R., & Sweat, M. (2006). Systematic review of the effectiveness of mass communication programs to change HIV/AIDS-related behaviors in developing countries. *Health Education Research, 21*(4), 567–597.

Cohen, J. (1988). *Statistical power analysis for the behavioral sciences* (2nd ed.). Hillsdale, NJ: Lawrence Erlbaum.

Coyle, K. K., Kirby, D. B., Marin, B. V., Gomez, C. A., & Gregorich, S. E. (2004). Draw the line/respect the line: A randomized trial of a middle school intervention to reduce sexual risk behaviors. *American Journal of Public Health, 94*(5), 843–851.

Donohew, L., Lorch, E., & Palmgreen, P. (1991). Sensation seeking and targeting of televised anti-drug PSAs. In L. Donohew, H. E. Sypher, & W. J. Bukoski (Eds.), *Persuasive communication and drug abuse prevention* (pp. 209–226). Hillsdale, NJ: Lawrence Erlbaum.

Donohew, L., Zimmerman, R., Cupp, P. S., Novak, S., Colon, S., & Abell, R. (2000). Sensation seeking, impulsive decision-making, and risky sex: Implications for risk-taking and design of interventions. *Personality and Individual Differences, 28*(6), 1079–1091.

Everett, M. W., & Palmgreen, P. (1995). Influences of sensation seeking, message sensation value, and program context on effectiveness of anticocaine public service announcements. *Health Communication, 7*(3), 225–248.

Hornik, R. C. (2002). *Public health communication: Evidence for behavior change.* Mahwah, NJ: Lawrence Erlbaum.

Hoyle, R. H., Fejfar, M. C., & Miller, J. D. (2000). Personality and sexual risk taking: A quantitative review. *Journal of Personality, 68*(6), 1203–1231.

Hoyle, R. H., Stephenson, M. T., Palmgreen, P., Lorch, E. P., & Donohew, R. L. (2002). Reliability and validity of a brief measure of sensation seeking. *Personality and Individual Differences, 32*(3), 401–414.

Lewis-Beck, M. S. (1986). Interrupted time series. In W. D. Berry & M. S. Lewis-Beck (Eds.), *New tools for social scientists: Advances and applications in research methods* (pp. 209–240). Beverly Hills, CA: Sage.

Lorch, E. P., & Palmgreen, P. (1994). Program context, sensation seeking, and attention to televised anti-drug public service announcements. *Human Communication Research, 20*(3), 390–412.

Myhre, S. L., & Flora, J. A. (2000). HIV/AIDS communication campaigns: Progress and prospects. *Journal of Health Communication, 5*(Suppl. 1), 29–45.

Noar, S. M. (2006). A 10-year retrospective of research in health mass media campaigns: Where do we go from here? *Journal of Health Communication, 11*(1), 21–42.

Noar, S. M. (2007). An interventionist's guide to AIDS behavioral theories. *AIDS Care, 19*(3), 392–402.

Noar, S. M. (2008). Behavioral interventions to reduce HIV-related sexual risk behavior: Review and synthesis of meta-analytic evidence. *AIDS & Behavior, 12*(3), 335–353.

Noar, S. M. (2009). The utility of "old" and "new" media as tools for HIV prevention. In C. Pope, R. T. White, & R. Malow (Eds.), *HIV/AIDS: Global frontiers in prevention/intervention* (pp. 343–353). New York: Routledge.

Noar, S. M. (in press). An audience-channel-message-evaluation (ACME) framework for health communication campaigns. *Health Promotion Practice.*

Noar, S. M., Palmgreen, P., Chabot, M., Dobransky, N., & Zimmerman, R. S. (2009). A 10-year systematic review of HIV/AIDS mass communication campaigns: Have we made progress? *Journal of Health Communication, 14*(1), 15–42.

Noar, S. M., Palmgreen, P., Zimmerman, R. S., Lustria, M. L. A., & Lu, H.-Y. (2010). Assessing the relationship between perceived message sensation value and perceived message effectiveness: Analysis of PSAs from an effective campaign. *Communication Studies, 61*(1), 21–45.

Noar, S. M., Palmgreen, P. C., Zimmerman, R. S., & Cupp, P. K. (2008). Formative research and HIV/AIDS mass media campaigns: Applications and insights from the field. In M. U. D'Silva, J. L. Hart, & K. L. Walker (Eds.), *HIV/AIDS: Prevention and health communication* (pp. 10–25). United Kingdom: Cambridge Scholars.

Noar, S. M., Zimmerman, R. S., & Atwood, K. A. (2004). Safer sex and sexually transmitted infections from a relationship perspective. In J. H. Harvey, A. Wenzel, & S. Sprecher (Eds.), *The handbook of sexuality in close relationships* (pp. 519–544). Mahwah, NJ: Lawrence Erlbaum.

Noar, S. M., Zimmerman, R. S., Palmgreen, P., Lustria, M., & Horosewski, M. L. (2006). Integrating personality and psychosocial theoretical approaches to understanding safer sexual behavior: Implications for message design. *Health Communication, 19*(2), 165–174.

Palmgreen, P. (2009). Interrupted time-series designs for evaluating health communication campaigns. *Communication Methods and Measures, 3*(1–2), 29–46.

Palmgreen, P., & Donohew, L. (2003). Effective mass media strategies for drug abuse prevention campaigns. In Z. Sloboda & W. J. Bukoski (Eds.), *Handbook of drug abuse prevention: Theory, science, and practice* (pp. 27–43). New York: Kluwer Academic/Plenum Publishers.

Palmgreen, P., Donohew, L., & Harrington, N. G. (2001). Sensation seeking in antidrug campaign and message design. In R. E. Rice & C. K. Atkin (Eds.), *Public communication campaigns* (3rd ed., pp. 300–304). Thousand Oaks, CA: Sage Publications.

Palmgreen, P., Donohew, L., Lorch, E. P., Hoyle, R. H., & Stephenson, M. T. (2001). Television campaigns and adolescent marijuana use: Tests of sensation seeking targeting. *American Journal of Public Health, 91*(2), 292–296.

Palmgreen, P., Donohew, L., Lorch, E. P., Rogus, M., Helm, D., & Grant, N. (1991). Sensation seeking, message sensation value, and drug use as mediators of PSA effectiveness. *Health Communication, 3*(4), 217–227.

Palmgreen, P., Lorch, E. P., Stephenson, M. T., Hoyle, R. H., & Donohew, L. (2007). Effects of the office of national drug control policy's marijuana initiative campaign on high-sensation-seeking adolescents. *American Journal of Public Health, 97*(9), 1644–1649.

Palmgreen, P., Stephenson, M. T., Everett, M. W., Baseheart, J. R., & Francies, R. (2002). Perceived message sensation value (PMSV) and the dimensions and validation of a PMSV scale. *Health Communication, 14*(4), 403–428.

Randolph, W., & Viswanath, K. (2004). Lessons learned from public health mass media campaigns: Marketing health in a crowded media world. *Annual Review of Public Health, 25,* 419–437.

Romer, D., & Hennessy, M. (2007). A biosocial-affect model of adolescent sensation seeking: The role of affect evaluation and peer-group influence in adolescent drug use. *Prevention Science, 8*(2), 89–101.

Romer, D., Sznitman, S., DiClemente, R., Salazar, L. F., Vanable, P. A., Carey, M. P., et al. (2009). Mass media as an HIV-prevention strategy: Using culturally sensitive messages to reduce HIV-associated sexual behavior of at-risk African American youth. *American Journal of Public Health, 99*(12), 2150–2159.

Slater, M. D., Kelly, K. J., Edwards, R. W., Thurman, P. J., Plested, B. A., Keefe, T. J. . . . Henry, K. L. (2006). Combining in-school and community-based media efforts: Reducing marijuana and alcohol uptake among young adolescents. *Health Education Research, 21*(1), 157–167.

Snyder, L. B., Hamilton, M. A., Mitchell, E. W., Kiwanuka-Tondo, J., Fleming-Milici, F., & Proctor, D. (2004). A meta-analysis of the effect of mediated health communication campaigns on behavior change in the United States. *Journal of Health Communication, 9,* 71–96.

Worden, J. K., & Flynn, B. S. (2002). Using mass media to prevent cigarette smoking. In R. C. Hornik (Ed.), *Public health communication: Evidence for behavior change* (pp. 23–33). Mahwah, NJ: Lawrence Erlbaum.

Zimmerman, R. S., Cupp, P. K., Donohew, L., Sionean, C. K., Feist-Price, S., & Helme, D. (2008). Effects of a school-based, theory-driven HIV and pregnancy prevention curriculum. *Perspectives on Sexual & Reproductive Health, 40*(1), 42–51.

Zimmerman, R. S., Noar, S. M., Feist-Price, S., Dekthar, O., Cupp, P. K., Anderman, E., et al. (2007). Longitudinal test of a multiple domain model of adolescent condom use. *Journal of Sex Research, 44*(4), 380–394.

Zimmerman, R. S., Palmgreen, P., Noar, S. M., Lustria, M. L., Lu, H.-Y., & Horosewski, M. L. (2007). Effects of a televised two-city safer sex mass media campaign targeting high-sensation-seeking and impulsive-decision-making young adults. *Health Education & Behavior, 34*(5), 810–826.

Zuckerman, M. (1994). *Behavioral expressions and biosocial bases of sensation seeking.* Cambridge; New York: Cambridge University Press.

Public Communication Campaigns to Promote Organ Donation

Theory, Design, and Implementation

Susan E. Morgan

Author's Note: The author would like to gratefully acknowledge the assistance of Andy J. King and Tyler R. Harrison in the preparation of this chapter.

Theory-grounded public communication campaigns to promote health are increasingly common. Even the small effect sizes often associated with campaigns that target large populations (see Snyder & LaCroix, Chapter 8) can translate into many lives saved. Organ donation is an example of a health-related issue that has benefitted from the collaborative efforts of scholars and practitioners to produce effective campaigns.

There are many challenges associated with promoting nonliving organ donation (that is, organ donation that takes place after the donor's death has been declared); it has taken decades to identify these myriad challenges and to develop ways to address them. With the transplant waiting list growing to over 100,000 people (United Network for Organ Sharing, 2010), an increased sense of urgency has developed among researchers pursuing the knowledge needed to create effective campaigns. When a potential donor, who typically suffers from traumatic brain injury, dies without actually donating, up to eight people will die as a result. Advocates express distress that people willingly bury "perfectly good organs" that could have saved lives. While this shortage could not be fully met even if every eligible donor declared an intent to donate by joining a statewide registry or by carrying a signed donor card, many of the thousands who die each year could be saved. The immediate need for increased numbers of people to declare a willingness to donate organs necessitates the continued development of innovative, theory-based campaigns that will allow the public to make informed decisions about becoming potential organ donors.

Following a discussion of theoretical foundations of organ donation campaigns, this chapter will focus on the results of several types of theory-based strategic campaigns that have been successful in increasing organ donation. These include worksite campaigns, campaigns that target specific populations (including university students, future physicians, and members of minority racial and ethnic groups), and campaigns that center on drivers license bureaus. Issues surrounding the design and implementation of those campaigns will also be discussed.

THEORETICAL FOUNDATIONS OF ORGAN DONATION CAMPAIGNS

The theoretical foundations of organ donation campaigns have varied considerably. Theories such as the Theory of Planned Behavior (TPB), Theory of Reasoned Action (TRA), and the Transtheoretical Model (the *stages of change* approach) have predominated. The Transtheoretical Model has proved popular but not particularly successful as a foundation for public communication campaigns to promote deceased donation, while TRA (and related models) has proven to be far more useful.

A review of the social scientific literature on the predictors of the willingness to donate organs reveals a general consensus that donation-related behaviors are a function of attitudes toward organ donation and toward becoming a donor, knowledge about organ donation (particularly knowledge that counters popular myths about donation), and the influence of family and friends (Horton & Horton, 1991; Feeley, 2007; Kopfman & Smith, 1996). These, of course, are the same variables that comprise TRA. There are additional factors that appear to contribute to the willingness to donate, including existential variables such as the perception that organ donors "survive" death, a concern about saving the lives of "bad" people, the fear that signing a donor card will tempt fate and possibly bring on premature death, and a general sense of disgust from the idea of putting the organs from one person into the body of another person (see Morgan, Harrison, Long, Afifi, & Stephenson, 2008; Morgan, Stephenson, Harrison, Afifi, & Long, 2008). Morgan and colleagues have added these noncognitive variables to TRA to create a model tailored to organ donation (Morgan, Stephenson et al., 2008).

The operationalization of both cognitive and noncognitive variables has resulted in specific messages for organ donation campaigns. Formative research with both general and minority populations, for example, has provided important information about the specific points of knowledge that were most predictive of the willingness to donate. These include knowledge about the organ allocation system, that an organ donor can have an open-casket funeral, that a black market does not exist in the United States, and that potential donor status will not affect the quality of medical care in an emergency (Morgan & Miller, 2002; Morgan, Miller, & Arasaratnam, 2003). Because of this formative evaluation research (see Atkin & Freimuth, Chapter 4), these campaigns have focused on providing details about these specific points of knowledge rather than overwhelm individuals with unnecessary general information about organ donation.

Although superstitions about bringing on premature death by signing a donor card or a visceral-level disgust response at the idea of organ transplantation would be difficult to overcome through a communication campaign, concerns about the deservingness of potential recipients is more easily addressed. By having transplant recipients and others affected by organ donation involved with campaign outreach activities, nondonors are able to establish a greater sense of connection with the sort of people who might be potential recipients of their own organs. In other words, a number of successful campaigns (Harrison, Morgan, Chewning, Williams, Barbour, Di Corcia et al., 2011; Morgan, Harrison, Chewning, Di Corcia, & Davis, 2010; Morgan & Miller, 2002; Morgan, Stephenson, Afifi, Harrison, Long, & Chewning, 2011) have not relied solely on messages that presume that the reluctance to register as an organ donor is the result of rational cognitive processes or a lack of factual knowledge. These campaigns attempt to take into account target audiences' fears, emotions, and beliefs about donation rather than simply "educating" people about donation.

WORKSITE CAMPAIGNS

Because workplaces are communities where people spend many of their waking hours, health educators have long assumed that they would be productive contexts for public education about a wide variety of health issues, including smoking cessation, health screening, and general health promotion, including physical activity, dietary improvements, and multivitamin use (Campbell, Tessaro, DeVellis, Benedict, Kelsey, & Belton, 2002; Emmons, Linnan, Shadel, Marcus, & Abrams, 1999; Grosch, Alterman, Petersen, & Murphy, 1998; Sorensen, Barbeau, Stoddard, Hunt, Kaphingst, & Wallace, 2005). Professionals seeking to disseminate compelling and accurate information about organ donation have been similarly attracted to the prospect of worksite campaigns not only because they provide a large, captive audience for information about organ and tissue donation but because information can be framed in ways that matter to employees.

Morgan and colleagues conducted a series of projects in diverse organizations (including health care, manufacturing, finance, law, education, and municipalities) that have resulted in increased knowledge about donation, improved attitudes toward donation, and most importantly, an average of 12% of employees who were previously nondonors joining the donor registry (Harrison, Morgan, Chewning, Williams, Barbour, Di Corcia et al., 2011; Morgan, Harrison et al., 2010; Morgan & Miller, 2002; Morgan et al., 2011). The reasons for the success of these interventions can be distilled into several campaign practices described below.

First, the project used a combination of mass media messages with interpersonal outreach activities. Outreach activities typically included site visits by volunteers (accompanied by a campaign staff member who ensured intervention fidelity) who were transplant recipients or donor family members. The team staffed information tables that typically featured a panel of a donor family quilt that honors the lives of individual donors. Generally, employees stopped by the table to collect small giveaways, at which time they were given a donor registration form. Any misgivings about organ donation were then discussed; these discussions often resulted in an employee registering to become a potential donor.

Second, the best results were found with larger organizations (at least 500 employees but as many as 4,000+ employees). Although multilevel modeling did not point to a structural relationship between size and the magnitude of the relative increase in registrations, the participation of large organizations created the greatest efficiency of efforts in organizing and conducting campaigns and thus produced the greatest real numbers of new registrations. Increasing actual organ donation is a matter of obtaining very large numbers of registrations because so few people die in ways that make them eligible to become organ donors. Additionally, because approximately 35% to 40% of people (depending on socioeconomic status, ethnicity, and geographic region) are already registered as potential donors, the number of employees who are the true audience for organ donation interventions is reduced by a rather large number.

Conducting campaigns in workplaces that offer more opportunities for social interaction (and thus social influence and diffusion through opinion leaders and peers) and that have a relatively large number of information channels through which messages can be disseminated maximizes the likelihood that potential donors will be reached with information that is tailored to the goals of the campaign (Harrison, Morgan, & Williams, 2010; Harrison, Morgan, Chewning et al., 2011). Thus, mere size is not the key predictor of a successful campaign, but it does ensure a greater efficiency of effort and likelihood of communicating about the topic.

Third, organizations' own employees who were affected by organ donation were prominently featured in promotional materials such as brochures, posters, and newsletter stories to help drive home the personal relevance of the issue. These individuals included donor family members, individuals waiting for transplants, transplant recipients (or their family members), and family members of those who have died while waiting for transplants. Not incidentally, finding people who have been touched by the issue of organ donation tends to be easier in larger organizations.

Fourth, volunteers from the regional nonprofit organ procurement organizations were trained to follow scripts to address common myths and misconceptions, which produced maximum efficiency, persuasion, and intervention fidelity. Volunteers and staff members alike delivered campaign messages that targeted the key barriers to the willingness to register as organ donors. It should be noted that it is not uncommon for organ procurement organizations to encourage transplant recipients to share their stories of being saved from death by the generosity of an organ donor (Morgan, 2009). Unfortunately, not only does this message not target the actual barriers people perceive when considering becoming potential donors, but it also opens the door to rather graphic displays of recipients' surgical scars or often-grotesque descriptions of surgical procedures. Training staff and volunteers to stay on message ensures greater intervention fidelity.

Fifth, campaign organizers harnessed the power of internal (free!) media, including e-mail, cafeteria table tents, newsletters, posters, paycheck stuffers, and LCD boards. Larger organizations have a number of channels of internal communication that are effective in reaching virtually 100% of the targeted population. Organizations provide the opportunity to attain the breadth of campaign reach that is so important in achieving results. An additional advantage of this setting is that the only cost associated with this use of media is the time it takes to make messages appropriate for each type of channel.

Finally, the researchers avoided the trap of the time-honored worksite campaign tradition of *lunch and learns.* This type of outreach strategy involves creating an hour-long educational session, typically held in a company meeting room; the presentation is publicized through fliers and e-mail, and employees attend only if they are interested in the topic. Such practices result in campaigns that preach to the choir that already understands the importance of organ donation rather than reaching the people who need the information the most (see Quinn, Alexander, Hollingsworth, O'Connor, & Meltzer, 2006).

An important limitation of worksite campaigns is the amount of planning and coordination that is required of researchers and practitioners. Negotiating access to the organization, reviewing acceptable campaign messages, determining the location of information tables (to ensure a central location), creating tailored materials for a particular organization, gaining permission to distribute written materials, and scheduling and supervising specially trained volunteers are not challenges that should be taken lightly. These represent real expenses in terms of both time and energy that many organizers often underestimate, and organizations resist.

CAMPAIGNS FOR TARGETED POPULATIONS

There are three types of targeted populations that have been the focus of organ donation interventions: university students on college campuses, future physicians enrolled in medical school, and members of racial and ethnic minority groups.

University Campaigns

There are several examples of successful campaigns that have centered on university campuses that were designed to increase the number of students who joined a state donor registry. Feeley and colleagues (Feeley, Anker, Vincent, & Williams, 2010; Feeley, Anker, Watkins, Rivera, Tag, & Volpe, 2009) partnered with regional organ procurement organizations (OPOs) and universities in New York to harness the expertise and enthusiasm of communication students to create materials that were used in a subsequent campus campaigns. More than 4,500 new registrations were completed as a result of these campaigns.

For example, Feeley and colleagues (2009) used active learning methods to significantly improve attitudes, knowledge, and behavioral outcomes among the students who designed and implemented a campus campaign. The campaign itself resulted in over 1,000 students joining the New York donor registry. These successes appear to be due primarily to several key elements of the campaign. First, a high level of involvement was required of students who designed the campaign, which helped them create effective messages to reach other university students (Marshall, Reinhart, Feeley, Tutzauer, & Anker, 2008). Second, there is homophily between the designers of the intervention and the target of that intervention. Thus, messages designed and delivered by students seem to resonate strongly and have positive influence with members of the target audience (see also Lederman & Stewart, 2005, for a similar approach to college alcohol campaigns).

Medical Students

Not surprisingly, physicians are seen as high-credibility sources of information about organ donation, and patients indicate that they would like to be able to express their concerns and ask questions about donation with their physicians (Saub, Shapiro, & Radecki, 1998).

Unfortunately, studies have repeatedly demonstrated that physicians' levels of knowledge about organ donation do not differ appreciably from those of their patients (Bardell, Hunter, Kent, & Jain, 2003; Schaeffner, Windisch, Freidel, Breitenfeldt, & Winkelmayer, 2004). These findings may be less shocking upon examination of medical school curricula; organ donation is rarely discussed.

To help remedy the situation, Feeley, Anker, Soriano, and Friedman (2010) developed interventions targeting medical students. In one intervention (Feeley, Tamburlin, & Vincent, 2008), medical students were given carefully selected information about donation based on the types of questions physicians might be asked about, focusing particularly about donor eligibility, the process of organ matching, organ allocation policies and procedures, and the roles of physicians versus transplant surgeons and staff after a potential donor is declared brain dead. After the information was delivered in a standard lecture format, medical students were asked to participate in a small group interaction where a trained confederate patient asked questions about donation. The interactions were coded to assess medical students' knowledge and communication about organ donation. Based on pretest and posttest data, the intervention was successful in increasing knowledge, perceived self-efficacy in engaging in donation discussions, and medical students' own intentions to donate.

A more in-depth examination of the use of confederate patients to train future physicians to communicate about organ donation was conducted by Feeley and colleagues (2010). Researchers asked trained patients to embed some of their questions in the context of concerns they had after viewing an episode of "ER" that depicted physicians hastening the death of a patient in order to recover organs. This strategy forced medical students to try to produce accurate messages about donation that counter common misconceptions rather than merely providing a straightforward listing of facts about donation. The findings indicated that medical students needed further education, whether through targeted outreach efforts or through the medical school curriculum, about state health care proxies, a patient's ability to choose specific organs for transplantation, and how organ donation might affect the timing of funeral arrangements in order to be effective in their conversations with patients expressing typical fears fostered by in the media.

Members of Racial and Ethnic Minority Groups

While a great deal is known about the differences in knowledge, attitudes, and behaviors among African-Americans, Hispanics, Asians, and Whites (Morgan et al., 2003; Siminoff, Burant, & Ibrahim, 2007), few well-evaluated campaigns actually target the specific concerns or address the needs of minority populations. This may, of course, be a result of the nature of the concerns held by members of racial and ethnic minority groups, including deeper levels of medical mistrust and increased worries about the afterlife consequences of donation. Such concerns would be exceptionally difficult to target in a communication campaign. Early interventions led by Washington, D.C., transplant surgeon Clive Callender (and the organization he founded, the Minority Organ and Tissue Transplant Education Program) used community outreach workers to go door-to-door in predominantly African-American neighborhoods to educate residents and offer the opportunity to ask questions and express fears about donation (Callender, Bey, Miles, & Yeager, 1995; Callender, Burston, Burton, & Miles, 1996). While positive attitudes toward organ donation increased and the rate of self-reported willingness to donate improved, these interventions were not evaluated using accepted social scientific methods. Nonetheless, Callender's work inspired other researchers to build upon these strategies to create more sophisticated, theory-based campaigns for minority communities.

Although there are few published studies describing campaigns that specifically attempt to reach African-Americans, Harrison, Morgan, King, and Williams (2011) recently reported on their campaign in Detroit to compare the effectiveness of mass media messages with an interpersonal outreach intervention at drivers license bureaus. As Figure 15.1 shows, combining all of the various campaign elements produced dramatic increases in actual donor registration rates of 1,258%. This increase is relative to very stable, long-term historical baseline rates; the results are similarly dramatic when paired against control sites. This campaign demonstrated the additive effects of theory-driven point-of-decision materials, mass media messages, and interpersonal communication on organ donation registrations.

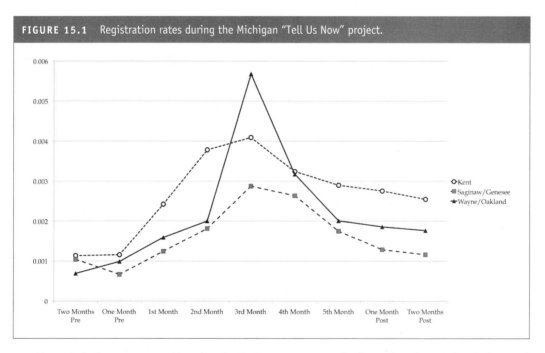

FIGURE 15.1 Registration rates during the Michigan "Tell Us Now" project.

Note: The vertical axis represents monthly registration figures as a percentage of each group's total population. The horizontal axis represents the point in the sequence of the interventions. Mass media campaigns and point-of-decision materials were used during Months 1 and 2; mass media campaigns, point-of-decision materials, and on-site outreach events were conducted during Months 3 and 4; point-of-decision materials were used in Month 5. Interventions in the three sets of counties were conducted sequentially over a 22-month period.

Similarly, there are very few actual campaigns detailed in the published literature that target Hispanics. Alvaro, Jones, Robles, and Siegel (2006) and Frates, Bohrer, and Thomas (2006) both used Spanish-language mass media campaigns, which were evaluated using a standard pretest and posttest design. While neither campaign included a control group comparison, both were able to increase knowledge, favorable attitudes, and self-reported donation intentions. It remains to be seen whether actual registrations or other "hard" behavioral outcomes can be improved through specifically targeted Spanish-language campaigns that use the mass media but do not include an interpersonal communication component.

DRIVERS LICENSE BUREAU CAMPAIGNS

Perhaps the most impressive organ donation campaigns in terms of the results of the numbers of new potential donors are those that are target customers of drivers license bureaus. Campaigns centering on drivers license bureaus have been conducted in Kentucky, Michigan, Florida, and Illinois (Harrison, Morgan, & Di Corcia, 2008; Harrison, Morgan, King et al., 2010; Harrison et al., 2011). Based on the success of these campaigns, additional states are currently implementing similar strategies. With over 60,000 new donor designations in the span of 16 months, one particular campaign in Michigan is by far the most successful. An alternating time-series design entailed groups of intervention counties receiving a phased campaign consisting of mass media ads combined with point-of-decision materials in each drivers license bureau, followed by the addition of an on-site interpersonal intervention component, and concluding with only point-of-decision materials. The results were compared across three groups of intervention counties as well as control counties and historical levels for each set of counties. Results indicated that the percentage of county residents who agreed to join the Michigan donor registry increased in intervention counties by 200 to 1,200%, depending on the intervention components. Details of the campaigns as well as specific statistical analyses of the results are reported elsewhere (Harrison, Morgan, King, Di Corcia et al., 2010; Harrison et al., 2011), but a few of the elements that were shown to contribute to the success of the campaigns warrant brief explication.

The Michigan drivers license bureau campaigns were grounded in key principles of communication design and media priming theory (Harrison et al., 2011). Communication design principles focus on "transforming something given . . . into something preferred" (Aakhus, 2007, p. 112) through the process of structuring the communication protocols governing interactions between clerks and customers (see also Dervin & Foreman-Wernet, Chapter 10). For the Michigan campaigns, this meant consciously and deliberately crafting messages that customers encountered as they progressed through the process of their transactions. At the same time that these new protocols were introduced, mass media messages primed residents to think about donation before arriving at drivers license bureaus. The intention was to strengthen the relationship between generally positive attitudes toward donation and behaviors leading to donor registration.

Although campaign organizers were unable to conduct a direct educational intervention with the clerks who interact with customers (as was the case in a Kentucky campaign; Harrison et al., 2008), this particular strategy for creating a new communication protocol was replaced by a more direct approach with customers as they entered offices. In larger branches, customers first check in with a clerk to ensure that they have all the necessary paperwork to get a driver's license, vehicle registration, and so on. A display at the check-in desk was added that contained laminated cards that told customers to "Tell Us Now" that they wanted to join the organ donor registry. The card was added to the customer's paperwork, which was then given to the clerk who actually performed the tasks associated with vehicle licensing or registration. Throughout the office, "Tell Us Now" materials were prominently displayed on posters (which highlighted the story and photo of a local resident who had been touched by organ donation), counter mats, and brochures that contained additional information about organ donation. The media component of the campaign included bus ads, PSAs, and billboards on the routes customers would have to drive in order to get to the branch office. The interpersonal campaign component followed the same principles outlined in the worksite campaigns described above (e.g., volunteers sharing personal stories, addressing each customer's individual concerns about donation). While each component alone increased registration rates, the greatest change was associated with a combination of point-of-decision materials displayed at the licensing bureau, mass media campaign messages, and an interpersonal campaign component, with the interpersonal component being especially important in African-American populations.

Conclusion

No one on the transplant waiting list wishes for the death of a potential donor. Instead, what they wish for desperately is that individuals and their loved ones will make the choice to not "bury perfectly good organs" after they die. Why so many people choose not to be organ donors after death is a mystery to some, but research has identified a number of key cognitive, noncognitive, and affective factors that act as important barriers to the decision to donate. Unfortunately, it appears that many nondonors have fears about donation that are created by entertainment media depictions of organ donation and transplantation (Morgan, Harrison et al., 2010; Morgan, Movius, & Cody, 2009) that are robbing them of the opportunity to make an informed decision about donation based on concrete realities.

The facts of the organ donation process are often complicated. For example, it begins with the intricacies of the organ allocation system, including hospital transplant committees that qualify patients for the transplant waiting list and involves medical testing procedures for blood and tissue typing which minimize the chances of transplant rejection. It also involves a complex computerized system administered by UNOS, which takes into account tissue type, how ill a potential recipient is, how long they have been waiting, the hardiness of an organ (e.g., kidneys vs. lungs), and the geographic distance that a particular organ would have to travel in order to be transplanted. Clearly, this system would be difficult to explain to the public in sound bites or on billboards.

Conversely, entertainment media tell far simpler stories that depict corrupt surgeons who kill their patients in order to sell their organs on the black market or steal the organs for favored patients (Harrison, Morgan, & Chewning, 2008). It should come as no shock that these are among the most commonly reported beliefs by the general public (Morgan, King, Smith, & Ivic, 2010). Campaigns (such as those described in this chapter) to repudiate these myths lack the funding available to Hollywood writers and producers, but media advocacy groups such as Donate Life Hollywood in Los Angeles are attempting to proactively help writers and producers create accurate organ donation story lines. To the extent that the efforts of advocacy groups, academic researchers, and professionals who work for OPOs succeed, people who would have died while languishing on the transplant waiting list will live.

References

Aakhus, M. (2007). Communication as design. *Communication Monographs, 74*(1), 112–117.

Alvaro, E. M., Jones, S. P., Robles, A. S., & Siegel, J. T. (2006). Hispanic organ donation: Impact of a Spanish-language organ donation campaign. *Journal of the National Medical Association, 98*, 28–35.

Bardell, T., Hunter, D. J. W., Kent, W. D. T., & Jain, M. K. (2003). Do medical students have the knowledge needed to maximize donation rates? *Canadian Journal of Surgery, 46*, 453–457.

Callender, C. O., Bey, A. S., Miles, P. V., & Yeager, C. L. (1995). A National Minority Organ/Tissue Transplant Education Program: The first step in the evolution of a national minority strategy and minority transplant equity in the USA. *Transplantation Proceedings, 27*, 1441–1443.

Callender, C. O., Burston, B. W., Burton, L. W., & Miles, P. V. (1996). An assessment of the impact of the National Minority Organ/Tissue Transplant Education Program (MOTTEP). *Transplantation Proceedings, 28*, 394–397.

Campbell, M. K., Tessaro, I., DeVellis, B., Benedict, S., Kelsey, K., & Belton, L. (2002). Effects of a tailored health promotion program for female blue-collar workers: Health works for women. *Preventive Medicine, 34*, 313–323.

Emmons, K. M., Linnan, L. A., Shadel, W. G., Marcus, B., & Abrams, D. B. (1999). The working healthy project: A worksite health promotion trial targeting physical activity, diet, and smoking. *Journal of Occupational and Environmental Medicine, 41*, 545–555.

Grosch, J. W., Alterman, T., Petersen, M. R., & Murphy, L. R. (1998). Worksite health promotion programs in the U.S.: Factors associated with availability and participation. *American Journal of Health Promotion, 13*, 37–45.

Feeley, T. H. (2007). College students' knowledge, attitudes, and behaviors regarding organ donation: An integrated review of the literature. *Journal of Applied Social Psychology, 37*, 243–271.

Feeley, T. H., Anker, A. E., Soriano, R., & Friedman, E. (2010). Using standardized patients to educate medical students about organ donation. *Communication Education, 59*, 249–262.

Feeley, T. H., Anker, A. E., Vincent, D. E., & Williams, C. R. (2010). Promoting organ donation through college student campaigns. In J. T. Siegel & E. M. Alvaro (Eds.), *Understanding organ donation: Applied behavioral science perspectives* (pp. 200–220). Hoboken, NJ: Wiley-Blackwell.

Feeley, T. H., Anker, A. E., Watkins, B. Rivera, J., Tag, N., & Volpe, L. (2009). A peer-to-peer campaign to promote organ donation among racially diverse college students in New York City. *Journal of National Medical Association, 101*, 1154–1162.

Feeley, T. H., Tamburlin, J., & Vincent, D. E. (2008). An educational intervention on organ and tissue donation for first-year medical students. *Progress in Transplantation, 18,* 103–108.

Frates, J., Bohrer, G. G., & Thomas, D. (2006). Promoting organ donation to Hispanics: The role of the media and medicine. *Journal of Health Communication, 11,* 683–698.

Harrison, T. R., Morgan, S. E., & Chewning, L. V. (2008). The challenges of social marketing of organ donation: News and entertainment coverage of donation and transplantation. *Health Marketing Quarterly, 25,* 33–65.

Harrison, T. R., Morgan, S. E., Chewning, L. V., Williams, E., Barbour, J., Di Corcia, M., & Davis, L. (2011). Revisiting the worksite in worksite health campaigns: Evidence from a multisite organ donation campaign. *Journal of Communication, 61*(3), 535–555.

Harrison, T. R., Morgan, S. E., & Di Corcia, M. (2008). The impact of organ donation education and communication training for gatekeepers: DMV clerks and organ donor registries. *Progress in Transplantation, 18,* 301–309.

Harrison, T. R., Morgan, S. E., King, A. J., Di Corcia, M. J., Williams, E. A., Ivic, R. K., & Hopeck, P. (2010). Promoting the Michigan Organ Donor Registry: Evaluating the impact of a multifaceted intervention utilizing media priming and communication design. *Health Communication, 25*(8), 700–708.

Harrison, T. R., Morgan, S. E., King, A. J., & Williams, E. A. (2011). Saving lives branch by branch: The effectiveness of drivers licensing bureau campaigns to promote organ donor registry sign ups to African-Americans in Michigan. *Journal of Health Communication, 16,* 805–819.

Harrison, T. R., Morgan, S. E., & Williams, E. A. (2010). A method for assessing the interaction environment of organizations. In G. Allard (Ed.), *Proceedings of the 9th European Conference on Research Methods for Business and Management Studies, Spain,* 166–174.

Horton, R. L., & Horton, P. J. (1991). A model of willingness to become a potential organ donor. *Social Science & Medicine, 33,* 1037–1051.

Kopfman, J. E., & Smith, S. W. (1996). Understanding the audiences of a health communication campaign: A discriminant analysis of potential organ donors based on intent to donate. *Journal of Applied Communication Research, 24,* 33–49.

Lederman, L. C., & Stewart, L. P. (2005). *Changing the culture of college drinking: A socially situated health communication campaign.* Cresskill, NJ: Hampton Press.

Marshall, H. M., Reinhart, A. M., Feeley, T. H., Tutzauer, F., & Anker, A. (2008). Comparing college students' value-, outcome-, and impression-relevant involvement in health-related issues. *Health Communication, 23,* 171–183.

Morgan, S. E. (2009). The challenges of conducting and evaluating organ donation campaigns. In J. T. Siegel & E. M. Alvaro (Eds.), *Understanding organ donation: Applied behavioral science perspectives* (pp. 234–246). Hoboken, NJ: Wiley-Blackwell.

Morgan, S. E., Harrison, T. R., Chewning, L. V., Di Corcia, M. J., & Davis, L. A. (2010). The Workplace Partnership for Life: The effectiveness of high- and low-intensity work site campaigns to promote organ donation. *Communication Monographs, 77,* 341–356.

Morgan, S. E., Harrison, T. R., Long, S. D., Afifi, W. A., & Stephenson, M. T. (2008). In their own words: The reasons why people will (not) donate organs. *Health Communication, 23,* 23–33.

Morgan, S. E., King, A. J., Smith, J. R., & Ivic, R. (2010). A kernel of truth? The impact of storylines exploiting myths about organ donation on the public's willingness to donate. *Journal of Communication, 60,* 778–796.

Morgan, S. E., & Miller, J. (2002). Communicating about gifts of life: The effect of knowledge, attitudes, and altruism on behavior and behavioral intentions regarding organ donation. *Journal of Applied Communication Research, 30,* 163–178.

Morgan, S. E., Miller, J., & Arasaratnam, L. A. (2003). Similarities and differences between African-Americans' and European-Americans' attitudes, knowledge, and willingness to communicate about organ donation. *Journal of Applied Social Psychology, 33,* 693–715.

Morgan, S. E., Movius, L., & Cody, M. (2009). The power of narratives: The effect of organ donation entertainment television storylines on the attitudes, knowledge, and behaviors of donors and nondonors. *Journal of Communication, 59,* 135–151.

Morgan, S. E., Stephenson, M. T., Afifi, W., Harrison, T. R., Long, S. D., & Chewning, L. V. (2011). The University Worksite Organ Donation Campaign: A comparison of two types of worksite campaigns on the willingness to donate. *Clinical Transplantation, 25,* 600–605.

Morgan, S. E., Stephenson, M. T., Harrison, T. R., Afifi, W. A., & Long, S. D. (2008). Facts versus "feelings": How rational is the decision to become an organ donor? *Journal of Health Psychology, 13,* 644–658.

Quinn, M. T., Alexander, G. C., Hollingsworth, D., O'Connor, K. G., & Meltzer, D. (2006). *Progress in Transplantation, 16*(3), 253–256.

Saub, E. J., Shapiro, J., & Radecki, S. (1998). Do patients want to talk to their physicians about organ donation? Attitudes and knowledge about organ donation: A study of Orange County, California, residents. *Journal of Community Health, 23,* 407–417.

Schaeffner, E. S., Windisch, W., Freidel, K., Breitenfeldt, K., & Winkelmayer, W. C. (2004). Knowledge and attitude regarding organ donation among medical students and physicians. *Transplantation, 77,* 1714–1718.

Siminoff, L. A., Burant, C. J., & Ibrahim, S. A. (2007). Racial disparities in preferences and perceptions regarding organ donation, *Journal of General Internal Medicine, 21,* 995–1000.

Sorensen, G., Barbeau, E., Stoddard, A. M., Hunt, A. K., Kaphingst, K., & Wallace, L. (2005). Promoting behavior change among working-class multiethnic workers: Results of the health directions–small business study. *American Journal of Public Health, 95,* 1389–1395.

United Network for Organ Sharing. (2010). Retrieved December 1, 2010, from www.unos.org

Transdisciplinary Approaches for Twenty-First Century Ocean Sustainability Communication

Ronald E. Rice and Julie A. Robinson

The ocean, Earth's life support system, is under siege. Human actions threaten ocean health at unprecedented scales. No area of the ocean remains pristine or untouched by human activities, from industrialized fishing and aquaculture, oil and natural gas extraction, mineral mining, coastal development, nutrient and toxic pollution, the introduction of pathogens, invasive species, marine transport, overfishing and species extinction, and military testing to perhaps the most destructive of all, climate change (see Jackson, 2008). The interconnectivity and severity of these impacts threaten the very foundation of the ocean food web and consequently pose profound, negative, and irreversible implications for human health and well-being. The International Programme on the State of the Ocean (Rogers & Laffoley, 2011) assessed the combined impacts of ocean stressors such as pollution, warming, acidification, overfishing, and hypoxia and recently concluded that ocean degeneration is occurring much faster than predicted, and similar combinations of factors have been associated with major extinctions.

Given this context, it is unfortunate that, basically, concerning ocean issues, people are only slightly concerned and essentially unaware or uninformed (Edge Research, 2002; Steel, Smith, Opsommer, Curiel, & Warner-Steel, 2005). Media coverage of environmental issues is generally slight and, like all news, subject to corporate and political biases and interests, limits on timing and space, framing, journalistic norms, deadlines, low science journalism training, and low audience interests (Ashlin & Ladle, 2007; O'Donnell & Rice, 2008). In general, the public's knowledge and awareness of ocean topics is negligible, superficial, and unchanging since 1999 (The Ocean Project, 2009). Over a third feel that the environmental issue of ocean health is overstated; people do not associate ocean issues with climate change; and there is little to no awareness of ocean issues apart from the vacation beach.

Solutions to these complex ocean environmental problems, including the need to develop greater ocean literacy (discussed below), seem scarce. But crises, fortunately, can also create opportunities for new paradigms to emerge such as with the subdiscipline of environmental communication (EC). This is the focus of this chapter. However, we use the term *environmental communication strategy* here instead of *campaign,* which offers a better representation of the dimensions and context for our discussion. Misgivings over the use of the term *campaign* and especially *social marketing* are especially common in environmental circles where debates abound over the role of science and scientists in influencing public opinions, policies, promoting social change, and related threats to the reputation of scientific credibility due to actual or perceived advocacy positions. While this debate is needed, and frankly overdue, the focus of this chapter is to elaborate the synergies that exist among three disciplinary branches: *sustainability science, ocean literacy* (from environmental education), and *communication for change strategies* (from health and development communication) in order to provide a clearer framework for fostering collaboration in developing, implementing, and evaluating more holistically conceived (from a systems perspective), but clearly defined, practical, and applied environmental communication strategies for sustainability (defined below).

With a special focus on ocean systems and sustainability, this chapter summarizes five disciplinary blind spots, portrayed in Figure 16.1, that can impair a holistic view of environmental issues and thus critical components that need to be considered when designing environmental communication strategies for ocean sustainability. The chapter then briefly applies this model to assess one campaign aimed at improving seafood sustainability awareness.

REVEALING AND DEALING WITH BLIND SPOTS IN OCEAN COMMUNICATION THROUGH TRANSDISCIPLINARY APPROACHES

Blind Spot One: The Need to Diagnose the Dimensions of Environmental Problems (Scale, Scope, and Fit)

Environmental communication efforts often fail to adequately address the issues of and between problems, solutions, and change strategies. Scale, in this context, refers to the dimensions of the environmental problem. Scope represents the interface boundaries (systems of governance, time, technology, and effort or technology needed to solve the problem, for example). The principle of fit refers to the variables considered in the communication intervention to avoid or minimize spatial and temporal mismatches relative to the biophysical systems, socioeconomic activities, and governance practices at hand (Young, Osherenko, Ekstrom, Crowder, Ogden, Wilson et al., 2007). Environmental science must inform communication and education efforts by providing diagnoses of the scope and scale of problems (and probability measures, whenever possible) before the best–fit, theory-based change strategy can be determined and for which level—local (individual- or household-level behavior change), regional (community- or industry-level change), or global (national and international governance regimes). Likewise, communication theory can inform strategies for scaling environmental solutions from top-down management approaches to bottom-up individual and community-based approaches, an important focus of sustainability research (see "Blind Spot Three").

FIGURE 16.1 Ocean communication model for sustainability.

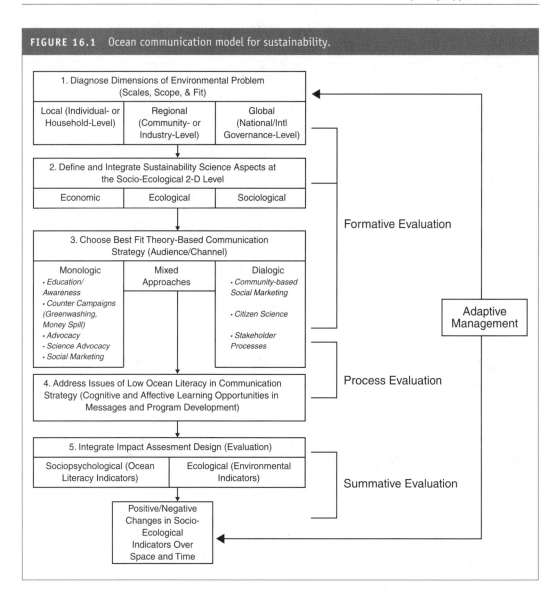

Blind Spot Two: The Need to Define and Integrate Sustainability Science Aspects at the Socioecological Level

development is "development that meets the needs of the present without compromising the ability of future generations to meet their own needs" (United Nations Food and Agricultural Organization, 1995, which extended this into the marine resources arena). While certainly challenging (Filho, 2000), embedding sustainability principles into 21st-century communication strategies is vital for at least two reasons. First, sustainability science represents a broader spectrum of valuations for deconstructing conflicts around common pool resource use by considering three dimensions—environmental stewardship, economic development, and societal equity (Sikdar, 2003)—intersections among each, and among all three. Second, this three-dimensional sustainability science approach emphasizes sociological, economic, and ecological performance indicators, such as changes in attitudes toward an environmental problem, the market value of an ecosystem resource, and change over space and time.

Critics of sustainability science, however, point out that it can mean vastly different things to different people (Hilborn, Punt, & Orensanz, 2004). In some corners of the developing world, for example, sustainability has become associated with neocolonialism; in the nongovernmental organization (NGO) world as a panacea; and in the pragmatic world of resource management, a quaint, but unattainable ideal. However, much of this confusion could be alleviated if an emphasis were placed on clearly outlining the sociopsychological, ecological, and economic goals and metrics of sustainability in planning frameworks. For example, in considering the environmental aspect of Sikdar's (2003) model, resource use or impact indicators for ocean health could be species abundance or the presence and ratio of nutrient pollution in a watershed. Social indicators include predictors of environmental behavior, such as knowledge, attitudes, skills, intention, and efficacy relevant to ocean sustainability (Graedel & Allenby, 2002).

Blind Spot Three: Choosing Best-Fit, Theory-Based Communication Strategies (Audience/Channel)

Broadly speaking, communication theories and models can be characterized as more or less *monologic* or *dialogic* (Mefalopulos, 2008, pp. 22–24). The categorization of the following approaches into these categories is somewhat artificial as there are many forms of each type of campaigns; the modes are not mutually exclusive and can be complementary (shown in Figure 16.1 as "Mixed Approaches").

Monologic Modes

The *monologic mode* is a one-way or linear transmission of information to raise awareness, educate, or persuade. Special care is taken in determining the target audience, the message development and source, and the most appropriate channels of communication.

Awareness, information, and persuasion. For example, strategists might choose to integrate the Elaboration Likelihood Model (ELM) for its power to predict and explain how members of the intended audience may process a message (motivation and ability) and the extent to which they'll think about issue-relevant arguments in a persuasive message. The ELM posits that, when situational and individual factors positively influence motivation, the ability for issue-relevant thinking or the elaboration likelihood will be high and therefore recipients are more likely to follow a central or argument-based route to persuasion. Resulting persuasion is more persistent, resistant to change, and predictive of behavior. When elaboration likelihood is low, however, recipients are more likely to follow the peripheral route to persuasion by "any variable capable of affecting persuasion without affecting argument scrutiny" (Petty & Cacioppo, 1986, p. 134). These variables may take the form of mechanisms or cues such as social norms, identity, source attractiveness, celebrity, trusted authority, and so forth. Resultant persuasion is more ephemeral. Gaining attention to an issue through the peripheral route may be an important first step in an environmental communication strategy, but achieving long-term, ongoing sustainability objectives requires a more comprehensive approach.

Entertainment–education (E–E) is the intentional placement of education content in entertainment messages to prompt conversations and create socially constructed learning environments in which previously held ideas are evaluated and changes in thinking and behavior occur (Singhal, Wang, & Rogers, Chapter 22). It is important to distinguish between the nonfiction genre of wildlife and natural history films, however, which may be considered and theoretically constructed E–E strategies. Very few films in the wildlife genre incorporate E–E designs. And, there is very little evidence to suggest that wildlife films, though entertaining and in some cases informational, actually promote environmental literacy in viewers (Dingwall & Aldridge, 2006). For example, the classic Cousteau television specials constituted one of the best-known media programs about the ocean. A study of viewer knowledge and attitudes before, directly after, and a few weeks after the broadcast of one of the documentary specials found that knowledge increased significantly and remained high for two weeks but then declined to baseline levels (Fortner & Lyon, 1985). The integration and evaluation of E–E in environmental television programs and films would certainly seem to warrant greater investigation; however, barriers within sectors of the mainstream media industry actually preclude such efforts. New media, unencumbered by some types of these barriers, may be more valuable for developing and disseminating environmental E–E content and for evaluating effects. Also, traditional E–E campaigns may involve quite dialogic components, such as radio show call-ins or performance attendance.

Countercampaigns to green washing and money spill. Green washing and money spill strategies are used by large corporations to counter the public's negative association with a polluting industry or product. One example of *green washing* is the case of the Exxon Valdez and Deepwater Horizon Gulf oil spills, where Exxon created an extensive public relations campaign to replace the facts and narrative of destruction with a clear signal of quickly dissipating damages and recovering ecology (Ott, 2008). A *money spill* strategy is another type of divergence tactic. Ott describes that in the disaster aftermath in Alaska, "Exxon dumped money into all the communities to hire people for its cleanup. Not everyone worked the cleanup. So there were 'haves' and 'have-nots.' A lot of people thought Exxon purposely created division, because people in oiled towns knew the cleanup was mostly a charade" (p. 240). BP's response to the oil spill in the Gulf of Mexico received similar criticism. Developing effective countercampaigns to green washing and money spill strategies can be very challenging because corporations nearly always have the upper hand in terms of financial and legal resources compared to their victims. However, in a small number of cases, well-organized grassroots activists, especially those philosophically aligned with and supported by the environmental justice movement, have been able to generate sufficient pressure from the base to counter money spill strategies and influence policy makers to adopt proenvironment positions for community health.

Advocacy. Environmental advocacy campaigns are usually conducted by noninstitutional sources (individuals, environmental organizations, community action groups) and seek to change external conditions or governmental or institutional policy or practice (not individual attitudes or behaviors). Environmental advocacy can involve 1) political and legal channels, including political advocacy, litigation, and electoral politics, 2) direct appeal to public audiences, including public education, direct action, media events, and community organizing, and 3) consumers and the market, including green consumerism and corporate accountability (Cox, 2006, p. 244). A major change in environmental advocacy campaigns occurred as a result of the first Earth Day in 1970: a shift from primarily educational to strategic campaigns to achieve specific goals, more participation by citizens, and systematic mobilization of members to create political pressure. Yet, advocacy generates persuasion dilemmas for environmental activists mobilizing public support, such as whether extreme rhetoric and actions are useful (because they can make mainstream groups appear more reasonable and thus acceptable) or damaging (because they give environmentalism a bad name).

Science advocacy. Scientific research results and conclusions are frequently and widely misrepresented in the news, either by heightening the consequences and shortening the time scales or by criticizing the foundational science—even the scientific approach itself. Further, the ways stories or studies are framed foster agendas and legitimize (or delegitimize) particular actions or policies (Ashlin & Ladle, 2007). This raises the paradoxical situation that scientists who wish the public to know more about their (objective, accurate) results through media may see science itself becoming delegitimized in the process. Ladle, Jepson, and Whittaker (2005, p. 231) label this a " 'struggle for legitimacy' between environmentalist and antienvironmentalist groups, with potential negative consequences for public trust in science." Scientists must become engaged in this struggle (Cole & Waltrous, 2007) and implement successful information translation models (Meeson, McDonnell, Kohut, Litchenwahler, & Helling, 2006) (such as developing stories with visuals about scientific research in forms ready for broadcast and print journalists).

Social marketing. Social marketing integrates theory, research, and practice from both social science public communication and commercial marketing campaigns (see Kotler & Lee, 2007; Bracht & Rice, Chapter 20). This approach conceptualizes socially beneficial ideas (e.g., recycling) as attractive, accessible, affordable, and appropriate products. Takahashi (2009) categorizes environmental social marketing articles and campaigns from 1971 to 2006. Bates (2010) organizes her review of ocean campaigns by the primary stages in a social marketing approach: audience analysis; audience segmentation; consumer orientation; theory; appropriate and realistic objectives; message and channel design; and formative, process, and summative research throughout emphasizing the four Ps of social marketing (product, pricing, placement, and promotion). She argues that a primary goal of such campaigns must be to increase public responsibility for ocean resources (e.g., Pew Oceans Commission, 2003). A social marketing approach allows some campaigns (such as the "Give Swordfish a Break" campaign—Brownstein, Lee, & Safina, 2003) to achieve both immediate and wider success.

Dialogic Modes

The dialogic two-way or participatory mode describes discourse, information exchanges, mutual understanding, and consensus development that occur in community-based social marketing initiatives, citizen science programs, or stakeholder-driven processes (Bracht & Rice, Chapter 20; Dietz & Stern, 2002; McKenzie-Mohr, 2010; Mefalopulos, 2008; United Nations Environment Programme, 2007). Three important components of participatory communication are capacity building through personal responsibility, efficacy to deal with environmental threats, and inclusion: Omitting groups from assessments and participation can create resentments, limit valuable information sources, and undermine the legitimacy and outcomes of stakeholder efforts. But, dialogic communication for ocean sustainability is a relatively new concept and requires a strong willingness on the part of designers and participants to fully engage in an often thorny, time-, and resource-consuming process involving conflicting goals. These problems are especially common in fisheries management settings where the primary focus of maintaining reproductively viable fisheries through the management of fishing activities creates conflict and where marine spatial planning relies heavily on science-based modeling and multistakeholder involvement in establishing management zones to protect and restore ocean health through measures such as marine-protected areas.

Community-based social marketing. As we have been arguing, many ocean environmental campaign issues and goals are socially complex and integrated with many other factors, and communities have many potentially relevant resources and motivations for becoming involved. Further, social-psychological principles indicate that behavior change efforts will be more successful if they involve direct interactions with people and are implemented at the community level. Thus, there is a growing emphasis on a community-based approach to social marketing campaigns, from problem definition through interventions (Bracht & Rice, Chapter 20; McKenzie-Mohr, 2010). Jonick, Anderson, Lin, Bruni, Schultz, Groner, and colleagues (2010) applied a community-based social marketing perspective (emphasizing direct contact with individual anglers in their social contexts) to change a single behavior to reduce a specific risk: Release back or stop fishing white croaker from the vast waters of the Palos Verdes Shelf Superfund Site. The central communication strategy was a tip card for identifying the fish and emphasizing the health risks, based on formative evaluation of the audience, the salient fishing locales, costs and benefits, and motivators and barriers. Pre- and postpersonal surveys at the treatment and a control pier also collected measures of actual fish catch and fishing techniques and accuracy in identifying white croakers. The effects were substantial: a 93 % reduction in number of white croakers taken from the treatment pier by anglers compared with a small increase in the control pier and a 22 % decrease in anglers from the intervention site reporting eating white croaker with no change in the control site.

Citizen science and community-based research. The citizen science model links expert input and citizen input in collecting and sharing data. Community-based research (CBR) goes further, by integrating community members (grassroots activists, resource users, community-based organizations, etc.) in the development of research protocols that are credible, relevant, and transparent to all participants (Mackinson, 2001).

Blind Spot Four: Addressing Issues of Low Ocean Literacy in Communication Strategies (Cognitive and Affective Learning Opportunities in Messages and Program Development)

Educators and policy makers have proposed that tackling the problem of rapidly declining ocean health requires a massive effort toward developing an ocean-literate society—in other words, broad awareness, understanding, and concern among the world's citizenry for the ocean's influence on human health and our influence on the ocean (Cava, Schoedinger, Strang, & Tuddenham, 2005; Pew Oceans Commission, 2003). The Ocean Literacy Network (n.d.) has developed a consensus definition of an ocean-literate person as someone who "understands ocean science, can communicate about the ocean, and is able to make informed decisions that affect the ocean" (see also National Geographic Society, 2006). While ocean literacy is gaining traction in a small number of environmental education circles, it hasn't as yet been well integrated into mainstream science education, informal environmental programs, and communication strategies. As a result, many efforts (and resources) remain directed at increasing ecological awareness and knowledge despite evidence that these objectives alone are insufficient to create enduring behavior changes (Coyle, 2005; Moser & Dilling, 2007).

In a model of environmental citizenship developed by Hawthorne and Alabaster (1999), personal responsibility and locus of control, in addition to knowledge, are prerequisites for individuals to engage in solving environmental problems. Important research on environmental literacy (Bamberg & Moser, 2007) suggests that proenvironmental behaviors are linked both to cognitive understanding (knowledge and awareness of issues) as well as, importantly, affective attunement (attitudes, skills, intention, and efficacy). Further, research from the field of behavior change communication and risk perception has demonstrated the value of considering affective dimensions as predictors of behavior.

An example of a program that included an evaluation of cognitive, attitudinal, and behavioral measures was the Cairns Section (of the Great Barrier Reef in Australia) campaign. Between 1985 and 1991, this study tracked changes in infringement and public participation in review of zoning plans to support for management practices, the reduction of fish catches, and wiser use of reef resources (Alder, 1996). It also collected cost data to assess the relative costs and benefits of education (measured through a total awareness score based on recalling any of a wide range of media and messages about the park) versus enforcement (via a stratified random sampling of infringement surveillance) in helping to protect the Cairns Section of the Great Barrier Reef. Although public use of the reef did not change over time, awareness of the park's existence and total awareness significantly increased. All but one of the measured attitudes improved significantly. While education costs increased and exceeded enforcement costs overall, costs per direct contact were around 10% of the cost of each infringement detection. Meanwhile, although infringement declined during the first three years, it leveled off after that.

Blind Spot Five: The Need to Integrate Impact Assessment in Designs (Evaluation)

In considering the sociopsychological aspects of Sikdar's three-dimensional sustainability model, ocean literacy measures should be included in the design and implementation of environmental communication strategies along with other cross-cutting metrics. Unfortunately, a review of environmental education programs by Flemming and Easton (2010) concluded that a majority of those failed to include routine evaluations, and there is a widespread lack of rigorous program design (see also Takahashi, 2009; and evaluation chapters in this book).

EXAMINING THE CASE OF SUSTAINABLE SEAFOOD USING THE OCEAN COMMUNICATION MODEL

Industrial-scale fishing, which became prominent in the early 19th century, is leading to serial depletion of target species (Seafood Choices Alliance, 2008). Further, as one target species is removed from an ecosystem, fishing efforts are often redirected toward a different species, called *fishing down the food web,* a clearly unsustainable practice. Thus, campaigns seek to change consumer behavior, including using sustainable fish identification and the *buycotting,* or boycotting, of unsustainable species products. A related awareness campaign approach encourages adding *eco-labeling* (such as dolphin safe symbols) to the Marine Stewardship Council's development of fishery sustainability criteria (Jacquet & Pauly, 2007). We apply our Ocean Communication Model to the Seafood Watch campaign initiated in 2000 (Kemmerly & Macfarlane, 2009).

Step 1: Diagnose Dimensions of Environmental Problem (Scales, Scope, and Fit)

Seafood recommendations produced by the Marine Stewardship Council and Seafood Watch are based on an assessment of the overall health of a commercial fish stock considering multiple variables and vast amounts of scientific data reviewed and synthesized through expert analyses. Because catch reporting methods and accuracy can vary widely by agency and country, recommendations are more frequently being oriented at smaller scales with care given to educate consumers about the regional distinctions.

Step 2: Define and Integrate Sustainability Science Aspects at the Socioecological 2-D Level

As a buycott campaign, Seafood Watch was designed to leverage consumer (individual) spending to support more ocean-friendly fisheries (mostly targeted at local and industry levels). It reflects three dimensions of sustainability: consumer behaviors, market incentives, and environmental objectives. The globalization of fisheries and associated issues (lack of traceability, relabeling, illegal catches), however, preclude direct and easy correlations between consumer behaviors and improved ocean health, so effects can only be assumed instead of directly measured (Kemmerly & Macfarlane, 2009, p. 410). This complex situation represents a mismatch of sorts between the scale and scope of the problem and fit of the communication solution,

Step 3: Choose Best-Fit, Theory-Based Communication Strategy (Audience, Message, and Channel)

Kemmerly and Macfarlane (2009) do not mention a specific theory-based model underlying the development of Seafood Watch, yet the design reflects a classic monologic awareness, information, and persuasion approach with some social marketing aspects included. Visitors to the Monterey Bay Aquarium are the primary audience and represent the first point of campaign contact for the message that "fishing practices worldwide are damaging our oceans—depleting fish populations, destroying habitats and polluting the water . . . [but that] informed consumers can help turn the tide" (Monterey Bay Aquarium Seafood Watch, 2010). The prescription is provided in the form of a free, wallet-sized printed guide to sustainable seafood choices for consumers (also available through a website—http://www.montereybayaquarium.org/cr/cr_seafoodwatch/download.aspx— and recently a mobile phone app) as well as tools that provide specific information on problems and solutions and specific activities that promote self-efficacy and provide a road map for action with a trigger or prompt that is available at the time of entry ticket purchase and a reduction in barriers at the point of action by working with restaurateurs, the seafood industry, and other organizations in the sustainable seafood movement to increase knowledge and available options.

Step 4: Address Issues of Low Ocean Literacy in Communication Strategy (Cognitive and Affective Learning Opportunities in Messages and Program Development)

The Monterey Bay Aquarium's environmental education mission "to integrate the relationships between personal actions and the oceans into its messaging" (Kemmerly & Macfarlane, 2009, p. 399) is well embedded in the Seafood Watch strategy. As such, the campaign aims to increase the knowledge and awareness of sustainable seafood issues among aquarium visitors but also attempts, through interactive science exhibits and the seafood pocket guide, to build skills and motivations to empower consumers to follow through with conservation actions.

Step 5: Integrate Impact Assessment Design (Evaluation) With Sociopsychological Indicators, Environmental Indicators, and Resources

More than 32 million pocket guides have been distributed since the launch of Seafood Watch (Monterey Bay Aquarium, 2009). While the program materials highlight planning, collaboration, and evaluation as adaptive tools, a specific theory-based communication strategy was not elaborated in the early design.

Referencing the ELM, for example, it could be predicted that an involved audience such as aquarium visitors would be more likely to have sufficient motivation and ability to attend to and process the campaign message through a science-based argument (central channel of persuasion). Interestingly, a comparative analysis of pre- (on-site surveys) and post- (telephone interviews) tests with 400 interviewees four months later reflect ELM-like outcomes:

> 91% of respondents reported that the pocket guide had influenced their thinking or awareness. . . . The pocket guide helped to educate them, made them more aware of issues or the status of a particular type of seafood, made them question where their seafood comes from and how it was caught, or verified their own beliefs on the subject. (Kemmerly & Macfarlane, 2009, p. 403)

Respondents indicated they not only used the guides to make their own decisions and change their buying habits but also to help educate others (by showing them or giving them the guide or helping with seafood purchase decisions).

The Monterey Bay Aquarium's (2009) survey results indicate that Americans believe their seafood choices impact ocean health and that they are willing to pay more for healthy, sustainable seafood; it also reports that print media coverage of sustainable seafood issues increased eightfold between 2002 and 2008. However, an absence of ecological indicators reflecting related changes over time precludes the possibility of determining the real effectiveness of these campaigns on ocean sustainability. Further, the amount of manipulation in the seafood market renders "seafood wallet cards and other related tools . . . ineffective in fulfilling their aims" and "the Monterey Bay Aquarium conducted a self-study that revealed no overall change in the market and that fishing pressures have not decreased for targeted species" (Jacquet & Pauly, 2007, p. 301).

Therefore, while the Seafood Watch campaign has clearly made substantial and important inroads in raising consumer awareness and influencing buying behaviors, direct correlations between the intervention and positive sustainability outcomes are elusive. However, applying the ocean communication model in a Seafood Watch-type planning framework might lead to the development of a regional scale pilot (linking sociological and ecological indictors such as promoting a specific consumer buying goal linked to a measurable, local seafood indicator) to evaluate campaign effectiveness. Pilot results could inform how to scale up the campaign over space and time or whether, in fact, the campaign goals are actually achievable and how to best use organizational resources.

Conclusion: The Holistic View

Modern ocean health problems are becoming increasingly complex, and solutions involve difficult socioeconomic trade-offs. An effective communication strategy to reach diverse goal audiences and secure difficult-to-achieve sustainability outcomes requires planners and researchers to accurately identify the linkages between the ecological, physical, economic, and social aspects (including values) related to a particular environmental issue. Consequently, 21st-century environmental communication efforts require more substantive strategies than simple monologic (silver bullet or knowledge-deficit) designs relied upon in former decades. Responding effectively to the challenges posed by today's crises demands the transdisciplinary convergence of social and environmental science perspectives to formulate innovative, theory-based communication models and assessment techniques, such as those presented here.

References

Alder, J. (1996). Costs and effectiveness of education and enforcement, Cairns section of the Great Barrier Reef Marine Park. *Environmental Management, 20*(4), 541–551.

Ashlin, A., & Ladle, R. J. (2007). "Natural disasters" and newspapers: Post-tsunami environmental discourse. *Environmental Hazards: Human and Policy Dimensions, 7*(4), 330–341.

Bamberg, S., & Moser, G. (2007). Twenty years after Hines, Hungerford, and Tomera: A new meta-analysis of psychosocial determinants of proenvironmental behaviour. *Environmental Psychology, 27,* 14–25.

Bates, C. H. (2010). The use of social marketing concepts to develop ocean sustainability campaigns. *Social Marketing Quarterly, 16*(1), 71–96.

Brownstein, C., Lee, M., & Safina, C. (2003). Harnessing consumer power for ocean conservation. *Conservation in Practice, 44*(4), 39–42.

Cava, F., Schoedinger, S., Strang, C., & Tuddenham, P. (2005). *Science content and standards for ocean literacy: A report on ocean literacy.* National Geographic Society, National Oceanic and Atmospheric Administration, Lawrence Hall of Science, University of California College of Exploration. Retrieved August 20, 2011, from http://coexploration.org/oceanliteracy/documents/OLit2004-05_Final_Report.pdf

Cole, N., & Waltrous, S. (2007). Across the great divide: Supporting scientists as effective messengers in the public sphere. In L. Dilling & S. C. Moser (Eds.), *Creating a climate for change: Communicating climate change and facilitating social change* (pp. 180–199). Cambridge, MA: Cambridge University Press.

Cox, R. (2006). Environmental advocacy campaigns. In *Environmental communication and the public sphere* (pp. 243–281). Thousand Oaks, CA: Sage.

Coyle, K. (2005). *Environmental literacy in America: What ten years of NEETF/Roper research and related studies say about environmental literacy in the U.S.* Retrieved August 20, 2011, from the National Environmental Education & Training Foundation website: http://www.neefusa.org/pdf/ELR2005.pdf

Dietz, T., & Stern, P. C. (Eds.). (2002). *New tools for environmental protection: Education, information, and voluntary measures.* Washington, DC: National Academy Press.

Dingwall, R., & Aldridge, M. (2006). Television wildlife programming as a source of popular scientific information: A case study of evolution. *Public Understanding of Science, 15,* 131–152.

Edge Research. (2002). *Public knowledge and attitudes about coral reefs.* Retrieved August 20, 2011, from the Coral Reef Foundation and SeaWeb website: http://www.oceanfdn.org/index.php?tg=fileman&idx=get&inl=1&id=5&gr=Y&path=&file=CoralReefPoll.pdf

Filho, W. L. (2000). Communicating sustainability: Some international considerations and challenges. In W. L. Filho (Ed.), *Environmental education, communication and sustainability* (pp. 11–23). Frankfurt: Peter Lang.

Flemming, M. L., & Easton, J. (2010). Building environmental educators' evaluation capacity through distance learning. *Evaluation and Program Planning, 33,* 172–177.

Fortner, R., & Lyon, A. E. (1985). Effects of a Cousteau television special on viewer knowledge and attitudes. *Journal of Environmental Education, 16*(3), 12–20.

Graedel, T. E., & Allenby, B. R. (2002). Hierarchical metrics for sustainability: Monitoring environmental progress across the corporate, regional, national, and global levels. *Environmental Quality Management, 12*(2), 21–30.

Hawthorne, M., & Alabaster, T. (1999). Citizen 2000: Development of a model of environmental citizenship. *Global Environmental Change, 9,* 25–43.

Hilborn, R., Punt, A. E., & Orensanz, J. (2004). Beyond band-aids in fisheries management: Fixing world fisheries. *Bulletin of Marine Science, 74*(3), 493–507.

Jackson, J. B. C. (2008). Ecological extinction and evolution in the brave new ocean. *Proceedings of the National Academy of Sciences, 105*(1), 11458–11465.

Jacquet, J. L., & Pauly, D. (2007). The rise of seafood awareness campaigns in an era of collapsing fisheries. *Marine Policy, 31*(3), 308–313.

Jonick, T., Anderson, E. L., Lin, S., Bruni, C. M., Schultz, P. W., Groner, S., et al. (2010). What's the catch? Reducing consumption of contaminated fish among anglers. *Social Marketing Quarterly, 16*(1), 32–51.

Kemmerly, J. D., & Macfarlane, V. (2009). The elements of a consumer-based initiative in contributing to positive environmental change: Monterey Bay Aquarium's Seafood Watch program. *Zoo Biology, 28*(5), 398–411.

Kotler, P., & Lee, N. (2007). *Social marketing: Influence behaviors for good* (3rd ed.). Thousand Oaks, CA: Sage.

Ladle, R. J., Jepson, P., & Whittaker, R. J. (2005). Scientists and the media: The struggle for legitimacy in climate change and conservation science. *Interdisciplinary Science Reviews, 30*(3), 231–240.

Mackinson, S. (2001). Integrating local and scientific knowledge: An example in fisheries science. *Environmental Management, 27*(4), 533–545.

McKenzie-Mohr, D. (2010). *Fostering sustainable behavior: An introduction to community-based social marketing* (4th ed.). Gabriola Island, British Columbia, Canada: New Society Publishers and Washington, DC: Academy for Education Development.

Meeson, B. W., McDonnell, J., Kohut, J., Litchenwahler, S., & Helling, H. (2006). More than one way to catch a fish: Effective translation of ocean science for the public. *Proceedings of Oceans 2006, Boston, MA,* 1–5.

Mefalopulos, P. (2008). *Development communication sourcebook: Broadening the boundaries of communication.* Retrieved August 20, 2011, from the International Bank for Reconstruction and Development/The World Bank website: http://siteresources.worldbank.org/EXTDEVCOMMENG/Resources/DevelopmentCommSourcebook.pdf

Monterey Bay Aquarium. (2009). *Turning the tide: The state of seafood.* Retrieved August 20, 2011, from http://www.montereybayaquarium.org/cr/cr_seafoodwatch/content/media/MBA_SeafoodWatch_StateofSeafoodReport.pdf

Monterey Bay Aquarium Seafood Watch. (2010). Retrieved August 20, 2011, from http://www.montereybayaquarium.org/cr/seafoodwatch.aspx?c=ln

Moser, S. C., & Dilling, L. (2007). Toward the social tipping point: Creating a climate for change. In S. C. Moser & L. Dilling (Eds.), *Creating a climate for change: Communicating climate change and facilitating social change* (pp. 491–516). New York: Cambridge University Press.

National Geographic Society. (2006). *Ocean literacy: The essential principles of ocean sciences, K-12.* Retrieved February 28, 2011, from http://www.coexploration.org/oceanliteracy/documents/OceanLitChart.pdf

O'Donnell, C., & Rice, R. E. (2008). Coverage of environmental events in U.S. and U.K. newspapers: Frequency, hazard, specificity, and placement. *International Journal of Environmental Studies, 65*(5), 637–654.

Ocean Literacy Network. (n.d.). Retrieved August 20, 2011, from http://oceanliteracy.wp2.coexploration.org/

Ott, R. (2008). *Not one drop: Betrayal and courage in the wake of the Exxon Valdez oil spill.* White River Jct., VT: Chelsea Green Publishing.

Petty, R. E., & Cacioppo, J. T. (1986). *Communication and persuasion: Central and peripheral routes to attitude change.* New York: Springer-Verlag.

Pew Oceans Commission. (2003). *America's living oceans: Charting a course for sea change. A report to the nation.* Retrieved August 20, 2011, from http://www.pewtrusts.org/uploadedFiles/wwwpewtrustsorg/Reports/Protecting_ocean_life/env_pew_oceans_final_report.pdf

Rogers, A. D., & Laffoley, D. d'A. (2011). *International Earth system expert workshop on ocean stresses and impacts.* Retrieved August 20, 2011, from http://www.stateoftheocean.org/ipso-2011-workshop-summary.cfm

Seafood Choices Alliance. (2008). *The marketplace for sustainable seafood: Growing appetites and shrinking seas.* Retrieved August 20, 2011, from http://64.130.1.197/resources/documents/reports_sustainableseafood.pdf

Sikdar, S. K. (2003). Sustainable development and sustainability metrics. *AIChE Journal, 49*(8), 1928–1932.

Steel, B. S., Smith, C. Opsommer, L., Curiel, S., & Warner-Steel, R. (2005). Public ocean literacy in the United States. *Ocean & Coastal Management, 48*(2), 97–114.

Takahashi, B. (2009). Social marketing for the environment: An assessment of theory and practice. *Applied Environmental Education & Communication, 8*(2), 135–145.

The Ocean Project. (2009). *America, the ocean, and climate change: New research insights for conservation, awareness, and action—Executive summary.* Retrieved August 20, 2011, from the Ocean Project website: http://www.theoceanproject.org/resources/environmental.php

United Nations Environment Programme. (2007). *Sustainability communications: A toolkit for marketing and advertising courses.* Retrieved August 20, 2011, from http://www.uneptie.org/shared/publications/pdf/DTIx0886xPA-EducationKitEN.pdf

United Nations Food and Agricultural Organization. (1995). *Living marine resources and their sustainable development: Some environmental and institutional perspectives.* Retrieved August 20, 2011, from the FAO Fisheries and Aquaculture Department website: http://www.fao.org/docrep/003/v5321e/V5321E01.htm

Young, O. R., Osherenko, G., Ekstrom, J., Crowder, L. B., Ogden, J., Wilson, J. A., et al. (2007). Solving the crisis in ocean governance: Place-based management of marine ecosystems. *Environment, 49*(4), 21–32.

Sociocognitive Approaches for AIDS Prevention

Explicating the Role of Risk Perceptions and
Efficacy Beliefs in Malawi

Rajiv N. Rimal and Rupali Limaye

The global burden of AIDS is disproportionately borne by countries in southern Africa. In 2009, approximately 11 million people were living with HIV in this region, which constituted a 31% increase from a decade earlier (Joint United Nations Programme on HIV/AIDS, 2010). Approximately 34% of the world's population living with HIV in 2009 resided in 10 countries in southern Africa, and 40% of all HIV-positive adult women live in southern Africa (Joint United Nations Programme on HIV/AIDS, 2010). In 2008, HIV prevalence among adults in sub-Saharan Africa was approximately 11%, as compared to 3.25% worldwide (Joint United Nations Programme on HIV/AIDS, 2008).

Malawi is a country in this region hit particularly hard by the epidemic. Approximately 7% of adults (ages 15 to 49) are living with HIV/AIDS in Malawi (United Nations General Assembly, 2010), and 68,000 deaths were attributable to this pandemic in 2007 (Joint United Nations Programme on HIV/AIDS, 2008). AIDS is the leading cause of death among Malawians aged 15 to 49 (Government of Malawi, 2005). This disease has greatly affected the average life expectancy, which currently stands at just 43 years (United Nations General Assembly, 2010). Although estimated prevalence of HIV infection in the country as a whole is 11%, prevalence in the Southern region, where more than half of the country's population lives, is 19% (Joint United Nations Programme on HIV/AIDS, 2010).

The primary driver of the epidemic in Malawi (and in the greater sub-Saharan African region) is unprotected sex: 90% of infections stem from heterosexual transmission (Joint United Nations Programme on HIV/AIDS, 2010). Sub-Saharan Africans are less likely to wear condoms in relationships characterized by a sense of trust (Hearst & Chen, 2004), including relationships with long-term partners, a practice that greatly increases HIV risk exposure (Macaluso, Demand, Artz, & Hook, 2000). In Malawi, condom use is low. Among nonmarried Malawians, approximately 39% of women and 46% of men reported using a condom during their last sexual intercourse (Malawi Demographic Health Survey, 2004). Some Malawians believe that condoms deprive them of pleasure, are ineffective in preventing HIV/AIDS, and are actually tainted with AIDS (Kaler, 2004). Condom use is also often associated with stigma, and many Malawians are embarrassed to request condoms in shops (Conroy, Blackie, Whiteside, Malewezi, & Sachs, 2006).

ROLE OF BEHAVIOR CHANGE

Behavior change is a critical factor in HIV prevention, and a number of psychosocial and economic factors affect behaviors that put Malawians at risk for HIV/AIDS (Joint United Nations Programme on HIV/AIDS /World Health Organization, 2008). Not only is condom use low, but other high-risk behavioral factors include early sexual debut, high levels of transactional sex without the use of condoms (Malawi Demographic Health Survey, 2004), multiple partnerships (Leclerc-Madlala, 2009), multiple concurrent partnerships (Halperin & Epstein, 2007), and nonmarital sex or sex with a noncohabitating partner (Malawi Demographic Health Survey, 2004). (Transactional sexual relationships are sexual relationships where the giving of gifts or services is an important factor. Transactional sex relationships are distinct from other kinds of prostitution in that the transactional sex provides only a portion of the income of the person providing the sex. Those offering sex may or may not feel affection for their patrons.)

As the search for an effective vaccine continues, prevention remains the most effective long-term strategy for reducing the burden of AIDS in Malawi and elsewhere (Rain-Talijaard, Lagarde, Talijaard, Campbell, Macphail, Williams et al., 2003). Improvements in prevention inevitably require people's behaviors to change, and interventions can bring about such change through the use of theory (Noar & Zimmerman, 2005). Which theory one uses for accomplishing this goal depends, of course, on the appropriateness of the theory to tackle key underlying drivers of the behavior in question.

Using our prior experience in Malawi as the backdrop, this chapter illustrates the use of a sociocognitive approach in promoting behavior change for HIV prevention. Extensive formative evaluation conducted before the start of the intervention (Rimal, Tapia, Böse, Brown, Joshi, & Chipendo, 2004) revealed that Malawians harbored low perceptions of personal risk to HIV infection, despite living in a country severely hit by the epidemic, and their overall sense of personal efficacy to bring about change was low. The campaign focused on enhancing risk and strengthening personal efficacy; the theoretical perspective unifying this effort, and subsequently described in this chapter, is the risk perception attitude (RPA) framework (Rimal & Real, 2003).

THEORETICAL BACKGROUND

The idea that people are motivated to reduce their risks is both intuitive and theoretically compelling. Intuitively, it appears reasonable to assume that people would want to reduce dangers that impinge on their lives, particularly if they perceive they have the ability to do so. This is not to deny the fact that people also like to court danger and seek thrills from activities that are risky, as the literature on sensation seeking suggests (Horvath &

Zuckerman, 1993; Zuckerman & Neeb, 1979). But, people have their own tolerance levels for certain risks they are willing to take, and when the nature of that risk changes—if, for example, the negative outcomes become cognitively proximal or when the risk magnitude crosses a certain threshold—people tend to act in ways to minimize exposure to those risks (Nightingale & Fischhoff, 2001).

Perception of risk has a strong theoretical basis as well. It is a central construct in a number of theories of behavior change, including the health belief model (Janz & Becker, 1984), protection motivation theory (Rogers, 1975), and the extended parallel process model (Witte, 1992). In the broader health behavior literature, the role of risk perception in behavioral modification is considered to be important, but empirical findings are inconsistent (Weinstein & Nicolich, 1993), with some studies showing a positive relationship (Weinstein, Sandman, & Roberts, 1990), others showing a negative relationship (Weinstein, Grubb, & Vautier, 1986), and still others showing no relationship (Svenson, Fischhoff, & MacGregor, 1985). In Africa, HIV prevention efforts have focused on perceptions of risk as key motivators of behavior change (Kaler, 2004; Watkins & Smith, 2005). Reflecting the broader literature in other health domains, findings on the role of HIV-related risk perception and behavior change have also been mixed; some studies show a positive association between risk perception and HIV prevention behaviors (Lindan, Allen, Carael, Nsengumuremyi, Van de Perre, Serufilira, 1991), whereas others do not (Moyo & Mbizvo, 2004).

Part of the inconsistency in the relationship between risk perception and self-protective behavior can be attributed to methodological factors. Because a majority of the studies in the literature are based on cross-sectional data, it is difficult to disentangle cause from effect (Weinstein & Nicolich, 1993). Risk perceptions can drive behavioral actions—as when those who feel vulnerable to HIV infection wear condoms (Johnston, O'Bra, Choptra, Mathews, Townsend, Sabin et al., 2008)—but behavioral actions can also affect risk perceptions—as when those who do not wear condoms perceive that they are at greater risk to HIV (Maticka-Tyndale & Tenkorang, 2010)—and the net observation, in cross-sectional data, would be the attenuation of correlation between the two factors.

It is also essential to specify what exactly is thought to change as a result of enhanced risk perceptions. For example, if the behavior in question is complex or novel—one that individuals have not previously encountered or one they do not know very much about—then increasing risk perceptions may motivate greater information seeking about the underlying issue (Afifi & Weiner, 2004). For other topics—ones in which individuals perceive they have adequate levels of knowledge—one would not expect greater information seeking to result from heightened risk perceptions.

Another explanation for the lack of consistency in the relationship between risk perceptions and behavioral action pertains to perceived control. When individuals believe that they are powerless to avert a threat (either because they do not have the ability to act or because they believe their actions would be futile), they are not motivated to act, in which case, high perceived risks will not translate into corresponding behaviors (Bandura, 1995). Similarly, believing that performing a behavior will produce beneficial outcomes is not adequate to motivate people to act if they are not confident in their ability to bring about change (Kraft, Rise, Sutton, & Roysamb, 2005). This is also the premise behind the RPA framework (Rimal & Real, 2003).

THE RISK PERCEPTION ATTITUDE FRAMEWORK

According to the RPA framework, perceptions about the risk to a disease are usually not sufficient to motivate people to take preventive action. Rather, when high-risk perceptions are coupled with strong efficacy beliefs, people are motivated and able to engage in self-protective behaviors. In accordance with the extended parallel process model (Witte, 1992), the RPA framework conceptualizes perceived risk as a motivator of change. This motivation, however, needs to be facilitated by strong efficacy, a belief that something can be done to avert the threat.

Apart from constituting one of the most reliable predictors of behavior change, self-efficacy also affects choices people make. When people feel efficacious, they take on challenging tasks to further enhance their abilities, whereas those with lower levels of efficacy take on tasks that they know they can achieve without expending much effort (Bandura, 1986). Similarly, higher levels of efficacy also affect the construal processes of individuals in how they interpret successes and failures. Those with higher levels of efficacy tend to construe failures as consequences of inadequate effort, whereas those with lower levels of efficacy construe similar (negative) outcomes as further evidence of their inability to bring about change (Bandura, 1977).

Based on individuals' perceptions of risk and beliefs about efficacy, the RPA framework classifies people into one of four groups (Table 17.1). First, those with low risk perceptions and weak efficacy beliefs are classified as the *indifference* group. Because they neither perceive that they are at risk, which results in low motivation for action (Witte, 1992), nor believe that they have the ability to bring about change, members of this group are thought to be least likely to take preventive action. Although no prior research has specifically focused on this issue, we suspect that people belong in the indifference group largely because the issue at hand is not perceived to be of particular relevance to them (young people's perceptions about heart disease, for example). Bringing about change among this group is challenging because it requires action on two fronts: enhancing risk perceptions and strengthening efficacy beliefs.

Second, those with low risk perceptions and strong efficacy beliefs are classified as the *proactive* group. It is interesting to think about what it means that individuals perceive they are not at risk to a particular disease but at the same time also believe that they can do a lot to avert the threat. Given that prior accomplishments are one of the strongest predictors of efficacy beliefs (Bandura, 1977), it is likely that members of the proactive group

TABLE 17.1 Four-Group Classification of the RPA Framework

Risk perception	Efficacy beliefs	
	Weak	Strong
Low	Indifference	Proactive
High	Avoidance	Responsive

have enacted behavioral changes in the past and enhanced their efficacy beliefs as a result. Furthermore, their low risk perceptions are likely the results of self-reflections they have made because of having taken risk-ameliorating actions in the past. Thus, members of the proactive group are expected to have greater familiarity with and more likely to take on the appropriate behaviors.

Third, the *avoidance* group is characterized by weak efficacy beliefs and high risk perceptions. This group is thought to be subjected to two opposing forces. On the one hand, the heightened sense of risk perceived by this group can stimulate motivations for action. On the other hand, weak efficacy beliefs can engender a sense of futility in taking appropriate steps to mitigate the risk. In prior research (Turner, Rimal, Morrison, & Kim, 2006), this group has been found to be characterized by high levels of anxiety, which stimulates information seeking but also suppresses information retention. It is also likely that members of the avoidance group, motivated to take action because of the heightened risk, are more discriminating in the specific types of action they take, choosing those behaviors that do not tax their efficacy and avoiding those that do.

Finally, those with high risk perceptions and strong efficacy beliefs are classified as the *responsive* group. High risk perceptions among members of this group increase their motivation to act, and translating these motivations into actual action is facilitated by their strong sense of efficacy. Both the responsive and proactive groups are characterized by strong efficacy beliefs, but differences in their risk perceptions are instructive to consider. The proactive group members' low risk perceptions are likely the result of having taken appropriate courses of action (indications of having taken previous action are also provided by their strong efficacy beliefs), whereas the responsive group members' high risk perceptions indicate either that they believe their prior actions have not mitigated their risk or that reducing risk is an ongoing activity and not a one-time event.

Central propositions of the RPA framework have been tested across a number of health domains: skin cancer (Rimal & Real, 2003), diabetes (Turner et al., 2006), breast cancer prevention (Rimal & Juon, 2010), breast cancer information seeking (Lee, Hwang, Hawkins, & Pingree, 2008), breast cancer information processing (Leshner, Cheng, Song, Choi, & Frisby, 2006), workplace safety (Real, 2008), food safety (Kennedy, Worosz, Todd, & Lapinski, 2008), and nutrition promotion (Sullivan, Beckjord, Rutten, & Hesse, 2008). The RPA framework has also provided the underlying theoretical structure for the Malawi BRIDGE Project (Rimal, Böse, Brown, Mkandawire, & Folda, 2009; Rimal et al., 2009), a long-term program to promote HIV-prevention behaviors.

THE MALAWI BRIDGE PROJECT: A MULTILEVEL APPROACH

Multiple Influences on Sexual and HIV-Prevention Behaviors

It is important to note that risk perceptions and efficacy beliefs, factors at the individual level, are critical influences but not the only determinants of HIV-prevention behaviors. There are clearly other practices at the sociocultural level that increase Malawians' vulnerability. These include, for example, the practice of *Chokolo* or *wife inheritance,* whereby a surviving brother marries his widowed sister-in-law, and *Fisi,* a ritual associated with initiation rites for adolescent boys, following which they are encouraged to have sex with multiple partners (Bisika, 2008). Similarly, poverty among women has been implicated as a driver of commercial sex work (Chirwa, 1997), which further increases their susceptibility to HIV infection. In Malawi, the prevalent practice of intergenerational sex has also been implicated as an important driver of HIV infection among women (Stirling, Rees, Kasedde, & Hankins, 2008). Finally, religious institutions also play a large role: In Malawi, some faith-based organizations have been known to undermine state-sponsored messages about condom use, casting them as sinful (Rankin, Lindgren, Kools, & Schell, 2008).

Thus, in the fight against HIV and AIDS, important behavioral determinants reside at multiple levels beyond just those at the individual level. Our focus in this chapter on risk perceptions and efficacy beliefs is not meant to deny the important role that interpersonal, cultural, and structural-level factors play in health behavior change (see, for example, Rice & Foote, Chapter 5). Rather, we have limited our discussion to risk perceptions and efficacy beliefs for three reasons. First, these are the theoretically based proximal determinants that are also amenable to change through a behavior-change intervention. Second, risk perceptions and efficacy beliefs themselves are determined by the larger sociocultural and structural factors impinging on people's lives. For example, in Malawi, one can imagine that the extent to which people internalize their efficacy to use condoms is determined by, among other things, the role that important religious institutions play in supporting or sanctioning the use of condoms (Rankin et al., 2008). Third, recognizing the role that important community and state institutions play in HIV prevention in Malawi, the BRIDGE Project included the Malawi National AIDS Commission as an integral partner right from the beginning of the project, which allowed us to work with many of the affiliated organizations (and others, including women's groups, youth clubs, and religious institutions) at the village, district, and national levels. Thus, even though the overall project adopted a multilevel perspective, the underlying theoretical approach was based on the idea that the role of sociocultural and structural factors will be incorporated in campaign goals to change HIV-prevention behaviors.

Strategies for Increasing Risk and Self-Efficacy

The Malawi BRIDGE Project, a six-year mass media and community-based campaign initiated in 2003 to reduce HIV/AIDS-related high-risk behaviors, adopted a two-prong strategy for promoting behavior change. First, it sought to increase people's awareness about their risk to HIV/AIDS, linking specific actions (e.g., having multiple sexual partners) with outcomes (getting infected). Second, this campaign for increasing risk perception was supplemented with efforts to promote self-efficacy among the target audience. Indeed, given the central role of efficacy beliefs in promoting behavior change, the BRIDGE Project incorporated this concept as an overarching intervention strategy early in the conceptualization and implementation of the program. As noted earlier, findings from the formative evaluation conducted before the start of the campaign (Rimal et al., 2004) showed that efficacy beliefs among Malawians were weak. Many Malawians felt overwhelmed by a number of factors, including the lack of control in their lives, the extent to which poverty intruded into their ability to make healthy decisions, and their inability to engage in open discussion about sex and sexuality (Rimal, Gibson, & Smith, 2008). Strengthening people's perceptions of control and efficacy was thus critical and in line with the central propositions from the RPA framework. The overall campaign tagline *"Nditha!"* (meaning *I can* in Chichewa) was developed on this basis.

From the perspective of the BRIDGE Project, the campaign needed to move individuals to the bottom right cell—corresponding to the responsive group—shown in Table 17.1. This meant that those in the indifference group had the most to achieve—their risk perceptions needed to be increased, and their efficacy beliefs needed to be strengthened. Similarly, individuals in the proactive group, characterized by low risk perceptions and strong efficacy beliefs, could be moved to become responsive by increasing their perceptions of risk. Finally, those in the avoidance group had heightened levels of risk, but they lacked efficacy, and hence, the goal here was to strengthen their personal efficacy.

Impact of the BRIDGE Project

Data from the baseline survey in 2003 (before the start of the campaign) and at midterm (2006) both showed that the RPA framework did a reasonable job in predicting HIV-prevention behaviors. At baseline (Rimal, Böse, et al., 2009), risk perceptions and efficacy beliefs jointly affected individuals' intentions to remain monogamous, though not their intentions to use condoms (for which only self-efficacy was a significant predictor). At midterm (Rimal, Brown, et al., 2009), the responsive group had the highest knowledge, HIV testing behaviors, and condom use behaviors; the relative positioning of the other groups, however, was mixed.

Figure 17.1 shows the distribution of the four RPA framework groups, configured according to their risk perceptions and efficacy beliefs with regard to condom use, at four points in time—at baseline (2003), before the start of the intervention; at the first midterm (2006); the second midterm (2007); and at end-line (2008), some five years after the baseline. There were significant changes in the distribution across the four waves, $x^2(n = 6,517,$ d.f. $= 9) = 1417, p < .001$. As shown in the figure, the percentage of individuals classified in the indifference group (low risk, weak efficacy) decreased significantly across the four waves—from 65% at baseline to only 13% at end-line. By contrast, the proportion of individuals classified in the responsive group (high risk, strong efficacy) increased significantly from only 3% at baseline to 41% at end-line. Figure 17.1 also shows a greater proportion of individuals in the proactive group (low risk, strong efficacy) than in the avoidance group (high risk, weak efficacy). Thus, it appears that, over the life of the campaign, a significant number of people moved to the responsive and proactive groups (both groups characterized by strong efficacy).

Figure 17.2 shows whether the differential configuration of individuals in the four RPA framework groups was associated with a behavioral outcome—in this case, intentions to use a condom at next sex, controlling for age, gender, and education. Across the four groups, there were significant differences in condom use intentions, $F(6, 6503) = 240.6,$ $p < .001$. Among members of the indifference group, 60% expressed an intention to use a condom, whereas the corresponding figure among members of the responsive group was

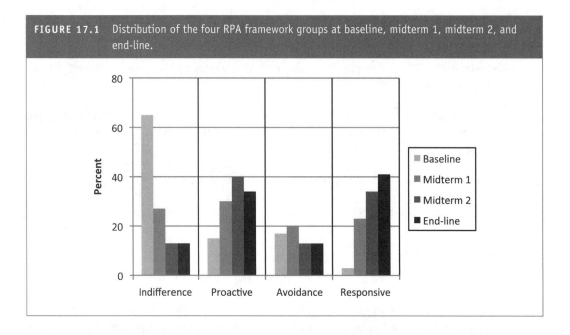

FIGURE 17.1 Distribution of the four RPA framework groups at baseline, midterm 1, midterm 2, and end-line.

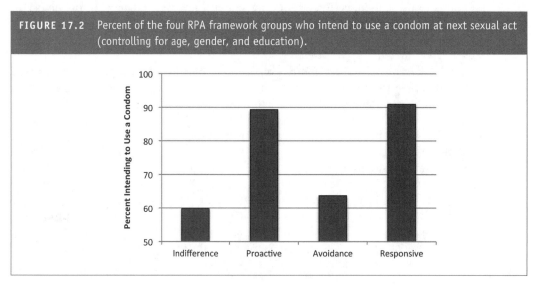

FIGURE 17.2 Percent of the four RPA framework groups who intend to use a condom at next sexual act (controlling for age, gender, and education).

91%. Members of the proactive group, who share the same level of efficacy with those of the responsive group, also had high intentions, at 89%.

A number of implications emerge from these results. First, it appears that, by enhancing perceptions of personal risk and strengthening efficacy beliefs, interventions can successfully move people to adopt a responsive outlook. In the districts where the BRIDGE Project was active, the proportion of respondents in the responsive group had changed from 3%

at baseline to 41 % at end-line. Second, individuals in the responsive and proactive groups exhibited the highest levels of positive behavioral intentions, as compared to the other groups. Both of these groups are characterized by strong efficacy beliefs, which implies that the primary driver of behavioral intentions was personal efficacy.

A methodological artifact may also be responsible for the strong efficacy effects—and relatively weaker effects of risk perception—that we observed. In our operationalization, efficacy beliefs were pegged specifically around the particular behavior in question—in this case, use of condoms. We asked questions about respondents' ability to initiate discussions about condom use, propose the use of condoms to their partners, and insist that a condom be used during sex. By contrast, perceptions of risk were not behavior specific; we only asked individuals about their likelihood of getting infected with HIV. Hence, the health domain specificity was greater in the assessment of efficacy in comparison to risk. The next section raises this issue and proposes a finer-grained conceptualization of the behavior in question as well as its determinants.

A FINER FOCUS ON BEHAVIORS: A CASE STUDY OF CONDOM USE

ABC behaviors is a term used by HIV prevention scholars and practitioners to refer to the three behaviors thought to be critical in reducing the sexual transmission of HIV: abstinence, being faithful, and using condoms, respectively (Shelton, Halperin, Nantulya, Potts, Gayle, & Holmes, 2004). At first blush, these three behaviors seem straightforward. Abstinence refers to refraining from sex unless one is in a long-term, committed relationship. For youth, this is usually operationalized as delaying sexual debut. Being faithful incorporates the idea of remaining monogamous but also of reducing the total number of sexual partners. Condom use refers to consistent and correct use of condoms during each sexual act. Upon closer scrutiny, however, these three behaviors are more accurately described as behavioral categories, each one comprising a number of subcomponent behaviors. Most behaviors can be broken down into their constituent components, which can be further broken down into subcomponents, and so on. For example, even a behavior one might normally think of as unitary—riding a bicycle—has a number of sub-behaviors, including getting on the bicycle, pedaling, stopping, controlling one's speed, and so on. The approach we are advocating is not simply to break down the behavior into smaller ones until no smaller behaviors can be found; such an approach would be tedious and theoretically meaningless. Rather, the disentanglement of behaviors makes sense to the extent that the configuration of underlying predictors—in this case, people's perceptions of risk and beliefs about personal efficacy—differs for each component behavior.

The critical point, from an intervention perspective, is the level at which the behavior is to be conceptualized in order to create an isomorphic connection between the theoretical construct and the operational definition. This is a slightly different argument from the need to ensure that the behavior in question means the same to all parties (program designers, implementers, target audiences, etc.). Instead, we are arguing for greater specificity in the behaviors we normally ask respondents to enact in order to align them more closely with the specificity of their determinants.

Condom use provides an excellent case study. When interventions urge individuals to use condoms to protect themselves from HIV infection, the behavior in question seems specific enough. Looking more closely, however, one sees numerous behaviors—both preceding and following the actual use of condoms—that are relevant for ensuring their consistent use. In order to use a condom during sex, partners have to agree to do so, which means they have to seek the compliance of the other person. They also have to ensure that a condom is available at the time of sex. Seeking compliance to gain agreement and ensuring availability, in turn, are two separate behaviors whose sociocognitive antecedents may be different.

Seeking compliance to gain agreement requires that at least one person initiates the discussion pertaining to condom use. The literature shows that, in many parts of Africa, women are shy about doing so, and they generally perceive that their male partners will disapprove of them initiating these discussions (Nalwadda, Mirembe, Byamugisha, & Faxelid, 2010). This suggests that efficacy beliefs pertaining to initiating discussions about condom use may be considerably weaker among females than among males. Self-efficacy to purchase condoms is also lower among females in many parts of Africa (Meekers & Klein, 2002). Risks associated with initiation of discussions about condom use (fear that the partner will perceive mistrust) are also likely different than risks associated with purchasing condoms (knowledge that others in one's community will know that one is sexually active). Thus, our conceptualization of risk perceptions and efficacy beliefs—around condom use as the composite behavior—needs to be modified in order to incorporate the more proximal sociocognitive determinants of the subcomponent behaviors.

It is known that frequency of regular condom use tends to lessen over the course of the relationship (Moyo, Levandowski, MacPhail, Rees, & Pettifor, 2008), signifying either that partners' HIV risk perceptions also diminish as relationships mature or that, once in a stable relationship, partners feel reluctant to request condom use for fear of being construed as lacking trust or questioning the partner's fidelity (Heise, 2009; St. Lawrence, Eldridge, Reitman, Little, Shelby, & Brasfield, 1998). This suggests that the unit of meaningful influence itself may have different configurations across the different subcomponent behaviors. For example, ensuring availability of a condom by purchasing it in advance could have an individual-level determinant (one of the partners' self-efficacy to do so) as well as a structural-level determinant (availability in one's neighborhood). Similarly, actual use of the condom may be a function of the individual user (perceptions about physical pleasure) or the nature of the relationship in terms of its duration or amount of mutual trust. Risks at the individual level (potential loss of privacy) associated with purchasing condoms are also likely different from those at the relationship level.

Conclusions and Future Research

In this chapter, we have explicated the role that individuals' risk perceptions and efficacy beliefs play in their behaviors pertaining to HIV prevention. We have also argued for the need to be specific in the conceptualization of the behavior being promoted for change by interventions; behaviors often contain subcomponents whose determinants, including risk perceptions and efficacy beliefs, are likely to vary across the components. Although social cognitive theory (Bandura, 1986) has made the case for behavioral specificity in conceptualizing and operationalizing the corresponding efficacy beliefs (Bandura, 1995, 1997), the literature on risk perception is more ambiguous in this regard. Furthermore, determinants of efficacy beliefs are well articulated in social cognitive theory (Bandura, 1977), and they include *performance accomplishment* (the idea that individuals' prior behavioral actions enhance subsequent efficacy), *vicarious reinforcement* (learning by observing the behaviors of others), *verbal persuasion* (greater efficacy that results from positive reinforcement one receives from others), and *emotional arousal* (positive affect that accompanies accomplishments). We have less guidance for improving individuals' risk perceptions.

Thus, through the next generation of research, there is great need to learn how individuals develop perceptions of personal vulnerability to specific behavioral outcomes. The literature on optimistic bias (Weinstein, 1980) shows that individuals tend to underestimate the likelihood of negative events and exaggerate the likelihood of positive events happening to them. This represents a significant challenge to health communication experts—who seek to enhance people's perceptions of risk—and there is little guidance on what factors actually promote perceptions of risk. Individuals who engage in healthy behaviors may look to their daily practices and conclude, correctly, that their risks are low, as might be the case when nonsmokers assess their risks to lung cancer. One can also understand why individuals' low perceptions of risk can often be protective; they make it easier for people to face life's challenges in an optimistic manner. But, refusing to acknowledge real risks with severe consequences—as might be the case for HIV infection when one lives in a high-prevalence country—can limit individuals' motivations to make healthy changes in their lives.

In our surveys in Malawi, we have consistently found that individuals' perceptions of personal susceptibility to HIV tends to be rather low (below the midpoint of the scale), and their perceptions of severity tends to be high (reaching almost the maximum point on the scale). This likely indicates a defensive mechanism that individuals use to remain optimistic in life. It is difficult to deny the severity of AIDS, given that many have seen the devastation that the disease has wrought. If one believes in the highly severe nature of the disease's consequences, then it would be rather difficult to believe simultaneously that one is also vulnerable to the disease and still be able to get on in one's life. Hence, we suspect, low personal susceptibility is the consequence of perceptions of high severity. But, this is speculative and certainly worthy of further research.

As we noted earlier, it is difficult to disentangle cause from effect when most of the data on the relationship between risk perceptions and health behaviors come from cross-sectional studies. Hence, there is a great need for longitudinal studies that can better inform these complex relationships.

Finally, it should be noted that we have assumed risk perceptions and efficacy beliefs are independent of each other. Indeed, the RPA framework is based on this assumption, and future research should empirically test the validity of this proposition. It appears likely, for example, that individuals who feel efficacious in their ability to enact certain behaviors, and thus keep themselves healthy, may also perceive that their risks are low.

Similarly, those who perceive that their risks are high (in the likelihood of getting heart disease because of family history or age, for example) may also believe they have no personal efficacy to avert the threat. The extent to which risk perceptions and efficacy beliefs affect each other in this manner remains to be investigated through future research. Nevertheless, it appears that a focus on risk perceptions and efficacy beliefs provides a theoretically meaningful lens through which health interventions can conceptualize preventive behaviors targeted for change.

References

Afifi, W. A., & Weiner, J. L. (2004). Toward a theory of motivated information management. *Communication Theory, 14,* 167–190.

Bandura, A. (1977). *Social learning theory.* Englewood Cliffs, NJ: Prentice Hall.

Bandura, A. (1986). *Social foundations of thought and action.* Englewood Cliffs, NJ: Prentice Hall.

Bandura, A. (1995). Exercise of personal and collective efficacy in changing societies. In A. Bandura (Ed.), *Self-efficacy in changing societies* (pp. 1–45). Cambridge, UK: Cambridge University Press.

Bandura, A. (1997). *Self-efficacy: The exercise of control.* New York: W.H. Freeman.

Bisika, T. (2008). Cultural factors that affect sexual and reproductive health in Malawi. *Journal of Family Planning and Reproductive Health Care, 34,* 79–80.

Chirwa, W. C. (1997). Migrant labour, sexual networking and multi-partnered sex in Malawi. *Health Transition Review, 7* (Suppl. 3), 5–15.

Conroy, A., Blackie, M., Whiteside, A., Malewezi, J., & Sachs, J. (2006). *Poverty, AIDS and hunger: Breaking the poverty trap in Malawi.* New York: Palgrave Macmillan.

Government of Malawi. (2005). *Malawi HIV & AIDS: Monitoring and evaluation report.* Lilongwe, Malawi: Department of Nutrition, HIV & AIDS, Office of the President and Cabinet.

Halperin, D., & Epstein, H. (2007). Why is HIV prevalence so severe in Southern Africa? The role of multiple concurrent partnerships and lack of male circumcision: Implications for HIV prevention. *Southern African Journal of Medicine, 8,* 19–25.

Hearst, N., & Chen, S. (2004). Condom promotion for HIV prevention in the developing world: Is it working? *Studies in Family Planning, 35,* 39–47.

Heise, L. (2009). Transforming AIDS prevention to meet women's needs: A focus on developing countries. *Social Science & Medicine, 40,* 931–943.

Horvath, P., & Zuckerman, M. (1993). Sensation seeking, risk appraisal, and risky behavior. *Personality & Individual Differences, 14,* 41–52.

Janz, N. K., & Becker, M. H. (1984). The health belief model: A decade later. *Health Education Quarterly, 11,* 1–47.

Johnston, L., O'Bra, H., Choptra, M., Mathews, C., Townsend, L., et al. (2008). The associations of voluntary counseling and testing acceptance and the perceived likelihood of being HIV-infected among men with multiple sex partners in a South African township. *AIDS & Behavior, 14,* 922–931.

Joint United Nations Programme on HIV/AIDS. (2008). *2008 report on the global AIDS epidemic.* Geneva: Joint United Nations Program on HIV/AIDS.

Joint United Nations Programme on HIV/AIDS. (2010). *UNAIDS report on the global AIDS epidemic.* Retrieved June 15, 2011, from http://www.unaids.org/globalreport/Global_report.htm

Kaler, A. (2004). AIDS-talk in everyday life: The presence of HIV/AIDS in men's informal conversation in Southern Malawi. *Social Science and Medicine, 59,* 285–297.

Kennedy, J., Worosz, M., Todd, E. C., & Lapinksi, M. K. (2008). Segmentation of U.S. consumers based on food safety attitudes. *British Food Journal, 110,* 691–705.

Kraft, P., Rise, J., Sutton, S., Røysamb, E. (2005). Perceived difficulty in the theory of planned behaviour: Perceived behavioural control or affective attitude? *British Journal of Social Psychology, 444,* 479–496.

Leclerc-Madlala, S. (2009). Cultural scripts for multiple and concurrent partnerships in southern Africa: Why HIV prevention needs anthropology. *Sexual Health, 6,* 103–110.

Lee, S. Y., Hwang, H., Hawkins, R., & Pingree, S. (2008). Interplay of negative emotion and health self-efficacy on the use of health information and its outcomes. *Communication Research, 35,* 358–381.

Leshner, G., Cheng, I-H., Song, H. J., Choi, Y., & Frisby, C. (2006). The role of spiritual health locus of control in breast cancer information processing between African American and Caucasian women. *Integrative Medicine Insights, 2,* 35–44.

Lindan, C., Allen, S., Carael, M., Nsengumuremyi, F., Van de Perre, P., Serufilira, A., et al. (1991). Knowledge, attitudes, and perceived risk of AIDS among urban Rwandan women: Relationship to HIV infection and behavior change. *AIDS, 5,* 993–1002.

Macaluso, M., Demand, M., Artz, L., & Hook, E. (2000). Partner type and condom use. *AIDS, 14,* 537–546.

Malawi Demographic Health Survey. (2004). *Malawi demographic and health survey 2004.* Calverton, MD: NSO and ORC Macro.

Maticka-Tyndale, E., & Tenkorang, E. Y. (2010). A multilevel model of condom use among male and female upper primary school students in Nyanza, Kenya. *Social Science & Medicine, 71,* 616–625.

Meekers, D., & Klein, M. (2002). Understanding gender differences in condom use self-efficacy among youth in urban Cameroon. *AIDS Education and Prevention, 14,* 62–72.

Moyo, W., & Mbizvo, M. T. (2004). Desire for a future pregnancy among women in Zimbabwe in relation to their self-perceived risk of HIV infection, child mortality, and spontaneous abortion. *AIDS Behavior, 8,* 9–15.

Moyo, W., Levandowski, B. A., MacPhail, C., Rees, H., & Pettifor, A. (2008). Consistent condom use in South African youth's most recent sexual relationships. *AIDS & Behavior, 12,* 431–440.

Nalwadda, G., Mirembe, F., Byamugisha, J., & Faxelid, E. (2010). Persistent high fertility in Uganda: Young people recount obstacles and enabling factors to use of contraceptives. *BMC Public Health, 10,* 530.

Nightingale, E. O., & Fischhoff, B. (2001). Adolescent risk and vulnerability: An overview. In B. Fischhoff, E. O. Nightingale, & J. G. Iannotta (Eds.), *Adolescent risk and vulnerability: Concepts and measurement* (pp. 1–14). Washington, DC: National Academy Press.

Noar, S. M., & Zimmerman, R. S. (2005). Health behavior theory and cumulative knowledge regarding health behaviors: Are we moving in the right direction? *Health Education Research, 20*(3), 275–290.

Rain-Talijaard, R., Lagarde, E., Talijaard, D., Campbell, C., Macphail, C., Williams, B., et al. (2003). Potential for an intervention on male circumcision in a South African town with high levels of HIV infection. *AIDS Care, 15,* 315–327.

Rankin, S. H., Lindgren, T., Kools, S. M., & Schell, E. (2008). The condom divide: Disenfranchisement of Malawi women by church and state. *Journal of Obstetric, Gynecologic, & Neonatal Nursing, 37,* 596–606.

Real, K. (2008). Information seeking and workplace safety: A field application of the risk perception attitude framework. *Journal of Applied Communication Research, 36,* 339–359.

Rimal, R. N., Böse, K., Brown, J., Mkandawire, G., & Folda, L. (2009). Extending the purview of the risk perception attitude (RPA) framework: Findings from HIV/AIDS prevention research in Malawi. *Health Communication, 24,* 210–218.

Rimal, R. N., Brown, J., Mkandawire, G., Folda, L., & Creel, A. H. (2009). Audience segmentation as a social marketing tool in health promotion: Use of the risk perception attitude (RPA) framework in HIV prevention in Malawi. *American Journal of Public Health, 99,* 2224–2229.

Rimal, R. N., Gibson, S. L., & Smith, K. A. (2008). Explication of barriers to effective HIV prevention: Using counterarguments as indicators of barriers to behavior change in Malawi. Paper presented at the International Communication Association annual meeting, Montreal, Canada.

Rimal, R. N., & Juon, H. S. (2010). Use of the risk perception attitude (RPA) framework to understand attention paid to breast cancer information and prevention behaviors among immigrant Indian women. *Journal of Applied Social Psychology, 40,* 287–310.

Rimal, R. N., & Real, K. (2003). Perceived risk and efficacy beliefs as motivators of change: Use of the risk perception attitude (RPA) framework to understand health behaviors. *Human Communication Research, 29,* 370–399.

Rimal, R.N., Tapia, M., Böse, K., Brown, J., Joshi, K., & Chipendo, G. (2004). *Exploring community beliefs, attitudes and behaviors about HIV/AIDS in 8 Malawi BRIDGE districts.* Baltimore, MD: Center for Communication Programs, Johns Hopkins University.

Rogers, R. W. (1975). A protection motivation theory of fear appeals and attitude change. *Journal of Psychology, 91,* 93–114.

Shelton, J. D., Halperin, D. T., Nantulya, V., Potts, M., Gayle, H. D., & Holmes, K. K. (2004). Partner reduction is crucial for balanced "ABC" approach to HIV prevention. *British Medical Journal, 328,* 891–893.

St. Lawrence, J. S., Eldridge, G. D., Reitman, D., Little, C. E., Shelby, M. C., & Brasfield, T. L. (1998). Factors influencing condom use among African American Women: Implications for risk reduction interventions. *American Journal of Community Psychology, 26,* 7–28.

Stirling, M., Rees, H., Kasedde, S., & Hankins, C. (2008). Addressing the vulnerability of young women and girls to stop the HIV epidemic in southern Africa. *AIDS, 22,* S1–S3.

Sulllivan, H. W., Beckjord, E. B., Rutten, L. J. F., & Hesse, B. W. (2008). Nutrition-related cancer prevention cognitions and behavioral intentions: Testing the risk perception attitude framework. *Health Education & Behavior, 35,* 866–879.

Svenson, O., Fischhoff, B., & MacGregor, D. (1985). Perceived driving safety and seatbelt usage. *Accident Analysis and Prevention, 17,* 119–133.

Turner, M. M., Rimal, R. N., Morrison, D., & Kim, H. (2006). The role of anxiety in processing risk information: Testing the risk perception attitude framework in two studies. *Human Communication Research, 32,* 130–156.

United Nations General Assembly. (2010). *Malawi HIV and AIDS monitoring and evaluation report: 2008–2009.* (Special Session Country Progress Report) Geneva, Switzerland: Author.

Watkins, S. C., & Smith, K. P. (2005). Perceptions of risk and strategies for prevention: Responses to HIV & AIDS in rural Malawi. *Social Science & Medicine, 60,* 649–660.

Weinstein, N. D. (1980). Unrealistic optimism about future life events. *Journal of Personality and Social Psychology, 39*(5), 806–820.

Weinstein, N. D., Grubb, P. D., & Vautier, J. (1986). Increasing automobile seatbelt use: An intervention emphasizing risk susceptibility. *Journal of Applied Psychology, 71,* 285–290.

Weinstein, N. D., & Nicolich, M. (1993). Correct and incorrect interpretations of correlations between risk perceptions and risk behaviors. *Health Psychology, 12,* 235–245.

Weinstein, N. D., Sandman, P. M., & Roberts, N. E. (1990). Determinants of self-protective behavior: Home radon testing. *Journal of Applied Social Psychology, 20,* 783–801.

Witte, K. (1992). Putting the fear back in fear appeals: The extended parallel process model. *Communication Monographs, 59,* 225–249.

Zuckerman, M., & Neeb, M. (1979). Sensation seeking and psychopathology. *Psychiatry Research, 1,* 255–264.

Corporate Social Responsibility Campaigns

What Do They Tell Us About Organization–Public Relationships?

Maureen Taylor

The field of public relations has evolved in a cocreational direction over the last two decades (Botan & Taylor, 2004; Heath, 2010). Public relations was once considered a functional organizational activity that worked mainly toward generating positive media coverage. Today, a cocreational approach to public relations suggests that organizations work to create shared meaning with stakeholders. Public relations activities in a cocreational approach build relationships with stakeholders, engage in dialogue, and counsel organizational leaders on how to make ethical, long-term decisions (Botan & Taylor, 2004). A new role for the public relations function that exemplifies the cocreational approach is *corporate social responsibility* (CSR).

The purpose of this chapter is to briefly explore the literature in public relations, organizational communication, and management literature to better understand the role of CSR campaigns in building organization–public relationships (OPR) that create social capital. As a strategic communication function, CSR provides insight into the challenges and opportunities in building OPRs. The first part reviews the different discussions underway about CSR as a business and relationship-building strategy. The second section of the chapter provides three examples of CSR campaigns that have been undertaken to build customer loyalty, address public and media criticisms, and help an organization to recover from a very damaging crisis. The final section of the chapter reflects how CSR campaigns in general may help organizations contribute to a fully functioning society (Heath, 2006) through creating and enhancing community social capital.

CORPORATE SOCIAL RESPONSIBILITIES CAMPAIGNS

As other chapters in this book show, communication campaigns are strategic efforts to accomplish specific objectives. Health campaigns seek to inform and persuade people to make better health decisions. Political communication campaigns seek to move people to vote a certain way. Likewise, advertising campaigns hope to move people toward a certain purchasing behavior. CSR campaigns are similar to these other campaigns in that organizations undertake certain socially desirable activities (an institutional perspective) and then communicate that activity to the media and the world on the belief that the activity will build goodwill (promotional perspective). CSR is a public relations activity in the most fundamental sense of what modern public relations has become: building OPRs (Botan & Taylor, 2004).

CSR is premised on the idea that an organization's behaviors should contribute to society (Bhattacharya & Sen, 2004). CSR practices vary across the world with some governments taking larger roles in its enactment (Glob & Bartlett, 2007). The term *corporate social responsibility* can mean different things to different ideological perspectives. For business ethicists and public relations managers espousing a cocreational approach, CSR is a normative, socially desirable activity (Duhe, 2009). For free market advocates, calls for CSR are tantamount to calls for socialism (Friedman, 1970). A quick look at the business ethics, management, and public relations journals suggests that the debate about CSR's value as a business communication function is far from settled.

PERSPECTIVES ON CORPORATE SOCIAL RESPONSIBILITY AS A BUSINESS FUNCTION

Each day, consumers encounter dozens of CSR messages. Have you seen someone wearing a shirt with the word (RED)™ on it? That term and image represent a branding campaign from a variety of clothing retailers to support HIV/AIDs education and medications in Africa. Have you purchased a product with a pink ribbon logo? That image represents the Susan G. Komen for the Cure Foundation. The pink ribbon has appeared on products ranging from women's vitamins to buckets of Kentucky Fried Chicken.

Corporate support of nonprofit and social cause groups is commonplace. Indeed, some nonprofit organizations have the power to pick which corporations to work with and which ones to reject. Nonprofit websites provide clear instructions for corporations on how to become a partner, how to use the logo, and how they should act as corporate sponsors. A visit to almost any corporation's website will find a company's CSR relationships. This information can be on the home page or is usually found within one click of the home page. Obviously, CSR has become a popular business activity.

Advocates of Corporate Social Responsibility

CSR is based on the idea that "corporations have obligations to society that extend beyond mere profit-making activities" (Godfrey & Hatch, 2007, p. 87). Social responsibility actions can range from minimizing societal harm to implementing a strategic function (Porter & Kramer, 2006). Harvard professors Porter and Kramer noted that when "used strategically corporate social responsibility can become a source of tremendous social process, as the business applies its considerable resources, expertise, and insights to activities that benefit society" (p. 80). Although they identified moral obligation as a key reason for adopting a socially responsible agenda, sustainability, reputation, and freedom to operate have emerged as additional compelling reasons for CSR. Improved reputation and customer loyalty are core economic rationales that prompt organizational behavior on many levels. When CSR campaigns are tied to an organization's core business goals, they become investments that improve the operating environment of the corporation. For instance, when community members have better educations or are healthier, they make better and more productive employees. When a community has an excellent school system, then companies can attract higher-qualified employees because highly educated people want their children to attend high-performing schools. CSR campaigns that address these topics are an investment because they generate a return that helps the organization to achieve its core business goals.

Jones and Chase (1979) alluded to the concept of CSR in issues management, telling communication managers in the 1970s:

> society is asking whether material progress is enough, whether private enterprise, especially large public corporations, should not also be expected to fill a complex mix of social goals. Second, new corporate stakeholders are demanding action on issues such as environmental protection, community renewal, corporate influence overseas, energy conservation, and employment of women and minorities. These new stakeholders (consumers, employees, and the community) want the resources and economic power of the corporation used to build a better society. (pp. 7–8)

The concept of CSR is grounded in the belief that organizations have an obligation to their employees, community, and consumers based on the concept of *stakeholder* obligations rather than *stockholder* obligations.

In the 21st century, the public's perception of an organization matters. There is a monetary value for the organization to have a favorable reputation and earn legitimacy. Indeed, legitimacy can only be conferred upon an organization by the public. Porter and Kramer's (1979) research showed that doing good may contribute to an organization's bottom line. As a tangible good, corporate reputation and legitimacy can be created, maintained, and changed by strategic communication, including CSR campaigns.

The public responds favorably when organizations place community interests over financial interests (Seeger & Ulmer, 2002; Sellnow, Ulmer, & Snider, 1998; Ulmer, Sellnow, & Seeger, 2007). In a study evaluating measures commonly found in CSR communication, O'Connor and Meister (2008) concluded that being honest ranked first in importance for survey participants drawn from middle-aged mothers from Midwest states. Top rankings also included producing quality products and services, treating employees fairly, giving back to the community, and conducting business in an environmentally friendly manner. Interestingly, generating a profit actually ranked as the lowest category for these respondents. Veil, Liu, Erickson, and Sellnow (2005) contextualized this finding by noting that "regardless of how competent an organization is financially, it must still satisfy the social expectations of its stakeholders to maintain legitimacy"

(p. 19). Consumers state they are more willing to buy from socially responsible organizations (Altman, 1998; Mescon & Tillson, 1987; Smith, 1996). Pfau, Haigh, Sims, and Wigley (2008) argued that CSR can improve public opinion about an organization's image, reputation, and credibility.

When societal problems arise from accidents attributable to a corporation, poor decisions by CEOs, or immoral behavior by organizational members, CSR may help to diminish negative press or mitigate activist boycotts. Alsop (1999) found that 25% of the respondents in a large reputation survey reported that they had boycotted products and indeed had urged others to boycott the organizations when they did not agree with that organization's policies. Thus, "corporate social responsibility sounds as unobjectionable as motherhood and apple pie" (Freeland, 2010, para. 10).

Criticisms of Corporate Social Responsibility

Yet, not everyone thinks CSR or philanthropy is an acceptable use of an organization's resources. For economists such as Milton Friedman (1970), CSR is a "fundamentally subversive doctrine" in a free society because corporations are expected to give away hard-won resources. This approach is based on a pure capitalist model. In this model, a corporation's imperative is to maximize profit and minimize risk. Friedman (1970) noted that:

> there is one and only one social responsibility of business—to use its resources and engage in activities designed to increase its profits so long as it stays within the rules of the game, which is to say, engages in open and free competition without deception or fraud. (p. 6)

The main point in the free market approach argument rests on the legal statute that corporations have no personal responsibility to anyone or anything other than shareholders. Additionally, free market critics of CSR argue that corporate philanthropy gives away profits from business activity. The profits do not belong to the corporation; rather, profits belong to the shareholders.

Intersection Between Advocacy and Criticism of Corporate Social Responsibility

The two perspectives of CSR are not irreconcilable. If we accept some aspects of the free market approach, then we can accept that businesses and corporations have an imperative to increase their "capital." Likewise, we can also accept aspects of the ethical business approach that argues that corporations have obligations to society. The point of intersection is the acknowledgement that there are different types of capital that are as valuable to organizations as monetary resources. Communication campaigns for CSR create a form of *social capital* that can strengthen a society and, in the end, improve the environment (legal, economic, community) in which corporations operate.

CORPORATE SOCIAL RESPONSIBILITY AS A RELATIONSHIP-BUILDING AND SOCIAL CAPITAL FORMATION FUNCTION

Ferguson (1984) proposed that public relations should be studied and practiced as a relationship management function, providing the foundation for one of the recent theoretical shifts in public relations research that exemplifies the cocreational approach. Research on CSR outcomes suggests that some stakeholders are interested in engaging organizations when they do good deeds while simultaneously being willing to hold organizations accountable when they violate social norms. The field of public relations has explored this phenomenon through the *organization–public relationship* literature.

Organization–Public Relationships

Broom, Casey, and Ritchey (1997) explicated the concept of OPRs from a variety of research literatures. They tied the concept of relationships back to interpersonal communication, psychotherapy, interorganizational research, and systems theory. Ledingham and Bruning (1998, 2000) extended Broom and colleagues' work by quantifying and measuring various relationships and relationship outcomes and continuing to refine relationship management theory. Grunig and Huang (2000) and Huang (2001) have further added to our understanding of OPR by identifying the antecedents to relationships, public relations strategies, and relationship outcomes. Their work has attempted to fold the study of relationships into an extension of the excellence theory framework (Grunig & Huang, 2000, p. 49). The study of relationship management has also been applied to various relational contexts. Jo and Kim (2003) have applied relationship management theory to website development. Jo (2006) has also used relationship management theory to study interorganizational relationship management. Hall (2006) explored specific result outcomes for relational partners, and Coombs and Holladay (2001) applied the theory to crisis management. An emergent stream in the OPR literature focuses on the social capital that is created by relationship building.

Social Capital as an Outcome of Relationships

Social capital research is "in vogue in contemporary social sciences" (Chen, 2009, p. 193). Social capital research has provided both micro and macro level approaches to studying social relations, individual and collective behaviors, economic growth, and political participation (Bourdieu, 1986, Coleman, 1988). *Social capital* is generally viewed as the norms, cultural values, and trust intrinsic to groups, organizations, or communities. Social capital theory was popularized by Robert Putnam (2000) in *Bowling Alone: The Collapse and Revival of American Community*. Social capital researchers question how groups or communities "develop and maintain their social networks and enhance their collective interests and identity" (Hsung & Breiger, 2009, p. 5).

Social capital is not much different from monetary capital in that it is a "certain kind of capital that can create advantages for individuals or groups pursuing their own ends"

(Chen, 2009, p. 194) and includes the "investment of resources with expected returns in the marketplace" (Lin, 2001). Lin posited that the notion of capital could be and has been extended to considerations of social relations. Social capital can be understood as the social relationships that involve the exchange of resources. Thus, social capital includes the resources that individuals or organizations can mobilize and profit from because of their roles in a network of relationships (Castiglione, 2008). Social capital facilitates the successful actions of an individual or organization. There are different types of social capital benefits. Weak social capital, created by interactions in small groups, provides resources to individuals. Strong social capital provides wider returns to both groups and communities. Both types of social capital can be created through CSR campaigns.

Organizations benefit from high levels of social capital in various ways. Social capital can enhance an organization's capacity for action (Nahapiet & Ghosal, 1998), and it can also contribute to organizational survival (Pennings, Lee, & van Witteloostujin, 1998). Public relations enables organizations to create and maintain relationships that ultimately help the organization to achieve desirable goals (Kennan & Hazelton, 2006). Organizational relationships can be conceptualized as mechanisms for acquiring, exchanging, or consuming resources. Ihlen (2005) contended that, as the public relations literature and practice have become more relationship oriented, the quantity and quality of the relationships an organization possesses should now be perceived as the social capital of an organization.

There are many ways to build internal and external social capital. Kennan and Hazelton (2006) linked internal social capital of the public relations practitioner to effectiveness in public relations communication. Sommerfeldt and Taylor (2011) conducted a study of internal social capital of the public relations function in a large government organization and found that "a public relations department or practitioner must have access to or reserves of social capital before it can be expended in either internal or external communications aimed at building a collective social capital" (p. 198). For internal relationships, public relations practitioners need to be perceived as trusted communication experts who can offer advice and action plans to members of their organization. Externally, practitioners must build relationships with different stakeholder groups that create trust, commitment, satisfaction, autonomy, and mutuality that the organization can draw upon. CSR campaigns are one way that public relations practitioners can build those key internal and external relations that create social capital.

The next section illustrates three CSR campaigns that have worked to build internal and external relationships, confront media criticisms, and assist organizations recovering from crisis. The three campaigns highlight the realities of CSR and provide insight into the OPR literature.

CASE STUDIES OF CORPORATE SOCIAL RESPONSIBILITY

As alluded to in the introduction, there are thousands of CSR campaigns. Organizations lend their support to recycling, health, education, women's and human rights, safe driving, safe sex, safe texting, and a myriad of other prosocial topics. Some campaigns are afforded significant public relations attention by their organizations with advertising budgets, social media tactics, and high-profile announcements. Other campaigns are quietly enacted with merely a paragraph or two noted on a website or in the annual report. The following sections highlight three different types of CSR campaigns that illustrate some of the opportunities and challenges in building OPRs through CSR efforts.

Crate & Barrel Partners With Nonprofit to Build Customer Loyalty

The OPR literature advocates for relationship-building communication that engages stakeholders. Engagement builds trust, commitment, autonomy, mutuality, satisfaction, and loyalty. Much of the research highlighting the empirical value of OPR comes from studies with undergraduates at large universities, surveys of public relations practitioners, or case studies of organizations that have allowed researchers access to staff and strategy sessions. These studies are valuable, but their findings are somewhat removed from the reality of conducting CSR as a business communication function. However, a *Wall Street Journal* article (Steel, 2006) that reported on the effectiveness of home retailer Crate & Barrel's DonorsChoose CSR campaign adds real-world insight into the value of CSR in OPR.

DonorsChoose is an education-based nonprofit organization that had initially solicited donations from individuals to help support teachers' request for school supplies. In 2005, the nonprofit changed its fund-raising strategy and began to seek support from corporations. Its partners have included Crate & Barrel, Chevron, American Express, and HP, which have integrated DonorsChoose into their broad CSR programs.

In 2006, Crate & Barrel created a CSR effort that sent certificates to customers who had purchased home furnishings. The certificates could be used by the customers to make donations to DonorsChoose. The CSR program was created to allow customers to decide what types of educational products to support though their certificates. The design of this campaign addressed two parts of OPR: autonomy and commitment. Crate & Barrel's customers were encouraged to visit the DonorsChoose website to donate the money from the certificates to teachers and schools. Teachers and schools posted their requests for items such as microscopes, school supplies, and books on the DonorsChoose website. Crate & Barrel's customers could choose any project that suited their interests.

Crate & Barrel hired a market research firm to track the impact of the CSR program. The findings are useful to understand the impact of CSR campaigns in building customer loyalty:

> 11% of the certificates it sent were redeemed—a high percentage compared with the typical direct-mail redemption rate for coupons, which averages about 2%, according to NCH Marketing Services. They also found that the program slightly strengthened customers' ties to the retail chain, as 82% of customers who redeemed the certificates were "very likely to consider Crate & Barrel for next home furnishings or accessories purchase" compared to 76% of a control group of customers that didn't get certificates. While just 21% of the control group perceived Crate & Barrel as community minded, 75% of gift-certificate redeemers had that perception. More than half of the redeemers said they told someone else about Crate & Barrel giving them a gift certificate. (Steel, 2006, p. B1)   .

The tangible outcome created by the campaign, in the form of school supplies, is also evidence that CSR provides social capital. This CSR effort appears to have incorporated several of the foundational assumptions of the OPR literature and clearly illustrates how a public good was created out of CSR efforts.

Western Union Addresses Criticisms Through Corporate Social Responsibility Campaign Engaging Migrant Workers and Employees

Some CSR campaigns are created to respond to criticisms from media, politicians, or activist groups. In 2007, Western Union was criticized in a five-part series in the *New York Times,* which profiled the role that money transfer services such as Western Union play in supporting remittances (sending money home). Funds from immigrants, especially illegal immigrants who do not have bank accounts, can be sent safely and quickly through wire transfer services. The series of articles highlighted the high fees associated with wire transfers from migrant workers, which can run "from about 4% to 20% or more" (DeParle, 2007, para. 7) and also charged that the company "profits from, or even promotes, illegal immigration."

Western Union responded with a five-year Our World, Our Family program that partnered with a respected international NGO, Mercy Corps. "Western Union set out to recast its image, portraying itself as the migrants' trusted friend after settling a damaging lawsuit that accused it of hiding large fees" (Helping migrant communities, 2009, p. 4). The company hired the cause-branding agency Cone to assist with its CSR and reputation rebuilding efforts. The Our World, Our Family CSR campaign engaged migrants living in the United States to raise funds to help the communities that they left behind. Additionally, Western Union matched the funds from employees ($1 for every $1). *PR News* reported that nearly half of all Western Union employees have contributed to the fund. Western Union has also formally asked national governments in the home countries of large migrant populations to match the donated funds.

The campaign shows how OPR can create both economic and social capital. Western Union engaged with multiple stakeholders (employees, governments) to create a greater impact in the fund-raising part of the campaign. The money raised helps to strengthen communities in Mexico and Latin America. The campaign also performed another task: It addressed the core criticisms in the *New York Times* series. Western Union reduced its fees and rallied employees and customers to give back to the communities they left behind. In February 2009, the Our World, Our Family CSR campaign received the *PR News* award for outstanding stakeholder engagement.

BP Learns How Much (or How Little) Its Past Corporate Social Responsibility Helps in a Crisis

OPR is premised on the assumption that long-term relationships are mutually beneficial to organizations and stakeholders. One question about CSR is whether or not it creates a reservoir of goodwill (social capital) that an organization can draw upon during a crisis. Luo and Bhattacharya (2009) tested if there is a "goodwill refund" for organizations with strong CSR records, finding that a goodwill refund is not guaranteed. Other factors may mediate the effects of campaigns. For instance, Tillman, Lutz, and Weitz (2009) studied the effect of hypocrisy on public perceptions of CSR programs. Their findings suggest the existence of a:

> destructive effect of inconsistent CSR information, which can trigger consumers' perceptions of corporate hypocrisy and thus jeopardize their positive CSR beliefs and attitudes toward the firm. Specifically, proactive CSR strategies may bear a hidden risk if they convey a firm's standards of social responsibility, which may be followed by the revelation of actions violating such principles. (p. 89)

A real-world case study of the potential goodwill refund (or, alternatively, perceived hypocrisy) occurred in spring 2010. British Petroleum (BP), a global energy supplier that had publicized its long-term track record of CSR, learned firsthand how much its past CSR programs can influence media coverage and public opinion during a high-profile crisis. Prior to the recent crisis, Pirsch, Gupta, and Grau (2007) noted that BP had consistently promoted itself as a strong corporate citizen worldwide:

> [BP] organized itself largely around the concept of being a strong corporate citizen worldwide, and provides an excellent example of a firm that has institutionalized its commitment to corporate social responsibility. This commitment is employed liberally throughout company policies, and reflects the company's commitment to demonstrating social responsibility across all stakeholder groups. For example, BP conducts research on renewable energy, has a stated long-term goal of reduced emissions for their products, and links up with governments, local businesses and organizations and nongovernmental organizations to protect worker rights and ensure lawful use of resources. BP also supports local arts and culture, has built a diverse employee base, remains committed to the health and safety of employees, generates human rights safeguards, maintains a stated policy on business ethics, and utilizes two independent external auditing firms to monitor their environmental and social reporting. (p. 128)

BP's reputation as a good corporate citizen was challenged on April 20, 2010, when the Deepwater Horizon oil-drilling rig exploded in the Gulf of Mexico, killing 11 people and creating a five-month crisis that appeared nightly on television news programs across the world. All of BP's past policies and CSR programs could not stop the extensive environmental damage of the oil spill. Indeed, many opinion pieces in business journals and blogs actually used BP's reputation as a leader in CSR as ammunition against the organization. Critics of CSR noted the falling stock price, Congressional inquiry, and relentless media coverage of the crisis as evidence that CSR does not work. For example, a *Washington Post* op-ed piece by Chrystia Freeland (2010) questioned the value of CSR activities and argued that real social responsibility is about safety and minimizing harm to society in the course of doing business. Reflecting on the Deepwater Horizon spill, Freeland noted that "safety turns out to have had much greater social value than any number of creative CSR drives" (para. 5).

Did BP gain any benefit from its long history of CSR? It is too early to tell. One year after the spill, the stock price was still much lower (about 20%) than before the accident. A November 2010 poll of people living in the affected region conducted by the University of South Alabama showed that 60% of respondents did not trust the information from BP (Thomas, 2010). Very little positive media attention was focused on BP's earlier CSR efforts, providing free market economists and critics alike with an argument against CSR as a goodwill-building function that has tangible benefits during a crisis.

Sellnow (2010) noted that another part of BP's operational strategy, cost-cutting decisions that increase profits but may also increase safety risks, became the dominant theme of the media coverage of the disaster. Sellnow points out that BP has an opportunity for redemption by undertaking

> an ongoing commitment to resurrecting the ecosystem in the gulf, attending to the financial needs of gulf residents, and addressing the complex and lasting emotional toll on residents are essential. Simply put, BP must recognize the urgency and necessity of entrenching itself in a long-term commitment to the healing and recovery of the gulf coast and its residents. (para. 11)

Sellnow's suggestion of a CSR approach that focuses on "righting the wrongs" is not about promotional activities but calls for CSR activities that help the people and ecosystem affected by the spill.

Summary

The three case studies help to answer the question posed at the beginning of the chapter: What can CSR campaigns tell us about OPRs? The answer to this question is simple. CSR campaigns create social capital when organizations engage their stakeholders and communities. The direct effect of CSR on OPRs is still unknown due to the complexity of organizational systems, public perception, and multiple mediating factors. Yet, it is clear that CSR creates a public good that would not exist otherwise. CSR creates individual, organizational, and community social capital with real benefits. CSR campaigns such as the ones mentioned in the earlier part of this chapter contribute to a fully functioning society (Heath, 2006). The final section of this chapter situates CSR and social capital within a larger framework that shows why CSR is a valuable and necessary organizational and societal activity.

CORPORATE SOCIAL RESPONSIBILITY CAMPAIGNS CONTRIBUTE TO A FULLY FUNCTIONING SOCIETY

As public relations research and practice have evolved, researchers and practitioners have, at times, walked an awkward path between its functional past and its current cocreational orientation embodying aspirational objectives of what public relations can be. We have looked for a way to show public relations' value to organizations and society beyond generating publicity, such as fostering civil society (Taylor, 2009, 2010). Civil society is premised on interorganizational relationships among the societal partners including non-governmental organizations, nonprofits, media, businesses, and government (Taylor & Doerfel, 2011). CSR is one way to create these interorganizational relationships.

In the "Onward Into More Fog" article in 2006, Heath identified seven premises of fully functioning society theory (FFST) that can help us understand the value of CSR campaigns to corporations. At the operational level, Heath called for the following: 1) management teams must commit to making decisions that bring order and control to uncertainty, 2) organizations must use their power responsibly, 3) an organization's legitimacy is tied to its capacity to meet or exceed the normative expectations of stakeholders, 4) all people and organizations operate with self-interest and an organization's interests are served when it attempts to coordinate and manage risk, 5) organizations should work for *communitas* and not only *corporatas* where two-way communication between parties creates trust, cooperation, and aligned interests, 6) organizations need to have internal communication processes that allow for coordination of external effort, and 7) organizations should engage in advocacy because enlightened choice for the public comes from the wrangle of the marketplace of ideas.

Taylor (2011) argued that Heath's image of a fully functioning society makes an implicit claim that relationships among organizations and groups create social capital that makes both the organization and its community stronger. When tied to an organization's core business goals, communication campaigns for CSR are investments that improve the operating environment of the corporation. Clean water and clear air are public goods that everyone can benefit from. Smarter, healthier people make better employees. Communities with good schools and a comprehensive calendar of cultural events attract a better pool of employees. Additionally, new businesses will locate to towns that are good places to live. CSR campaigns are an investment. They create a return that facilitates organizational action.

Conclusion

CSR is a necessary and positive activity for organizations in the 21st century. A socially responsible business record, in both words and deeds, has become a requirement in maintaining organizational legitimacy. One way that organizations enact their responsibility is through CSR campaigns that create social capital. The public relations function facilitates CSR by developing campaigns as one part of the organization's overall communication and business strategy. Second, the public relations function uses various tactics—relationship building, publicity, websites, and social media—to communicate to the media, employees, or various stakeholders about the campaign. CSR generates significant media and public attention for the organization.

The neoliberal or capitalist argument is not irreconcilable with the pro-CSR argument. Businesses seek to amass capital, but it is important to acknowledge that some capital is not monetary in form. Social capital is an asset. A respected reputation, public legitimacy, and the opportunity to recruit and retain highly skilled employees are outcomes of CSR campaigns. The recipients of CSR campaigns, such as the teachers and students helped by DonorsChoose or the communities in Latin America that were helped by Western Union's Our World, Our Family campaign, have been enriched. When organizations invest resources in CSR to create social capital, they are making an investment that builds their own capacity, reputation, and legitimacy. Social capital is every bit as valuable to an organization and the community in which it operates as the monetary capital of dollars, euros, or yen. Strategic communication campaigns based on CSR principles can do so much to contribute to organizational and societal well-being. Yet, as the BP example shows, CSR is not an antidote for bad organizational behavior. CSR campaigns, like all public relations campaigns, need to be based on the principles of the OPR literature, where relationship building is the objective. It is then, and only then, that the organization's actions will create long-lasting social capital that benefits both stockholders and stakeholders.

What do CSR campaigns tell us about OPRs? They tell us that CSR activities and relationships build social capital that benefit individuals, organizations, and communities.

References

Alsop, R. (1999, September 23). The best corporate reputations in America—just as in politics, trust, reliability pay off over time. *Wall Street Journal,* p. B1.

Altman, B. W. (1998). Corporate community relations in the 1990s: A study in transformation. *Business and Society, 37*(2), 221–227.

Bhattacharya, C. B., & Sen, S. (2004). Doing better at doing good: When, why, and how consumers respond to corporate social initiatives. *California Management Review, 47,* 9–24.

Bourdieu, P. (1986). The forms of capital. In J. G. Richardson (Ed.), *Handbook of theory and research for the sociology of education* (pp. 241–258). New York: Greenwood.

Botan, C. H., & Taylor, M. (2004). Public relations: The state of the field. *Journal of Communication, 54*(4), 645–661.

Broom, G. M., Casey, S., & Ritchey, J. (1997). Toward a concept and theory of organization—public relationships. *Journal of Public Relations Research, 9,* 83–98.

Castiglione, D. (2008). Introduction: Conceptual issues in social capital theory. In D. Castiglione, J. W. Van Deth, & G. Wolleb (Eds.), *The handbook of social capital* (pp. 1–10). Oxford, UK: Oxford University Press.

Chen, C. J. (2009). The distribution and return of social capital in Taiwan. In R. Hsung, N. Lin, & R. L. Breiger (Eds.), *Contexts of social capital: Social networks in markets, communities, and families* (pp. 193–227). New York: Routledge.

Coleman, J. S. (1988). Social capital in the creation of human capital. *American Journal of Sociology, 94,* 95–120.

Coombs, W. T., & Holladay, S. (2001). An extended examination of the crisis situations: A fusion of the relational management and symbolic approaches. *Journal of Public Relations Research, 13,* 321–340.

DeParle, J. (2007, November 22). Western Union empire moves migrant cash home. [Electronic version]. *New York Times.* Retrieved July 10, 2011, from http://www.nytimes.com/2007/11/22/world/22western.html

Duhe, S. C. (2009). Good management, sound finances, and social responsibility: Two decades of U.S. corporate insider perspectives on reputation and the bottom line. *Public Relations Review, 35,* 77–78.

Ferguson, M. A. (1984, August). *Building theory in public relations: Interorganizational relationships as public relations paradigm.* Paper presented to the conference of the Association for Education in Journalism and Mass Communication. Gainesville, FL.

Freeland, C. (2010, July 18). What's BP's responsibility? [Electronic version]. *Washington Post.* Retrieved July 15, 2011, from http://www.washingtonpost.com/wp-dyn/content/article/2010/07/16/AR2010071604070.html

Friedman, M. (1970, September 13). The social responsibility of business is to increase its profits. *The New York Times Magazine,* pp. 122–126.

Glob, U., & Bartlett, J. L. (2007). Communicating about corporate social responsibility: A comparative study of CSR reporting in Australia and Slovenia. *Public Relations Review, 33,* 1–9.

Godfrey, P. C., & Hatch, N. W. (2007). Researching corporate social responsibility: An agenda for the 21st century. *Journal of Business Ethics, 70,* 87–98.

Grunig, J. E., & Huang, Y. H. (2000). From organizational effectiveness to relationship indicators: Antecedents of relationships, public relations strategies, and relational outcomes. In J. A. Ledingham & S. D. Bruning (Eds.), *Public relations as relationship management: A relational approach to the study and practice of public relations* (pp. 23–53). Mahwah, NJ: Lawrence Erlbaum.

Hall, M. R. (2006). Corporate philanthropy and corporate community relations: Measuring relationship-building results. *Journal of Public Relations Research, 18,* 1–21.

Heath, R. L. (2006). Onward into more fog: Thoughts on public relations' research directions. *Journal of Public Relations Research, 18,* 93–114.

Heath, R. L. (2010). (Ed.). *The SAGE handbook of public relations.* Thousand Oaks, CA: Sage.

Helping migrant communities: Western Union targets global customer base for massive CSR campaign. (2009, December 21). *PR News, 65*(48), 4–5.

Huang, Y. H. (2001). OPRA: A cross-cultural, multiple-item scale for measuring organization–public relationships. *Journal of Public Relations Research, 13,* 61–90.

Hsung, R., & Breiger, R. L. (2009). Position generators, affiliations, and the institutional logics of social capital: A study of Taiwan firms and individuals. In R. Hsung, N. Lin, & R. L. Breiger (Eds.), *Contexts of social capital: Social networks in markets, communities, and families* (pp. 3–27). New York: Routledge.

Ihlen, O. (2005). The power of social capital: Adapting Bourdieu to the study of public relations. *Public Relations Review, 31*(3), 492–496.

Jo, S. (2006). Measurement of organization–public relationships: Validation of measurement using a manufacturer–retailer relationship. *Journal of Public Relations Research, 18,* 225–248.

Jo, S., & Kim, Y. (2003). The effect of web characteristics on relationship building, *Journal of Public Relations Research, 15,* 199–224.

Jones, B. L., & Chase, W. H. (1979). Managing public policy issues. *Public Relations Review, 2,* 3–23.

Kennen, W. R., & Hazelton, V. (2006). Internal public relations, social capital, and the role of effective organizational communication. In C. H. Botan & V. Hazelton. (Eds.), *Public relations theory 2* (pp. 311–340). Hillsdale, NJ: Lawrence Erlbaum.

Ledingham, J. A., & Bruning, S. D. (1998). Relationship management in public relations: Dimensions of an organization–public relationship. *Public Relations Review, 24,* 55–65.

Ledingham. J., & Bruning, S. (2000). (Eds.). *Public relations as relationship management: A relational approach to the study and practice of public relations.* Hillsdale, NJ: Lawrence Erlbaum.

Lin, N. (2001). *Social capital.* Cambridge, UK: Cambridge University Press.

Luo, X., & Bhattacharya, C. (2009). The debate over doing good: Corporate social performance, strategic marketing levers, and firm-idiosyncratic risk. *Journal of Marketing, 73*(6), 198–213.

Mescon, T. S., & Tillson, D. J. (1987). Corporate philanthropy: A strategic approach to the bottom line. *California Management Review, 29*(2), 49–61.

Nahapiet, J., & Ghoshal, S. (1998). Social capital, intellectual capital, and the organizational advantage. *The Academy of Management Review, 23*(2), 242–266.

O'Connor, A., & Meister, M. (2008). Corporate social responsibility attribute rankings. *Public Relations Review, 34,* 49–50.

Pennings, J. M., Lee, K., & van Witteloostujin, A. (1998). Human capital, social capital, and firm dissolution. *Academy of Management Journal, 41*(4), 425–440.

Pfau, M., Haigh, M. M., Sims, J., & Wigley, S. (2008). Influence of corporate social responsibility campaigns on public opinion. *Corporate Reputation Review, 11*(2), 145–154.

Porter, M. E., & Kramer, M. R. (2006). Strategy & society: The link between competitive advantage and corporate social responsibility. *Harvard Business Review, 84*(12), 78–92.

Pirsch, J., Gupta, S., & Grau, S. L. (2007). A framework for understanding corporate social responsibility programs as a continuum: An exploratory study. *Journal of Business Ethics, 70,* 125–140.

Putnam, R. (2000). *Bowling alone: The collapse and revival of American community.* New York: Simon & Schuster.

Seeger, M. W., & Ulmer, R. R. (2002). A postcrisis discourse of renewal: The cases of Malden Mills and Cole Hardwoods. *Journal of Applied Communication Research, 30,* 126–142.

Sellnow, T. (2010). BP's crisis communication: Finding redemption through renewal. *Communication Currents, 5*(4). Retrieved August 1, 2011, from http://www.natcom.org/CommCurrentsArticle.aspx?id=1344

Sellnow, T. L., Ulmer, R. R., & Snider, M. (1998). The compatibility of corrective action in organizational crisis communication. *Communication Quarterly, 46,* 60–74.

Smith, C. (1996, September 8). Corporate citizens and their critics. *New York Times,* p. A11.

Steel, E. (2006, December 20). Novel program blends charity and marketing. *Wall Street Journal,* p. B1.

Sommerfeldt, E. J., & Taylor, M. (2011). A social capital approach to improving public relations' efficacy: Diagnosing internal constraints on external communication. *Public Relations Review, 37*(3), 197–206.

Taylor, M. (2009). Civil society as a rhetorical public relations process. In R. Heath, E. L. Toth, & D. Waymer (Eds.), *Rhetorical and critical approaches to public relations II* (pp. 76–91). Hillsdale, NJ: Lawrence Erlbaum.

Taylor, M. (2011). Building social capital through rhetoric and public relations. *Management Communication Quarterly, 25*(2), 436–454.

Taylor, M., & Doerfel, M. L. (2011). The Croatian civil society movement: Implications, recommendations, and expectations for donors and NGOs. *Voluntas: The International Journal of Voluntary Associations, 22,* 311–334.

Tillmann, W., Lutz R. J., & Weitz, B. A. (2009). Corporate hypocrisy: Overcoming the threat of inconsistent corporate social responsibility perceptions. *Journal of Marketing, 73,* 77–91.

Thomas, C. (2010, November 1). *Oil spill survey: Public trust in BP, Feds diminished.* Retrieved August 12, 2011, from http://www.usavanguard.com/news/oil-spill-survey-public-trust-in-bp-feds-diminished-1.1738668

Ulmer, R. R., Sellnow, T. L., & Seeger, M. W. (2007). *Effective crisis communication: Moving from crisis to opportunity.* Thousand Oaks, CA: Sage.

Veil, S. R., Liu, M., Erickson, S. L., & Sellnow, T. L. (2005). Too hot to handle: Competency constrains character in Chi-Chi's green onion crisis. *Public Relations Quarterly, 50*(4), 19–22.

CHAPTER 19

Designing Digital Games, Social Media, and Mobile Technologies to Motivate and Support Health Behavior Change

Debra A. Lieberman

Author's Note: Preparation of this chapter was supported by a grant from the Pioneer Portfolio of the Robert Wood Johnson Foundation.

There are now thousands of digital games designed to motivate and support health behavior change. Health games appear in social media, virtual worlds, mobile apps (applications), health insurers' websites, home-to-clinic telehealth systems, museum exhibits, medical devices, and robots in addition to computers and video game consoles. Public communication campaigns are increasingly using games as part of their media mix to promote and improve, for example, physical activity (Murphy, Carson, Neal, Baylis, Donley, & Yeater, 2009), nutrition (Baranowski, Baranowski, Cullen, Marsh, Islam, Zakeri, et al., 2003), mental health (Andrews, Joyce, & Bowers, 2010; Griffiths, 2003; Walshe, Lewis, Kim, O'Sullivan, & Wiederhold, 2003; Wilkinson, Ang, & Goh, 2008), safer sex negotiation (Read, Miller, Appleby, Nwosu, Reynaldo, Lauren, et al., 2006; Thomas, Cahill, & Santilli, 1997), and disease self-management and adherence to one's treatment plan (Kato, Cole, Bradlyn, & Pollock, 2008; Lieberman, 2001).

Health games are advancing in quantity and quality, but we are far from achieving consistently high standards of research and design that can assure that new games will be engaging, challenging, and effective and will provide game experiences that are especially appealing and impactful for the specific target population, health topic, and game play environment. This chapter offers evidence-based ideas for the design and implementation of digital games in health campaigns that have health behavior change as their central goal.

ADVANTAGES OF GAMES FOR HEALTH PROMOTION AND BEHAVIOR CHANGE

Well-designed games can be powerful environments for learning and behavior change because they are highly interactive and experiential (Hansen, 2008; Ritterfeld, Cody, & Vorderer, 2009). Essentially, a game is a rule-based activity that involves challenge to reach a goal and provides feedback on the player's progress toward that goal (Lieberman, 2006, 2009). Digital games include any form of digital media that uses the core elements of rules, challenge, and feedback to engage players in interactive play with the intention to reach a goal.

Games present compelling problems to solve, and they usually provide a great deal of feedback on the player's progress toward the goal. In a well-designed game, players have a sense of agency. They feel they are making things happen, they have control within the game, they have plenty of possible choices to make, they have access to information and tools as needed, and everything they do changes their game state and the game's story line in interesting ways. Games are usually structured and incremental, so the player feels a sense of progress and accomplishment. Some games adapt to the player's performance, adjusting the difficulty level as the player develops more skills so that the game remains continuously challenging and never too difficult and frustrating or too easy and boring. Game players welcome feedback, even when they fail, because failing is a way to learn and improve. Failure is not an end point, as it is in classroom test taking; rather, it is an opportunity to learn and start again. The learning mode in many games is simply to try things out and see what happens, to experiment and take risks, and to venture out with new approaches to discover how to triumph over the problems posed by the game challenge.

Games have many features that designers could potentially use to enhance health-related learning and behavior change, such as interaction with socially complex game characters; teamwork with other players; interfaces that require physical exertion (exergames such as the dance pad game Dance Dance Revolution and motion-detecting games on the Kinect or Wii game platforms); downloading of one's own health data into the game so that self-care is the game mechanic or game-playing strategy; and rehearsal of decision-making skills that would help players avoid relapse in their own lives by experiencing realistic game scenes that trigger, for example, cravings for tobacco, alcohol, or other drugs. The list of game features is extensive and growing as new technologies appear that enable games to sense the environment, detect players' emotions while playing, involve them in social media, aggregate data from many players, and individualize and tailor the game experience to match the player's interests and abilities.

Challenge to reach a goal, which is the central premise and impetus of a great game, makes games highly motivating. Most players in the target population will be intensely motivated to win it (Bogost, 2007; Brown, Lieberman, Gemeny, Fan, Wilson, & Pasta, 1997; Vorderer & Bryant, 2006) and will enthusiastically learn and rehearse any skills needed in order to win. Games give players compelling challenges, interactive experiences, and feedback using the rich graphics and media production techniques that digital media can deliver. Once they motivate players to take on challenges, games can then develop and assess their skills, stretch their capabilities, transport them to new environments, simulate complex systems that players can manipulate and test, immerse them in intriguing stories, and enable them to show off their talents to others to create experiences that are enthralling and fun. Well-designed games prompt players to make decisions and solve problems, and they deliver progress monitoring, recognition, and rewards in addition to the enjoyment of trying out new experiences and the inherent pleasure of learning and developing new skills and succeeding with new strategies.

The decision to develop a game for a health campaign, and which style of game to develop, depends to a great extent on the outcomes the team desires. It is easy to produce a low-cost casual game that will appear on the campaign website and will take a few minutes to play. This type of game would be fine if the goal were to attract people to the website, keep them coming back at least a few more times, and expose them to key concepts, messages, and characters used elsewhere in the campaign. A game like this could also convey that the campaign understands the target population by reaching them where they live in their media world—on their mobile phones, in their social networks, and on the web—using artwork and animations and sounds that reflect the population's tastes and preferences. However, a casual, low-budget game would not likely be enough to change in significant ways a player's attitudes, risk perceptions, knowledge, skills, self-concepts, social relationships, perceived social norms, or any of the many other factors that are known to lead to health behavior change and improved health outcomes. A game intended to change behavior would be more expensive and time-consuming to produce and evaluate and would require a team of experts in game design, interactive and media-based processes of learning and behavior change, the health topic, medicine, behavioral health, the target age group, and formative and summative research, but if the game led to players' improved health behaviors and outcomes, especially those aligned with the campaign's overall goals, it could be well worth the investment.

WIDE RANGE OF DIGITAL GAME FORMATS

Digital games can appear entirely on digital media, where the player interacts only with the technology (technology-based games) or they can be supported by or partially played with digital media, such as a game that tracks one's daily physical activity, nutrition, and calories using a mobile phone to record and display progress, milestones, and achievements, and to serve as a communication medium among friends who coach each other along the way (technology-supported games).

A game can consist of a single quiz question or puzzle to solve, or it can involve hundreds of thousands of people who play for many hours a day in a narrative- and graphics-rich, massive, multiplayer, online team-based game that continues indefinitely. Health games have been made for almost every game genre and on almost every form of digital technology. Following are descriptions of a few game types and worlds that have been used for health games, including puzzle, eye-hand coordination, action and adventure, scenario-based, simulation, virtual world, mobile, active, context-aware, alternate reality, and community collaboration. Many have elements that can be combined with others, so they are not mutually exclusive categories, and there are many others not mentioned here.

Puzzle games use the interactivity and rich graphics of digital media to challenge players to solve puzzles that involve using visual, mathematical, word, memory, or logical skills, among others. Puzzle formats have been used to introduce health-related concepts to players and to help them keep those concepts in mind. They can reinforce the message of a campaign and can draw people to a campaign's website. Some puzzle games are designed to diagnose cognitive disorders, maintain or improve cognitive skills, or help delay the onset of dementia.

Eye-hand coordination games involve, for example, hitting targets, catching objects, rolling or maneuvering an object while staying within bounds, or racing while picking up certain items for more points or to gain increased speed and then avoiding other items that reduce points or decrease speed. These games can involve the player in health-related decision making and display general consequences of those decisions. Usually, they involve simpler tasks, such as catching healthy foods as they fall and avoiding the unhealthy foods or picking up all the diabetes self-care supplies. Like puzzle games, they can attract people to a campaign's website and teach them basic concepts. Eye-hand coordination games can be incorporated as mini games into other game formats to provide some arcade game fun and perhaps to win items that can be used in the main game.

Action and adventure games enable the player to take the role of a character and move through a complex and varied game world. This format is effective for portraying role model characters and for supporting learning by doing. If players are challenged to make crucial health decisions in an action and adventure game, their expertise and skills can increase through repetition and practice, and this can improve their perceived self-efficacy, or self-confidence, to carry out in real life the tasks they rehearsed in the game (Bandura, 1986, 1997). Studies of health games that have used an action and adventure format have found improvements in players' health-related knowledge, skills, self-efficacy, and health behaviors, for example, in the area of cancer self-care and adherence to a treatment plan (Kato et al., 2008) and in the self-management of type 1 diabetes (Brown et al., 1997) and asthma (Lieberman, 2001).

Scenario-based games put the player into a realistic situation within a digital game world and involve decision making that results in positive or negative health consequences. Examples include games that use dating scenarios to rehearse and teach safe sex negotiation (Read et al., 2006) and alcohol abuse relapse prevention games that present the social scenarios that tend to trigger a desire for a drink so that the player can rehearse avoidance and refusal skills (Andrews et al., 2010). Scenario-based formats are designed to help players perceive their own health risks more accurately as they see the consequences of their health decisions, understand the benefits of good prevention and self-care, and practice the skills they will need when confronting the same scenarios in their daily lives.

A *simulation* is a model of a system or environment—with interrelated, interdependent elements—that responds system-wide to any change the user makes within it. A simulation becomes a game when the user is given the goal to achieve at least one specific outcome within the simulated system. For example, a diabetes self-management game (Brown et al., 1997; Lieberman, 1997, 2001) simulated several factors that contributed to the diabetic main character's blood glucose level, including the amount of insulin taken before certain meals, the types of food eaten (classified as food exchanges, such as fruits, grains, dairy, etc.) for meals and snacks, and the number of servings eaten for each type of food. The game challenged players to keep the character's blood glucose readings in the normal range through proper insulin use and food choices, and it provided a cumulative record showing the blood glucose readings over time. By achieving the goal of keeping blood glucose neither too high nor too low, the player's game character was not slowed down by diabetes-related problems and was therefore better able to win the game.

A *virtual world,* such as Second Life, Club Penguin, Webkins, or Whyville, is an online environment in which participants can create characters, places, and events. In Second Life, the world is constructed by the participants, who interact with each other, develop friendships, share media and entertainment, collaborate, build things, buy and sell things, hold discussions and support group meetings, and find and share information. Games can take place in virtual worlds. In the virtual world Whyville, the CDC introduced an infectious disease called the Whypox, which appeared as red splotches on the faces of some of the participants' avatar characters. Whyville participants realized that they needed to learn how to treat Whypox, learn how to prevent it community-wide, and figure out what individuals could do to avoid catching it. The CDC provided information and resources within the virtual word so that participants could find it and address their health crisis during this teachable moment about epidemics and infectious disease (Kafai, Quintero, & Feldon, 2010).

Mobile games are playable on mobile phones and tablet computers. As these technologies become increasingly multipurpose, multimedia, networked, and powerful, there will be increasingly rich opportunities to develop on-the-go gaming. The number of mobile health games and health apps is growing fast. In the first quarter of 2011, there were more than 8,000 of them available for mobile phones (MobiHealth News, 2011).

Active games are designed to get the player moving. They could be technology-based exergames that require physical exertion to interact with the game, or they could be technology-supported games that monitor the player's real-world physical activity (for example, by using a global positioning system (GPS) to monitor distances walked each day or by using a pedometer or accelerometer that counts daily steps and transmits the step counts to a computer or mobile phone that uses step counts as part of the game challenge). Exergames involve the player in dance moves, step aerobics, kickboxing, sports moves, balancing, Hula-Hooping, martial arts, stationary biking, virtual window washing, and many other forms of physical activity. Players may interact with these games on dance pads, balance platforms, or through gestures detected by cameras or by handheld remote controls. Research finds that exergames can be appealing, motivating, and fun and offer compelling game challenges, a chance to perform for an audience athletically or expressively, and a way to meet and interact with others in friendships and communities. Some exergames improve players' stress management, weight management, fitness, and health (Lieberman, Chamberlin, Medina, Jr., Franklin, McHugh Sanner, & Vafiadis, 2011; Murphy et al., 2009). Some have used exertion interfaces to deliver therapies such as physical therapy and stroke rehabilitation (Fritz, Rivers, Merlo, & Duncan, 2009), and others have used breathing as the interface to the game to improve cystic fibrosis patients' skills and motivation to take inhaled medication and engage in breath therapy and, in so doing, increased their frequency of engaging in these important self-care activities (Bingham, Bates, Thompson-Figueroa, & Lahiri, 2010).

Context-aware games take place in the physical world, and they use data and information from the environment as inputs into the game. Motion-detecting games enable players to gesture and move as a way to interface with the game. Brain wave sensors used in biofeedback games such as Journey to Wild Divine and the use of heart rate and blood pressure data taken in real time during game play are examples of the physiological monitoring that can be input into context-aware games. GPS is used in location-based games such as the Japanese game Mogi, in which players explore their physical surroundings to collect hidden virtual items. Players interact with the Mogi world via software on their GPS-equipped mobile phones. As they move throughout the (real) city, the software updates their positions and lets them know when they are near any (virtual) tokens they could collect. Their goal is to gather as many tokens as possible, trade them with other players for rarer tokens, and build the ultimate Mogi collection. Context-aware games that use the player's location as an input to the game are sometimes called *pervasive games* because they extend the game experience off the screen and into the player's natural, physical world. These games can be designed to be played anywhere, making the entire world into a game environment. When this happens, daily life could take on an added dimension of being a game itself. Normal activities such as driving to work, shopping in the grocery store, or crossing a street could affect players' progress in a game. Players could play alone or receive ideas, clues, opinions, and expertise from other players as they make choices and take action. Context-aware games offer many novel and interesting opportunities to integrate into the world of a game the player's physiological data, geographic location, physical activity, and any other activities or physical or emotional states that could be detected by sensors.

Alternate reality games take place in the physical world with technology delivering information and facilitating communication. In these games, people interact with each other via media and face-to-face, and they are immersed as players in a dramatic fictional story that unfolds in the real world. Some games insert fictional content into the same media and technologies that players use mainly for real-world, nonfiction purposes, including newspapers, magazines, the web, e-mail, and phones. For instance, a player may receive a phone call from a fictional character, and the player is suddenly interacting in a fictional alternate reality in the middle of a nonfictional day. Examples of alternate reality games for health include Epidemic Menace, Can You See Me Now?, and The Skeleton Chase.

Community collaboration games bring people together online to address important issues, participate in new scientific discoveries, and solve problems. This form of interaction is also known as *crowdsourcing,* which involves using the collective knowledge and skills of the crowd to arrive at groundbreaking solutions. By adding game elements such as teamwork, prizes, and clearly defined rules and goals, people become more urgently engaged and motivated to succeed, and they enjoy the social recognition when they succeed and the deeply felt pleasure of making a contribution to society. Two popular community collaboration games related to health are FoldIt and EteRNA. FoldIt involves the general public in the complex task of protein folding to discover new proteins that can aid medical research and lead to cures for a variety of diseases. Players work alone, and they collaborate in an online community to share ideas and strategies. EteRNA challenges players to design RNAs and involves them in an online community. There is a weekly competition, and each RNA submitted is synthesized and then scored by how well it folds. Both games, with the involvement of researchers at Carnegie Mellon University and Stanford University, help advance medical science by harnessing the wisdom of crowds, bringing many people together to work on labor-intensive searches for important discoveries. A third example is Breakthroughs to Cures, a crowdsourced game developed by the Institute for the Future to gather ideas for new ways to approach the process of medical research and to accelerate the development of research findings into lifesaving disease treatments.

THEORY AND RESEARCH: OBESITY PREVENTION EXAMPLE

Health games and game technologies can be especially successful when they implement theories of human information processing, motivation, attitude change, learning, and behavior change into their game design strategies drawn from a wide variety of fields, including psychology, communication, public health, education, bioengineering, human–computer interaction, kinesiology, and medical informatics, to name just a few. Well-researched theories can be the source of evidence-based game design principles to guide the design of health games. As an example, following is a discussion of a few theories and research findings that could be used in health games for obesity prevention.

Obesity has reached epidemic proportions in the United States. It continues to rise, and it can be prevented or ameliorated to a certain extent when individuals improve their health habits and daily lifestyles. Innovative games are already motivating and supporting players' lifestyle changes related to physical activity (Biddis & Irwin, 2010; Fasola & Mataric, 2010; Graf, Pratt, Hester, & Short, 2009; Lieberman et al., 2011; Murphy et al., 2009; Papastergiou, 2009; Unnithan, Houser, & Fernhall, 2005) and healthy eating (Baranowski et al., 2003; Mackert, Kahlor, Tyler, & Gustafson, 2009; Norman, Zabinski, Adams, Rosenberg, Yaroch, & Atienza, 2007; Thompson, Baranowski, Cullen, & Baranowski, 2007), but there is a great deal more that could be done.

One approach to changing health behaviors, including those that help people maintain a healthy weight, is to increase perceived risk and, concurrently, to increase people's sense of personal efficacy or self-confidence that they could successfully carry out risk-reducing health behaviors and that those behaviors could actually lead to better health. In the case of obesity, a game would help people understand the personal health risks of being obese and, at the same time, would help them develop the confidence that they can successfully take action to prevent or reduce obesity. The Extended Parallel Process Model (Witte, Meyer, & Martell, 2001) identifies two components of risk perception and two components of efficacy perception that are essential for behavior change to occur. First, regarding risk perception, people must perceive that they are personally susceptible to the health problem (perceived susceptibility) and that the problem is severe enough to do significant harm to them (perceived severity). If even one of these perceptions is not very strong, health behavior change is not likely to occur. Second, on the efficacy perception side of the equation, it is essential that people feel a strong sense of personal capability to carry out the recommended behaviors (self-efficacy) and must believe that the behaviors will truly lead to better health (response efficacy). The Extended Parallel Process Model integrates theories such as the Theory of Reasoned Action (Fishbein & Ajzen, 1981), which explains how changing people's beliefs about the risks and consequences of their current behaviors can motivate them to improve their behaviors, and Social Cognitive Theory (Bandura, 1986, 1997), which focuses on the crucial role of efficacy beliefs and outcome expectations in people's willingness to engage in behavior change.

A health game could be designed to increase players' perceived susceptibility to a health problem and their perceived severity of the problem by requiring them to play the role of a game character that has many of the same characteristics as the player and also has an obesity-related health problem, such as type 2 diabetes. The game must be very appealing to the target audience and fun or compelling to play because, if people will not play the game, it can never be effective no matter how much theory and evidence went into its design. In the game, players experience the problems of obesity by playing the role of the obese, diabetic character, and in so doing, they develop deeper understanding of the health effects of carrying too much weight. If the game is designed well, players will identify with the character and will see that the same health problems could happen to them, and as a result, they will perceive that they are susceptible to the problem and that the problem is a severe one. In the game, they must take care of their characters' health problems through blood sugar monitoring and medication, and their game challenge is to improve their characters' physical activity and food choices in order to manage weight and improve health and well-being, perhaps even to remove the need for any more medication. That same game could increase the player's self-efficacy for improving obesity-related health behaviors by repeatedly involving the player in appropriate self-care decisions and healthy lifestyle habits as strategies to win the game, and it could improve response efficacy by demonstrating, through the depiction of cause-and-effect events in the normal course of the game, that the healthy lifestyle habits the player has participated in can indeed lead to better health outcomes and that unhealthy habits can lead to worse health outcomes. Several studies have found that health games involving this type of experiential learning by doing, in which the player's health choices are clearly linked to realistic health outcomes, have led to improvements in perceived self-efficacy and response efficacy related to the positive health behaviors that were learned and rehearsed in the game (Brown et al., 1997; Kato et al., 2008; Lieberman, 2006, 2009).

A related theoretical area and program of research that holds great promise for the design of obesity prevention games and health games in general is the Proteus Effect (Yee, Bailenson, & Duchenaut, 2009), which finds that people tend to identify with their avatars, which are virtual representations of them as characters in a game or other digital virtual environment. People identify so strongly, and they are influenced so much by the self-modeling that their avatars provide, especially when the avatars look somewhat like them, that they begin to take on characteristics of their avatars in their face-to-face interactions with other people and in their everyday behaviors, conforming to the expectations that people might have of them based on the attributes of their avatars. Imagine a game character avatar that looks like the player but is more physically active, eats more nutritious foods, and is full of vitality, and imagine what would happen if the player then began to behave that way in daily life due to the effects of self-modeling by the avatar. Research on the Proteus Effect suggests that this can happen at least in the short term, and it finds, for example, that when avatars provide virtual self-modeling of physical activity, there is an increase in people's physical activity in real life (Fox & Bailenson, 2009).

There are many other studies of avatars and identification with media characters (see Blascovich & Bailenson, 2011; Cohen, 2001; Lewis, Weber, & Bowman, 2008) that show, for example, that we identify with our avatars even when they age. When we see our older avatars, we make better decisions that impact our futures, such as saving more money for retirement. Having a clear image of ourselves as older might also influence our health habits, not just our financial habits, in similar ways. A variation on this theme involves the use of aspirational avatars, which are not necessarily older than the user, but they reflect the user's ideal self: what the user aspires to be. A study randomly assigned each participant either to create an avatar that looks like 1) his or her actual self or 2) his or her ideal self. Then, when the participant played a game as the avatar, the study found that players with aspirational, idealized avatars were more immersed in game play, perceiving more interactivity while they played (Jin, 2009). Developing an aspirational avatar, then, could trigger the effects of self-modeling mentioned earlier, and it could also immerse the player in the game more deeply so that self-modeling effects might be strengthened as a result.

Research on video game self-representation finds that game players who are allowed to select avatars to represent themselves in a game are more aroused and attentive during game play than players who are not allowed to select their avatars, especially when the game is played in a third-person over-the-shoulder view so that each player sees the avatar instead of playing with a first-person view through the eyes of the avatar (Lim & Reeves, 2009). Arousal and attentiveness are associated with higher levels of learning, persuasion, attitude change, and behavior change, all of which are often integrated into the design and intended outcomes of health games.

3-D BODY MODEL: YOUR GAME CHARACTER OR GAME WORLD COULD BE . . . YOU

Here is a scenario of converging media that could be built with today's technologies. It is presented here as an example of the way theory and research can drive the design of health games.

Imagine having a digital, 3-D model of your own body, inside and out. It looks exactly like you, displaying photorealistic images. You can peel away layers of your digital body and isolate various organ systems or specific arteries or bones or glands as you wish, viewing them from any angle and zooming in to take a closer look. You can zoom down to the level of nerve endings or bronchial tubes or capillaries or go deeper to the cellular or molecular level in any location in the body, zoom out to see the outside of the body, and then continue out further to see the body in its social, cultural, economic, and environmental context.

This model is a representation of your own current health status and external health environment. You, your clinic, and various meters and sensor devices all supply specific data that the digital 3-D body model system gathers and dynamically displays in this realistic representation of your body at the present time. When data are not available—say, for example, you don't have any scans showing whether your coronary arteries are narrowed down with plaque—powerful algorithms (formulas using if–then decision rules) will display those arteries as they are likely to appear given your age, gender, health habits, health record, and genetic profile. The system will indicate whether a display is based on real data about your body or is based on probabilities, and you can use the model as the interface to search for information related to your health risks and your displayed probable health status to learn more about the topic and find out how your risks were calculated.

Your digital, 3-D body model can appear on a mobile phone, medical device, tablet, desktop computer, TV, or immersive virtual display. In addition to zooming in and out of the body from an external point of view, you can go inside the body and change your position and viewpoint to see it from within, moving around from the inside of one organ to the inside of another, to see what the inside surfaces of your organs probably look like and to understand how body parts are connected, how they work and interact, and how fluids, gasses, hormones, and nerve signals travel. The visual representation of your body can be augmented with displays of vital signs, meter readings, and lab test results. Cumulative data about a body part or body system can be displayed using images, words, numbers, or graphs that show how your readings and results have progressed over time.

Also imagine how you might play with your digital, 3-D body model. You can use it as a simulation and tinker with the body, asking what-if questions and seeing their outcomes. You can go backward or forward in time to see your body as it was 10 years ago or how it might be 30 years from now and then change some parameter, such as average daily fruit and vegetable servings, fat grams per day, hours of vigorous exercise per week, or weekly sun exposure without sunscreen, to see what your body parts might look like and your health status might be in the future if you changed your health behavior starting today. The model will show you becoming slimmer or pudgier based on the various food and physical activity changes you try out in the simulation and project into the future. Make the wrong choices, and your digital, 3-D body model becomes a health risk message and a negative role model showing the negative consequences of harmful behaviors as your health, fitness, and appearance deteriorate. Make improved choices, and your model is now a positive role model showing how changes in health behaviors can lead to better, more rewarding outcomes.

Now, here we arrive at games. What a powerful game character or game world this digital, 3-D body model would make! You can play any game as yourself, maneuvering an avatar character that has all the physical and physiological attributes of your own body, in your body's current state of health and with its actual health strengths and vulnerabilities. Body sensors could feed the game your current vital signs, stress level, and emotional state to add a real-time health component to game play. The game, as all games do, gives you a challenge to reach a goal. The game goal could focus on achieving a desirable lifestyle habit related to, say, nutrition or physical activity or stress management or cancer prevention in order to maintain or improve your health, or the goal could involve self-care choices, following a treatment plan, or managing a chronic condition. Your game goals would be health goals, so that good health choices are essential in order to win. The body's ultimate health status, based on your actions in the game, would determine whether you win or lose.

Another way to use the 3-D body model in health games would be to make it the game world itself. You can maneuver your character in and around a body that has your own health characteristics. Take a dive into the lungs to see whether lung tissues are healthy or blackened by years of smoking and then maneuver into the heart to see if there are any problems there. While doing this inside the body, you carry out game challenges in which you keep the body healthy or treat its diseases and conditions. The special appeal is that the body is your own 3-D body model. The game world is . . . you.

The 3-D body model provides immersive experiences that motivate better health behaviors. The theory discussion in the previous section can be integrated into the design of each player's 3-D body model avatar character to enhance, for example, self-modeling and at times visualizing oneself as older or as an ideal version of oneself now or in the future. Risk perceptions and efficacy perceptions can also be enhanced in games using the 3-D body model, where players learn and rehearse important self-care skills in response to severe health threats. Many groundbreaking health games contain features of this system already (e.g., Brown et al., 1997, Kato et al., 2008; Tingen, Grimling, Bennett, Gibson, & Renew, 1997), but integrating these features into one system could potentially yield more extensive benefits and increase player engagement, learning, and behavior change. The 3-D body model would be useful as a character or as a game world in any games that involve health simulations, role playing in fictional or nonfictional settings, role modeling or self-modeling, or a focus on health outcomes as game outcomes.

Here are a few more spin-offs of the 3-D body model idea.

Spinoff #1: Play With Diagnoses

Your digital, 3-D body model develops troubling symptoms, and it is up to you to diagnose what might be wrong and decide what to do: Engage in self-care (including decisions about what self-care actions to take), make a nonurgent appointment with your doctor, or get immediate urgent or emergency care. You could search for information to learn more that would help you make decisions. Diagnostic simulations are used to train medical professionals, but this one would be made for individuals who are not medical experts and who need to decide whether to take care of a health problem themselves or see a doctor. However, this idea could easily be adapted to give more complex diagnostic challenges to health care professionals, and their decisions could involve determining which tests and treatments to give.

Spinoff #2: Play With Self-Care

To learn more about a problem such as a broken leg or the flu or drug addiction or heart disease, your digital, 3-D body model develops a health problem, and you play a game in which you can learn and rehearse skills and habits that would enable you to treat your condition the best way possible by following your doctor's recommendations, and you would be challenged to use those skills at the appropriate times in the game.

Spinoff #3: Invite a Friend to Play a Collaborative Two-Player Game

Using your digital, 3-D body model, you and a friend could work together to take care of "your" health in a challenging health game. If you have asthma, for example, you and your friend would keep your character's asthma under control and avoid asthma triggers while engaging in other game challenges. Not only would you both learn how to take care of asthma, but the game could be a springboard for social support and discussion about your condition, and it could help your friend understand what is involved in your daily asthma care.

Spinoff #4: Play a Game as a Different Character With Different Health Attributes

Sometimes, it is interesting to walk in someone else's shoes and play the role of another character. Instead of nurturing yourself in the game, you can nurture another person. This enables new kinds of vicarious experience not possible with one's own 3-D body model avatar and provides a way to develop empathy and insight. For example, a healthy, young woman who is not overweight could play a game as an older woman, or as a young man, or as a young woman who is overweight, or as a woman with a chronic disease to manage.

Conclusion

Digital games are interactive media that motivate and engage players by challenging them to reach a goal. They are immersive, social, "cool," and fun, and the digital technologies that deliver games are becoming more advanced, affordable, and easier to access and use. As a popular leisure-time activity in the United States, games can be an important component of a health communication campaign when designed to address a specific target demographic group and health issue (see Lustria, Cortese, Noar, & Glueckauf, 2009, and Noar, 2006, for overviews of research on tailored health messages and mass media health campaigns and to gain insights into issues that also pertain to the use of games in health campaigns). Games can be designed to bring people to a website and serve as a gateway to additional campaign content; to supplement and reinforce campaign messages that are also disseminated via other media and events; or to stand on their own and provide in-depth game-play experiences that change health behaviors by helping players develop new attitudes, improve self-concepts, strengthen self-efficacy, give and receive social support in social networks, learn and rehearse skills, and increase motivation.

A growing body of theory and research is discovering game design strategies that can motivate health behavior change, and there is more work to be done, especially as new health topics, game formats, technologies, and game-play environments continue to emerge. For example, physiological sensors placed on the player's body can transmit data wirelessly into games, enabling players to put themselves into digital games with their game characters having the same physiological states that they have in any given moment, as the discussion of the 3-D body model illustrated. Games can also use sensor data to adjust, for example, the content or pace or difficulty level of game play in response to the player's state so that a relaxed and alert player might be presented with a very different version of a game than a player who is anxious, distracted, or tired. Also, game displays are migrating off the TV screen or computer monitor and onto our networked mobile phones, which are always with us, and onto augmented reality displays that hover in space in our fields of vision wherever we move throughout the day. New ways of playing and researching digital games are enabling us to develop new strategies to enhance learning and behavior change through game play, while at the same time, fundamental questions about processes of human learning and behavior continue to be relevant.

As the design strategies and technological capabilities of digital games evolve, research should continue to investigate both intended and unintended outcomes so that designers of entertainment games can avoid teaching undesirable lessons and designers of health games can improve players' learning experiences and behavioral and health outcomes (see Isbister & Schaffer, 2008, to learn about game usability testing and play testing). Health messages in mainstream entertainment games are also a legitimate focus for health game researchers and designers, because these games often convey health-related information, role modeling, attitudes, and consequences, and it is important to make sure that the lessons they teach are desirable ones.

A new standard is needed in which there is widespread agreement that health games should be theory and evidence based in their design and well researched both during and after game development. This standard should be held not only by game designers and publishers but also by the decision makers who fund, recommend, purchase, and disseminate health games and by end users and consumers as well. Digital games offer a tremendous opportunity to motivate and support health behavior change in fun, engaging, and impactful ways, and we can make the most of that opportunity by producing, researching, and implementing health games that draw upon our best sources of knowledge, creativity, and understanding.

References

Andrews, A., Joyce, R. T., & Bowers, C. A. (2010). *Using serious games for mental health education.* In J. Cannon-Bowers & C. Bowers (Eds.), *Serious game design and development: Technologies and training for learning (pp. 246–259).* Hershey, PA: IGI Global.

Bandura, A. (1986). *Social foundations for thought and action: A social cognitive theory.* Englewood Cliffs, NJ: Prentice Hall.

Bandura, A. (1997). *Self-efficacy: The exercise of control.* New York: W.H. Freeman and Company.

Baranowski, T., Baranowski, J., Cullen, K. W., Marsh, T., Islam, N., Zakeri, I., Honess-Morreale, L., & deMoor, C. (2003). Squire's Quest! Dietary outcome evaluation of a multimedia game. *American Journal of Preventive Medicine, 24*(1), 52–61.

Biddis, E., & Irwin, J. (2010). Active video games to promote physical activity in children and youth. *Archives of Pediatric and Adolescent Medicine, 164*(7), 664–672.

Bingham, P. M., Bates, J. H. T., Thompson-Figueroa, J., & Lahiri, T. (2010). A breath biofeedback computer game for children with cystic fibrosis. *Clinical Pediatrics, 49,* 337–342.

Blascovich, J., & Bailenson, J. (2011). *Infinite reality: Avatars, eternal life, new worlds, and the dawn of the virtual revolution.* New York: HarperCollins.

Bogost, I. (2007). *Persuasive games: The expressive power of videogames.* Cambridge, MA: MIT.

Brown, S. J., Lieberman, D. A., Gemeny, B. A., Fan, Y. C., Wilson, D. M., & Pasta, D. J. (1997). Educational video game for juvenile diabetes: Results of a controlled trial. *Medical Informatics 22*(1), 77–89.

Cohen, J. (2001). Defining identification: A theoretical look at the identification of audiences with media characters. *Mass Communication and Society, 4*(3), 245–264.

Fasola, J., & Mataric, M. (2010). Robot motivator: Increasing user enjoyment and performance on a physical/cognitive task. Paper presented at the International Conference on Development and Learning, Ann Arbor, MI.

Fishbein, M., & Ajzen, I. (1981). Acceptance, yielding and impact: Cognitive processes in persuasion. In R. E. Petty, T. M. Ostrom, & T. C. Brock (Eds.), *Cognitive responses in persuasion* (pp. 339–359). Hillsdale, NJ: Lawrence Erlbaum.

Fox, J., & Bailenson, J. N. (2009). Virtual self-modeling: The effects of vicarious reinforcement and identification on exercise behaviors. *Media Psychology, 12,*1–25.

Fritz, S. L, Rivers, E. D., Merlo, A. R., & Duncan, B. M. (2009). Examining the effects of commercially available video game systems, the Nintendo Wii and Sony Playstation 2, on balance and mobility in individuals with chronic stroke. *Journal of Neurologic Physical Therapy Abstracts, 33*(4), 224–232.

Graf, D. L., Pratt, L. V., Hester, C. N., & Short, K. R. (2009). Playing active video games increases energy expenditure in children. *Pediatrics, 124,* 534–540.

Griffiths, M. (2003). The therapeutic use of videogames in childhood and adolescence. *Clinical Child Psychology & Psychiatry, 8*(4), 547–554.

Hansen, M. M. (2008). Versatile, immersive, creative and dynamic virtual 3-D health care learning environments: A review of the literature. *Journal of Medical Internet Research, 10*(3), e26.

Isbister, K., & Schaffer, N. (2008). *Game usability: Advancing the player experience.* San Francisco: Morgan Kaufmann.

Jin, S. A. (2009). Avatars mirroring the actual self versus projecting the ideal self: The effects of self-priming on interactivity and immersion in an exergame, Wii Fit. *CyberPsychology & Behavior, 12*(6), 761–765.

Kafai, Y. B., Quintero, M., & Feldon, D. (2010). Investigating the "Why" in Whypox: Casual and systematic explorations of a virtual epidemic. *Games and Culture, 5*(1), 116–135.

Kato, P. M., Cole, S. W., Bradlyn, A. S., & Pollock, B. H. (2008). A video game improves behavioral outcomes in adolescents and young adults with cancer: A randomized trial. *Pediatrics, 122*(2), e305–e317.

Lewis, M. L., Weber, R., & Bowman, N. D. (2008). "They may be pixels, but they're MY pixels:" Developing a metric of character attachment in role-playing video games. *CyberPsychology & Behavior, 11*(4), 515–518.

Lieberman, D. A. (1997). Interactive video games for health promotion: Effects on knowledge, self-efficacy, social support, and health. In R. L. Street, W. R. Gold, & T. Manning (Eds.), *Health promotion and interactive technology: Theoretical applications and future directions* (pp. 103–120). Mahwah, NJ: Lawrence Erlbaum.

Lieberman, D. A. (2001). Management of chronic pediatric diseases with interactive health games: Theory and research findings. *Journal of Ambulatory Care Management, 24*(1), 26–38.

Lieberman, D. A. (2006). What can we learn from playing interactive games? In P. Vorderer & J. Bryant (Eds.), *Playing video games: Motives, responses, and consequences* (pp. 379–397). Mahwah, NJ: Lawrence Erlbaum.

Lieberman, D. A. (2009). Designing serious games for learning and health in informal and formal settings. In U. Ritterfeld, M. Cody, & P. Vorderer, P. (Eds.), *Serious games: Mechanisms and effects* (pp. 117–130). New York: Routledge, Taylor and Francis.

Lieberman, D. A., Chamberlin, B., Medina, Jr., E., Franklin, B. A., McHugh Sanner, B. M., & Vafiadis, D. K. (2011). The Power of Play: Innovations in Getting Active Summit 2011: A science panel proceedings report from the American Heart Association. *Circulation, 123*(21), 2507-2516.

Lim, S., & Reeves, B. (2009). Being in the game: Effects of avatar choice and point of view on psycho-physiological responses during play. *Media Psychology, 12*(4), 348-370.

Lustria, M. L. A., Cortese, J., Noar, S., & Glueckauf, R. L. (2009). Computer-tailored health interventions delivered over the web: Review and analysis of key components. *Patient Education and Counseling, 74*(2), 156-173.

Mackert, M., Kahlor, L., Tyler, D., & Gustafson, J. (2009). Designing e-health interventions for low health literate culturally diverse parents: Addressing the obesity epidemic. *Telemedicine and e-Health, 15*(7), 672-677.

MobiHealth News. (2011). *Mobile health Q1 2011: State of the industry.* Boston: MobiHealthNews.

Murphy, E. C., Carson, L., Neal, W., Baylis, C., Donley, D., & Yeater, R. (2009). Effects of an exercise intervention using Dance Dance Revolution on endothelial function and other risk factors in overweight children. *International Journal of Pediatric Obesity, 4,* 205-214.

Noar, S. M. (2006). A 10-year retrospective of research in health mass media campaigns: Where do we go from here? *Journal of Health Communication, 11*(1), 21-42.

Norman, G. J., Zabinski, M. F., Adams, M. A., Rosenberg, D. E., Yaroch, A. L., & Atienza, A. A. (2007). A review of ehealth interventions for physical activity and dietary behavior change. *American Journal of Preventive Medicine, 33*(4), 336-345.

Papastergiou, M. (2009). Exploring the potential of computer and video games for health and physical education: A literature review. *Computers & Education, 53,* 603-622.

Read, S. J., Miller, L. C., Appleby, P. R., Nwosu, M. E., Reynaldo, S., Lauren, A., et al. (2006). Socially optimized learning in a virtual environment: Reducing risky sexual behavior among men who have sex with men. *Human Communication Research, 32*(1), 1-34.

Ritterfeld, U., Cody, M., & Vorderer, P. (Eds.). (2009). *Serious games: Mechanisms and effects.* New York: Routledge, Taylor and Francis.

Thomas, R., Cahill, J., & Santilli, L. (1997). Using an interactive computer game to increase skill and self-efficacy regarding safer sex negotiation: Field test results. *Health Education & Behavior, 24,* 71-86.

Thompson, D., Baranowski, J., Cullen, K., & Baranowski, T. (2007). Development of a theory-based internet program promoting maintenance of diet and physical activity change to 8-year-old African-American girls. *Computers & Education, 48*(3), 446-459.

Tingen, M. S., Grimling, L. F., Bennett, G., Gibson, E. M., & Renew, M. M. (1997). A pilot study of pre-adolescents to evaluate a video game-based smoking prevention strategy. *Journal of Addictions Nursing, 9*(3), 118-124.

Unnithan, V. B., Houser, W., & Fernhall, B. (2005). Evaluation of the energy cost of playing a dance simulation video game in overweight and nonoverweight children and adolescents. *International Journal of Sports Medicine, 26,* 1-11.

Vorderer, P., & Bryant, J. (Eds.). (2006). *Playing video games: Motives, responses, and consequences.* Mahwah, NJ: Lawrence Erlbaum.

Walshe, D. G., Lewis, E. J., Kim, S. I., O'Sullivan, K., & Wiederhold, B. K. (2003). Exploring the use of computer games and virtual reality in exposure therapy for fear of driving following a motor vehicle accident. *CyberPsychology & Behavior, 6*(3), 329-334.

Wilkinson, N., Ang, R. P., & Goh, D. H. (2008). Online video game therapy for mental health concerns: A review. *International Journal of Social Psychiatry, 54*(4), 370-382.

Witte, K., Meyer, G., & Martell, D. (2001). *Effective health risk messages.* Thousand Oaks, CA: Sage.

Yee, N., Bailenson, J., & Ducheneaut, N. (2009). The proteus effect: Implications of transformed digital self-representation on online and offline behavior. *Communication Research, 36,* 285-312.

CHAPTER 20

Community Partnership Strategies in Health Campaigns

Neil Bracht and Ronald E. Rice

This chapter reviews lessons learned from numerous community studies and experiences that have employed a community involvement orientation. Commitment of campaign planners and professionals to community empowerment and capacity building not only adds to the material and human resources needed for any given campaign but also increases the likelihood that campaign results endure beyond the campaign or project period (Thompson & Winner, 1999). The chapter discusses four major themes: 1) community collaboration, 2) community change theory, 3) a five-stage model of basic strategies in planning and organizing at the community level, and 4) a summary of lessons learned and future research implications.

COMMUNITY COLLABORATION: PERSPECTIVES ON PARTNERSHIP APPROACHES

Looked at broadly, the concept of *citizen participation* is a fundamental aspect of civic life and democratic tradition. Numerous examples of community improvement are initiated through civic action and volunteer effort (sometimes with and sometimes without professional input). Some health problems clearly require a community orientation and involvement, such as for disaster preparedness and management (International Federation of Red Cross and Red Crescent Societies, n.d.). When disparate community resources and talents are mobilized for a specific campaign goal, the larger community can be energized for action, utilizing all institutional sectors (e.g., media, schools, work sites, government, business, civic groups, etc.). This intersecting integration allows for the incorporation of campaign goals throughout several sectors of daily community life.

This paradigm shift to community-wide or population-based models of intervention has fostered hundreds of community health promotion and research projects. Chapters in Bracht (1999) provide international examples, while Mittelmark (1999) reviewed many diverse projects. In keeping with the goal of community empowerment and capacity

289

building, many community-based projects use lay volunteers and leaders to deliver campaign interventions. Nearly 50% of Americans volunteer annually (Review and outlook, 1999). This citizen pool is an enormous resource of talent and energy and has been used to achieve many of the goals of the health promotion movement (Breslow, 1999), such as church group involvement in heart health campaigns (Lasater, Abrams, Artz, Beaudin, Cabrera, Elder et al., 1984) or local citizens advocating enforcement of alcohol sale ordinances for minors (Veblen-Mortenson, Rissel, Perry, Forster, Wolfson, & Finnegan, 1999). Basing a campaign within a local community context also generates opportunities for members to observe other members engaging in the promoted behaviors, leading to greater compliance with (here, televised and workplace) media messages, as in the case of a community-based, physical activity campaign in Yuma County, Arizona (Renger, Steinfelt, & Sydney, 2002).

The use of community-based organizations and associations to assist in broad public health work is, of course, not a new phenomenon (see Paisley & Atkin, Chapter 2). Starting in the late 1800s, block committees of local mothers were organized in support of early maternal and child health clinic goals (e.g., Hull House in Chicago). Also in Chicago, in the 1890s, two community organizations (one founded by women) worked for citywide reform of garbage collection (Knight, 2007). The National Citizens' Committee on Prevention of Tuberculosis worked closely with public health professionals to combat infectious diseases in the early 1900s. The National Mental Hygiene movement of the 1930s was a citizen-based group that was instrumental in achieving important reforms in the treatment of the mentally ill. Today, hundreds of voluntary health and social reform groups (e.g., The American Cancer Society, Mothers Against Drunk Drivers) bring outstanding volunteer resources to community improvement programs.

A very extensive and influential example of community-oriented campaigns was the Stanford Five City Project (1978 to 1992) to reduce cardiovascular disease. Underlying premises were that 1) attempts to change behavior must go beyond individuals and include the family, social, and cultural contexts, 2) affecting the interactions between personal and environmental factors requires intervention strategies in multiple community domains, and 3) all community members could benefit (Flora, 2001; Fortmann, Flora, Winkelby, Schooler, Taylor, & Farquhar, 1995; Schooler, Farquhar, Fortmann, & Flora, 1997).

In addition to standard campaign goals of 1) knowledge and attitude change, 2) behavior change (e.g., diet, activity, smoking cessation, and weight reduction), and 3) risk reduction (e.g., cholesterol level), it also included an educational program and extensive community mobilization. The community mobilization orientation applied principles of consensus development with community constituencies (e.g., to institutionalize education programs), social actions to mobilize community members (e.g., advocacy to create smoke-free environments), and social planning through use of community-collected objective data to guide system-wide change. The project's formative evaluation included an organizational needs analysis based on interviews with leaders, gatekeepers, and workplace personnel to identify community resources and readiness for change. Community organizations were then brought into project advisory groups, helped develop institutional programs, and promoted the project. Community organizations played a supplemental role as metachannels of health information via mechanisms of instrumental material support and affinity-oriented social support (Stephens, Rimal, & Flora, 2004).

Intervention components (each evaluated) included: 1) media (TV programs and PSAs, radio series, doctors' columns in newspapers, mass mailings, information booklets, and self-help kits), 2) more than 800 sessions of formal and informal, face-to-face education (delivered by community teachers and health educators), 3) workplace programs (distributing print materials, providing workshops, sponsoring contests, and measuring environmental risks), 4) educational programs involving schools, school administrators, teachers, students, and families, 5) implementation of health food programs and menu labeling in restaurants, cafeterias, and grocery stores, 6) health professionals who participated in training programs, received and distributed materials, and applied risk reduction programs in their practices, 7) contests in both work sites and the general community with incentives to change smoking, exercise, nutrition, and weight control behaviors, and 8) sustainability of program components through cooperative learning methods to community health educators.

In an application of this model in two South Carolina communities, Croft, Temple, Lankenau, Heath, Macera, and Eaker (1994) described how a comprehensive, community-based nutrition intervention to reduce risk of cardiovascular disease included classes, grocery store tours, a supermarket point-of-purchase program, a restaurant labeling program, speakers' bureaus, home study courses, work site nutrition programs, and mass media coverage (such as local radio and TV PSAs, talk shows, and newspaper articles).

Internationally, NGOs play similar roles in providing citizen input and leadership. One of the pioneering community-based studies to reduce heart disease, the North Karelia Project in Finland (Puska, Nissinen, Tuomilehto, Salonen, Koskela, McAlister, et al., 1985), utilized the local voluntary heart association as a major partner in conducting the campaign to inform the citizens of very high rates of heart-related mortality in the region. Other groups in agriculture and food processing were also involved. The Global Transport Knowledge Partnership (http://www.gtkp.com/theme.php?themepgid = 93) also reinforces the notion that community partnership in campaigns (here, road safety) avoids the limited effects and lack of engagement in traditional top-down public health campaigns, illustrated through case examples ranging from Bangladesh to Thailand and South Africa.

COMMUNITY CHANGE THEORY: MULTIPLE APPROACHES

Community Change Theory

Thompson and Kinne (1999) reviewed and integrated various change theories (e.g., behavioral, organizational, environmental, etc.), including both community and wider environmental and societal factors. A unifying construct in the application of social change theory to population health is the view of the community as a dynamic system in which change or alteration in one segment or institutional sector will have influence on one or more other sector(s) (a systems perspective; see also Rice and Foote, Chapter 5). The health promotion movement generally targets multiple sectors (churches, work sites, schools, etc.) of the entire community system in order to maximize intervention dissemination throughout the broader population. Community collaboration also helps to integrate the program in existing social and administrative structures (Bryant, McCormack Brown, McDermott, Forthofer, Bumpus, Calkins, et al., 2007). Of course, enhanced marketing or organizing strategies can simultaneously occur in selected sectors (e.g., special outreach efforts or involvement of Hispanic churches in the religious sectors of a city).

Behavioral and Advocacy Approaches

Many of the earlier health promotion projects focused on behavioral change outcomes only (e.g., smoking cessation, improved diet and exercise). The overall results have been mixed (see Fortmann et al., 1995; Kottke, 1995; Mittelmark, 1999; Seedhouse, 1997; Shea & Basch, 1990; Snyder & LaCroix, Chapter 8).

Recent social advocacy approaches (e.g., stronger enforcement of penalties in proven illegal tobacco or alcohol sales to minors) have offered alternative strategies (see Dorfman & Wallack, Chapter 23). For example, a community alliance in a small city in Western Australia developed a public health advocacy campaign to deal with increased road traffic (Gomm, Lincoln, Pikora, & Giles-Corti, 2006). It was successful in pressuring key stakeholders (via attracting public attention, reframing media messages, and providing alternative policies) to alter road policies. Increasingly, both behavioral and social advocacy approaches are being combined in community campaigns.

Social Marketing Approaches

Another trend is to combine social marketing with community campaigns (Grier & Bryant, 2005; Middlestadt, Schechter, Peyton, & Tjugum, 1997). The social marketing perspective highlights the audience's balance between barriers and benefits and the components of commitment, prompts, norms, effective messages, incentives, design, and evaluation (McKenzie-Mohr, 2010). This perspective involves five primary domains (Andreason, 2005; Kotler & Lee, 2007). The first is a philosophy of *exchange,* where consumers (or at-risk populations, campaign audiences, etc.) enter into a fair arrangement with providers and campaign sponsors so that both meet their needs. This means that campaign designers must understand those needs and construct messages and interventions that provide exchange value rather than imposing their values or presuming what constitutes a satisfying exchange. The second is an ongoing, *iterative research* strategy as needs, subgroups, and external conditions change over time. The third is the *marketing mix,* or the appropriate emphasis upon the combination of the 4 Ps: *product benefits* (perceptions, uses, attributes), *price* (including all individual, social, and institutional barriers to change), *place* (the infrastructure and social system enabling or preventing one from engaging the service, product, or behavior, including training, sales, advice, etc.), and *promotion* (including not just the traditional campaign message but also user education, interpersonal support, public relations, conferences, etc., provided through appropriate channels and media). Finally, social marketing emphasizes the importance of *positioning* the message, product, or service within the context of competing messages, products, services, attitudes, fears, expectations, and norms (such as from friends or advertisements advocating cigarette smoking) and oriented toward relevant and changing audience segments.

The combined principles from community-based campaigns and social marketing are being applied to community-based prevention marketing (CBPM) projects such as the University of Florida's Prevention Research Center's program to prevent initiation of smoking and alcohol consumption among middle-school students in one county, with parents, school staff, and youth-oriented community organizations as secondary audiences (Bryant, Forthofer, Brown, Landis, & McDermott, 2000; Bryant et al., 2007; Bryant, McCormack Brown, McDermott, Debate, Alfonso, Baldwin, et al., 2009). This project team essentially helps bring together and train community partners and coalitions in social marketing concepts and practices, but the community's advisory committee leads the stages. Another project extended the national media campaign promoting physical activity (the VERB™ campaign during 2002 through 2006) by developing a Summer Scorecard (http://www.cdc.gov/youthcampaign/partners/scorecard/scorecard.htm) as one way to reduce childhood obesity. The program provided tweens a card with 24 physical activity squares, upon which an authorized adult could confirm each activity. Upon completion, they could turn in their card for prizes (also related to physical activity). The program also aimed to increase awareness of activity possibilities and provide a handy way for parents to remind their children to exercise. From 2002 to 2007, surveys involving from 2,600 to 4,000 respondents showed that awareness of the Summer Scorecard rose from 35% to 79%, and the number of scorecards submitted went from 355 to 1,720, although completion of the scorecard rose only from 25% to 30%.

Community-Based Social Marketing (http://cbsm.com) is an online guide describing how to use community-based social marketing to design and evaluate programs to foster sustainable behavior in the areas of agriculture and conservation, energy, transportation, waste and pollution, and water (see also McKenzie-Mohr, 2010).

BASIC STRATEGIES IN ORGANIZING COMMUNITY CAMPAIGNS: A FIVE-STAGE MODEL

We now consider the stages and key tasks of community mobilization and campaign implementation using a five-stage model, summarizing Bracht, Kingsbury, and Rissel's (1999) detailed description and the many activities associated with each stage. It should be noted that these stages are overlapping, and some tasks may need to be repeated in later stages. For example, planning tasks for durability of effort should begin in the analysis phase, but progress and finalization of plans need to be assessed in the maintenance and dissemination stages as well.

Stage One: Conduct a Community Analysis

Commitment to community participation in campaigns requires above all else a knowledge of the assets, capacity, and history of a local community. While all communities share certain definable functions (e.g., social participation, social control, etc.), a careful mapping of the community brings forth the unique qualities, norms, and modes of organization in each community (McKnight, 1988), allowing realistic matching of goals with citizen readiness, expectations, and resources. The product of community analysis is a dynamic profile that blends health and illness statistics with demographic, political, and sociocultural factors.

Key Task 1: Define the Community

Community is a term that has different meanings and interpretations. Hillery (1955) studied 94 definitions of community and found that 73% of the definitions agreed that social interaction, area, and common ties were frequently found features. Rissel and Bracht (1999) discuss the implications of using differing conceptual approaches to the study of a community. Clarity about target audience or geographical boundaries, and so on, must be achieved early and in consultation with local representatives. If more than one community in a region is to be involved, patterns of cooperation, commerce, jurisdictions, and regulations among and across the communities may need special analysis.

Key Task 2: Initiate Data Collection

Community analysis requires the collection and analysis of a wide range of data in order to achieve a comprehensive profile of the campaign area or target group. Rissel and Bracht (1999) summarize these various data needs—generalized community characteristics, structure and history; health–wellness outcomes assessment; health risk profile (behavioral, social, and environmental risks); community health promotion survey; and specialized studies (gatekeepers, influentials)—and the likely sources of such information. In a community approach, citizens and local organizations are directly involved in this study process. Some of the information required may have already been compiled locally or is available from past community projects in the area.

Key Task 3: Assess Community Capacity and Readiness for Change

A primary assessment focus in community-wide health promotion programs is the study of social institutions or organizational sectors (education, health, recreation business and labor, etc.) and the possibilities for coordinating community-wide programs of health action. Leadership persons are often the source of this information, and their willingness to cooperate is another indicator of community support or readiness for program initiation. Rissel and Bracht (1999) discuss techniques and approaches used to study leadership patterns. Community readiness for change can be measured by a combination of factors, such as past history of cooperative community action, degree of support and enthusiasm among community influentials for the current project, willingness to commit organizational resources, local skill level (e.g., quit smoking counseling) of lay citizens and professionals available for use in the campaign, and the presence of motivated advocates or visionaries supporting the project.

Stage Two: Design and Initiation of a Campaign

A core planning group of citizens and professionals will usually begin the process of establishing a more permanent organizational structure (e.g., coalition) to elicit and coordinate broader citizen support and involvement. This group's responsibilities may also include calling public attention to the data analysis and identified community needs, writing a mission statement, and selecting a community-based project coordinator. Some preliminary decisions will likely have to be made about campaign objectives and initial intervention design(s). Later, these decisions will be approved by the permanent citizen organization.

Key Task 1: Develop an Organizational Structure for Collaboration

There are several alternative structures for organizing community involvement and participation, including an advisory board, coalition, lead agency, informal network, and so on, each with pros and cons (Thompson & Winner, 1999). Sometimes, existing agencies or coalitions can be used as collaboration structures for campaigns, thus avoiding the start-up time required for new organizations. The type of structure chosen should be based on community factors such as culture and history of change efforts, past decision-making styles, and any competing events or programs. Final choice of organizational structure usually rests with the community and its representatives. However, some funding agencies often prescribe in advance the community structure most preferred or recommended (e.g., coalition). This can be risky because one model seldom fits all communities, and citizen-based structures are dynamic, with organizational patterns often evolving into new or modified arrangements.

Coalitions involving multiple community groups and health organizations have become increasingly popular structures for implementing community health promotion efforts. *Coalition* has been defined as an organization of individuals representing diverse organizations, factions, or constituencies who agree to work together in order to achieve a goal, often in response to a specific issue or legislative goal. The major advantage of the coalition is that it involves a breadth and diversity of membership that may make, at times, for strange bedfellows but can cut across ideologies and constituencies in order to achieve results not attainable by more narrowly focused groups. Bracht and colleagues (1999) reviewed the literature on coalition effectiveness and found the following functions important to overall coalition productivity: leadership, management, communication, conflict resolution, perception of fairness, shared decision making, and perceived benefits versus costs (see also Dluhy & Kravitz, 1990). The Florida Kidcare campaign (Ray, White, Cannon, Powen, & O'Rourke, 2006) created coalitions involving child advocacy groups, community partners, and government agencies to inform families about a very short time frame in 2005 for enrolling their children in a state health insurance program. It succeeded in enrolling almost five times the average for any prior enrollment period.

Key Task 2: Increase Community Participation and Membership in the Organization

The core planning group contacts individuals to assess interest in serving on task forces or the executive committee of the new organization. Such collaboration may raise issues of both visible and invisible power relations, which emerged during a process evaluation of a community public health media campaign on HIV prevention for women (Champeau & Shaw, 2002). Thus, such issues should be raised and discussed very early on.

The experience and skill of a paid coordinator or community organizer is frequently used in health promotion programs. The person employed for this purpose must understand how change occurs in communities and must be knowledgeable about local history and values. Past experience in facilitating organizational collaboration, including good management skills, and in deploying volunteers is critical.

Key Task 3: Develop Early Intervention Design and Plans

During this phase of work, collaboration between community groups and outside professionals usually begins on intervention goals and design. A review of data collected from the analysis stage is a good beginning point for such deliberations. A heart disease prevention intervention(s) will require a close look at prevalence and incidence data to answer questions such as what the focus of intervention work should be (e.g., nutrition education, exercise, smoking cessation, rapid treatment). A task force of citizens and professionals can usually develop a preliminary plan within two to three months. The plan should include a preliminary evaluation and monitoring strategy as well. Pirie (1999) (and the evaluation chapters in this volume) provides a helpful guide to evaluation strategies in community-based health promotion. Later, the intervention goals and objectives will need the approval and support of the wider community group as mentioned above.

Stage Three: Campaign Implementation

Implementation turns theory and ideas into action, translating design into effectively operating programs. Organizations and citizens are mobilized and involved in the planning of a sequential set of activities that will accomplish campaign objectives. For example, a project in Haiti included community members in the design and implementation of disaster preparedness information campaigns through 22 local civil protection committees, each receiving technical and funding support during 2003 and 2004 (http://www.comminit. com/node/277293). Overall, these campaigns developed both public awareness as well as capacity building and contributed to developing a culture of safety.

Written intervention action plans with specific timelines have been shown to be critical forerunners of successful change efforts (Fawcett, Paine-Andrews, Francisco, Schultz, Richter, Lewis et al., 1995). Intervention cost estimates should be included in the plan, along with monitoring and feedback strategies. The key element in this stage is determining priority intervention activities and focusing efforts for maximum impact. Based on experience from other community projects, it has been learned that some community members may want to rush the intervention implementation process. There is a tendency to want to jump in with both feet and get the project going. Organizers need to channel enthusiasm, helping task forces and work groups to select, evaluate, and plan for best practices in implementation. While such "delays" can dampen the enthusiasm of more action-oriented volunteers, it is probably better to have to deal with this motivational issue than to see interest and commitment to the project dampened by early reports of negative results of interventions caused by poorly operationalized and delivered campaign strategies.

Key Task 1: Clarify Roles and Responsibilities of All Partners

Complex community campaigns require the coordinated effort of many people and resources. Role clarification at the outset is essential if the project is to unfold smoothly and systematically. For example, in a community stop-smoking campaign, how will the role of the local Heart Association be coordinated with the ongoing antismoking activities of the American Lung Association? A written understanding of intervention roles is often helpful, especially in large, coalition-led programs. A formal process called *responsibility charting* (explained in detail in Bracht, 1999, p. 99) helps participants to review some 30 tasks associated with campaign implementation—such as determine goals and priorities, community and public relations, staff hiring, design evaluation strategies, plan for durability, and so on—and decide on which person or group will be accountable for completion of required activities.

Key Task 2: Provide Orientation and Training

Effective citizen and volunteer involvement usually requires some level of additional training and skill development. For example, special classes in smoking cessation techniques for community professionals may be in order. Such training adds to community capacity building and also enhances the likelihood of the durability of ongoing campaign and community objectives.

Key Task 3: Refine Intervention Plan to Local Situation

No matter how good an intervention looks on paper or reported in the literature, when it is implemented in a community, it must speak that community's language (Vincent, Clearle, Johnson, & Sharpe, 1988). The approaches and messages must be acceptable to the community. For example, Ramirez (1997) and colleagues have developed a most useful training manual on mass media messages and community outreach for minority groups. Their work shows how to better integrate community values into the programs, materials, and messages of the campaign.

Key Task 4: Generate Broad Citizen Participation

Throughout the implementation process, continuing efforts to reach out to people and encourage their participation is required. Special attention to ways of involving minority communities may be needed if there is a history of noninclusion or lack of participation in health projects. Interviews with key community minority participants will help in this process and shed light on current or past difficulties with trust and collaboration (Kone & Sullivan, 1998).

Stage Four: Program Maintenance and Consolidation

During this stage, the citizen organization should be developing a solid foundation and acceptance in the community. Problems in implementation (e.g., media misses coverage of certain key events) will obviously have been encountered, but an indicator of community capacity building will be the ability to overcome and improve future intervention activities. Campaign program elements should be more fully incorporated into the established structures of the community (e.g., exercise programs become a regular part of work site culture). Task forces of the local citizen organization need to reassess past efforts and determine any new tasks or directions of the program.

Key Task 1: Maintain High Levels of Volunteer Effort

Turnover of volunteers and even of paid staff is to be expected in multiyear projects. To counteract this, one needs to establish a plan to identify, recruit, and involve new people in the project on an ongoing basis. New sources of energy and commitment can be helpful to volunteers who may be experiencing some burnout characteristics. Typically, a small percentage of individuals provides much of a project's volunteer needs, and such projects may experience tensions between their needs and those volunteers' expectations, especially when there are racial differences (Boyle & Sawyer, 2010). Florin and Wandersman (1990) found that participation was more prevalent in people who were concerned about their neighborhood, had more experience in community leadership, and felt that other competent colleagues could be engaged in order to reach project goals. Peer support and morale are critical factors in group cohesion and continued participation. Appreciation letters to volunteers, celebratory luncheons, and training retreats are ways of enhancing volunteer morale and commitment to the project.

Key Task 2: Continue to Integrate Intervention Activities Into Community Networks

Integration of intervention activities into established community structures creates a broad context for the acceptance and adoption of health-promoting behaviors and norms. In one Midwest heart disease prevention project, local churches initiated a monthly exercise Sunday project into their routine service schedule. The project encouraged families to leave the car at home and walk, bike, or jog to church. Key influentials and stakeholders often assist in this kind of organizational adoption and integration of programs. For more discussion of this process, see Rissel, Finnegan, and Bracht (1995).

Stage Five: Dissemination and Durability

Communities and citizens need to receive clear, succinct messages describing what has been accomplished and what continuing effort may be required. Such messages are reinforcing when community influentials and decision makers, as opposed to professional experts, are involved in their presentation. How this dissemination process occurs is a basic element of a durability plan along with a vision for future programming.

Key Task 1: Reassess Campaign Activities and Outcomes

Final results of campaigns may not always be available in time for citizens and communities to act on future directions. Processes or formative evaluations that have been done during the campaign (for example, participation rates in health-risk screening programs, etc.) can help assist the project group in reassessing interventions that have worked and those that have experienced difficulty. Steps in implementation can be retraced and ana-lyzed. A report to the community should be drafted and submitted to the overall citizen group for review and comment. When complete, this report on campaign results becomes the foundation of a durability plan.

The CBPM project team discussed earlier evaluated the CBPM approach (Bryant et al., 2000, 2007) through process and impact evaluation. The process evaluation assessed the feasibility of the elements, community perceptions of the value of the elements, and the extent to which the project was managed in accord with community-based research and action. The impact evaluation assessed changes in community competence, durability, and sustainability; control and social capital; the use of social and prevention marketing in other community problems; and the extent to which the smoking prevention objectives were met. They also explained lessons learned, involving constituting the lead agency and coalition board, awareness of community profile information by board members, tensions and decision processes in selecting the risk and preventive behavior, increasing flexibility in applying policies, varying expertise and commitment by members, develop-ing a valid marketing strategy, finding an appropriate company or agency to develop the materials, assuring sufficient board diversity, and requirements for sufficiently rigorous mixed-methods evaluation that did not exceed community members' patience and under-standing (Bryant et al., 2007). Based upon these CBPM projects, Bryant and colleagues (2007) developed a revised nine-stage campaign process: Mobilize the community, develop a community profile, select the target behavior, enhance community capac-ity, conduct formative evaluation, develop a marketing strategy, develop the program, implement the program, track and evaluate, and provide feedback and adjust the stages (Fig. 1, p. 156).

Key Task 2: Refine the Durability Plan

The citizen group needs to address several important questions: What has been accom-plished to date, and what do citizens desire to continue? What is the vision of the project for the future? What human resources would be required to continue interventions or modi-fications of same? Are any new skills required for the future, and what kinds of trainings might be required to finalize community capacity for maintaining such efforts? Finally, what kind of citizen structure will work for the future? The process of answering these questions may take several weeks or months, so it should be started as soon as possible.

Key Task 3: Update the Community Analysis

Part of durability planning may require updating the community analysis and profile. This involves looking for changes that have occurred in leadership, resources, and orga-nizational relationships in the community. Key community members, opinion leaders, and organizations in a community will change over time. Reviewing these changes may point to a need for new collaborators and for efforts to recruit new board and task force members. Based on this new review of resources, programs are modified, expanded, or abandoned. Thompson and Winner (1999) developed a strategic planning model to be used by communities that wish to develop a detailed plan for durability of project effort.

Conclusion

The participatory community approach to campaigns in health promotion seeks to stimulate and fuse citizen energies, interests, and resources into a collective response for change. Often, this is done in collaboration with professional or research groups, but the decision-making role of community groups should remain paramount. The theories and principles of community organization and empowerment (Minkler & Wallerstein, 1997) are central to this approach.

Community-based campaigns are taking good advantage of the Internet to provide online tools and resources. For example, The Community Guide (http://www.thecommunityguide.org/index.html) of the CDC provides systematic evaluations, recommendations, evidence, and materials (including slides and promotional materials) based on more than 200 public health interventions in 18 topic areas. The Community Tool Box from the University of Kansas (http://ctb.ku.edu/en/default.aspx) offers extensive materials on all aspects of community campaigns, with 46 chapters and 300 sections including models for promoting community health and development, community assessment and agenda setting, promoting interest and participation, developing a strategic plan and organizational structure, leadership and management, designing or adapting community interventions, implementing community interventions, community building, effective advocacy, evaluating community programs, maintaining quality, generating and sustaining financial resources, social marketing, program sustainability, and research design and data collection. The Community Initiative (http://www.comminit.com/en/about-global.html) is an example of an online metacampaign community, which provides a wide array of resources for people and organizations applying communication for economic and social development change.

The Benton Foundation (http://www.benton.org/node/6173) applies its focus on community media and telecommunication to its New Routes to Community Health program, which uses local media to improve new immigrants' health. The Obesity Prevention Program of the CDC, University of North Carolina (http://www.center-trt.org/index.cfm?fa = opstrategies.pa &page = community) supports community-wide campaigns that engage mass media, social support programs, individual education, health fairs, physical activity events, and environmental changes to increase physical activity. Earthworks (http://www.earthworksaction.org/communitysupport.cfm) collaborates with local campaigns and community-based organizations concerned with implications and risks of proposed or existing mines. The Centers for Disease Control and Prevention (2009) provides very detailed guidelines and resources (what they call procedural guidance) for a range of community-based campaigns and interventions related to HIV/AIDS.

The key factors that seem to contribute most to successful citizen mobilization and community collaboration in campaigns, based on a wide range of national and international studies and experiences (e.g., see Bracht, 1999; Hopkins, Briss, Ricard, Husten, Carande-Kulis, Fielding et al., 2001; Norris, Nichols, Caspersen, Glasgow, Engelgau, Jack, Jr., et al., 2002; Shults, Elder, Sleet, Nichols, Alao, Carande-Kulis et al., 2001; Thompson, Corbet, Bracht, & Pehacek, 1993; Zaza, Sleet, Thompson, Sosin, Bolen, & Task Force on Community Preventive Services, 2001), include:

1. Early commitment of project leaders to partnership and community development approaches should be established.

2. Decision-making authority of citizen groups should be clearly defined. Resources to carry out designated roles and functions must be available and adequate and include skill development training opportunities.

3. A strong volunteer management and training program must be in place at the start of a campaign. This includes things such as regularly scheduled performance assessments, clearly stated time commitments, and planned recognition and celebratory events.

4. Timely use of conflict resolution strategies should be implemented when disagreements arise over project goals, research objectives, or implementation issues.

References

Andreason, A. R. (2005). *Social marketing in the 21st century.* Thousand Oaks, CA: Sage.

Boyle, M. P., & Sawyer, J. K. (2010). Defining volunteering for community campaigns: An exploration of race, self perceptions, and campaign practices. *Journal of Community Practice, 18*(1), 40–57.

Bracht, N. (Ed.). (1999). *Health promotion at the community level: New advances* (2nd ed.). Thousand Oaks, CA: Sage.

Bracht, N., Kingsbury, L., & Rissel, C. (1999). A five-stage community organization model for health promotion: Empowerment and partnership strategies. In N. Bracht (Ed.), *Health promotion at the community level: New advances* (2nd ed., pp. 83–104). Thousand Oaks, CA: Sage.

Breslow, L. (1999). Foreword. In N. Bracht (Ed.), *Health promotion at the community level: New advances* (2nd ed., pp. ix–xii). Thousand Oaks, CA: Sage.

Bryant, C. A., McCormack Brown, K., McDermott, R. J., Debate, R. D., Alfonso, M. A., Baldwin, J. L., et al. (2009). Community-based prevention marketing: A new framework for health promotion interventions. In R. DiClemente, R. A. Crosby, & M. C. Kegler (Eds.), *Emerging theories in health promotion practice and research: Strategies for improving public health* (2nd ed., pp. 331–356). San Francisco: Jossey-Bass.

Bryant, C. A., McCormack Brown, K., McDermott, R. J., Forthofer, M. S., Bumpus, E. C., Calkins, S., et al. (2007). Community-based prevention marketing: Organizing a community for health behavior intervention. *Health Promotion Practice, 8,* 154–163.

Bryant, C., Forthofer, M., Brown, K. Mc., Landis, D., & McDermott, R. (2000). Community-based prevention marketing: The next steps in disseminating behavior change. *American Journal of Health Behavior, 24*(1), 61–68.

Centers for Disease Control and Prevention. (2009). *Provisional procedural guidance for community-based organizations.* Retrieved July 15, 2011, from http://www.cdc.gov/hiv/topics/prev_prog/ahp/resources/guidelines/pro_guidance/index.htm

Champeau, D. A., & Shaw, S. M. (2002). Power, empowerment, and critical consciousness in community collaboration: Lessons from an advisory panel for an HIV awareness media campaign for women. *Women and Health, 36*(3), 31–50.

Croft, J. B., Temple, S. P., Lankenau, B., Heath, G. W., Macera, C. A., Eaker, E. D., et al. (1994). Community intervention and trends in dietary fat consumption among black and white adults. *Journal of the American Dietetic Association, 94*(11), 1284–1290.

Dluhy, M., & Kravitz, S. (1990). *Building coalitions in the human services.* Newbury Park, CA: Sage.

Fawcett, S. B., Paine-Andrews, A., Francisco, V. T., Schultz, J. A., Richter, K. P., Lewis, R. K., et al. (1995). Using empowerment theory in collaborative partnerships for community health and development. *American Journal of Community Psychology, 23,* 677–697.

Flora, J. (2001). The Stanford Community studies: Campaigns to reduce cardiovascular disease. In R. E. Rice & C. K. Atkin (Eds.), *Public communication campaigns* (3rd ed., pp. 193–213). Thousand Oaks, CA: Sage.

Florin, P., & Wandersman, A. (1990). An introduction to citizen participation, voluntary organizations, and community development: Insights for empowerment through research. *American Journal of Community Psychology, 18*(1), 41–53.

Fortmann, S., Flora, J., Winkleby, M., Schooler, C., Taylor, C., & Farquhar, J. (1995). Community intervention trials: Reflections on the Stanford five-city experience. *American Journal of Epidemiology, 142,* 576–586.

Gomm, M., Lincoln, P., Pikora, T., & Giles-Corti, B. (2006). Planning and implementing a community-based public health advocacy campaign: A transport case study from Australia. *Health Promotion International, 21*(4), 284–292.

Grier, S., & Bryant, C. A. (2005). Social marketing in public health. *Annual Review Public Health, 26,* 319–339.

Hillery, G. A. (1955). Definitions of community: Areas of agreement. *Rural Sociology, 20*(2), 118–127.

Hopkins, D. P., Briss, P. A., Ricard, C. J., Husten, C. G., Carande-Kulis, V. G., Fielding, J. E., et al. (2001). Reviews of evidence regarding interventions to reduce tobacco use and exposure to environmental tobacco smoke. *American Journal of Preventive Medicine, 20*(2S), 16–66.

International Federation of Red Cross and Red Crescent Societies. (n.d.). Retrieved July 15, 2011, from http://www.ifrc.org/en/what-we-do/disaster-management/

Knight, L. W. (2007). Garbage and democracy: The Chicago community organizing campaign of the 1890s. *Journal of Community Practice, 14*(3), 7–27.

Kone, A., & Sullivan, M. (1998). *The community interview project: Promoting collaboration between communities and researchers.* Seattle, WA: King County Department of Public Health.

Kotler, P., & Lee, N. (2007). *Social marketing: Influence behaviors for good* (3rd ed.). Thousand Oaks, CA: Sage.

Kottke, T. (1995). Community-based heart disease prevention: The American experience. In P. Puska, J. Tuomilehto, A. Nissinen, & E. Vartiaianen (Eds.), *The North Karelia Project: 20-year results and experiences* (pp. 331–343). Helsinki, Sweden: National Public Health Institute.

Lasater, T., Abrams, D., Artz, L., Beaudin, P., Cabrera, L., Elder, J., et al. (1984). Lay volunteer delivery of a community-based cardiovascular risk factor change program: The Pawtucket experiment. In J. D. Matarazzo, S. H. Weiss, J. A. Herd, N. E. Miller, & S. W. Weiss (Eds.), *Behavioral health: A handbook of health enhancement and disease prevention* (pp. 1166–1170). New York: Wiley.

McKenzie-Mohr, D. (2010). *Fostering sustainable behavior: An introduction to community-based social marketing* (4th ed.). Gabriola Island, British Columbia: New Society Publishers.

McKnight, J. (1988). *Mapping community capacity.* Evanston, IL: Center for Urban Affairs and Policy Research, Northwestern University.

Middlestadt, S., Schechter, C., Peyton, J., & Tjugum, B. (1997). Community involvement in health planning: Lessons learned from practicing social marketing in a context of community control, participation, and ownership. In M. Goldberg, M. Fishbein, & S. Middlestadt (Eds.), *Social marketing: Theoretical and practical perspectives* (pp. 291–312). Mahwah, NJ: Lawrence Erlbaum.

Minkler, M., & Wallerstein, N. (1997). Improving health through community organization and community building. In K. Glanz, F. M. Lewis, & B. K. Rimer (Eds.), *Health behaviour and health education: Theory, research and practice* (2nd ed.). San Francisco: Jossey-Bass.

Mittelmark, M. (1999). Health promotion at the community-wide level: Lessons from diverse perspectives. In N. Bracht (Ed.), *Health promotion at the community level: New advances* (2nd ed., pp. 3–28). Thousand Oaks, CA: Sage.

Norris, S. L., Nichols, P. J., Caspersen, C. J., Glasgow, R. E., Engelgau, M. M., Jack, Jr., L., et al. (2002). Increasing diabetes self-management education in community settings: A systematic review. *American Journal of Preventive Medicine, 22*(4S), 39–66.

Pirie, P. (1999). Evaluating community health promotion programs: Basic questions and approaches. In N. Bracht (Ed.), *Health promotion at the community level: New advances* (2nd ed., pp. 127–134). Thousand Oaks, CA: Sage.

Puska, P., Nissinen, A., Tuomilehto, J., Salonen, J. T., Koskela, K., McAlister, A., et al. (1985). The community-based strategy to prevent coronary heart disease: Conclusions from the ten years of the North Karelia Project. *Annual Review of Public Health, 6,* 147–193.

Ramirez, A. (1997). *En accion training manual.* (NIH Pub. No 97–4260). Bethesda, MD: National Cancer Institute.

Ray, J., White, M., Cannon, P., Bowen, C., & O'Rourke, K. (2006). Implementing the Florida Kidcare open enrollment communications campaign: A framework for mobilizing community partners to reduce the number of uninsured children. *International Quarterly of Community Health Education, 26*(4), 365–377.

Renger, R., Steinfelt, V., & Sydney, L. (2002). Assessing the effectiveness of a community-based media campaign targeting physical inactivity. *Family & Community Health: The Journal of Health Promotion & Maintenance, 25*(3), 18–30.

Review and outlook. (1999). *Wall Street Journal,* December 17, p. 17.

Rissel, C., & Bracht, N. (1999). Assessing community needs, resources and readiness: Building on strengths. In N. Bracht (Ed.), *Health promotion at the community level: New advances* (2nd ed., pp. 59–71). Thousand Oaks, CA: Sage.

Rissel, C., Finnegan Jr., J., & Bracht, N. (1995). Evaluating quality and sustainability: Issues and insights from the Minnesota Heart Health Program. *Health Promotion International, 10*(3), 199–207.

Schooler, C., Farquhar, J. W., Fortmann, S. P., & Flora, J. A. (1997). Synthesis of findings and issues from community prevention trials. *Annals of Epidemiology, 7*(S7), 54–68.

Seedhouse, D. (1997). *Health promotion: Philosophy, prejudice and practice.* Chichester, England: Wiley.

Shea, S., & Basch, C. (1990). A review of five major community-based cardiovascular disease prevention programs. Part I: Rationale, design, and theoretical framework. *American Journal of Health Promotion, 4,* 202–213.

Shults, R. A., Elder, R. W., Sleet, D. A., Nichols, J. I., Alao, M. O., Carande-Kulis, V. G., et al. (2001). Reviews of evidence regarding interventions to reduce alcohol-impaired driving. *American Journal of Preventive Medicine, 21*(4S), 66–88.

Stephens, K. K., Rimal, R. N., & Flora, J. (2004). Expanding the reach of health campaigns: Community organizations as meta-channels for the dissemination of health information. *Journal of Health Communication, 9,* 97–111.

Thompson, B., Corbett, K., Bracht, N., & Pehacek, T. (1993). Lessons learned from the mobilization of communities in the Community Intervention Trial for Smoking Cessation (COMMIT). *Health Promotion International, 8,* 69–83.

Thompson, B., & Kinne, S. (1999). Social change theory: Applications to community health. In N. Bracht (Ed.), *Health promotion at the community level: New advances* (2nd ed., pp. 29–46). Thousand Oaks, CA: Sage.

Thompson, B., & Winner, C. (1999). Durability of community intervention programs: Definitions, empirical studies and strategic planning. In N. Bracht (Ed.), *Health promotion at the community level: New advances* (2nd ed., pp. 137–154). Thousand Oaks, CA: Sage.

Veblen-Mortenson, S., Rissel, C., Perry, C., Forster, J., Wolfson, M., & Finnegan, Jr., J. (1999). Lessons learned from project Northland: Community organization in rural communities. In N. Bracht (Ed.), *Health promotion at the community level: New advances* (2nd ed., pp. 105–117). Thousand Oaks, CA: Sage.

Vincent, M., Clearle, A., Johnson, C., & Sharpe, P. (1988). *Reducing unintended adolescent pregnancy through school-community educational interventions: A South Carolina case study.* Atlanta, GA: U.S. Department of Health and Human Services, Public Health Service, Centers for Disease Control.

Zaza, S., Sleet, D. A., Thompson, R. S., Sosin, D. M., Bolen, J. C., & Task Force on Community Preventive Services. (2001). Reviews of evidence regarding interventions to increase use of child safety seats. *American Journal of Preventive Medicine, 21*(4S), 31–47.

Closing the Gaps in Practice and in Theory

Evaluation of the Scrutinize HIV Campaign in South Africa

D. Lawrence Kincaid, Richard Delate, Douglas Storey,
and Maria Elena Figueroa

Authors' Note: The authors acknowledge the support of the U.S. Agency for International Development for financial assistance and encouragement for the programs described in this chapter. Special thanks to Johns Hopkins Health and Education in South Africa (JHHESA) for sharing its experiences and insights about implementing the campaign. We also would like to acknowledge the leadership and contribution of JHHESA's director Patrick Coleman. Thanks also to the many partners who generously gave their time: CADRE, Mat©hboxology, Levi's®, Mediology, DramAidE, Lighthouse Foundation, and the Western Cape Department of Health. Finally, thanks to Timothy Mah (USAID/Washington, DC), the General Population and Youth HIV Prevention Technical Working Group, and to Wendy Benzerga and Nellie Gqwaru (USAID/South Africa) for their assistance.

When applied to public health, communication campaigns need a conceptual framework that moves away from the idea of a one-time, one-way communication act to an iterative process that unfolds over an extended period of time. The health of a population involves a set of behaviors and social norms that are interrelated in complex ways. More than one campaign is usually required. The conventional definition specifies that its purpose is "(1) to generate specific outcomes or effects (2) in a relatively large number of individuals, (3) usually within a specified period of time, and (4) through an organized set of communication activities" (Rogers & Storey, 1987, p. 821). The purpose of this chapter is to expand on this definition by treating a single campaign as just one phase in a series of incrementally improved campaigns that eventually—if implemented and evaluated effectively—improve the health of a population.

Evaluation is not simply a matter of measuring the outcomes when the campaign is over (see Valente & Kwan, Chapter 6). If conceptualized as a *dialogue* with the audience, then a campaign can be reconceptualized as a self-correcting feedback process defined dynamically as a diminishing series of under- and-overcorrections converging on a goal (Kincaid, 2009; Rogers & Kincaid, 1981). Effective communication begins with the audience and continues over time as a process of mutual adjustment and convergence (Piotrow, Kincaid, Rimon, II, & Rinehart 1997). Formative research and pretesting of messages is a dialogue between members of the audience and those who design and conduct the campaign (Atkin & Freimuth, Chapter 4). It gives the audience a chance to speak first—to provide valuable information about their own situations, beliefs and values, current and past behavior, and hopes and dreams for a better life. Monitoring research tells us who and how many are listening or otherwise participating. Impact evaluation measures how many have been affected, in what ways, and why. The latter are required to improve the next iteration of communication. This process is designed to reduce the gap between the initial state of the audience and its desired state as specified by the audience itself and the objectives of the campaign (Rice & Foote, Chapter 5).

The notion of a diminishing gap rather than a closed gap implies that health communication is never perfect. Inherent imperfections (errors) can be reduced with effective research (i.e., *systematic listening* to the audience; see also Dervin & Foreman-Wernet, Chapter 10). When evaluation is theory driven rather than just methods driven (Chen, 1990), then measurement of the causal pathways applied to the design and evaluation of a campaign yields a different but related error, namely, the quantitative residual from the fit of the theory to the data. The size of this residual helps determine if the observed effects can be causally attributed to the campaign. With a valid causal inference, cost-effectiveness estimates are feasible, as are recommendations to improve the next campaign. Improvement means a reduction in the error communicating with the audience and a reduction in the error of the theoretical model used to design and estimate the impact of a campaign.

To illustrate how this framework can be applied, we use a case study of a recent communication campaign for HIV prevention in South Africa. The description of this case follows a new model of the campaign design and evaluation. The model is theory based, so we also present a new metatheory of health communication for campaign design and evaluation.

THEORY-BASED COMMUNICATION CYCLE OF EFFECTIVE HEALTH COMMUNICATION PROGRAMS

Figure 21.1 presents a six-stage model of the communication design, implementation, and evaluation cycle. Because theory plays a role in all six stages, it is treated as the central core of the model. There is no real beginning to this cycle; previous communication and its evaluation, along with new formative research, should both be used to design a new campaign. Several iterations of this cycle are usually required to accomplish the desired health objectives. The details of each stage and how they work together to produce an effective campaign are illustrated by means of the case study described below.

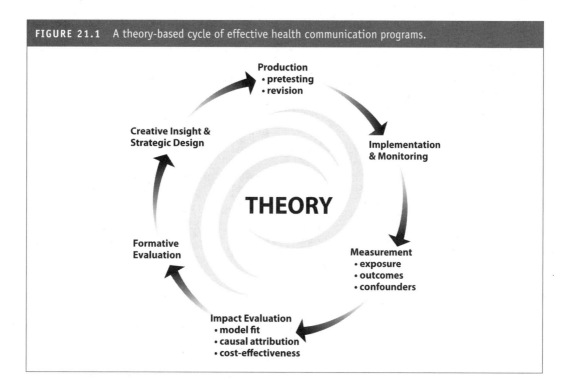

FIGURE 21.1   A theory-based cycle of effective health communication programs.

Strategic communication is based on facts and theories integrated by a visionary design that affects the most likely sources and barriers to social and behavioral change (Piotrow & Kincaid, 2001). But, which facts and which theory? What is the most likely source of change?

Figure 21.2 presents a metatheory of health communication that summarizes the contribution of a wide range of communication, social, and behavioral change theories and their interrelationships. Which one to apply depends on the nature of the problem and the ability to use them creatively. From left to right, the model provides a descriptive, explanatory, and predictive model of change that can be applied to practice and to theory-based evaluation research. Communication design, however, should move from right to left, starting with the nature of the health issue and working backward to the changes in behavior, ideation, and the communication approaches that are expected to have the desired effect.

The left-to-right order implies causal influences as indicated by the direction of the arrows among the four stages (boxes) of the model and the underlying environmental constraints. The vertical, top-to-bottom order implies a social-ecological theory of communication—from the individuals to social networks to institutions to societal and then to environmental supports and constraints. Each term in the metatheory indicates a variety of particular theories that can be used to design the content of the campaign and to specify the variables used to measure its impact and evaluate its effectiveness. The structure of the metatheory lends itself to a multivariate, multilevel regression analysis to evaluate the impact of the campaign. Statistical tests indicate how well the corresponding regression

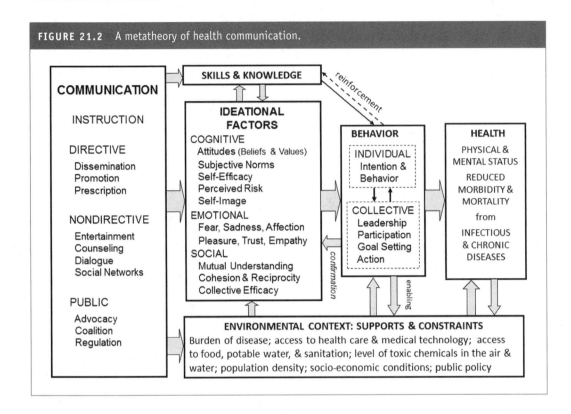

FIGURE 21.2 A metatheory of health communication.

model fits the data used to evaluate the campaign, how well the expected outcome(s) are predicted by the model, and how well the causal assumptions of the communication and the statistical model are supported by the data.

THE SCRUTINIZE HIV PREVENTION CAMPAIGN OF SOUTH AFRICA

Formative Evaluation

After studying the results of two national AIDS surveys in South Africa in 2005 and 2006, the professional communication staff of Johns Hopkins Health Education in South Africa (JHHESA) recognized that 1) the rate of increase in HIV prevalence was beginning to stabilize at around 16% (ages 15 to 54 years), 2) after 10 years of prevention campaigns, prevention knowledge and behavior, especially condom use among young people, especially men, had reached a level that could account for this leveling off, 3) HIV prevalence was still too high among youth ages 15 to 32 years and unacceptably high among women compared to men (38% and 10%, respectively), 4) condom use was relatively high with casual and multiple sex partners but declined when a relationship stabilized, and 5) awareness of the risk from having multiple sex partners was low (Kincaid, Parker, Schierhout, Connolly, & Pham, 2008; Shisana, Rehle, Simbayi, Parker, Zuma, Bhana, et al., 2005). Policy-oriented research pointed out the role of interlocking sexual networks to the spread of HIV infection (Halperin & Epstein, 2004). Eventually, the priority for prevention shifted to reducing the number of sexual partners, along with condom use and HIV testing.

The Centre for AIDS Development, Research and Evaluation (CADRE), an HIV research agency in Johannesburg, conducted 30 in-depth interviews and six focus group discussions to explore attitudes, norms, and practices related to multiple sexual partners (MSP) (Parker, Makhubele, Ntlabati, & Connolly, 2007). From the summary of the transcripts, 120 verbatim statements related to MSP were extracted, edited to improve clarity, and then pretested with 100 selected youth in Gauteng Province. Table 21.1 shows the set of 12 attitudinal statements that emerged from the factor analysis of these items. They offer a valuable insight into how South African youth think about MSP. Theory guided the audience research that led to the discovery of these statements. Theory states that that they should predict MSP behavior and that messages designed to change these attitudes would also change the behavior.

Creative Insight and Strategic Design

The challenge for the new campaign was to find a way to get young men and women, ages 16 to 32 years of age, to pay attention to new HIV prevention messages that focused on 1)

TABLE 21.1   List of Attitudes Toward MSP From Qualitative Research With Young People
Attitude Statements
1. It's OK to have sex with others as long as your main partner does not find out.
2. Having someone else for sex makes it easier to deal with your main partner when problems come up.
3. I sometimes have sex with someone one day and then another person the next day.
4. There are people I will have sex with whenever they call me.
5. I don't really feel a tie with anyone I have sex with.
6. I need someone else to fill the gap in case I ever break up with my main partner.
7. Now and then, I go to someone else besides my main partner because the sex is so good.
8. A real man tries to have a stable relationship with just one partner. (reversed)
9. If you wait to have sex, you will find the right person for yourself. (reversed)
10. If you have good communication with your partner, you can be sexually satisfied with one person. (reversed)
11. When a relationship ends, you should wait a few months and not rush into a new sexual relationship. (reversed)
12. I am confident that I can resist the temptation of having sex with anyone else besides my main sex partner. (reversed)

the risk of multiple sex partners, 2) the danger of failing to use condoms properly when drinking heavily, and 3) the importance of getting tested regularly for HIV. The initial idea, funded through the Levi's® Red for Life campaign (http://www.levi.co.za/RFL/) provided the foundation for JHHESA to work with Mat©hboxology, a commercial advertising firm in Johannesburg. Mat©hboxology applied its own version of social marketing—consumer social opportunity (CSO) thinking—to further elaborate on the design of an innovative television campaign to help prevent HIV. CSO treats society's needs as market needs and asserts that commercial brands and campaigns "have powerful social as well as commercial influence" (Mat©hboxology, n.d.).

The design team partnered with top animators, actors, and comedians to create something never seen on South African TV: Scrutinize, an animated, consumer-oriented campaign with a very high level of energy, humor, excitement, and highly memorable messages (for edu-entertainment campaigns, see Singhal, Wang, & Rogers, Chapter 22). The short, animated commercials, called *animerts,* featured two distinct "township" characters, Victor and Virginia, in unconventional mini-dramas that force audience members to face up to their own risky beliefs and behaviors. HIV itself was personified as a stealth-like ninja character "who sneaks around under the cover of ignorance and lack of vigilance, infecting those who fail to keep him at bay with safe behaviour" (Spina, 2009). The ninja character helped dramatize the risky, hidden nature of HIV, its penetration into interconnected sexual networks, and its acute, six-week infectious period, while reducing the stigma surrounding AIDS. All of the content was based on scientific facts about the disease and sound medical advice.

The brand name, Scrutinize, was proposed by the voice of the leading character as a way to remind people to look out for themselves and others. The primary slogan, "Eliminate the Element of Surprise—Scrutinize," had cognitive and emotional appeal as well as a call for action. The campaign logo depicted an eye embedded within an AIDS red ribbon that makes the connection of Scrutinize to HIV and emphasizes the need for the audience to look carefully at themselves and their partners' sexual behavior to avoid HIV infection. The payoff line—"Flip HIV to H.I. Victory"—was designed to counter the fatalism surrounding HIV and to reinforce the perceived efficacy of prevention behavior. Access to television in South Africa is over 80% (Kincaid et al., 2008), so the campaign was broadcast during prime time by the South African Broadcast Channel, SABC-1, and e.tv, the two most frequently watched stations in the country.

Two overlapping theories apply to these design decisions: the theory of reasoned action and planned behavior (Ajzen, 1991; Fishbein & Ajzen, 1975) and the extended parallel process model (Witte, 1992). The first specifies that behavior is a function of intention, which is determined by one's attitude toward the behavior, perception of social norms related to the behavior, and perceived control (self-efficacy) of the behavior. The second explains how one manages the danger and fear that is generated from communication about a threat. Communication motivates danger control behavior to the extent that it realistically portrays the severity of a threat and one's susceptibility to it, describes actions that can alleviate the threat, and increases confidence in the ability to perform those actions. If these cognitive conditions do not apply, then fear control may lead to responses to cope with the emotion of fear—defensive avoidance, perception of being manipulated, and so forth.

Production

Production of the animerts was directed by Cal Bruns, animated by Jill Slabbert, with music by The Rudimentals. Joey Rasdien, a well-known comedian, performed the voice for the lead character, a taxi driver called Victor. Victor was joined by Virginia, the *shebeen* (bar or nightclub) queen, whose voice was played by actress Welile Tembe. Small details in the animation, such as Victor's eye enlarging and popping forward like a magnifying glass, emphasized the concept of scrutinize. Showing the HIV ninja moving across and eventually infecting an entire sexual network dramatized the risk of MSP. "The animerts were peppered with slang and streetwise expressions. The characters and situations appeared 'real' to the audience. Celebrity involvement contributed star power to the campaign. . . . Rather than telling the audience what to do, it encouraged those in the audience to scrutinize their own behavior" (Spina, 2009, p. 7).

The first two animerts were pretested by means of focus group discussion and in-depth interviews in three different settings (urban, peri-urban, and rural) to determine audience acceptability (Hajiyiannis, 2008). The next five animerts were pretested with focus group discussions to check whether the intended meanings were consistent with audience members' interpretations and revised accordingly. A facilitator's guide for the community component was pretested with peer educators in several settings. DramAidE trained peer educators and other partners to engage in their own entertainment-education (E–E) activities related to the campaign. YouTube versions of the final seven animerts used in the campaign are available online at the JHHESA website, http://www.scrutinize.org.za, and the Mat©hboxology website, http://www.matchboxology.com/.

Scrutinize also included promotional items such as bar coasters, stickers, umbrellas, hats, HIV risk cards, and Levi's Scrutinize T-shirts, posters that showed how to use condoms correctly, including one that illustrated sexual networks and linked the Scrutinize theme to football (soccer). Unplanned publicity occurred when one of South Africa's most popular DJs, Cleo, showed dancers in one of his music videos wearing the Levi's® Scrutinize T-shirts. Coverage of the campaign also appeared in newspapers. Scrutinize was a multimedia campaign centered around a series of prime-time, animated television spots.

Implementation and Monitoring

From June 2008 to July 2009, the seven 40- to 60-second animerts were broadcast on all SABC television stations, e.tv, M-TV, and in 370 health clinics nationwide through Mindset Health. They were strategically placed in popular, prime-time television programs with high viewership, such as TV dramas, sports, music, and youth reality shows. The broadcast schedule coincided with national events and holidays. Scrutinize was the only HIV prevention message broadcast during the halftime of football matches during the 2009 Confederations Cup in June, 2009. Monthly broadcast schedules were provided by Mediology. The animerts were broadcast a total of 2,666 times, reaching 96% of South Africans aged 16 to 32 years who watched with an average frequency of 89.6 times. The most frequently broadcast animert, Undercover Lover (sexual networks) was broadcast

1,065 times; the least frequent animert, Undercover HIV (acute infectious period), was broadcast 107 times before being withdrawn when audience reception research indicated confusion about the final message.

Scrutinize Online initiated a Facebook page where the audience could engage in key issues themselves and a Scrutinize website where the YouTube versions of the animerts could be seen. More than 1,500 young people friended the site on Facebook, and 2,000 joined an unofficial Scrutinize Fan Group on the web. The *Scrutinize Live* events reached out to communities, schools, universities, postsecondary education and training institutions, and out-of-school youth with its own E–E approach. The last (fourth) day of the Scrutinize Live event involved celebrities and other prominent persons who used music and popular culture to engage the audience around the key themes of the campaign, with HIV testing facilities being provided through New Start (PSI). Ten college campuses participated. DramAidE trained more than 637 peer educators in the Scrutinize methodology; an estimated 71,000 students were reached by means of interpersonal communication, promotion of HIV prevention, counseling, and HIV testing. ABC Ulwazi and DramAidE reached 640,000 people through campus radio and other media outreach. Activities were monitored by participating partners who returned monthly reports on the number of individuals trained and reached.

Measurement

A nationally representative sample survey of 9,728 men and women ages 16 to 55 years was conducted between June and August of 2009. The overall results of the survey are available in the *Second National HIV and AIDS Communication Survey 2009* (Johnson, Kincaid, Laurence, Chikwava, Delate, & Mahlasela, 2010). Because the Scrutinize TV campaign was intended for youth 16 to 32 years of age who were sexually active, this subsample of 4,012 was used to measure the impact. The overall analysis showed that Scrutinize had statistically significant impacts on condom use, talking to one's friends and sexual partners about HIV testing, getting tested for HIV, and knowledge about the increased risk from having multiple sex partners (Kincaid, Delate, & Pearce, 2011). The case study presented here focuses only on the MSP objective.

To avoid acquiescence response set and social desirability bias, exposure was measured by means of a visual recognition and recall (VRR) methodology that included unaided recognition of still images captured from the video of four selected animerts, followed by unaided recall and interpretation of the relevant health content. For example, 32% recognized and then provided correct interpretations of the Undercover HIV animert about the acute infectious period, including: 1) Wait more than 6 weeks before having sex with anyone for the first time, 2) get tested for HIV before having sex with anyone for the first time, 3) get your partner tested for HIV before you have sex with him or her for the first time, 4) get tested often for HIV if you have many sex partners, and 5) always use a condom. Respondents were also asked (6 to 8) to complete the second part of the three slogans used in the animerts and 9) to identify the ninja character as a symbol for the virus. Together, these nine items were used to construct a reliable 0- to 9-point scale (alpha = .89). Correct recall of any one of the nine (overall exposure) was 77%, while the mean number of correctly recalled items was 4.2.

The following potentially confounding socioeconomic variables were measured in order to estimate the adjusted, net impact of Scrutinize: gender, age, marital status, education level, socioeconomic status, poverty, employment status, frequency of watching television (SABC1-3, e.tv) and listening to the radio, reading newspapers and magazines, Internet use, heavy drinking at bars, discussion of AIDS at local community meetings, type of residence (urban formal, urban informal, peri-urban, tribal, farming), province, and race.

MSP attitude was measured by means of a 4-point Likert-type scale of agreement or disagreement to the 12 items shown in Table 21.1. The average scale value ranged from 1 to 3.7 out of 4, so the scale (alpha = .81) was highly skewed toward the disagreement end (median = 1.33), indicating that a majority of youth do not hold attitudes that agree with MSP. The short duration of the animerts did not allow time to address this MSP attitude, so the campaign should not be held accountable for any MSP attitude change. It is included in the analysis as a theoretical variable and as another potential confounding variable in the regression analysis. However, the campaign was designed to increase knowledge of the risk of MSP. Respondents were asked how they could prevent HIV infection. Faithfulness (sticking to one partner) was mentioned spontaneously by 39.7%, and 13.7% mentioned reducing the number of sexual partners. The final measure was defined as mentioning either one or both of the two, which amounted to 46%.

Respondents were asked several questions about their relationships with their most recent sexual partners during the prior 12 months, followed by their next most recent partners, and so forth, up to a maximum of five partners. The total number of sex partners was transformed into a binary variable of two or more partners (MSP) versus one. Among youth ages 16 to 32 years, 16.2% (weighted) reported having two or more sexual partners. The rate was much higher for young men than women, 27.7% and 4.7% respectively. MSP is the primary outcome variable for this analysis. The full evaluation report describes the campaign's significant effects on the other two main objectives: condom use and getting tested for HIV (Kincaid et al., 2011).

IMPACT EVALUATION

A health communication intervention is a purposeful action designed to initiate one or more causal processes that may lead to expected effects (outcomes). Evaluation research determines if these effects actually occurred and then estimates what portion of these effects can be causally attributed to the intervention (Valente & Kwan, Chapter 6). A full-scale campaign is a field experiment without random assignment to treatment and control groups. This means that exposure is subject to self-selection bias, differences between exposed and unexposed members of the population that may be related to the expected outcomes. To justify a causal inference in this situation, multiple causal attribution (MCA) analysis was used with the data from the national cross-sectional survey. MCA combines structural equation modeling (SEM), multiple probit regression, propensity score matching (PSM), and sensitivity analysis to estimate the net impact of the intervention (Babalola & Kincaid, 2009; Kincaid & Do, 2006).

Model Fit

SEMs are multivariate, multiequation regression models in which a dependent variable in one equation is an independent predictor variable in another equation (Greene, 2007). When intervening theoretical terms, such as knowledge and attitude, are used, the causal process is represented by four interlinked regression equations. The relationship between the overall, continuous measure of Scrutinize and MSP was not statistically significant when controlling for other variables nor were any of its separate nine items except for the Undercover HIV animert that introduced the concept of the acute infectious period for HIV. This result was not expected because the broadcast of this animert was discontinued after the first two months of the campaign and because it had the lowest level of correct recall (32%). In spite of these limitations, recall of this single animert and the two intervening variables and the outcome measure of MSP attitude were used to fit the SEM model shown in the form of path diagram in Figure 21.3 to the survey data. The original continuous measure of MSP attitude was split at the median to create a binary (low or high) variable to eliminate skewness and so that multiple probit regression analysis could be used to estimate the parameters of all four equations.

Arrows in the path diagram indicate the direction and causal pathway among the four dependent variables. The probit regression coefficients for each relationship are shown

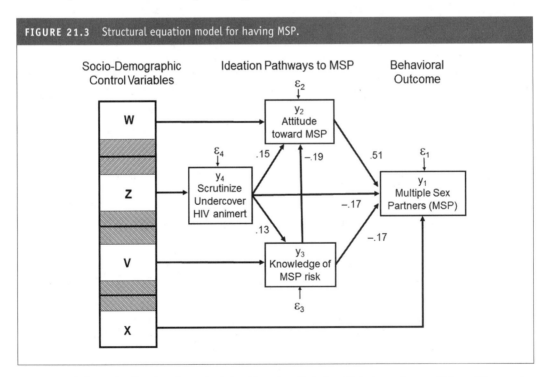

FIGURE 21.3 Structural equation model for having MSP.

Note: Arrows indicate the direction of causal relationships; the adjusted coefficients are from multiple probit regression analysis.

next to each arrow. Controlling for significant socioeconomic variables (shown as a single vector W, X, V, Z, for parsimony), the final SEM results indicate that correct recall of the Undercover HIV animert had a direct negative impact on MSP (–0.17) as hypothesized, a positive direct impact on MSP knowledge (0.13) as hypothesized, and an unexpected and unintended positive effect on MSP attitude (0.15). Knowledge had a direct negative effect on MSP attitude (–0.17) and on MSP behavior (–0.19) as hypothesized. MSP attitude had a direct positive effect on MSP behavior (0.51) as hypothesized. This means that the animert did have the expected indirect effect on MSP through its direct impact on MSP knowledge.

Causal Attribution

The fact that MCA was used after an experimental intervention (campaign) helps support a causal inference for the results (Pearl, 2009). Furthermore, MCA analysis is based on Mackie's (1980) theory of causality as "insufficient but nonredundant parts of an unnecessary but sufficient condition," which is consistent with the practice of apportioning causal attribution into independent variables by means of multiple regression analysis. Multivariate regression makes the underlying causal model multiple and probabilistic rather than singular and deterministic. If the regression model accounts for a sufficient amount of variance—fits the data well—then the direction of cause is justifiable.

To justify the causal inference statistically, each of the dependent variables (MSP attitude, knowledge, and Scrutinize) included in the equation of another dependent variable must be shown to be *exogenous*, independent from the states of the other dependent, or *endogenous,* variables in the model and hence determined by variables outside the causal system, such as the measured socioeconomic control variables and other variables not included in the model. This assumption was tested statistically by means of recursive bivariate probit regression (*biprobit* in STATA) for each pair of equations. This test also helps to rule out the possibility that *unobserved variables* (omitted or not measured) may be responsible for the observed relationship and the possibility that the relationship is *reciprocal* (e.g., MSP behavior influences attitude, knowledge, and recall of Scrutinize). These statistical requirements were met for each pair of equations in the SEM.

These tests are interrelated. When the set of predictor variables in the model fit the data well, the residual terms tend to function as random variables with respect to one another (little or no systematic variance). If both equations fit well, then the recursive biprobit test of rho will not be statistically significant, supporting exogeneity. The final model will then correctly classify (predict) the status of a substantial percentage of cases in the sample. When R. A. Fisher, the originator of the randomized experimental design, was asked how to take the "step from association to causation [when a randomized experimental design is not feasible], he replied: 'make your theories elaborate' " (Cox, 1992, p. 292). Only by specifying theoretically what influences communication, behavior, attitude, and knowledge can an adequate number of variables be measured and tested in an SEM to pass these rigorous statistical tests and justify a causal inference.

All the observed relationships were consistent with the theoretical model except for the unexpected positive effect of the Scrutinize animert on the MSP attitude. The design of the animerts did not explicitly address this attitude, so no significant impact was expected.

Separate analysis by gender revealed that the animert only had a significant positive effect on MSP attitude among men, not women, and only among those who believe that they are not likely to get infected (low perceived risk). Both men and women who understood the animert had a significantly higher knowledge of the risk of MSP. The direct negative impact on MSP behavior was statistically significant only among men and not women.

Counterfactual Analysis

After satisfying the causal assumptions of SEM, PSM was used to construct a counterfactual condition to estimate the net impact of the animert (Pearl, 2009; Kincaid & Do, 2006; Rosenbaum & Rubin, 1983). A counterfactual condition is what would have happened without exposure to the intervention (treatment). The results of PSM approximate those expected from a randomized control group design to the extent that no significant confounding variables are omitted from the analysis, known as the *strong ignorability assumption*. The SEM analysis reported above supports this assumption. The net difference (average treatment effect on the treated, ATT) was minus 3.2 percentage points (SE = .014; t = −2.35; p < .05). Among those who correctly recalled the animert, MSP was 14.7% compared to 17.9% among those in the matched control group who did not recall it.

Cost-Effectiveness

An estimate of the net impact makes it possible to conduct a valid cost-effectiveness analysis. The size of the population ages 16 to 32 years who had sex in the last 12 months was 10,784,684 (frequency weighted data). Of that population, 3,496,443 correctly interpreted the Undercover HIV animert (32.4%). Based on the PSM estimate, 3.2% of this group would have had multiple sexual partners without exposure and correct understanding of the animert. This amounts to 111,886 young people. This animert was broadcast 107 times at a total cost of $231,258. Thus, the cost-effectiveness of reducing MSP among those who would have had MSP without exposure was $2.07 per person. However, almost half of the broadcast costs were paid for by SABC and e.tv. If this is taken into count, then the cost-effectiveness of the animert was just $1.09 per number of fewer cases of MSP.

Isolation of the cost-effectiveness of this single animert ignores the possibility that exposure to some of the other animerts, though not significantly related to MSP, also may have helped people understand the acute infectious period. Even though it is impossible to take into account the role of the environment created by the other animerts and components of the campaign, they may still be a necessary condition for it to have been effective, thus increasing the overall cost-effectiveness.

Conclusion

The theory-based cycle of communication programs balances the contributions made by the production and evaluation components of communication and places emphasis on the key role of theory to both. Theories that inform the creative design process also guide the measurement of outcomes and the intervening causal pathways. Having an adequate number of theoretically relevant measures available for the multivariate analysis increases the fit of the structural equation model to the data. This fit increases the likelihood that the statistical tests of the assumptions for a causal inference for SEM and the assumption of strong ignorability in PSM are supported. Theory-driven statistical analysis of survey data maximizes external validity, in other words, the generalization of the findings to the population of interest.

The impact evaluation revealed a relatively high level of cost-effectiveness of the Undercover HIV animert on MSP. The primary message of this animert—the 6-week acute infectious period for HIV—was undoubtedly new information for most of the audience. It may have elicited a renewed, heightened level of fear related to MSP. Future animert development should elaborate on this message, simplify it, and find a way to make it clear while still increasing the audience's confidence (self-efficacy) for dealing with it in their own lives.

The SEM uncovered an unexpected positive effect of the animert on MSP attitudes among a subset of the population: young men and those who think that they are not at risk of getting infected. MSP attitude did not confound or adversely affect the animert's direct negative impact on MSP behavior. It is possible that showing entertaining animerts on television inadvertently legitimized and reinforced MSP attitudes among young men who already hold those attitudes and those who think they are not at risk (see Yzer, Southwell, & Stephenson, Chapter 11). Heavy emphasis on MSP may have made it appear to be the social norm when, in fact, it is not. Perhaps the animert provoked an emotional, psychological reactance because of the perceived threat to one's personal sense of freedom (Brehm & Brehm, 1981). These are explanations for what is called a boomerang effect of persuasive campaigns (see Hornik, Chapter 3) for outcomes that are the opposite of what is expected. Because MSP attitude was not an explicit objective of Scrutinize, it is simply an unintended effect and one that needs to be addressed in future campaigns.

The data available from the evaluation survey do not provide enough evidence to support or reject any of these potential explanations. That it occurred among young men who already have positive attitudes toward MSP supports the reactance theory. It is not likely that it occurred in response to a high perceived risk with low self-efficacy (EPPM theory). The positive relationship with MSP occurred among those with low perceived risk. The two main reasons given for low perceived risk were always being faithful to one partner (58%) and always using a condom (47%), which implies high perceived efficacy. High condom use may have created a sense of overconfidence, leading some to believe that MSP is not risky "for me," so "my favorable attitude" toward MSP is acceptable. Further analysis also revealed that MSP is a significant predictor of condom use. These results provide valuable new baseline information for next campaign communication cycle. New animerts need to emphasize that MSP is not the social norm while still conveying the increased risk of infection during the acute infectious period.

Future research and new communication programs need to take all of these potential threats and constraints into account. Fortunately, *Scrutinize* is not the only communication program that addresses HIV prevention in South Africa. In fact, JHHESA itself has already launched two new serial television dramas on television that prominently feature women and dramatize how MSP and unknown sexual networks increase their risk of infection. The cycle of campaign design and evaluation for the first Scrutinize campaign has identified how well and in what ways it affected the intended audience while at the same time providing new information to improve its effectiveness in the next cycle. Because the evaluation was theory driven as well as method driven, the results have also made contributions to the body of knowledge in several fields of scientific inquiry as well as to professional practice.

References

Ajzen, I. (1991). The theory of planned behavior. *Organizational Behavior and Human Decision Processes, 50*, 179–211.

Babalola, S., & Kincaid, D. L. (2009). New methods for estimating the impact of health communication programs [Special issue]. *Communication Methods and Measures, 3*(1), 61–83.

Brehm, S., & Brehm, J. W. (1981). *Psychological reactance: A theory of freedom and control.* New York: Academic Press.

Chen, H. T. (1990). *Theory-driven evaluations.* Newbury Park, California: Sage.

Cox, D. R. (1992). Causality: Some statistical aspects. *Journal of the Royal Statistical Society, 155*(2), 291–301.

Hajiyiannis, H. (2008). *Key findings from the field testing of the Scrutinize TV animerts: 2 ½ months postbroadcast.* (Research report). Johannesburg, South Africa: Centre for AIDS Development, Research and Evaluation (CADRE).

Halperin, D. T., & Epstein, H. (2004). Concurrent sexual partnerships help to explain Africa's high HIV prevalence: Implications for prevention. *Lancet, 364*(9428), 4–6.

Fishbein, M., & Ajzen, I. (1975). *Belief, attitude, intention and behavior: An introduction to theory and research.* Reading, MA: Addison-Wesley.

Greene, W. H. (2007). *Econometric analysis* (6th ed.). Upper Saddle River, NJ: Prentice Hall.

Johnson, S., Kincaid, D. L., Laurence, S., Chikwava, F., Delate, R., & Mahlasela, L. (2010). *Second national HIV communication survey 2009.* (Research report). Pretoria, South Africa: Johns Hopkins Health Education South Africa (JHHESA).

Kincaid, D. L. (2009). Convergence theory. In S. W. Littlejohn & K. A. Foss (Eds.), *Encyclopedia of communication theory.* Thousand Oaks, CA: Sage.

Kincaid, D. L., Delate, R., & Pearce, B. (2011). *Scrutinizing Scrutinize—A quantitative evaluation of the Scrutinize campaign in South Africa.* (Research report). Pretoria, South Africa: Johns Hopkins Health Education South Africa (JHHESA).

Kincaid, D. L., & Do, M. P. (2006). Multivariate causal attribution and cost-effectiveness of a national mass media campaign in the Philippines. *Journal of Health Communication, 11*(Suppl. 2), 1–21.

Kincaid, D. L., Parker, W., Schierhout, G., Connolly, C., & Pham, V. H. T. (2008). *AIDS communication programmes, HIV prevention, and living with HIV and AIDS in South Africa, 2006: A summary* (Research report). Pretoria, South Africa: Johns Hopkins Health Education South Africa (JHHESA).

Mackie, J. L. (1980). *The cement of the universe: A study of causation.* New York: Oxford University Press.

Mat©hboxology. (n.d.). Retrieved October 15, 2011, from http://www.matchboxology.com/index.php?option=com_content&task=view&id=20&Itemid=37

Parker, W., Makhubele, B., Ntlabati, P., & Connolly, C. (2007). *Concurrent sexual partnerships amongst young adults in South Africa: Challenges for HIV prevention communication* (Research report). Johannesburg, South Africa: Centre for AIDS Development, Research and Evaluation (CADRE).

Pearl, J. (2009). *Causality: Models, reasoning, and inference* (2nd ed.). New York: Cambridge University Press.

Piotrow, P. T., & Kincaid, D. L. (2001). Strategic communication for international health programs. In R. E. Rice & C. K Atkin (Eds.), *Public communication campaigns* (3rd ed., pp. 249–266). Thousand Oaks, CA: Sage.

Piotrow, P. T., Kincaid, D. L., Rimon, II, J. G., & Rinehart, W. E. (1997). *Health communication: Lessons from family planning and reproductive health.* Westport, CT: Praeger.

Rogers, E. M., & Kincaid, D. L. (1981). *Communication networks: Toward a new paradigm for research.* New York: Free Press.

Rogers, E. M., & Storey, J. D. (1987). Communication campaigns. In C. Berger & S. Chafee (Eds.), *Handbook of communication science* (pp. 817–846). Newbury Park, CA: Sage.

Rosenbaum, P. R., & Rubin, D. B. (1983). The central role of the propensity score in observational studies for causal effects. *Biometrika, 70*(1), 41–55.

Shisana, O., Rehle, T., Simbayi, L. C., Parker, W., Zuma, K., Bhana, A., et al. (2005). *South African national HIV prevalence, HIV incidence, behavior and communication survey.* Cape Town, South Africa: Human Sciences Research Council Press.

Spina, A. (2009). *The Scrutinize campaign: A youth HIV prevention campaign addressing multiple and concurrent partnerships* (Case Study Series). Arlington, VA: United States Agency for International Development, AIDS Support and Technical Assistance Resources, AIDSTAR-One, Task Order 1.

Witte, K. (1992). Putting the fear back into fear appeals: The extended parallel process model. *Communication Monographs, 59*, 329–349.

CHAPTER 22

The Rising Tide of Entertainment–Education in Communication Campaigns

Arvind Singhal, Hua Wang, and Everett M. Rogers

Authors' Note: The present chapter draws upon Lacayo and Singhal (2008), Singhal and Rogers (1999, 2002), and Wang and Singhal (2009).

THE ENTERTAINMENT–EDUCATION STRATEGY

The idea of combining entertainment with education goes as far back in human history as the timeless art of storytelling. For thousands of years, music, drama, dance, and various folk media have been used in many countries for recreation, devotion, reformation, and instructional purposes. However, *entertainment–education* (E–E) as a purposive communication strategy is a relatively new concept in that its conscious use in radio, television, popular music, films, and digital gaming has received attention only in the past few decades (Singhal, Cody, Rogers, & Sabido, 2004; Singhal & Rogers, 1999; Wang & Singhal, 2009).

In its initial decades, E–E was broadly defined as "the process of purposely designing and implementing a media message both to entertain and educate, in order to increase audience members' knowledge about educational issues, create favorable attitudes, shift social norms, and change overt behavior" (Singhal et al., 2004, p. 5; also see Singhal & Rogers, 1999, p. 9). However, in recent years, with the exponential growth in the development and popularity of digital interactive entertainment, especially gaming applications and practices, Wang and Singhal (2009) proposed a reformulation: "Entertainment–education is a theory-based communication strategy for purposefully embedding educational and social issues in the creation, production, processing, and dissemination process of an entertainment program, in order to achieve desired individual, community, institutional, and societal changes among the intended media user populations" (pp. 272–273).

In radio, the most well-known E-E application occurred in 1951, when BBC began broadcasting *The Archers,* a British radio soap opera that carried educational messages about agricultural development. As the world's longest-running radio soap opera, *The Archers* continues to be broadcast to this date, addressing contemporary issues such as

HIV/AIDS prevention and environmental conservation. In television, E–E was discovered more or less by accident in Peru in 1969, when the television soap opera *Simplemente María* (Simply Maria) was broadcast (Singhal, Obregon, & Rogers, 1994). The main character, María, a migrant to the capital city, worked during the day and enrolled in adult literacy classes in the evening. She then climbed the socioeconomic ladder of success through her hard work and strong motivation and later developed seamstress skills with a Singer sewing machine. *Simplemente María* attracted record audience ratings, and the sale of Singer sewing machines boomed in Peru. So did the number of young girls enrolling in adult literacy and sewing classes. When *Simplemente María* was broadcast in other Latin American nations, similar effects happened. Audience identification with María was strong, especially among poor, working-class women: She represented a Cinderella role model for upward social mobility.

Inspired by the audience success and the unintentional educational effects of *Simplemente María,* Miguel Sabido, a television writer–producer–director in Mexico, developed a production method for E–E soap operas. Its key elements include: a moral grid; a set of protagonists, antagonists, and transitional characters as role models; a narrative structure that confronts the status quo and progresses through stages of suffering, doubting, and overcoming obstacles to achieve the ultimate triumph; and the use of epilogues and infrastructure to facilitate public discourse and support social change (Sabido, 2004). Between 1975 and 1982, Sabido produced seven E–E *telenovelas* that helped motivate enrollment in adult literacy classes, encourage the adoption of family planning, and promote gender equality. These programs were also commercial hits for Televisa, the Mexican television network, earning audience ratings equivalent to Televisa's other soap operas (Nariman, 1993).

The Sabido production method snowballed globally, inspiring the development of television soap operas such as Hum Log (We People) in India, radio soap operas such as Twende Na Wakati (Let's Go With the Times) in Tanzania, and the use of rock music campaigns in Mexico and Nigeria (Singhal & Rogers, 1999). Since the mid-1980s, E–E has continued to expand at a rapid rate (Singhal & Rogers, 2002). In the past 25 years, it has spread to thousands of projects, spurred by the efforts of dozens of global and local organizations, notably, Population Communications International (now PCI Media Impact), Johns Hopkins University's Center for Communication Programs, BBC World Service Trust, Population Media Center, Search for Common Ground, Oxfam-Novib, University of Southern California's Norman Lear Center, Soul City Institute of Health and Development Communication, Heartlines, Puntos de Encuentro, Breakthrough, and Centrum Media & Gezondheid. E–E has also been widely adapted by creative media professionals in television, radio, film, print, theater, and new media.

Research has been built into E–E programs since early practice, and it routinely includes formative and summative evaluations (Singhal et al., 2004; Singhal & Rogers, 1999; see also Atkin & Freimuth, Chapter 4; Valente & Kwan, Chapter 6). A majority of the work from the mid-1980s to early 2000s focused on message design and delivery to close gaps in knowledge, attitude, and practice (KAP) and effects of the change mechanism through parasocial interaction, role modeling, self-efficacy, celebrity identification, and the mediation of interpersonal communication. Audiences find E–E to be highly engaging, and it often attracts widespread viewership or listenership as well as generating excellent audience response via handwritten letters, phone calls, and e-mails. Such campaigns are also proven to be effective for raising awareness and knowledge, changing individual attitudes and behaviors, and creating conditions to change social and cultural norms.

SOUL CITY: AN ENTERTAINMENT–EDUCATION EXEMPLAR

To better understand the role of E–E in large-scale, national-level communication campaigns, let us consider the case of the Soul City Institute of Health and Development Communication in South Africa, an institution regarded as an international leader in E–E (Lacayo & Singhal, 2008). The Soul City multimedia platform reaches 16 million South Africans regularly, influencing their norms, attitudes, and behaviors on a wide range of health and social topics. Its two flagship series are *Soul City* and *Soul Buddyz,* each containing a television series, a corresponding radio drama—broadcast in nine of South Africa's 11 official languages—as well as glossy print material, including comic books, life skills materials, and workbooks.

Soul City's origins go back to 1992, when Dr. Garth Japhet was working as a medical doctor at a clinic in Alexandra, a township just north of Johannesburg. The number one cause of child death in Japhet's clinic was diarrhea, which was easily preventable if mothers knew how to rehydrate their children (see also Rice & Foote, Chapter 5). Teaming up with another medical doctor, Dr. Shereen Usdin, Japhet launched Soul City, a health education initiative that was to reach the people through multimedia edutainment programming. Its television series *Soul City* became an instant hit, and the organization has continued to march forward ever since. In 1999, *Soul Buddyz,* a sister brand, was launched especially to serve the younger generation of 8- to 12-year-olds, addressing their problems and concerns in school, at home, and in their communities.

Soul City uses an exhaustive research process to create highly compelling story lines. For each of its series, Soul City chooses to prioritize three or four health and development issues to address and provides consultations with experts, civil society groups, medical doctors, and scholars. Its in-house researchers engage in a long consultative process with audiences, trying to understand what they know about the issue, how they feel, and what barriers prevent them from practicing desired behaviors. Accordingly, scripts are developed and pretested for their entertainment and educational value, clearing the way for production, broadcast, and distribution of multimedia materials.

A case in point is the fourth *Soul City* television series in which a well-respected character, Thabang, a school teacher, slapped his wife, Matlakala. As the story line progressed and the cycle of violence increased and began to take a heavy physical and emotional toll on Matlakala, she was advised by her mother to *bekezela,* that is, endure the abuse as it was primarily a woman's duty to make a marriage work. Thabang's father agreed, emphasizing that, as per tradition, a husband must discipline his wife. When Matlakala's beatings got worse, including a hospitalization, she learned about South Africa's new Domestic Violence Act and served Thabang a protection order. Matlakala's father, speaking on behalf of his abused daughter, and thereby modeling a new paternal behavior, explicitly urged the neighbors to not be "silent colluders," but rather to intervene. As the story unfolded, and when in an episode, Thabang began to beat Matlakala, her neighbors, collectively, stood outside Thabang's house beating their pots and pans. The loud noise of dozens of pots and pans sent a clear message to Thabang that the community disapproved of his actions and an assurance to Matlakala that her neighbors cared about her.

This pot-banging episode, which earned one of the highest audience ratings in South Africa in 1999, demonstrated the importance of creatively modeling collective efficacy in order to energize neighbors, who for social and cultural reasons, felt previously inefficacious. By watching the neighbors collectively act against an abuser on-screen, viewers learned and practiced new ways to break the cycle of spousal abuse (Usdin, Singhal, Shongwe, Goldstein, & Shabalala, 2004). Pot banging to stop partner abuse was reported in several communities in South Africa (including in Khayelitsha Township, Cape Town). Patrons of a local pub in Thembisa Township in South Africa self-organized to reinvent the new collective action they learned. Together, they banged bottles in the bar when a man physically abused his girlfriend (Singhal, 2010a).

In 2009, Soul City broke new ground in E–E by broadcasting *Kwanda, Communities With Soul* (www.kwanda.org/), a prime-time reality TV program that sought to transform dysfunctional social relationships in communities facing high unemployment and underemployment, HIV/AIDS, alcoholism, drug abuse, and gang warfare. *Kwanda,* an Nguni term meaning *to develop* or *to grow,* was a prosocial spin on the hit ABC television program *Extreme Makeover,* which depicts ordinary men and women experiencing plastic surgery, exercise regimes, new hairstyles, and wardrobes; at the end of the episode, they are revealed to their loved ones, evoking "jaw dropping" reactions (Lacayo & Singhal, 2008).

In a similar vein, *Kwanda* depicted five communities spread across South Africa (Pefferville in Eastern Cape, Mthwalume in Kwa-Zulu Natal, Tjakastad in Mpumalanga, Lephephane in Limpopo, and Kwakwatsi in Free State) that competed in an "extreme community makeover" competition in order to look better (e.g., removal of garbage dumps), feel better (e.g., young women feeling safe in their neighborhoods), and work better (e.g., a responsive local administration). *Kwanda's* larger goal was to build social capital among community members who were united by a common purpose and engaged in trusting, collaborative interactions for the greater public good. Toward this end, Soul City worked with some 50 men and women in each participating community, training them over a period of five weeks to attain the organizational skills needed to design, implement, and scale up local initiatives. Ten of the 50 participants in each community were especially trained in fashion design and sewing so that they could lead the *Kwanda Klothing* project that was launched alongside the TV show, allowing their communities to generate sustainable income and jobs. Designing a chic urban collection for both men and women, *Kwanda Klothing* incorporates indigenous designs involving denim, wraps, beads, and buttons to appeal to contemporary South African styles and tastes.

When *Kwanda* was broadcast in 2009, each community's "makeover" received an airtime of two reality TV episodes. *Kwanda's* final episode recognized the community of Kwakwatsi as the winner, and Team Kwakwatsi was applauded for their role in planting vegetable gardens for poor families; cleaning streets, garbage dumps, and graveyards; creating services and safety nets for disabled children; enrolling children in schools; and creating profitable sewing, beading, and other allied businesses (Mkhetho, 2009). They received a large amount of prize money from South Africa's National Development Agency and from state and local agencies to continue their good work. Postbroadcast, more than 2,000 people in the community of Kwakwatsi were working in Kwanda-related social and entrepreneurial enterprises, demonstrating that the entertainment component of the reality TV format could be harnessed for community organization, development, and transformation (see http://www.facebook.com/pages/Kwanda/118735351447?ref = ts).

EMERGING TRENDS IN ENTERTAINMENT–EDUCATION

There are six emerging trends in the practice of E–E, signifying its consolidation, growth, expansion, and integration with other approaches: 1) consultative social merchandizing, 2) social movements, 3) invitational approaches, 4) positive deviance, 5) digital technology, and 6) transmedia storytelling.

Trend #1: Entertainment–Education and Consultative Social Merchandizing

Up until the mid- to late 1990s, the E–E approach, barring some exceptions, was almost exclusively applied in the developing countries of Latin America, Africa, and Asia. Employing entertainment programs for health promotion and social change in media-saturated environments can be particularly challenging (Hether, Huang, Beck, Murphy, & Valente, 2008; Sherry, 2002). In recent years, E–E practitioners have found new consultative ways to work with the creative industry in media-saturated environments. Commonly referred to as *consultative social merchandizing,* in such an approach, an E–E institution consults with and serves as a resource for creative writers, producers, and entertainment professionals so that social topics can accurately be inserted and portrayed in the commercial media. Akin to the practice of product placement that commercial marketers employ, social merchandizing is about placing social and health topics in dramatic story lines. The telenovelas of TV Globo in Brazil are well known for employing the social merchandizing strategy (La Pastina, Patel, & Schiavo, 2004).

The Hollywood, Health & Society (HH&S) program at the University of Southern California's Norman Lear Center (www.usc.edu/hhs) in the United States, and the Centrum Media & Gezondheid in Gouda, Netherlands, represent two E–E institutions that serve as leaders in this approach. Since 2000, HH&S has partnered with a wide range of donor and government agencies, professional health institutions, and communication and public health researchers to serve as a 24-7 resource for Hollywood producers and writers. For millions of Americans, television is an important and often primary source of health information and a variety of health story lines have been used in prime-time and daytime television shows (Beck, 2004; Murphy, Hether, & Rideout, 2008). Viewers learn from these dramas despite the often inaccurate content (Morgan, Movius, & Cody, 2009). HH&S strives to help the creative community incorporate accurate health information and key messages for attitudinal and behavioral change in their entertainment programming in multiple ways: individual consultations with case examples and assistance to the development of specific story lines; group briefings on top issues in public health; quarterly "Real to Reel" newsletters with health headlines; an expanding list of writer's tip sheets; and panel discussions at Writers Guild of America, West (Beck, 2004; Movius, Cody, Huang, Berkowitz, & Morgan, 2007; Roberts, 2011). By serving as a consultative bridge, they connect health expertise with compelling storytelling to produce television drama with accurate portrayals and effective social modeling (e.g., Hether et al., 2008; Morgan et al., 2009; Movius et al., 2007; Wilkin, Valente, Murphy, Cody, Huang, & Beck, 2007).

Trend #2: Entertainment–Education and Social Movements

One emerging and encouraging trend in E–E is the harnessing of its ability to stimulate mass-mediated public discourse on important social topics and coupling them with on-the-ground alliances to create social movements. An exemplary organization in this realm is *Puntos de Encuentro* (Meeting Places or Common Ground), a Nicaraguan organization that promotes youth and women's rights primarily by challenging social norms and unequal power relationships (Lacayo & Singhal, 2008). Puntos combines cutting-edge media, leadership training, community education, and alliance building as tools for creating a just society. Its popular television soap opera *Sexto Sentido* (Sixth Sense) is part of a multimedia strategy that includes a daily radio talk show, a feminist magazine, billboards, and other allied activities.

Puntos takes a relatively nonprescriptive route: Through various media vehicles and outreach programs, it aims to influence the social contexts in which individuals live and create conversational spaces where citizens can discuss and decide the kind of change they wish to achieve (Rodriguez, 2005). Founded in 1991 by a small group of feminist activists, Puntos relentlessly links the personal with the political; questions power relations and shows alternatives; encourages networking, critical thinking, and private and public dialogue and debate; and builds social support systems to create an environment open to informed personal and collective change (Lacayo, 2006; Lacayo, Obregon, & Singhal, 2008).

Puntos' engagement with the media started modestly with the mimeographed newsletter *La Boletina,* which covered Nicaragua's women's movement. By 2007, *La Boletina* was the most widely circulated magazine in Nicaragua. Distributed to more than 1,000 women's groups by a volunteer network, *La Boletina* is Puntos' means for local organizing, consciousness-raising, and popular education. It is Puntos' most significant contribution to the Nicaraguan women's movement, connecting women and women's groups across the country, building a sense of belonging, and fostering visibility of the women's movement and its actions (Lacayo & Singhal, 2008).

Puntos also sought to develop a constituency among youth, who were equally silenced (as women) by authoritarianism and violence in Nicaraguan society. The organization launched *Sexto Sentido Radio,* a daily, youth-run, call-in radio program, which became an instant hit. In 2007, in its 15th year of live broadcast on 11 local stations and via the Internet, *Sexto Sentido Radio* is perhaps the longest-running radio program in Nicaragua of the youth, for the youth, and by the youth.

Puntos expanded into television with the indigenous television soap series *Sexto Sentido* (Sixth Sense). Running for four seasons (2001 to 2005) and watched by 70% of Nicaragua's television audience, *Sexto Sentido* addressed bold topics in sexual and reproductive health; overt and covert prejudice and discrimination; and rights of the weak, vulnerable, and the marginalized, personalizing them in stories that reflected the problems, decisions, triumphs, and challenges of a group of young Nicaraguans. Research evaluations of *Sexto Sentido* demonstrate the program's wide audience appeal, the spurring of new conversations among viewers on a variety of sensitive topics (such as abortion, incest, homosexuality, and others), and the synergistic effects of E–E drama within a social movement strategy (Lacayo & Singhal, 2008). In 2010, reruns of *Sexto Sentido* were broadcast on major television channels in Nicaragua, Costa Rica, Guatemala, Honduras, and Mexico. *Sexto Sentido* has won several international awards and has been featured in over 40 film festivals in the United States and internationally.

Beyond mediated television and radio fare, Puntos's media protagonists (e.g., major characters in *Sexto Sentido*) further break the silence about issues such as rape, abortion, and HIV stigma in real life: They take stands against abusive relationships, question gay stereotypes, and create visible and audible alternatives to unequal power relations. Building on platforms for public discourse created by popular television and radio, tours of the *Sexto Sentido* cast to high schools all across Nicaragua (and in other Central American countries), and the accompanying large-scale distribution of educational audiovisual and print materials, young people are provided safe spaces where they can facilitate dialogue and debates to voice opinions, share experiences, challenge biases, negotiate different viewpoints, and make decisions about how and where to create change in their lives (Lacayo & Singhal, 2008). In overall terms, Puntos strategically combines media and education with alliance-building partnerships with youth and women-friendly service providers to support on-the-ground social change movements in Nicaragua and Central America.

Trend #3: Invitational Entertainment–Education

Another trend in E–E is to incorporate the principle of invitation along with persuasion (Greiner & Singhal, 2009). In contrast to the element of push in persuasion, invitation is more of a pull strategy, acting on those who choose to willingly engage, seek, imagine, create, and generate (Greiner, 2009). The invitational approach, by definition, overcomes resistance to change, increasing people's participation, and spreads the burden of action across more shoulders (Foss & Griffin, 1995). The underlying assumption of invitational E–E is that any community members can be agents of change for themselves and for others.

The seeds of invitational E–E can be found in Augusto Boal's (1979) Theatre of the Oppressed (TO) movement, where audience members are invited to take control of situations rather than be passive consumers (Singhal, 2004). Inspired by the pedagogy of Paulo Freire (1970), Boal openly invited audience members to stop a theatrical performance and suggest different actions for the actors, who would then carry out the audience suggestions. During one such performance, a woman in the audience was so outraged that the actor could not understand her suggestion that she charged onto the stage and acted out what she meant. For Boal, this defining event marked the birth of the *spect-actor* (not spectator). From that day, audience members were invited onto the stage. Thus, passive spectators are changed into actors who then become transformers of the dramatic action. They are invited to assume a protagonist role, change the dramatic action, try out various solutions, discuss plans for change, and train themselves for social action in the real world.

The notion of invitational E–E is firmly embodied in the Scenarios From Africa project, which consists of three key components: a scriptwriting contest for young people ages 15 to 24 on themes related to HIV/AIDS, a juried selection of winning scripts, and production and distribution of short films created from the winning script ideas (Winskell & Enger, 2005). The Scenarios process is implemented by hundreds of international and community-based organizations across sub-Saharan Africa. Since its inception in 1997, there have been five completed editions of the Scenarios contest with a cumulative total of 55,072 scripts submitted by 145,875 young people from 47 different countries (D. Enger, personal communication, January 2, 2011).

Designed to invite young people to take part in a creative contest, Scenarios opens dialogue and debate on HIV/AIDS and sexuality topics among and between young people and a range of community interlocutors (Winskell & Enger, 2005). Story lines submitted by youth reflect their humor, compassion, perceptiveness, and ingenuity (Greiner & Singhal, 2009). For instance, in a short, award-winning script for a film *The Shop* presented by Olga Ouédraogo, a young man enters a shop to buy condoms but has little courage to do so publicly. Embarrassed to ask for condoms, he ends up purchasing several packets of biscuits until he watches an elderly man enter the shop and openly asks for condoms (Winskell & Enger, 2005). Overcoming his embarrassment, the young man purchases the condoms and arrives at his girlfriend's house. "It's too late!" she tells him and rides off on her moped. The film has proven so popular with audiences that it was dubbed into 19 languages and has been broadcast in dozens of countries including Fiji, Cyprus, Sri Lanka, and Haiti (Winkell & Enger, 2005).

Trend #4: Integrating Positive Deviance and Entertainment–Education

One approach that holds great promise of integration with E–E is the positive deviance (PD) approach to social change (Singhal, 2010a, b; Singhal, Buscell, & Lindberg, 2010; Singhal & Dura, 2009) that enables communities to discover the best practices and local wisdom they already have and then to act on it (Sternin & Choo, 2000). PD is an assets-based approach, identifying what's going right in a community in order to amplify it, as opposed to focusing on what's going wrong in a community and fixing it (see also Bracht & Rice, Chapter 20, for community-based campaigns).

From the perspective of E–E producers, there are important implications of conducting PD inquiries on the ground as part of formative research and then finding ways to incorporate these findings in the message design process by creating role models to exemplify the PD behaviors on E–E narrative. Such happened in North West Frontier Province of Pakistan where, in 2003 to 2004, a 13-episode entertaining magazine show called *Zindagi ki Dore* (Threads of Life) was broadcast to educate audiences about maternal and newborn care practices and included the role modeling of pregnancy-related PD behaviors. One example is a mother-in-law who hand stitches a small mattress for the baby to have a clean and warm surface immediately following delivery and the husband who gives the traditional birth attendant a clean blade to cut the umbilical cord.

These individuals are *deviants* because their behaviors are not the norm, and they are *positive* as they model the desirable maternal and newborn care behaviors. In *Zindagi ki Dore,* such PD behaviors were role modeled so that the audience members could observe them, consider them, and learn from them. As more people in the audience discover how to practice the new PD behaviors, the norm across institutions and communities can begin to shift.

The PD approach is now yielding home-grown insights on how to address diverse and intractable behavioral issues such as childhood anemia, increasing school retention rates, reducing hospital-acquired infections, promoting condom use among commercial sex workers, and a variety of child protection issues. These include the eradication of female genital cutting in Egypt, the curbing of girl trafficking in Indonesia, and the empowerment and reintegration of child mothers and vulnerable girl survivors in Northern Uganda. Insights gleaned from such ground-based understandings can directly inform mass-mediated role modeling in E–E programs. This is an area of high future potential. Not much of it has been tapped thus far.

Trend #5: Entertainment–Education and Digital Technology

As communication technologies become increasingly accessible, portable, and affordable, they offer important implications for the scholarship and practice of E–E. The prevalence and popularity of digital entertainment media such as games are astonishing (see Lieberman, Chapter 19). In 50 years, digital games have gone through phases to first become as a medium, then through public debates and industry development, a legitimate entertainment and social media platform, and now one of the largest and most profitable media industries with its products being integrated into contemporary, everyday life (Juul, 2010; Vorderer, Bryant, Pieper, & Weber, 2006; Williams, 2006). Meanwhile, tremendous interest and effort among the gaming, health, advocacy, and academic communities have generated a new field called serious games, which includes digital games for learning, health, and social change (Ritterfeld, Cody, & Vorderer, 2009). Wang and Singhal (2009) explicated five unique qualities of digital games to the advantage of the continued development of E–E: 1) experiential game play, 2) multimodality, 3) interactivity, 4) persuasive, interactive narrative, and 5) social interaction. Role taking, rather than the vicarious experience in traditional TV viewing and radio listening, is a distinctive characteristic of digital game play and can empower people through their own journeys of exploration, experimentation, and discovery (Peng, Lee, & Heeter, 2010). Applications such as *Re-Mission* by HopeLab and *ICED! I Can End Deportation* by Breakthrough are great examples to show the potential of digital games in E–E (Wang & Singhal, 2009).

Trend #6: Entertainment–Education Goes Transmedia

Another emerging trend in E–E is to engage audience members through a narrative that unfolds across different media platforms over time. *Transmedia* (or *cross-media*) *storytelling* is a complex process where elements of a narrative are strategically designed and implemented across different communication platforms to create a coherent entertainment experience (Davidson et al., 2010; Gomez, 2010; Jenkins, 2007). An example of transmedia storytelling is *The Matrix* franchise, where key bits of the overarching story line were conveyed through the trilogy movies, a series of animated shorts, two comic book story collections, and video game tie-ins (Jenkins, 2006). Such a format offers audiences different entry points. Each element stands as an independent media and narrative experience yet also contributes to the larger picture through the puzzles and clues that encourage people to extend their participation across multiple platforms over time. Therefore, unity and variety are two critical characteristics that enable transmedia storytelling to engage people from all walks of life via their own choices of media and art forms (Dena, 2010).

Communication campaigns (including many E–E programs) have often used more than a single mode of communication. However, the mind-set behind transmedia storytelling is centered on art, play, experimentation, cocreation, and collective action. Compared to traditional campaigns, it is rather open-ended, exploratory, nonlinear, process-oriented, and fun! The emergence of transmedia storytelling coincides with the rapid development of new information and communication technologies and the transformational practices of media convergence and participatory culture (Jenkins, 2006).

There have been numerous successful transmedia examples in recent years, ranging from commercial projects and educational programs to grassroots initiatives (Davidson et al., 2010). *EVOKE* (urgentevoke.com), a 10-week crash course in changing the world, uses a graphic novel as a textbook to broach a weekly global crisis, teaching players essential skills like creativity, collaboration, entrepreneurship, and sustainability to tackle intractable world problems such as hunger, poverty, and access to clean water. Developed by Jane McGonigal and the World Bank Institute, this project attracted 8,000 students in 120 countries within the first week of its launch in March 2010. Students are encouraged to come up with innovative solutions to urgent problems, report on their activities through blogs and videos, and at the end of the course, set themselves up to carry out an actionable project in the real world with others. *EVOKE* was awarded the #1 Social Impact Game by Games for Change in 2010. More organizations such as HH&S and Tribeca Film Institute are interested in using transmedia storytelling for health promotion and social advocacy.

LOOKING BACK AND LOOKING FORWARD

Communication campaigns need to engage members of the intended population group in compelling ways in order to accomplish their goals. Practice and research in the area of E–E have demonstrated that thoughtfully incorporating public health concerns and intractable social issues into entertainment programs and activities can foster desirable social change. Hundreds of E–E applications are currently underway in Latin America, Asia, Africa, Europe, and North America (Singhal & Rogers, 2004; Wang & Singhal, 2009).

E–E harnesses the appeal of entertainment formats, providing a communication platform for powerful storytelling as well as scripting of new possibilities and realities. By watching, listening to, and even participating in new stories, audience members are empowered to question their existing realities and encouraged to take new actions individually and collectively. As shown in the case of Soul City's ongoing, multiscalar, multimedia campaign, E–E can effectively work at different levels with diverse population groups, combining the on-air outreach of broadcast media with on-the-ground community engagement and social mobilization.

E–E scholars and practitioners must attend to six emerging trends: consultative social merchandizing, integration with social movements, invitational approaches, the PD approach to change, new digital technologies, and transmedia storytelling. These converging and powerful trends suggest that E–E is a highly flexible and versatile strategy for social change. As part of a communication campaign, E–E can be global and local, a standalone intervention and a component of a larger project. The field of E–E continues to keep an open and proactive perspective in its theoretically grounded and research-informed practices.

The digitization and hybridization of media-consuming experiences hold important implications for the future of E–E, especially in terms of scalability and interconnectivity. As the global digital networks expand and penetrate, communication campaigns incorporating E–E can simultaneously be developed at a much larger scale and in a more tailored manner, allowing for data sharing and tracking across geographies over a long period of time. The networked nature of new digital communication platforms offers unforeseen opportunities for leveraging E–E experiences across space–time scales.

References

Beck, V. (2004). Working with daytime and prime-time television shows in the United States to promote health. In A. Singhal, M. J. Cody, E. M. Rogers, & M. Sabido (Eds.), *Entertainment–education and social change: History, research, and practice* (pp. 207–224). Mahwah, NJ: Lawrence Erlbaum.

Boal, A. (1979). *The theatre of the oppressed.* New York: Urizen Books.

Davidson, D., et al. (2010). *Cross-media communications: An introduction to the art of creating integrated media experiences.* Pittsburg, PA: ETC Press.

Dena, C. (2010, September). *Dare to design* [Video file]. Retrieved on December 4, 2010, from http://tedxtransmedia.com/2010/

Freire, P. (1970). *Pedagogy of the oppressed.* New York: Continuum.

Foss, S., & Griffin, C. (1995). Beyond persuasion: A proposal for an invitational rhetoric. *Communication Monographs, 62,* 2–18.

Gomez, J. (2010, September). *Dare to change* [Video file]. Retrieved December 4, 2010, from http://tedxtransmedia.com/2010/

Greiner, K. (2009). Participatory communication processes as "infusions of innovation": The case of "Scenarios from Africa." In T. Tufte & F. Enghel (Eds.), *Teens changing the world: Youth, communication and social change* (pp. 267–282). Malmö, Sweden: NORDICOM.

Greiner, K., & Singhal, A. (2009). Communication and invitational social change. *Journal of Development Communication, 20*(2), 31–44.

Hether, H. J., Guang, G. C., Beck, V., Murphy, S. T., & Valente, T. W. (2008). Entertainment–education in a media-saturated environment: Examining the impact of single and multiple exposures to breast cancer storylines on two popular medical dramas. *Journal of Health Communication, 13,* 808–823.

Jenkins, H. (2006). *Convergence culture: Where old & new media collide.* New York: New York University Press.

Jenkins, H. (2007, March 22). Transmedia storytelling 101 [Web log message]. Retrieved December 4, 2010, from http://henryjenkins.org/2007/03/transmedia_storytelling_101.html

Juul, J. (2010). *A casual revolution: Reinventing video games and their players.* Cambridge, MA: The MIT Press.

La Pastina, A. C., Patel, D. S., & Schiavo, M. (2004). Social merchandizing in Brazilian telenovelas. In A. Singhal, M. J. Cody, E. M. Rogers, & M. Sabido (Eds.), *Entertainment–education and social change: History, research, and practice* (pp. 261–279). Mahwah, NJ: Lawrence Erlbaum.

Lacayo, V. (2006). *Approaching social change as a complex problem in a world that treats it as a complicated one: The case of Puntos de Encuentro, Nicaragua.* Unpublished master's thesis. Ohio University, Athens.

Lacayo, V., Obregon, R., & Singhal, A. (2008). Approaching social change as a complex problem in a world that treats it as a complicated one: The case of Puntos de Encuentro, Nicaragua. *Investgacion y Desarrollo, 16*(2), 126–159.

Lacayo, V., & Singhal, A. (2008). *Popular culture with a purpose! Using edutainment media for social change.* Den Haag, Netherlands: Oxfam-Novib.

Mkhetho, N. (2009, December 11). Project's mahala turns to millions. *Daily Sun,* p. 20.

Morgan, S. E., Movius, L., & Cody, M. J. (2009). The power of narratives: The effect of entertainment television organ donation storylines on the attitudes, knowledge, and behaviors of donors and nondonors. *Journal of Communication, 59,* 135–151.

Movius, L., Cody, M. J., Huang, G., Berkowitz, M., & Morgan, S. (2007). *Motivating television viewers to become organ donors. Cases in public health communication & marketing.* Retrieved December 4, 2010, from: http://www.casesjournal.org/volume1/peer-reviewed/cases_1_08.cfm

Murphy, S. T., Hether, H. J., & Rideout, V. (2008). *How healthy is prime time? An analysis of health content in popular prime time television programs.* Retrieved on December 4, 2010, from http://www.kff.org/entmedia/upload/7764.pdf

Nariman, H. (1993). *Soap operas for social change.* Westport, CT: Praegar.

Peng, W., Lee, M., & Heeter, C. (2010). The effects of a serious game on role-taking and willingness to help. [Electronic version]. *Journal of Communication, 60,* 723–742. DOI: 10.1111/j.1460-2466.2010.01511.x

Ritterfeld, U., Cody, M. J., & Vorderer, P. (Eds.). (2009). *Serious games: Mechanism and effects.* New York: Routledge.

Roberts, D. (2011, January 27). *How to get the boob tube to tell the truth about climate change.* Retrieved December 4, 2010, from http://www.grist.org/article/2011-01-27-how-to-get-tv-shows-to-tell-truth-about-climate-change

Rodríguez, C. (2005). From the Sandinista revolution to telenovelas: The case of Puntos de Encuentro. In O. Hemer & T. Tufte (Eds.), *Media and global change: Rethinking communication for development* (pp. 367–384). Sweden, NORDICOM, University of Göteborg.

Sabido, M. (2004). The origins of entertainment–education. In A. Singhal, M. J. Cody, E. M. Rogers, & M. Sabido (Eds.), *Entertainment–education and social change: History, research, and practice* (pp. 61–74). Mahwah, NJ: Lawrence Erlbaum.

Sherry, J. L. (2002). Media saturation and entertainment-education. *Communication Theory, 12,* 206–224.

Singhal, A. (2004). Entertainment-education through participatory theater. In A. Singhal, M. J. Cody, E. M. Rogers, & M. Sabido (Eds.), *Entertainment–education and social change: History, research, and practice* (pp. 377–398). Mahwah, NJ: Lawrence Erlbaum.

Singhal, A. (2010a). Communicating what works! Applying the positive deviance approach in health communication. *Health Communication, 25*(6), 605–606.

Singhal, A. (2010b). Riding high on *Taru* fever: Entertainment–education broadcasts, ground mobilization, and service delivery, in rural India. *Entertainment–Education and Social Change Wisdom Series, 1,*1–20.

Singhal, A., Buscell, P., & Lindberg, C. (2010). *Inviting everyone: Healing healthcare through positive deviance.* Bordentown, NJ: PlexusPress.

Singhal, A., Cody, M., J., Rogers, E. M., & Sabido, M. (Eds.). (2004). *Entertainment–education and social change: History, research, and practice.* Mahwah, NJ: Lawrence Erlbaum.

Singhal, A., & Dura, L. (2009). *Protecting children from exploitation and trafficking: Using the positive deviance approach in Uganda and Indonesia.* Washington D.C. Save the Children.

Singhal, A., Obregon, R., & Rogers, E. M. (1994). Reconstructing the story of *Simplemente María,* the most popular telenovela in Latin America of all time. *Gazette, 54,* 1–15.

Singhal, A., & Rogers, E. M. (1999). *Entertainment-education: A communication strategy for social change.* Mahwah, NJ: Lawrence Erlbaum.

Singhal, A., & Rogers, E. M. (2002). A theoretical agenda for entertainment-education. *Communication Theory, 12*(2), 117–135.

Singhal, A., & Rogers, E. M. (2004). The status of entertainment–education worldwide. In A. Singhal, M. J. Cody, E.M. Rogers, & M. Sabido (Eds.), *Entertainment–education and social change: History, research, and practice* (pp. 3–20). Mahwah, NJ: Lawrence Erlbaum.

Sternin, J., & Choo, R. (2000). The power of positive deviancy. *Harvard Business Review. January-February,* 2–3.

Usdin, S., Singhal, A., Shongwe, R., Goldstein, S., & Shabalala, A. (2004). No shortcuts in entertainment–education: Designing Soul City step-by-step. In A. Singhal, M. J. Cody, E. M. Rogers, & M. Sabido (Eds.), *Entertainment–education and social change: History, research, and practice* (pp. 153–176). Mahwah, NJ: Lawrence Erlbaum.

Vorderer, P., Bryant, J., Pieper, K. M., & Weber, R. (2006). Playing video games as entertainment. In P. Vorderer & J. Bryant (Eds.), *Playing video games: Motives, responses, and consequences* (pp. 1–8). Mahwah, NJ: Lawrence Erlbaum.

Wang, H., & Singhal, A. (2009). Entertainment–education through digital games. In U. Ritterfeld, M. J. Cody, & P. Vorderer (Eds.), *Serious games: Mechanism and effects* (pp. 271–292). New York: Routledge.

Wilkin, H. A., Valente, T. W., Murphy, S., Cody, M. J., Huang, G., & Beck, V. (2007). Does entertainment–education work with Latinos in the United States? Identification and the effects of a telenovela breast cancer story line. *Journal of Health Communication, 12,* 455–469.

Williams, D. (2006). A brief social history of game play. In P. Vorderer & J. Bryant (Eds.), *Playing video games: Motives, responses, and consequences* (pp. 259–274). Mahwah, NJ: Lawrence Erlbaum.

Winskell, K., & Enger, D. (2005). Young voices travel far: A case study of scenarios from Africa. In O. Hemer & T. Tufte (Eds.), *Media and global change: Rethinking communication for development* (pp. 403–416). Göteberg, Sweden: NORDICOM.

Putting Policy Into Health Communication

The Role of Media Advocacy

Lori Dorfman and Lawrence Wallack

Public communication campaigns are very seductive. They present knowledge as ultimate power: Armed with the right information, people can control their health destinies. However, by focusing almost exclusively on personal choice, the strategy systematically ignores the wide range of social forces that influence health. Thus, flaws are defined and remedied at the individual level, leaving important social, economic, and other environmental contributory factors unchanged.

In this chapter, we argue that this strategy is fundamentally inconsistent with the mission and goals of public health. Health communication campaigns evolve out of a desire to ensure that people have the right information about their health. Although information is important, traditional campaign approaches have been poor tools for improving health status. This chapter offers reasons for the lack of success of these approaches in improving the health of populations and suggests that media advocacy, a more policy-oriented approach, is necessary to create the environments in which information campaigns have better chances of achieving their goals.

HEALTH COMMUNICATION CAMPAIGNS

The use of mass media to improve public health has become increasingly sophisticated in the past generation. The careful application of behavior change theories and social marketing techniques has increased the potential of large-scale public education campaigns to achieve their goals. In addition, the use of paid rather than public service advertising, particularly in the area of tobacco and illicit drugs, has become more common. This helps to ensure repeated exposures to the desired message. Nonetheless, there are continuing questions as to whether such campaigns do, in fact, change behavior and contribute to improved population health status. Public education campaigns are largely governed by the idea that people need more and better personal information to navigate a hazardous health environment. This may seem intuitively reasonable, and the history of media campaigns demonstrates a primary focus on increasing personal knowledge rather than promoting collective action or policy change.

Mass-mediated health communication efforts generally flow from a pragmatic view that assumes an information gap in individuals: If people just knew and understood that certain behaviors were bad for them and others good, then these people would change to the behaviors that benefited their health. If enough people changed their behavior, then this would lead to a healthier society. The problem is operationally defined as people just not knowing any better. The goal, then, is to warn and inform people so they can change. To make this happen, campaigns fill the knowledge gap by focusing on developing the right message to deliver to the largest number of people through the mass media. Finding the right message is central to the campaign and extremely important. The message, however, is almost always about personal change rather than social change, institutional accountability, or collective action.

Although there are many ways in which a well-designed campaign can increase the potential for success, sustained evidence of behavior change has been elusive. In a comprehensive review of communication campaigns, Rogers and Storey (1987) noted, "The literature of campaign research is filled with failures, along with qualified successes—evidence that campaigns can be effective under certain conditions" (p. 817). This review, more optimistic than some and slightly more pessimistic than others, generally echoed previous reviews (Alcalay, 1983; Atkin, 1981; McGuire, 1986; Wallack, 1981, 1984) and anticipated later reviews (Abroms & Maibach, 2008; Brown & Walsh-Childers, 1994; DeJong & Winsten, 1998; Rice & Atkin, 2009; Salmon, 1989; Snyder & LaCroix, Chapter 8; Wallack & DeJong, 1995).

New Approaches and Current Challenges

Better health communication campaigns are characterized by at least three important factors. First, these campaigns are more likely to use mass communication and behavior change theory as a basis for campaign design. This means using a variety of mass communication channels, ensuring that the audience is exposed to the message, reducing barriers to change, and providing a clear and specific action for the individual to take. Second, they are more likely to use formative research such as focus groups to develop messages and inform campaign strategy (see Atkin & Freimuth, Chapter 4). Many better-designed interventions also include various social marketing strategies, such as market segmentation, channel analysis, and message pretesting (Kotler & Lee, 2008; McKenzie-Mohr, 2010). Third, they are more likely to link media strategies with community programs, thus reinforcing the media message and providing local support for desired behavior changes (Wallack & DeJong, 1995; see Bracht & Rice, Chapter 20). These three factors improve the traditional approach, but they do not remedy the fundamental problem of the focus on personal behavior change. Approaches that change the environment in which people make their health decisions have a better chance of improving health status across broad populations over the long term. Without this orientation, the potential of health communication campaigns will always be limited.

Limits of Health Communication Campaigns

Much of the reason for the lack of clear, consistent effects of mass media campaigns may be that they are just not comprehensive enough to affect public health problems. Such campaigns may fall short in at least three areas. First, many media campaigns are based on *risk factorology* (McKinlay & Marceau, 2000) and focus primarily on changing individual behavior. Even when the body of risk factors for specific diseases is aggregated, however, seldom is more than 50% of the variance explained. Lomas (1998) argues that individual risk factor modification, an approach at the core of most mass media campaigns, has been "spectacularly unsuccessful" (p. 1183). Even if campaigns are successful in changing risk factor behaviors in some intended audiences, they are unlikely to be effective in improving health status at the population level.

Second, the lessons from prototypical public education campaigns such as the Stanford Heart Disease Prevention Program clearly indicate that, to be successful, campaigns must be linked to broader community action, but this is seldom the case. For example, the ongoing antidrug campaign by the federal Office on Narcotics and Drug Control Policy (http://www.mediacampaign.org/) uses extensive paid advertising but has weak links to community participation (Hornik, Jacobsohn, Orwin, Piesse, & Kalton, 2008). The expectation is that local people will be motivated by the campaign to get involved in preventing drug use, but no resources are allocated to ensure that this happens (DeJong & Wallack, 1999).

Third, the mission of public health is to ensure "conditions in which people can be healthy" (Institute of Medicine, 1988, p. 140). Public policy to change the conditions that give rise to and sustain public health problems is fundamental to improving population health (Beauchamp, 1976; see Rice & Foote, Chapter 5, for a discussion of systems approaches). Few campaigns, however, move out of the behavioral context to the larger issue of policies that create the environment that determines the range of personal and behavioral choices available to individuals (however, see Rice & Robinson, Chapter 16). Motivating people to jog in neighborhoods riddled by violence or encouraging consumption of fresh fruits and vegetables where none are available, even if somehow successful in getting people's attention and motivating them to want to change, will do little to improve their overall life chances.

Certainly, there is a need for clear health-related information, well produced and widely distributed. Often, however, it is not an appropriate starting point for health promotion. For example, 5-a-Day campaigns have as their goal improving health status by increasing consumption of fruit and vegetables. This worthy goal will remain unattainable, despite the most persuasive communications campaign, if fruit and vegetables are not easily available and affordable, especially while fast food is. One local group in California wanted to initiate a local 5-a-Day campaign to improve the outcomes of teen pregnancies. When they sought our advice on administering a 5-a-Day campaign, we asked, "Where will the young women get the fruit and vegetables?" The major supermarkets had abandoned the inner-city neighborhoods that were home to the teens they wanted to reach, leaving nothing but corner liquor stores that stocked old and expensive fruit and vegetables, if they stocked them at all. We suggested they frame this from an economic development perspective and involve the teens in a campaign to demand the return of the grocers or to initiate a community garden or other effort to create an environment in which they could make healthy choices for themselves and their families. In this example, a 5-a-Day social marketing campaign would make sense only after a campaign had been carried out to ensure the local availability of fruits and vegetables.

Ultimately, a combination of communications will be required for chronic problems. Consider seat belts. It took public policy to require that seat belts be included in vehicles. Then, campaigns informed and educated the public about using seat belts. But, communication campaigns that asked people to buckle up had only limited success. Refinements led to a deeper understanding of the problem that links individual behavior to the broader policy environment. Seat belt use increased dramatically only after primary enforcement laws were in place combined with aggressive local law enforcement and education from various levels of government—including road signs and other publicity (Kotler & Lee, 2008). Over time, the issue moved from policy to personal behavior back to policy (Dorfman, Ervice, & Woodruff, 2002).

The mission of public health emphasizes the need to focus on public policy and not just personal habits (Chapman, 2001). This means that populations, rather than individuals, are the primary focus (Rose, 1992) and points to the importance of addressing the rules that shape the social and physical environments that largely determine health (Freudenberg, Bradley, & Serrano, 2009). When policy is understood as central to the mission of public health, then our understanding of media campaigns will shift. For example, the role of the news media in setting the public and policy agenda and framing public debate becomes critical.

If media campaigns are to move beyond a risk factor focus, if they are to connect people to community action and attend to the policies that create unhealthy conditions, then people need skills to better participate in the public policy process to make the environment less hazardous (Wallack, 2000). Health communication campaigns can contribute to this skill development if the audience is thought of as potential participants in the social change process rather than simply being viewed as vehicles for personal behavior change (see Bracht & Rice, Chapter 20).

Some Unintended Adverse Consequences of Campaigns

Overreliance on public education campaigns, even the better-designed ones, may actually be a barrier to the accomplishment of public health goals for three reasons. First, such an emphasis conflicts with the social justice ethic of public health that calls for a fair sharing of the burden for prevention (Beauchamp, 1976). The narrow behavioral focus of the campaign may deflect attention away from social and structural determinants of health by focusing exclusively on the behavior of individuals—in effect blaming the victim for the problem and placing the sole burden for change on him or her (Dorfman, Wallack, & Woodruff, 2005; Dorfman & Wallack, 1993; Ryan, 1976; Wallack, 1989, 1990).

Second, public policy or social action is seldom, if ever, a focus of public health media campaigns because these campaigns are usually supported with public money that makes advocacy for specific policies problematic. Also, many media outlets will not accept PSAs or even paid advertisements that are considered controversial—and policy issues that inevitably confront corporate interests are inherently controversial (Hammond, Freimuth, & Morrison, 1987). Campaigns that focus on individual behavior change appear apolitical as they uphold the default frame of individualism; personal responsibility is usually not considered controversial (Dorfman & Wallack, 1993). Tobacco control campaigns such as those supported by excise taxes in California and elsewhere are notable exceptions, but these campaigns appeared only after decades of consistent, persistent media advocacy assigning responsibility to the tobacco industry and designating a role for government in solving the problem.

Third, it is not logical or effective to define a problem at the community or societal level and then focus primarily on solutions at the personal or individual level. There are many definitions of public health, but one clear thread running through these is the fundamental idea that the primary focus must be on the health and well-being of communities or populations and not individuals (Mann, 1997; Rose, 1985, 1992). Environmental issues are glaringly community, nation, and world based, so campaigns increasingly focus on policy and macroactions (Rice & Robinson, Chapter 16).

The crucial issue, then, is what kinds of media approaches can increase the capacity of groups and broader communities to act on matters related to public health that potentially benefit the entire society? Media advocacy is one approach that provides a framework and a set of skills for shifting the focus to policy issues addressing population health.

MEDIA ADVOCACY

Media advocacy is the strategic use of mass media in combination with community organizing to advance healthy public policies. Media advocacy takes a citizen rather than a consumer approach to mass media. Instead of conceptualizing the audience as consumers of information, media advocates think of them as participants in democracy. The primary focus is on the role of news media with secondary attention to the use of paid advertising (Chapman & Lupton, 1994; Dorfman et al., 2005; Wallack, 1994; Wallack & Dorfman, 1996; Wallack, Dorfman, Jernigan, & Themba, 1993; Wallack & Sciandra, 1990–1991; Wallack, Woodruff, Dorfman, & Diaz, 1999; Winett & Wallack, 1996). Media advocacy seeks to raise the volume of voices for social change and shape the sound so that it resonates with the social justice values that are the presumed basis of public health (Beauchamp, 1976; Mann, 1997). It has been used by a wide range of grassroots community groups, public health leadership groups, public health and social advocates, and public health researchers (Wallack et al., 1993, 1999).

The practical origins of media advocacy can be traced to the late 1980s. It grew from a collaboration of public health groups working on tobacco and alcohol issues with public interest and consumer groups also working on these or similar issues (U.S. Department of Health and Human Services, 1988). The public interest and consumer groups brought a new array of strategies and tactics that were more common in political campaigns than in public health efforts. The public health perspective provided a clearer understanding of the substantive scientific issues and the importance of theory in creating change. The result has been an approach that blends science, politics, and advocacy to advance public health goals.

From a theoretical perspective, media advocacy borrows from mass communication, political science, cognitive linguistics, sociology, and political psychology to understand the role of news in policy making and to develop strategy. Central to media advocacy is the concept of *agenda setting* (Dearing & Rogers, 1997; McCombs & Shaw, 1972) and *framing* (Dorfman et al., 2005; Gamson, 1989; Iyengar, 1991; Lakoff, 1996; Ryan, 1991). Agenda setting research encourages the media advocacy approaches to focus attention on specific public health issues. Lessons from framing studies help shape the debate to reflect a public health perspective (Dorfman et al., 2005). Media advocacy also borrows from community organizing, key elements of formative research (i.e., focus groups and polling), and political campaign strategy (e.g., application of selective pressure on key groups or individuals) (Wallack et al., 1993). Blending theory with practice provides an overall framework for advocacy and social change.

Media advocacy differs in many ways from traditional public health campaigns. It is most marked by an emphasis on

1. linking public health and social problems to inequities in social arrangements rather than to flaws in the individual,

2. changing public policy rather than personal health behavior,

3. focusing primarily on reaching opinion leaders and policy makers rather than those who have the problem (the traditional audience of public health communication campaigns),

4. working with groups to increase participation in the democratic process and amplify their voices to influence policy change rather than providing health behavior change messages to individuals, and

5. having a primary goal of reducing the power gap rather than just filling the information gap.

Media advocacy is generally viewed as a part of a broader strategy rather than as a strategy per se. One of the fundamental rules of media advocacy is that it is part of the overall plan, but it is not the plan for achieving policy change. For example, a group in Oakland, California, effectively used media advocacy to advance a city ordinance to place a tax on liquor stores and institute a one-year moratorium on new licenses in the city (Seevak, 1997). Over four years, the group used media advocacy to provide legitimacy to the issue, to increase the credibility of their position and add urgency to the problem, and to let politicians know that the community was very concerned about the issue and would be following all votes. To achieve this, they used a variety of tactics to generate news coverage and discussion on the editorial pages. This increased the effectiveness of the grassroots coalition advancing the policy but would have made little difference if the coalition did not have strong community support for the issue, a clear and reasonable policy goal, research to support their claims, and a media strategy to advance the policy and support community organizing. Media advocacy helped amplify and accelerate their efforts; the news coverage provided a sense of urgency to their demands, increased legitimacy and credibility of the policy they were advancing, and attracted new supporters while reinforcing the commitment of the original supporters.

Media advocacy has four layers of strategy to support community organizing and policy development and advancement: developing overall strategy, media strategy, message strategy, and access strategy.

Overall Strategy: The Path to the Policy Change

Media advocacy understands and responds to problems as social issues rather than as personal problems. With this problem definition, the focus of the strategy is on elaborating policy options; identifying the person, group, or organization that has the power to create the necessary change; and identifying organizations that can apply pressure to advance the policy and create change. In the Oakland example, various elements of the community were organized to apply pressure on the zoning commission, the mayor's office, city council, and state legislature, which were all targets at various points in the campaign. In media advocacy, the target is the policy maker, organization, or legislative body that has the power to make the desired policy change rather than the individuals with the problem.

Media Strategy: The Mechanism for Reaching the Target

Policy battles are often long and contentious, and it is important to make effective use of the media to keep the issue on the media agenda. After the Oakland effort won the policy battle, the participants needed to refocus media attention to ensure the policy would be properly implemented. Thus, it is important to develop strategies to maintain the media spotlight on the policy issue on a continuing basis. This means identifying opportunities to reintroduce the issue to the media, such as key anniversaries of relevant dates, publication of new reports, and significant meetings, as well as linking the policy solution to breaking news.

Message Strategy: Shaping the Debate

The news media generally focus on the plight of the victim, whereas policy advocates emphasize social conditions that create victims. Media advocates frame policy issues using public health values that resonate with broad audiences. Some of the steps include "translat[ing] personal troubles into public issues" (Mills, 1959, p. 187); emphasizing social accountability and personal responsibility; identifying individuals and organizations that must assume greater burdens for addressing the problem; presenting a clear and concise policy solution; and packaging the story by combining key elements such as visuals, expert voices, authentic voices (those with experience of the problem), media bites, social math (creating a context for large numbers that are interesting to the press and understandable to the public), research summaries, fact sheets, policy papers, and so on. The challenge is to provide journalists with varied story elements that make it easier for them to tell the story from the population and policy perspective rather than just the individual or personal angle. In the Oakland example, the key messages and the story elements advocates provided were about the community health and safety issues related to the overconcentration of liquor stores and not pleas to stop drinking or warnings about the dangers of excessive drinking.

Media advocates further refine the concept as *framing for access,* where the objective is to capture journalists' attention by focusing on what is considered newsworthy, and *framing for content,* where the objective is to reframe a public health issue to highlight environmental factors and the desired policy solution. Typically, this means that media advocates must emphasize shared responsibility for solving problems across individuals and society, which Beauchamp (1976) defined as the difference between market justice and social justice. This frame tends to be deemphasized in news coverage that often highlights individuals and events. Iyengar (1991) finds that such episodic news results in audience interpretations that tend to blame the victim, while more thematic news helps audiences understand the impact of environments on personal outcomes. Because this interpretation is consistent with a public health approach, in media advocacy, the goal is often to reframe from episodic to thematic frames. Instead of stories framed as portraits focused narrowly on individuals or events, media advocates work with reporters to help them see individuals and events embedded in broader landscapes that can reveal the context surrounding individuals and events (Dorfman et al., 2005).

Framing for content wrestles with the core tension in our society between the personal and the environmental or social views of the world. Most public discourse reflects the default frame in America, which emphasizes rugged individualism and the value of personal responsibility. Consequently, the institutional accountability and role for government in solving public health problems is harder to see. For example, when the frames around obesity emphasize overeating, appearance, or health without some indication of the food and activity environments in which people make their eating and activity decisions, then the solutions to the problem will center on willpower and character; lack of willpower is a default frame for obesity (Dorfman & Wallack, 2007). Furthermore, the idea of willpower in relation to obesity prevention does not have to be overtly suggested because it is an expression of the dominant default frame of individualism (Lawrence, 2004; Wallack & Lawrence, 2005). However, the alternative perspective that brings the environment into view does have to be explicitly stated. Just as media advocates shifted the frame by talking about tobacco instead of smoking, we will need proactive efforts to be sure the larger environment is brought into the frame when we talk about obesity. Public health advocates concerned about obesity are starting to bring the environment into focus by talking about the need to improve the places where children and families live, learn, work, and play and by identifying policies in transportation, agriculture, land use, education, and economic development that can reshape those environments (Bell, Rogers, Dietz, Ogden, Shuler, & Popovic, 2010).

Access Strategy: Reaching Journalists

Getting an issue in the media can help set the agenda and provide legitimacy and credibility to the issue and group. Media advocacy involves understanding how journalism works so that access to the news media can be increased. This includes understanding when media attention can influence the policy process; maintaining a media list including reporters, bloggers, and producers; monitoring the print, broadcast, and electronic media; understanding the elements of newsworthiness, pitching stories, and holding news events; and developing editorial page strategies for reaching key opinion leaders. As news boundaries have become more fluid with the advent of web-based digital media, advocates themselves can create news and opinions to distribute. For example, in response to attacks on breast-feeding from prominent politicians, public health advocates moved quickly to post a blog that reframed the issue (Bartick & True, 2011). Social media had fewer gatekeepers, and the documents could be shared easily. However, traditional mainstream media still set the agenda for online and broadcast outlets, so they remain a key source for reaching policy makers (Pew Research Center, 2010).

Advancing the Policy

During the past 40 years, tobacco control advocates have used media advocacy approaches in efforts to increase the excise tax on tobacco, enact smoke-free workplace policies, outlaw vending machines, and give the Food and Drug Administration jurisdiction over tobacco in addition to other policies. In each of these efforts, the target has been the legislator, legislative body, or executive that had the power to enact the policy being sought. Although the specific target changed based on local circumstances, the overall framing has focused on the tobacco industry and the government body that regulates it rather than just on the smoker.

Media advocacy has since then been applied to many other public health and social issues, including affirmative action, child care, alcohol, tobacco, childhood lead poisoning, health promotion, nutrition, physical activity, violence, handgun control, and suicide prevention. Children's health advocates have used media advocacy to pressure policy makers to include prevention measures for childhood lead poisoning in national legislation. Disability rights advocates used media advocacy to fight for accessible public transportation and federal support for home attendant care (Hartman & Johnson, 1993). In New Zealand, alcohol control advocates used media advocacy to frame alcohol problems in terms of easy availability and to increase support for alcohol policies (Stewart & Casswell, 1993). In the United States, alcohol control advocates used media advocacy to reframe the problem as one of public safety and quality of community life and helped pass policy to reduce access to alcohol (Jernigan & Wright, 1996; Seevak, 1997). Violence prevention advocates promoted policies to reduce morbidity and mortality from firearms (Wallack, 1999). Housing activists used media advocacy to pressure a local housing authority to make repairs and improve conditions (University Research Corporation, 1996) and support local investments in affordable housing (Dean, 2006). These examples are emblematic of efforts that are using the media in its most powerful form: to change policy.

Common to all these media advocacy campaigns is a focus on policies that change the environment in which people live and make their health decisions. Media advocacy efforts may focus on statewide policy (e.g., the California ban on "Saturday night special" handguns; Wallack, 1999) or national policy (e.g., disability rights groups efforts to shift of 25% of the Medicare budget from nursing homes to attendant care).

Evaluating Media Advocacy

The ultimate outcome measure for media advocacy is whether or not the desired policy passed and implemented as the advocates intend. However, disentangling media advocacy's contribution to the policy process from the effects of community organizing or policy advocacy—or other events or secular trends—is challenging, especially because policies can take years, sometimes decades, to pass (Stead, Hastings, & Eadie, 2002). Thus, most evaluations of media advocacy have been case studies (Chapman & Lupton, 1994; Dean, 2006; DeJong, 1996; Jernigan & Wright, 1996; Wallack & Dorfman, 1996; Wallack et al., 1993, 1999; Woodruff, 1996). These case studies have shown that community groups trained in media advocacy can effectively gain access to the news media and enhance their participation in the process of public policy making.

In a more systematic evaluation of the role of media advocacy in a controlled study designed to advance community policies to reduce drinking and driving, Holder and Treno (1997) concluded that media advocacy was effective in several areas and "an important tool for community prevention" (p. S198). For example, local people trained in media advocacy were able to increase local news coverage in television and newspapers and presumably frame it around policy issues. They suggest that results of the media advocacy component of the intervention "can focus public and leader attention on specific issues and approaches to local policies of relevance to reducing alcohol involved injuries" (p. S198). In another evaluation of alcohol-related media advocacy, Harwood, Witson, Fan, and Wagenaar (2005) examined the relationship between newspaper coverage and legislative action restricting minors' alcohol consumption in Louisiana. They found that news coverage may be most beneficial in the early stages of a campaign to help frame the problem.

An evaluation of media advocacy in the Stanford Five City Heart Disease Prevention Project (Schooler, Sundar, & Flora, 1996) examined coverage of the issue, prominence of the article, framing of the article (e.g., prevention vs. treatment), and the impact on the media agenda (i.e., ratio of locally generated articles on heart disease vs. other health issues). The study concluded that "media advocacy efforts can be successful" (p. 361) but found that maintenance of the effects was weak.

In one of the few experiments testing the concepts underlying media advocacy, Major (2009) investigated the effects of news frames on the reader's perceptions of obesity and lung cancer as individual or societal responsibilities. By manipulating the content of news stories, Major compared the effect of thematic or episodic frames and gain (benefits such as lives saved) or loss (costs, such as lives lost) frames. The results showed that people exposed to news stories with thematic and loss framing attributed more responsibility to society, consistent with a public health approach.

Conclusion

Public education campaigns, even if successful in changing some individual behavior, are not sufficient to address significant public health problems. These problems are rooted in our social structure and linked primarily to how we make policy decisions as a society and not just personal health decisions as individuals. Media advocacy approaches designed to change policy must be integrated into public health interventions. Such approaches can make traditional health communication campaigns more comprehensive and more consistent with the missions and goals of public health.

As a society, we exalt the person that can beat the odds and succeed against adversity (Shorr, 1988). The triumphant individual story, in fact, is one of the dominant parables that guide political thought, rhetoric, and policy development in our society (Reich, 1988). Public health is a profession that should work to reduce the odds so that more people can succeed and not a profession that simply provides information, services, and encouragement to people so they might be among the few lucky ones to beat the odds (Beauchamp, 1981). In considering media approaches, we must include the kinds of strategies that have the long-range potential to change the odds.

References

Abroms, L., & Maibach, E. (2008). The effectiveness of mass communication to change public behavior. *Annual Review of Public Health, 29,* 1–16.

Alcalay, R. (1983). The impact of mass communication campaigns in the health field. *Social Science Medicine, 17,* 87–94.

Atkin, C. K. (1981). Mass media information campaign effectiveness. In R. E. Rice & W. Paisley (Eds.), *Public communication campaigns* (2nd ed., pp. 265–279). Beverly Hills, CA: Sage.

Bartick, M., & True, L. (2011). Retrieved October 15, 2011, from http://www.huffingtonpost.com/melissa-bartick/what-do-sarah-palin-and-m_1_b_825953.html

Beauchamp, D. (1976). Public health as social justice. *Inquiry, 8,* 3–14.

Beauchamp, D. (1981). Lottery justice. *Journal of Public Health Policy, 2*(3), 201–205.

Bell, J., Rogers, V. W., Dietz, W. H., Ogden, C. L., Shuler, C., & Popovic, T. (2011). CDC grand rounds: Childhood obesity in the United States. *Morbidity & Mortality Weekly Report, January 21, 60*(02), 42–46.

Brown, J. B., & Walsh-Childers, K. (1994). Effects of media on personal and public health. In J. Bryant & D. Zillmann (Eds.), *Media effects: Advances in theory and research* (pp. 389–416). Hillsdale, NJ: Lawrence Erlbaum.

Chapman, S. (2001). Advocacy in public health: Roles and challenges. *International Journal of Epidemiology, 30,* 1226–1232.

Chapman, S., & Lupton, D. (1994). *The fight for public health: Principles and practice of media advocacy.* London: BMJ.

Dean, R. (2006, October). Moving from head to heart: Using media advocacy to talk about affordable housing. *Berkeley Media Studies Group, 16.* Retrieved October 15, 2011, from www.bmsg.org/pdfs/Issue16.pdf

Dearing, J. W., & Rogers, E. M. (1997). *Agenda-setting.* Thousand Oaks, CA: Sage.

DeJong, W. (1996). MADD Massachusetts versus Senator Burke: A media advocacy case study. *Health Education Quarterly, 23*(3), 318–329.

DeJong, W., & Wallack, L. A. (1999). Critical perspective on the Drug Czar's antidrug media campaign. *Journal of Health Communication, 5,* 155–160.

DeJong, W., & Winsten, J. A. (1998). *The media and the message.* Washington, DC: The National Campaign to Prevent Teen Pregnancy.

Dorfman, L., Ervice, J., & Woodruff, K. (2002, November). *Voices for change: A taxonomy of public communications campaigns and their evaluation challenges.* Washington, DC: Communications Consortium Media Center.

Dorfman, L., & Wallack, L. (2007). Moving nutrition upstream: The case for reframing obesity. *Journal of Nutrition Education and Behavior, 39,* S45–S50.

Dorfman, L., & Wallack, L. (1993). Advertising health: The case for counter-ads. *Public Health Reports, 108*(6), 716–726.

Dorfman, L., Wallack, L., & Woodruff, K. (2005). More than a message: Framing public health advocacy to change corporate practices. *Health Education and Behavior, 32*(4), 320–336.

Freudenberg, N., Bradley, S. P., & Serrano, M. (2009). Public health campaigns to change industry practices that damage health: An analysis of 12 case studies. *Health Education and Behavior, 36*(2), 230–249.

Gamson, W. A. (1989). News as framing: Comments on Graber. *American Behavioral Scientist, 33*(2), 157–162.

Hammond, S., Freimuth, V., & Morrison, W. (1987). The gatekeeping funnel: Tracking a major PSA campaign from distribution through gatekeepers to target audience. *Health Education Quarterly, 14,* 153–166.

Hartman, T., & Johnson, M. (1993). *Making news: How to get news coverage for disability rights issues.* Louisville, KY: Advocado Press.

Harwood, E. M., Witson, J. C., Fan, D. P., & Wagenaar, A. C. (2005). Media advocacy and underage drinking policies: A study of Louisiana news media from 1994 through 2003. *Health Promotion Practice, 6*(3), 246–257.

Holder, H. D., & Treno, A. J. (1997). Media advocacy in community prevention: News as a means to advance policy change. *Addiction, 92*(Suppl. 2), S189–S199.

Hornik, R., Jacobsohn, L., Orwin, R., Piesse, A., & Kalton, G. (2008). Effects of the national youth anti-drug media campaign on youths. *American Journal of Public Health, 98*(12), 2229–2237.

Institute of Medicine. (1988). *The future of public health.* Washington, DC: National Academy Press.

Iyengar, S. (1991). *Is any one responsible?* Chicago: University of Chicago Press.

Jernigan, D. H., & Wright, P. A. (1996). Media advocacy: Lessons from community experiences. *Journal of Public Health Policy, 17*(3), 306–330.

Kotler, P., & Lee, N. (2008). *Social marketing: Influencing behaviors for good.* Thousand Oaks, CA: Sage.

Lakoff, G. (1996). *Moral politics: What conservatives know that liberals don't.* Chicago: University of Chicago Press.

Lawrence, R. (2004). Framing obesity: The evolution of public discourse on a public health issue. *Harvard International Journal of Press/Politics, 9*(3), 56–75.

Lomas, J. (1998). Social capital and health: Implications for public health and epidemiology. *Social Science Medicine, 47*(9), 1181–1188.

Major, L. H. (2009). Break it to me harshly: The effects of intersecting news frames in lung cancer and obesity coverage. *Journal of Health Communication, 14,* 174–188.

Mann, J. M. (1997). Medicine and public health, ethics and human rights. *Hastings Center Report, 27*(3), 6–13.

McCombs, M., & Shaw, D. (1972). The agenda-setting function of mass media. *Public Opinion Quarterly, 36,* 176–187.

McGuire, W. J. (1986). The myth of massive media impact: Savaging and salvagings. In G. Comstock (Ed.), *Public communication and behavior* (Vol. 1, pp. 173–257). New York: Academic Press.

McKenzie-Mohr, D. (2010). *Fostering sustainable behavior: An introduction to community-based social marketing* (4th ed.). Gabriola Island, British Columbia: New Society Publishers.

McKinlay, J. B., & Marceau, L. D. (2000). To boldly go. . . . *American Journal of Public Health, 90*(1), 25–33.

Mills, C. W. (1959). *The sociological imagination.* New York: Oxford University Press.

Pew Research Center. (2010). *New media, old media: How blogs and social media agendas relate and differ from the traditional press.* Washington, DC: Author.

Reich, R. B. (1988). *Tales of a new America: The anxious liberal's guide to the future.* New York: Vintage.

Rice, R. E., & Atkin, C. K. (2009). Public communication campaigns: Theoretical principles and practical applications. In J. Bryant & M. B. Oliver (Eds.), *Media effects: Advances in theory and research* (3rd ed., pp. 436–468). Hillsdale, NJ: Lawrence Erlbaum.

Rogers, E. M., & Storey, J. D. (1987). Communication campaigns. In C. R. Berger & S. H. Chaffee (Eds.), *Handbook of communication science* (pp. 817–846). Newbury Park, CA: Sage.

Rose, G. (1985). Sick individuals and sick populations. *International Journal of Epidemiology, 14*(1), 32–38.

Rose, G. (1992). *The strategy of preventive medicine.* New York: Oxford University Press.

Ryan, W. (1976). *Blaming the victim.* New York: Vintage.

Ryan, C. (1991). *Prime time activism.* Boston: South End Press.

Salmon, C. (1989). *Information campaigns: Balancing social values and social change.* Newbury Park, CA: Sage.

Schooler, C., Sundar, S. S., & Flora, J. (1996). Effects of the Stanford five-city project media advocacy program. *Health Education Quarterly, 23*(3), 346–364.

Shorr, L. (1988). *Within our reach.* New York: Anchor/Doubleday.

Seevak, A. (1997, December). Oakland shows the way: The coalition on alcohol outlet issues and media advocacy as a tool for policy change. *Berkeley Media Studies Group, 3.* Retrieved October 15, 2011, from www.bmsg.org/pdfs/Issue3.pdf

Stead, M., Hastings, G., & Eadie, D. (2002). The challenge of evaluating complex interventions: A framework for evaluating media advocacy. *Health Education Research, 17*(3), 351–364.

Stewart, E., & Casswell, S. (1993). Media advocacy for alcohol policy support: Results from the New Zealand Community Action Project. *Health Promotion International, 8*(3), 165–175.

U.S. Department of Health and Human Services. (1988, January). *Media strategies for smoking control.* Washington, DC: Government Printing Office.

University Research Corporation. (1996, August 14). *Henry Horner Mothers Guild: Tenants go public on public housing.* (OPM Contract No. 91–2960). Bethesda, MD: U.S. Office of Personnel Management and the Center for Substance Abuse Prevention.

Wallack, L. (1981). Mass media campaigns: The odds against finding behavior change. *Health Education Quarterly, 8*(3), 209–260.

Wallack, L. (1984). Drinking and driving: Toward a broader understanding of the role of mass media. *Journal of Public Health Policy, 5*(4), 471–498.

Wallack, L. (1989). Mass communication and health promotion: A critical perspective. In R. E. Rice & C. K. Atkin (Eds.), *Public communication campaigns* (2nd ed., pp. 353–367). Newbury Park, CA: Sage.

Wallack, L. (1990). Improving health promotion: Media advocacy and social marketing approaches. In C. Atkin & L. Wallack (Eds.), *Mass communication and public health: Complexities and conflicts* (pp. 147–163). Newbury Park, CA: Sage.

Wallack, L. (1994). Media advocacy: A strategy for empowering people and communities. *Journal of Public Health Policy, 15*(4), 420–436.

Wallack, L. (1999). The California violence prevention initiative: Advancing policy to ban Saturday night specials. *Health Education and Behavior, 26*(6), 841–857.

Wallack, L. (2000). The role of mass media in creating social capital: A new direction for public health. In B. D. Smedley & S. L. Syme, (Eds.), *Promoting health: Intervention strategies from social and behavioral research* (pp. 337–365). Washington, DC: National Academy Press.

Wallack, L., & DeJong, W. (1995). Mass media and public health. In U.S. Department of Health and Human Services (Ed.), *The effects of mass media on the use and abuse of alcohol* (pp. 253–268). Bethesda, MD: National Institutes of Health.

Wallack, L., & Dorfman, L. (1996). Media advocacy: A strategy for advancing policy and promoting health. *Health Education Quarterly, 23*(3), 293–317.

Wallack, L., Dorfman, L., Jernigan, D., & Themba M. (1993). *Media advocacy and public health: Power for prevention.* Newbury Park, CA: Sage.

Wallack, L., & Lawrence, R. (2005). Talking about public health: Developing America's "Second Language." *American Journal of Public Health, 95,* 567–570.

Wallack, L., & Sciandra, R. (1990–1991). Media advocacy and public education in the community trial to reduce heavy smoking. *International Quarterly of Community Health Education, 11,* 205–222.

Wallack, L., Woodruff, K., Dorfman, L., & Diaz, I. (1999). *News for a change: An advocate's guide to working with the media.* Thousand Oaks, CA: Sage.

Winett, L., & Wallack, L. (1996). Advancing public health goals through the mass media. *Journal of Health Communication, 1*(2), 173–196.

Woodruff, K. (1996). Alcohol advertising and violence against women: A media advocacy case study. *Health Education Quarterly, 23*(3), 330–345.

About the Contributors

Peter A. Andersen (PhD, Florida State University) is Professor Emeritus in the School of Communication at San Diego State University. He served as Coinvestigator on the Go Sun Smart projects. He was Director of Research of the Japan-US Telecommunications Research Institute, a research consortium funded by 42 multinational corporations and the Ministry of Telecommunication in Japan. He was President of the Western States Communication Association and Editor of the *Western Journal of Communication*. His research focuses on health communication, risk and crisis communication, homeland security, tobacco control, persuasion, nonverbal communication, instructional communication, and telecommunications.

Charles K. Atkin (PhD, University of Wisconsin) is Chair of the Department of Communication and University Distinguished Professor at Michigan State University. He has published seven books, including *Mass Communication and Public Health,* as well as the second and third editions of *Public Communication Campaigns,* and more than 165 journal articles and chapters relating primarily to media effects and health communication. He's served as a campaign design consultant or evaluation researcher on numerous public information programs in the health arena, including drunk driving, safety belts, alcohol and drug abuse, heart disease, AIDS, parasitic diseases, gun safety, violence, and organ donation; these projects have been carried out in Africa, South America, Europe, and the United States.

Neil Bracht (MA, University of Chicago; MPH, University of Michigan) is Professor Emeritus in the School of Public Health and School of Social Work at University of Minnesota and is an independent Community Health Consultant. He is the editor of *Health Promotion at the Community Level: New Advances, 2nd edition.* His chapter from *Public Communication Campaigns, 3rd edition,* was revised by Ronald Rice for this edition.

David B. Buller (PhD, Michigan State University) is a Senior Scientist at Klein Buendel, Inc., a health communication research firm located in Golden, Colorado. Dr. Buller was formerly a professor in the Department of Communication at the University of Arizona, and Director of Behavioral Sciences Section at the Arizona Cancer Center. His theory-based communication strategies employing various media in communities have been used to reduce the risk of chronic disease among children and adults by promoting sun protection, dietary behavior, physical activity, safe sexual behavior, HPV vaccination, and reduction of the use of tobacco and substance abuse.

Gary R. Cutter (PhD, University of Texas, Houston) is Professor of Biostatistics and Head of the Section on Research Methods and Clinical Trials at the University of Alabama at

Birmingham School of Public Health Department of Biostatistics. Dr. Cutter has directed numerous coordinating centers for national and international clinical trials and multiple cores on program projects and collaborative grants. His major research interests are in the design of clinical trials and epidemiological studies. He is currently directing the coordinating center of three National Institutes of Health (NIH)-sponsored randomized clinical trials, including the trial of Combination Therapy in Multiple Sclerosis.

William DeJong (PhD, Stanford University) is a Professor in the Department of Community Health Sciences at the Boston University School of Public Health, where he teaches courses in intervention planning, program evaluation, and health communications. For 9 years, Dr. DeJong was Director of the Higher Education Center for Alcohol, Drug Abuse, and Violence Prevention. He is also the Principal Investigator of the Social Norms Marketing Research Project, a five-year, $4-million study funded by the National Institute on Alcohol Abuse and Alcoholism.

Richard Delate (MA, University of KwaZulu-Natal) is the Country Programme Director for Johns Hopkins Health and Education in South Africa (JHHESA), an affiliate to the Johns Hopkins University, Bloomberg School of Public Health, Centre for Communication Programmes. There, he has overseen the development and implementation of strategic communication campaigns that combine mass media, social networking, community mobilization, and advocacy aimed at curbing new HIV infections. Prior to joining JHHESA, he served as the Global HIV Prevention Adviser at the Joint United Nations Programme on HIV/AIDS (UNAIDS). He has written extensively on HIV prevention and the use of the media in HIV and social and behavioral communication.

Brenda Dervin (PhD, Michigan State University) is Professor of Communication and Joan N. Huber Fellow in Social and Behavioral Sciences at Ohio State University. She is most widely known for the 35-year development of her Sense-Making Methodology (SMM) designed to study and research audiences in audience-oriented communicative ways and for designing system interfaces that respond better to audiences and users. Her work has been applied to diverse contexts (e.g., information seeking and use, health communication, pedagogy, development communication, citizen participation, peace negotiations, arts policy, museum studies, audience reception), as referenced in *Sense-Making Methodology Reader* and at http://communication.sbs.ohio-state.edu/sense-making.

Mark B. Dignan (PhD, University of Kentucky) is a Professor in the Department of Internal Medicine and Director of the Prevention Research Center at the University of Kentucky. Dr. Dignan was Professor of Public Health at University of Alabama, Birmingham, Chair of the Center for Community Studies at AMC Cancer Research Center, and Professor of Family and Community Medicine at Wake Forest University Health Sciences Center. His research has focused on community-based trials of interventions for low-income, minority populations, particularly populations in Appalachia and the Southeastern United States. He was Coinvestigator on the Go Sun Smart projects.

Lori Dorfman (DrPH, University of California Berkeley) directs the Berkeley Media Studies Group, a project of the Public Health Institute, where she oversees research, media advocacy training, strategic consultation, and professional education for journalists. Her research examines how the media portray health issues, including alcohol, tobacco, nutrition, children's health, health inequities, and violence, among others. She is part of a team that helps news organizations include a public health perspective in their crime and violence coverage. She has coauthored *Public Health and Media Advocacy* and *News for a Change* and edited *Reporting on Violence: A Handbook for Journalists.*

Maria Elena Figueroa (PhD, Johns Hopkins University) is Associate Faculty in the Department of Population and Family Health Sciences and Director of the Research and Evaluation Division of the Center for Communication Programs in the Johns Hopkins Bloomberg School of Public Health. She studies health behavior in support of health communication programs in Latin America, Africa, and most recently Asia. Her current work focuses on the understanding of ecological, household, and individual factors affecting hygiene behavior. Other research interests include the development of conceptual models and indicators to assess community-based and social change communication interventions.

Dennis Foote (PhD, Stanford University) is Vice President for Global Communications and Distance Learning at the Academy for Educational Development in Washington, D.C. There he is also Director of USAID's LearnLink Project, a five-year, $25-million effort, which helps USAID introduce appropriate learning, information, and communication technologies in development projects around the world. Dr. Foote has worked in more than 35 countries for USAID, the World Bank, the World Health Organization (WHO), and the United Nations Children's Fund (UNICEF). He has been an Assistant Professor at Stanford University, Associate Professor at the University of San Francisco, and Founder of Applied Communication Technology.

Lois Foreman-Wernet (PhD, Ohio State University) is Associate Professor of Communication at Capital University in Columbus. She spent nearly two decades managing communication programs in cultural and educational institutions, and she is an accredited member of the Public Relations Society of America (PRSA). She has coedited three books, including *Audiences and the Arts: Communication Perspectives,* and has published a number of book chapters and articles. Her research interests focus on audience-centered approaches to institutional communication, with a particular emphasis on the use of Dervin's Sense-Making Methodology in the study of arts and cultural audiences.

Vicki Freimuth (PhD, Florida State University) is Director of the Center for Health and Risk Communication at the University of Georgia, where she also holds a joint appointment as a Professor in the Department of Speech Communication and the Grady College of Journalism and Mass Communication. She earlier served as Director of Communication at the Centers for Disease Control and Prevention (CDC). Her research focuses on the role of communication in health behavior change programs. She is author of *Searching for Health Information* and coeditor of two books on HIV/AIDS and communication.

Robert C. Hornik (Ph.D., Stanford University) is the Wilbur Schramm Term Professor of Communication and Health Policy at the Annenberg School for Communication, University of Pennsylvania. Since 2003, he has directed Penn's National Cancer Institute-funded

Center of Excellence in Cancer Communication Research. Previously he led the evaluation of the US National Youth Antidrug Media Campaign as well as more than 20 evaluations of public health communication campaigns in the United States and throughout the world. He is the author of *Development Communication*, editor of *Public Health Communication: Evidence for Behavior Change* and co-editor of *Prediction and Change of Health Behavior* as well as more than 100 refereed articles and papers. He has served on four Institute of Medicine Committees. He is Past Chair of the Faculty Senate at Penn.

D. Lawrence Kincaid (PhD, Michigan State University) is a Senior Advisor for the Research and Evaluation Division and Associate Scientist in the Faculty of Social and Behavioral Sciences at the Johns Hopkins Bloomberg School of Public Health. He has worked in Asia, Latin America, and South Africa. He developed and tested the ideational model for health communication evaluation as well as many other methodological and theoretical contributions to health communication. He coauthored the first book in the field on communication networks, and he edited the first book on communication theory from both Eastern and Western perspectives.

Patchareeya P. Kwan (PhD, University of Southern California) is a part-time lecturer in the Master of Public Health Program at the University of Southern California's Keck School of Medicine. She is also currently serving as a consultant for Claremont Graduate University's School of Global and Community Health doing evaluation work. Her research interests include social network influences, particularly positive social influences among high-risk and minority groups. She is also interested in program evaluation that focuses on measuring program impact—both effectiveness and ineffectiveness.

Jessica M. LaCroix received a dual degree in mathematics and psychology from Quinnipiac University and completed her master's degree at the University of Idaho. She has worked on meta-analytic projects focusing on HIV/AIDS, family planning, mass media communication, and the relationship between exercise and the psychological well-being of cancer survivors. LaCroix is an affiliate of the Center for Health, Intervention, and Prevention (CHIP) and is currently working toward her PhD at the University of Connecticut.

Debra A. Lieberman (PhD, Stanford University) is a communication researcher at the University of California, Santa Barbara, where her research focuses on processes of learning and behavior change with interactive media, with special interests in digital games, health media, and children's media. She consults for health organizations, education agencies, and media and technology companies to help design and evaluate media for entertainment, learning, and health behavior change, and she directs Health Games Research, a national program funded by the Robert Wood Johnson Foundation's Pioneer Portfolio to improve and advance the research, design, and effectiveness of health games.

Rupali Limaye (MA, MPH, George Washington University) is a doctoral student at the Johns Hopkins Bloomberg School of Public Health, in the Department of Health, Behavior, and Society. She has extensive experience in strategic behavior change communication, focusing on HIV/AIDS, in a number of countries, including Nigeria, Kenya, Tanzania, Haiti, Malawi, and Ethiopia.

William J. McGuire's (1925 to 2007) research focused on attitude change, the self-concept, and the structure of thought systems. He authored *Constructing Social Psychology* and coedited *Explorations in Social Psychology*. He received the annual award for Distinguished Scientific Contribution from the American Psychology Association (APA), from the Society for Experimental Social Psychology, and from the International Society of Political Psychology. McGuire passed away in 2007. His chapter from *Public Communication Campaigns, 3rd edition,* was revised by Ronald Rice and Charles Atkin for this edition.

Susan E. Morgan (PhD, University of Arizona) is Professor in the Department of Communication, Purdue University. Her research involves the design and evaluation of persuasive messages targeting health behavior change in multicultural populations. Her research has been supported by NIDA, the National Institute for Occupational Safety and Health (NIOSH), and the Department of Health and Human Services (DHHS). Her latest research involves conducting and evaluating multimedia campaigns to promote organ donation in worksite and community settings, analyzing how the mass media frames organ donation, and the effects of that framing on public attitudes and behaviors.

Lisa Murray-Johnson (PhD, Michigan State University) is Program Director of Patient Education and Adjunct Assistant Professor of Undergraduate Studies in the College of Nursing, Ohio State University Medical Center. She won the joint ICA-NCA Health Division MA Thesis of the Year and the Dissertation of the Year. Her research areas include health education theories, application of the extended parallel process model, social support in online health groups, cultural factors in AIDs-related fear appeals, and noise-induced hearing loss.

Seth M. Noar (PhD, University of Rhode Island) is an Associate Professor in the School of Journalism and Mass Communication, University of North Carolina, and a member of the Lineberger Comprehensive Cancer Center. His work addresses health behavior theories, message design and media campaigns, computer-based interventions, tailored communication, and methodological topics, including meta-analysis and evaluation. Dr. Noar is the Principal Investigator of a National Institute of Mental Health (NIMH)-funded study to develop a computer-tailored, safer-sex intervention for at-risk African Americans. He recently coedited *Communication Perspectives on HIV/AIDS for the 21st Century.*

William Paisley (PhD, Stanford University) was an original coeditor of this volume (1981) and taught in the Stanford University Communication Department from 1965 to 1985. He later cofounded and codirected Knowledge Access Inc., an electronic publishing company. His research and writing continues to focus on American public knowledge in its social-historical context. His chapter from *Public Communication Campaigns, 3rd edition,* was revised by Charles Atkin for this edition.

Philip C. Palmgreen (PhD, University of Michigan) is Professor of Communication at the University of Kentucky. He has served as Principal or Co-Principal Investigator on a series of projects supported by NIDA and NIMH investigating the design and targeting of televised public service announcements for populations at risk for drug abuse or HIV/STD infection. Dr. Palmgreen also served as a primary scientific advisor for the Office of National Drug

Control Policy's $2-billion National Youth Antidrug Media Campaign. He is the winner of the Gerald M. Phillips Award for Distinguished Applied Communication Scholarship and the Prevention Science Award.

Ronald E. Rice (PhD, Stanford University) is the Arthur N. Rupe Chair in the Social Effects of Mass Communication in the Department of Communication and Codirector of the Carsey-Wolf Center at University of California, Santa Barbara. His coauthored or coedited books include *Organizations and Unusual routines, Media Ownership, The Internet and Health Care, Social Consequences of Internet Use, The Internet and Health Communication, Accessing and Browsing Information and Communication, Public Communication Campaigns* (three editions), *Research Methods and the New Media, Managing Organizational Innovation,* and *The New Media.* He has published more than 100 refereed journal articles and 60 book chapters.

Rajiv N. Rimal (PhD, Stanford University) is Associate Professor in the Department of Health, Behavior, and Society in the School of Public Health with a Joint Appointment in the School of Medicine at Johns Hopkins University. Dr. Rimal conducts and evaluates the effectiveness of health promotion campaigns for AIDS prevention in sub-Saharan Africa and for family planning practices in India. He is part of a team of U.S. researchers who study how health communication can inform emergency preparedness efforts. His work has been funded by the USAID, the NIH, the CDC, and the Bill and Melinda Gates Foundation.

Julie A. Robinson (PhD, University of California Santa Barbara) is a Research Scientist cross-trained in marine ecology and communication. Her research interests include the design, implementation, and evaluation of environmental communication strategies and ocean literacy programs as capacity-building tools to support environmental problem solving. Robinson also produces science documentaries for Public Broadcasting Service (PBS) and National Geographic and has coauthored an award-winning book about America's National Marine Sanctuaries.

Everett M. Rogers (1931 to 2004) was Professor Emeritus, Department of Communication and Journalism, University of New Mexico (UNM), at the time of his passing. Professor Rogers distinguished himself as one of the foremost thinkers in the field of communication and social change. Author of many books, he was internationally recognized for his work in many areas, including diffusion of innovations, communication networks, and the entertainment-education strategy. He had also served as the Walter H. Annenberg Professor at the University of Southern California and the Janet M. Peck Professor of International Communication at Stanford University.

Charles T. Salmon (PhD, University of Minnesota) is Professor in the School of Communication and Information at Nanyang Technological University, Singapore, and Past Dean of the College of Communication Arts and Sciences at Michigan State University. He has served as a Rockefeller Foundation Fellow at Bellagio, Italy, Fulbright Fellow at Tel Aviv University, Visiting Professor at the Norwegian School of Management, Visiting Scientist at the CDC, and Social Marketing Trainer for UNICEF in Kazakhstan. His research focuses on the intersection of public information, public health, and public opinion.

Michael D. Scott (PhD, University of Southern California) is Professor Emeritus in the School of Communication at California State University, Chico, and President and Founder of Mikonics, Inc., a health communication firm. He has been a consultant to the ski and snow sports industry for 20 years, helping them to improve communication skills among mountain operations personnel, improve marketing and diffusion, and enhance instruction in ski schools. He served as Coinvestigator on the Go Sun Smart projects. Dr. Scott's research also concerns interdependencies among persuasive messaging, diffusion, instructional design, and relational communication.

Arvind Singhal (PhD, University of Southern California) is the Samuel Shirley and Edna Holt Marston Professor of Communication and Director of the Social Justice Initiative in the University of Texas-El Paso's Department of Communication. He is also a William J. Clinton Distinguished Fellow at the Clinton School of Public Service, Little Rock, Arkansas. Singhal teaches and conducts research in the diffusion of innovations, organizing for social change, and the entertainment-education strategy. Singhal's 11 books include *Inviting Everyone: Healing Health Care Through Positive Deviance; Protecting Children from Exploitation and Trafficking; Popular with a Purpose; Entertainment-Education Worldwide; Combating AIDS;* and *Entertainment-Education.*

Sandi W. Smith (PhD, University of Southern California) is Director of the Health and Risk Communication Center and Professor in the Department of Communication at Michigan State University. Her work has been funded by agencies and foundations such as the Health Resources and Services Administration (HRSA), the National Cancer Institute (NCI), the National Institute of Environmental Health Sciences (NIEHS), the U.S. Department of Education, and the Fetzer Institute. Smith's research interests include the impact of memorable messages on health behavior, such as the prevention and detection of breast cancer, organ donation, and how to encourage college students to consume alcohol moderately. She coedited *New Directions in Interpersonal Communication Research.*

Leslie B. Snyder (PhD, Stanford) is Professor of Communication Sciences at University of Connecticut. She is also affiliated with the Academy of Global Economic Advancement, the Center for Health and HIV Intervention and Preventions, and Center for Survey Research and Analysis. Her research in health campaigns and risk reduction has been funded by the CDC, the NIMH, USAID, Johns Hopkins University, and the U.S. Department of the Interior, among others. Dr. Synder's research includes meta-analyses, methodology, health (such as HIV and alcohol) and development campaigns, and agenda setting.

Brian G. Southwell (PhD, University of Pennsylvania) is Senior Research Scientist at RTI International, and Research Professor at the School of Journalism and Mass Communication at the University of North Carolina at Chapel Hill. Southwell's research interests include the intersection of interpersonal communication and mass media effects and campaign measurement and evaluation. His work has been funded by the National Science Foundation and the NIH. Southwell is Senior Editor for *Health Communication* and serves on the editorial boards of *Public Opinion Quarterly, Communication Research, Science Communication,* and a number of other journals.

Michael T. Stephenson (PhD, University of Kentucky) is Professor of Communication and Associate Dean in the College of Liberal Arts at Texas A&M University. His most recent research focuses on the effective design and implementation of antidrug ads directed at parents and youth. He has conducted CDC-funded research to prevent secondhand smoke exposure among children living in *colonias* along the Texas-Mexico border. He has served as Coinvestigator on a Division of Transplantation grant to investigate the promotion of organ donation as well as Coinvestigator on a NIDA grant aimed at preventing marijuana use among adolescent sensation seekers.

Douglas Storey (PhD, Stanford University) is Associate Director for Program Research, The Health Communication Partnership. His work ranges from individual health behavior change theory, to the political economy of media and development, to grassroots participation and community mobilization. Dr. Storey has done research on a wide range of health communication issues including malaria, TB, HIV/AIDS, nutrition, hypertension, immunization, family planning, and many others. He has designed and carried out research for all phases of the communication project life cycle from small-scale qualitative formative studies for program design and message development to large-scale quantitative studies for summative impact evaluation.

Maureen Taylor (PhD, Purdue University) is Professor and Gaylord Family Chair of Strategic Communication in the Gaylord College of Journalism and Mass Communication at the University of Oklahoma. Professor Taylor's research interests are in international public relations, nation building and civil society campaigns, and new communication technologies. She has traveled extensively around the world conducting research in Malaysia, Taiwan, Bosnia, Croatia, Kosovo, Serbia, Jordan, Liberia, and Sudan. Her work has appeared in journals such as *Journal of Public Relations Research, Public Relations Review, Communication Monographs, Human Communication Research, Journal of Communication,* and *Management Communication Quarterly.*

Thomas W. Valente (PhD, University of Southern California) is a Professor and Director of the Master of Public Health Program in the Department of Preventive Medicine, Keck School of Medicine, University of Southern California. He is author of *Social Networks and Health, Evaluating Health Promotion Programs, Network Models of the Diffusion of Innovations,* and more than 100 articles and chapters on social networks, behavior change, and program evaluation. Valente uses social network analysis, health communication, and mathematical models to implement and evaluate health promotion programs designed to prevent tobacco and substance abuse, unintended fertility, and STD/HIV infections.

Barbara J. Walkosz (PhD, University of Arizona) is a Senior Scientist at Klein Buendel, Inc. She was formerly a Professor in the Department of Communication at the University of Colorado Denver. Dr. Walkosz was a Coinvestigator on the Go Sun Smart projects. She is currently a Multiple Principal Investigator on the Sun Safe Worksite Project, an NCI-funded project to design and test a campaign promoting sun protection policies to public employers in Colorado. She is a member the Colorado Physical Activity and Nutrition Council (COPAN) Worksite Task Force, the Metro Denver Health and Wellness Commission, and the Health Disparities Task Force and Skin Cancer Task Forces of the Colorado Cancer Coalition.

Lawrence Wallack (PhD, University of California Berkeley) is Dean, College of Urban and Public Affairs, Portland State University, and Emeritus Professor, Public Health University of California, Berkeley. He was Founding Director of the Berkeley Media Studies Group, which conducts research and training in the use of media to promote healthy public policies. Dr. Wallack is one of the primary architects of media advocacy—an innovative approach to working with mass media to advance public health. He is the principal author of *News for a Change* and *Media Advocacy and Public Health* and coeditor of *Mass Media and Public Health.*

Hua Wang (PhD, University of Southern California) is Assistant Professor in the Department of Communication at the University at Buffalo, the State University of New York. Her research interests include communication technology, health promotion, and social change with a focus on the design and evaluation of new information and communication technology (ICT)-based interventions. She studies the social dynamic and transformation of communication technologies for the well-being of individuals, groups, and societies at large in contexts such as the social impact of new media in everyday life, digital games beyond pure entertainment, participation in online communities, and social network sites.

Marco C. Yzer (PhD, University of Groningen) is Associate Professor of Communication at the University of Minnesota, where he also has an adjunct appointment with the School of Public Health. His research focuses on motivational processes that explain how mass-mediated and interpersonal communication may lead or inhibit health behavior. His work includes studies funded by NIDA and the NCI and has appeared in communication, psychology, and health outlets.

Rick S. Zimmerman (PhD, University of Washington) is Professor and Chair of the Department of Global and Community Health at George Mason University. His work focuses on understanding why individuals do or do not engage in risky or protective health behaviors. In addition to HIV prevention work in the United States and South Africa, Dr. Zimmerman and his colleagues have been involved in HIV prevention research in Ethiopia, Thailand, and India. He has more than 70 publications and has received over $10 million in NIH grants as a Principal Investigator, most on HIV and pregnancy prevention.

Index

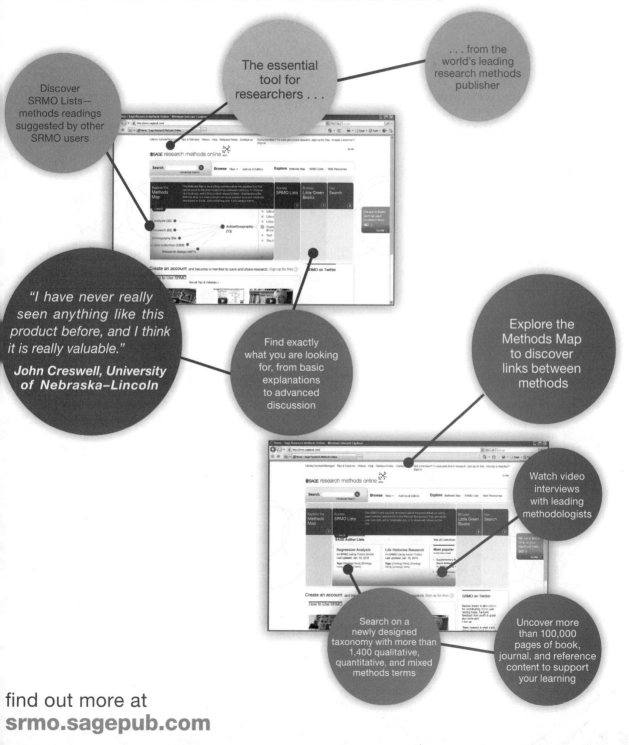